Matthew 24–25 as Prophetic-Apocalyptic

Matthew 24–25 as Prophetic-Apocalyptic

Structure, Function, and Eschatology

Kennedy K. Ekeocha

☙PICKWICK *Publications* • Eugene, Oregon

MATTHEW 24–25 AS PROPHETIC-APOCALYPTIC
Structure, Function, and Eschatology

Copyright © 2024 Kennedy K. Ekeocha. All rights reserved. Except for brief quotations in critical publications or reviews, no part of this book may be reproduced in any manner without prior written permission from the publisher. Write: Permissions, Wipf and Stock Publishers, 199 W. 8th Ave., Suite 3, Eugene, OR 97401.

Pickwick Publications
An Imprint of Wipf and Stock Publishers
199 W. 8th Ave., Suite 3
Eugene, OR 97401

www.wipfandstock.com

PAPERBACK ISBN: 978-1-6667-8385-8
HARDCOVER ISBN: 978-1-6667-8386-5
EBOOK ISBN: 978-1-6667-8387-2

Cataloguing-in-Publication data:

Names: Ekeocha, Kennedy K. [author].

Title: Matthew 24–25 as prophetic apocalyptic : structure, function, and eschatology / by Kennedy K. Ekeocha.

Description: Eugene, OR: Pickwick Publications, 2024 | Includes bibliographical references and index.

Identifiers: ISBN 978-1-6667-8385-8 (paperback) | ISBN 978-1-6667-8386-5 (hardcover) | ISBN 978-1-6667-8387-2 (ebook)

Subjects: LCSH: Bible.—Matthew, XXIV–XXV—Criticism, interpretation, etc. | Eschatology—Biblical teaching. | Bible.—Matthew—Criticism, interpretation, etc. | Jesus Christ—Biblical teachings.

Classification: BS2575.2 E34 2024 (paperback) | BS2575.2 (ebook)

VERSION NUMBER 01/05/24

All Greek Scripture citations are taken from SBL Greek New Testament. Copyright © 2010 Society of Biblical Literature and Logos Bible Software.

Unless otherwise indicated, Scripture quotations are taken from Revised Standard Version of the Bible, copyright © 1971 the Division of Christian Education of the National Council of the Churches of Christ in the United States of America. Used by permission. All rights reserved.

Citations from the Septuagint are either the author's translations and/or taken from *The Old Testament in Greek According to the Septuagint* by Henry Barclay Swete. Fourth Edition. © 1909 Cambridge University Press.

To my late Father, Edward N. Ekeocha, for his encouragements and immense personal investments in my life

Contents

Tables and Figures | ix
Acknowledgments | xi
Abbreviations | xiii

1. Introduction and Historical Overview | 1
2. Statement of Problem, Purpose, and Methodology | 33
3. Matthew 24–25: Form and Hermeneutics | 52
4. Structures of Matthew and the Eschatological Discourse | 86
5. An Interpretation of Matt 24:3—25:46 | 123
6. The Function of the Eschatological Discourse in Matthew | 237
7. Conclusions and Correlation within the NT | 260

Appendix 1: My Diagrammatical Representation of Carson's Structure of Matt 24 | 283
Appendix 2: Comparative Analysis of Matt 2:19—4:18 | 285
Appendix 3: Proposed Structure of Matthew | 287
Appendix 4: Salvation-Historical Outline Arising from the Interpretation of Matt 24–25 | 289
Bibliography | 291
Ancient Document Index | 313

Tables and Figures

Tables

Table 1: Matera's Narrative Blocks of Matthew | 97

Table 2: Comparing Matera's and Carter's Structures of Matthew | 98

Table 3: Weren's New Proposal on Matthew's Structure | 98

Table 4: Preliminary Structure of the Eschatological Discourse | 111

Table 5: Proposed Structure of the Eschatological Discourse | 122

Table 6: Showing Relation between Christological Titles and Matthew's Structure | 253

Figures

Figure 1: Extended *Inclusio* Framing the Eschatological Discourse | 113

Figure 2: Grammatical Arrangement and Connections of 24:3 | 115

Figure 3: Interchange of Particulars within the Eschatological Discourse | 121

Figure 4: Matt 24:4–14 in Panoramic View | 141

Figure 5: A Diagrammatic Representation of Matt 24:21 | 173

Figure 6: "Those Days" in Context | 194

Figure 7: Gathering Terminology in Context | 208

Figure 8: Connecting the Analogies of Matt 24:45—25:30 | 221

Figure 9: Showing Matt 24:31 and 25:32 as Two Parts of the Same Event | 233

Acknowledgments

THIS MONOGRAPH IS THE fruit of years of reflection and research for my PhD degree at Asbury Theological Seminary, Wilmore, Kentucky. I want to express my profound gratitude to the founder of West Africa Theological Seminary, Lagos, Nigeria, Prof. Gary S. Maxey, the American missionary with an African heart. I am deeply indebted to his encouragement and support, which enabled me to embark on this study program. My sincere appreciation goes to the provost, the entire family of WATS, Lagos, and Friends of WATS, USA, for their support throughout the period.

Throughout my time at Asbury, I experienced grace from many individuals and bodies. Pastor Mark Horton and his church, Faith United Community Church in Nicholasville, KY, embraced my wife and me with much openness and warmth. They made us feel at home with lots of encouragement, fellowship, and financial support. Rev. Dr. William Sillings, former chairmen of Friends of WATS and my superintendent at the International Fellowship of Bible Churches (IFBC) USA, Drs. Mark and Marybeth Leavell, and Gary and Phillis Hedges were all part of the support team. I thank Dr. Vic Reasoner for assisting me with research materials. Ryan Smith and his family did me much good. His friendship and prayers were an immense blessing. May the Lord richly reward him for his labor of love. I am thankful to my doctoral mentor, Dr. David R. Bauer, for his excellent guidance throughout. The world-class faculty at Asbury are appreciated, especially Dr. Fredrick J. Long, my reader, Dr. Craig S. Keener, and Dr. Ben Witherington III, all with whom I shared inspiring conversations in and outside of class throughout my study. Many thanks to Patti Walker, our amiable Advanced Research Program coordinator and Dr. Jim Miller, my examiner from the Orlando campus.

At a critical time during my studies, I accepted the call through the IFBC to serve as resident pastor at Community Fellowship Church,

Corydon, Indiana. It was quite a challenging task, but I owe the church much gratitude for their understanding and sacrificial commitment toward my studies. Words are not enough to describe the love and hospitality of a group of Jesus-loving people who became my family and spiritual backbone. My lovely wife, Grace, is ever so amazing. She embodied grace at home throughout the duration of my studies. Her patient love, prayers, and sacrifice were instrumental to this milestone. There is no way I could have accomplished this feat without her warm, caring, and steadfast support. I love you, Darling; this is your success!

And to God the Father, the supplier of all grace, and Jesus my Lord and Savior, the Coming One, be all glory forever. Maranatha!!

Abbreviations

Primary Sources

Old Testament/Hebrew Bible

Gen	Genesis	Isa	Isaiah
Exod	Exodus	Jer	Jeremiah
Lev	Leviticus	Lam	Lamentations
Num	Numbers	Ezek	Ezekiel
Deut	Deuteronomy	Dan	Daniel
Josh	Joshua	Hos	Hosea
Judg	Judges	Joel	Joel
1–2 Sam	1–2 Samuel	Amos	Amos
1–2 Kgs	1–2 Kings	Obad	Obadiah
1–2 Chr	1–2 Chronicles	Mic	Micah
Ezra	Ezra	Nah	Nahum
Neh	Nehemiah	Hab	Habakkuk
Esth	Esther	Zeph	Zephaniah
Job	Job	Hag	Haggai
Ps/Pss	Psalms	Zech	Zechariah
Prov	Proverbs	Mal	Malachi
Eccl (or Qoh)	Ecclesiastes (or Qoheleth)		

Old Testament Apocrypha

Jdt	Judith	Tob	Tobit
1 Macc	1 Maccabees	Sir	Sirach/Ecclesiasticus
2 Macc	2 Maccabees	Wis	Wisdom of Solomon

Pseudepigrapha

Apoc. El.	Apocalypse of Elijah
Apoc. Zeph.	Apocalypse of Zephaniah
2 Bar.	2 Baruch
1 En.	1 Enoch
2 En.	2 Enoch
4 Ezra	4 Ezra
Jub.	Jubilees
Liv. Pro.	Lives of the Prophets
3 Macc	3 Maccabees
Ps.-Philo, Bib. Ant.	Pseudo Philo, Biblical Antiquities
Pss. Sol.	Psalms of Solomon
T. Job	Testament of Job
T. Jos.	Testament of Joshua
T. Jud.	Testament of Judah
T. Levi	Testament of Levi
T. Mos.	Testament of Moses
Sib. Or.	Sibylline Oracle

Philo

Aet.	*De aeternitate mundi* (*On the Eternity of the World*)
Legat.	*Legation ad Gaium* (*On the Embassy to Gaius*)
Spec.	*De specialibus legibus* (*On Special Laws*)

Josephus

J.W.	*Jewish Wars*
Ant.	*Jewish Antiquities*
Ag. Ap.	*Against Apion*

New Testament

Matt	Matthew		Gal	Galatians		
Mark	Mark		Eph	Ephesians		
Luke	Luke		Phil	Philippians		
John	John		Col	Colossians		
Acts	Acts		1–2 Thess	1–2 Thessalonians		
Rom	Romans		1–2 Tim	1–2 Timothy		
1–2 Cor	1–2 Corinthians		Titus	Titus		

Heb	*Hebrews*	*1–2 John*	*1–2 John*
Jas	*James*	*Rev*	*Revelation*
1–2 Pet	*1–2 Peter*		

Dead Sea Scrolls

1QpHab	*Pesher Habakkuk*
1QM	*War Scroll*
1QH	*Hodayot or Thanksgiving Hymns*
1QS	*Rule of the Community*
4Q225	*Pseudo-Jubilees*
4Q174	*Florilegium or Midrash on Eschatology*

Greco-Roman Writings

Aelian

Nat. an.	*De Natura animalium*

Aristotle

Hist. an.	*Historia Animalium* (History of Animals)
Poet.	*Poetica*
Rhet.	*Rhetorica*

Diogenes Laertius

Diog. Laert.	
Vit. philos.	*Vitae philosophorum*

Lucian

Nav.	*Navigium*

Pliny the Elder

Nat.	*Naturalis historia*
Ps. Soph. fr.	Pseudo-Sophocles Fragment

Seneca

Ep. *Epistolae morales*

Early Christian Writings

Apollinaris

Frag. *Fragments*

Clement of Rome

1 Clem. 1 Clement

Augustine

Ep. Epistles

Clement of Alexandria

Strom. *Stromateis*

Chrysostom

Hom. Matt. *Homiliae in Matthaeun*

Cyril of Alexandria

Ths. *Thesaurus de Sancta et Consubstantiali Trinitate*
Frag. *Fragments*

Did. Didache

Eusebius

Dem. ev. *Demonstration evangelica*
Hist. eccl. *Historia ecclesiastica*
Praep. ev. *Preparatio evangelica*

Epiphanius

Pan. *Panarion*
Treat. *Treatise on Weights and Measures*

Hillary

Comm. Matt. *Commentary on Matthew*

Hippolytus

Matt. *Matthaeun*

Ignatius

Ign. *Phld.* *Ignatius, To the Philadelphians*

Irenaeus

Ad. Haer. *Adversus Haereses*

Jerome

Comm. Matt. *Commentariorum in Matthaeum*

Origen

Cels. *Contra Celsium*
Frag. *Fragmenta*

Theodoret of Cyrus

Comm. Paul. *Commentary on The Letters of St. Paul*

New Testament Apocrypha

Apoc. Pet. Apocalypse of Peter (Ethiopian)
Ep. Apos. Epistle of the Apostles
Gos. Pet. Gospel of Peter

Secondary Sources

ABCS *The Anchor Bible Commentary Series*
ABD *Anchor Bible Dictionary*
ACNT *Augsburg Commentaries on the New Testament*
ANTC *Abingdon New Testament Commentary*
BBR *Bulletin for Biblical Research*

BCBC	Believers Church Bible Commentary
BDAG	*Greek-English Lexicon of the New Testament and Other Early Christian Literature*. Edited by Walter Bauer et al. 3rd ed. Chicago: University of Chicago Press, 1999.
BECNT	Baker Exegetical Commentary on the New Testament
BET	Beiträge zur Evangelischen Theologie
BETL	Bibliotheca Ephemeridum Theologicarum Lovaniensium
Bib	*Biblica*
BibInt	*Biblical Interpretation*
BJRL	*Bulletin of the John Rylands University Library of Manchester*
BMSSEC	Baylor Mohr Siebeck Studies in Early Christianity
BSac	*Bibliotheca Sacra*
BT	*The Bible Translator*
BTB	*Biblical Theology Bulletin*
BW	*Biblical World*
BZNW	Beihefte zur Zeitschrift für die Neutestamentliche Wissenschaft
CBQ	*Catholic Biblical Quarterly*
CC	Concordia Commentary
CCSS	Catholic Commentary on Sacred Scripture
CNT	Commentaire du Nouveau Testament
CTL	Crown Theological Library
CTR	*Criswell Theological Review*
DJG	*Dictionary of Jesus and the Gospels*. Edited by Joel B. Green et al. Downers Grove, IL: InterVarsity, 1992.
DLNTD	*Dictionary of the Later New Testament and Its Development*. Edited by Ralph P. Martin and Peter H. Davids. Downers Grove, IL: InterVarsity, 1997.
EBC	The Expositor's Bible Commentary
EBib	Études Bibliques
EQ	*The Evangelical Quarterly*
ETL	*Ephemerides Theologicae Lovanienses*
Exp	*Expositor*
ExpTim	*The Expository Times*
GTJ	*Grace Theological Journal*
HBT	*Horizons in Biblical Theology*
HTKNT	Herders Theologischer Kommentar zum Neuen Testament

HTR	*Harvard Theological Review*
IDB	*Interpreter's Dictionary of the Bible*
Int	*Interpretation*
JAAR	*Journal of the American Academy of Religion*
JBL	*Journal of Biblical Literature*
JDT	*Jahrbücher für deutsche Theologie*
JETS	*Journal for the Evangelical Theological Society*
JGES	*Journal of the Grace Evangelical Society*
JIBS	*Journal of Inductive Biblical Studies*
JML	*Journal of Memory and Language*
JNES	*Journal of Near Eastern Studies*
JP	*Journal of Pragmatics*
JR	*Journal of Religion*
JRR	*Journal from the Radical Reformation*
JRS	*Journal of Roman Studies*
JSNT	*Journal for the Study of the New Testament*
JSNTSup	*Journal for the Study of the New Testament Supplement Series*
JSP	*Journal for the Study of the Pseudepigrapha*
JTI	*Journal of Theological Interpretation*
JTS	*Journal of Theological Studies*
LNTS	Library of New Testament Studies
LQHRev	*London Quarterly & Holborn Review*
MGC	Moody Gospel Commentary
MNTC	MacArthur New Testament Commentary
MSJ	*The Master's Seminary Journal*
NAC	The New American Commentary
NCB	New Century Bible
NCBC	New Cambridge Bible Commentary
NGS	New Gospel Studies
NIBC	New International Biblical Commentary
NICNT	New International Commentary on the New Testament
NIGTC	New International Greek Testament Commentary
NIVAC	The NIV Application Commentary
NovT	*Novum Testamentum*
NovTSup	Supplements to Novum Testamentum
NS	New Series
NTC	The New Testament Commentary
NTL	New Testament Library
NTM	New Testament Message

NTS	*New Testament Studies*
OTL	Old Testament Library
PCNT	Paideia Commentaries on the New Testament
PLAL	Perspectives on Linguistics and Ancient Languages
ResQ	*Restoration Quarterly*
RSB	*Religious Studies Bulletin*
SBibT	*Studia Biblica et Theologica*
SBLBMI	Society of Biblical Literature Bible and Its Modern Interpreters
SBLDS	Society of Biblical Literature Dissertation Series
SBLMS	Society of Biblical Literature Monograph Series
SBLSBS	Society of Biblical Literature Sources for Biblical Study
SBLSP	Society of Biblical Literature Seminar Papers
SBT	Studies in Biblical Theology
SNTSMS	Society for New Testament Studies Monograph Series
SPS	Sacra Pagina Series
START	*Selected Technical Articles Related to Translation*
TDNT	*Theological Dictionary of the New Testament*. Edited by Gerhard Kittel and Gerhard Friedrich. Translated by Geoffrey W. Bromiley. 10 vols. Grand Rapids: Eerdmans, 1964–76.
THNTC	Two Horizons New Testament Commentary
TJ	*Trinity Journal*
TJT	*Toronto Journal of Theology*
ThKNT	Theologischer Kommentar zum Neuen Testament
THKNT	Theologischer Handkommentar zum Neuen Testament
TNTC	Tyndale New Testament Commentaries
TS	*Theological Studies*
TynBul	*Tyndale Bulletin*
TZ	*Theologische Zeitschift*
WBC	Word Biblical Commentary
WMANT	Wissenschaftliche Monographien zum Alten und Neuen Testament
WTJ	*Westminster Theological Journal*
ZECNT	Zondervan Exegetical Commentary on the New Testament
ZNW	*Zeitschrift Für die Neutestamentliche Wissenschaft*

1

Introduction and Historical Overview

Introduction

THE NEW TESTAMENT IN general bears witness to the deeply eschatological consciousness that gave rise to it. Perhaps, nowhere else in the NT does the issue of eschatology come to a most complex head than in Matt 24–25 and its parallels. The Olivet Discourse, Eschatological Discourse, or Apocalyptic Discourse—as it has been variously identified—has always been the most critical and extensive starting point for reflections on Jesus' eschatology.[1] It is grounded in the inquiry of the disciples regarding the fate of the Jerusalem temple and "the sign of your *parousia* and the consummation of the age" (τὸ σημεῖον τῆς σῆς παρουσίας καὶ συντελείας τοῦ αἰῶνος [24:1–3]). Jesus' response addresses such eschatological themes as "the end" (τὸ τέλος [vv. 6, 13, 14]), "tribulation" (θλῖψις [vv. 9, 21]), "the coming of the Son of Man" (ἡ παρουσία τοῦ υἱοῦ τοῦ ἀνθρώπου [vv. 27, 37, 39]), and in 25:46, "everlasting punishment" (κόλασιν αἰώνιον) and "everlasting life" (ζωὴν αἰώνιον).

What exactly does the disciples' question mean, and what is the interpretation of Jesus' response? These two broad questions may be broken down into at least five particulars: numerical (what is the number of questions in Matt 24:3 and how many does Jesus answer in the response that follows?), linguistic/semantic (what is the meaning of *parousia* and other such themes or phrases within the Discourse?), chronological (what is the eschatological time referent—past, future, or both?), structural (what is the

---

1. In this study, these identifications will be used synonymously, abbreviated sometimes as "the Discourse."

exact relationship between the destruction of the Jerusalem temple in 70 CE and the *parousia* of Christ?), and theological (what overall eschatological view is communicated by the Discourse?).

The fact that there is hardly a consensus on any of these fronts may be quite surprising to the lay reader. But as centuries of scholarship show, Matt 24–25 (and parr.) can hardly be taken for granted as crystal clear. Thus, anyone approaching this passage must prepare to wrestle with some of the most difficult issues in the whole of the NT, bearing in mind the long and checkered history of interpretation. The history of scholarly engagement with the Eschatological Discourse has seen much frustration, leading some to charge the evangelists with either conspiracy or sheer ignorance. Some concluded that Jesus was in error, while others gave up eschatology altogether.

Although most interpreters today recognize the authenticity of the Discourse, at least two factors have stood in the way of a thorough interpretation of the Matthean version. The first is the knotty issue of synoptic relationships. Most scholars approach the Discourse with a rather too confident redaction-critical assumption regarding the direction of this relationship. The second issue is that many interpreters approach the Discourse from eschatological views too entrenched in presupposed theological frameworks to welcome new insights. Moreover, the few recent treatments have been rather piecemeal; certainly, many have been less than holistic.

To say that these have largely hampered the interpretation of Matt 24–25 is in no way to make light of the massive and painstaking effort that has been invested and continues to be invested into the passage and its synoptic parallels. Rather, it is to highlight the immense complexity of what is perhaps the most famous passage of the NT and the need not only to re-evaluate current interpretations but also to explore other hermeneutical approaches. This study is borne out of the conviction that to arrive at an accurate interpretation, Matt 24 and 25 must be taken together and the Discourse allowed to speak for itself in relation to Matthew's Gospel as a whole. It is an attempt at a holistic text-based approach that takes seriously the literary genre, seeks to discern the literary structure, and aims at a thorough and compelling interpretation of the Discourse.

Historical Overview

A detailed history of interpretation of the Eschatological Discourse is neither possible nor necessary for the main objective of the present investigation.[2]

---

2. An account of interpretations covering the entire length of Matt 24–25 through the ages has yet to be written. However, Gray makes a limited but most helpful

As such only a broad overview of interpretive trends will be undertaken here. In pursuit of this, I will survey the subject based on three considerations, namely: (1) pre-modern interpretations, (2) historical-critical currents, and (3) synopsis of evangelical positions. These considerations will reveal the prevailing need for further investigation of the passage. Since many interpretive moves in (1) reflect or influence the views in (3), I will reserve general critiques for the latter.

Premodern Interpretations

Many church fathers interpreted the Olivet Discourse largely futuristically.[3] As early as "the first or beginning of the second century," the *Didache*—"a church-manual of primitive Christianity or of some section of it"—declares in its sixteenth chapter:

> For in the last days *the false prophets* and corrupters shall be multiplied, and the sheep shall be turned into wolves, and love shall be turned into hate. For as lawlessness increaseth, *they shall hate one another and shall persecute and betray*. And then the world-deceiver *shall appear* as a son of God *and shall work signs and wonders*; and the earth shall be delivered into his hands and he shall do unholy things which have never been since the world began. Then all created mankind shall come to the fire of testing and many shall be offended and perish *but they that endure in their faith shall be saved* by the Curse Himself. And then shall *the signs of the truth appear*; first a sign of a rift in the heaven, then a sign of a voice of a trumpet, and thirdly a resurrection of the dead; yet not all, but as it was said: *The Lord shall come and all His saints with Him. Then shall the world see the Lord coming upon the clouds of heaven*.[4]

The *Didache*, drawing much from Matt 24 as some have argued,[5] interprets the tribulation as a future universal fiery test (πύρωσιν τῆς δοκιμασίας) of

---

contribution in her *Least of My Brothers*. See also Beasley-Murray, *Jesus and the Last Days*. First published in 1954 and written from the perspective of Mark 13, Beasley-Murray offers the most extensive critical history to date.

3. See commentaries by ancient fathers in Oden and Simonetti, *Ancient Christian Commentary*, 185–235; Aquinas, *Commentary*, 799–872.

4. Lightfoot, *Apostolic Fathers*, 215–16, 235.

5. See Balabanski, *Eschatology*, 180–205; Varner, "Didache 'Apocalypse' and Matthew 24," 309–22. Stanton states that the "*Didache* is undoubtedly dependent on Matthew and is both Jewish and Matthean in its ethos" (*Gospel for a New People*, 204–5); cf. marginal notes in Lightfoot, *Apostolic Fathers*, 224–25.

all humanity. Balabanski thinks that Didache's antichrist figure—the world-deceiver (κοσμοπλανής) may have developed from the combination of Matthew's "abomination of desolation" (Matt 24:15), the lawless watchers of the Enochian tradition (1 En. 7:2–6), and the *Nero redivivus myth*.[6]

While this judgment is uncertain as far as one can infer from the text itself, Irenaeus is known to be, perhaps, the first church father to move eschatology to the front burner in a systematic way by blending Dan 7, 2 Thess 2, and Matt 24:15 into a reference to a future Antichrist.[7] Origen and Hillary of Poitiers were mystical or fanciful at times, but they were also often futuristic in their interpretations.

However, it would be quite incorrect to simply label the church fathers as futurists. Origen himself relates aspects of the Discourse historically to the first century.[8] Hillary believes that of the threefold question of the disciples, Jesus answers the one concerning the destruction of the temple first,[9] even though, like Irenaeus, he views the abomination of desolation as a reference to some future Antichrist.[10]

Some of the church fathers were even more thoroughly historical. For example, relying heavily on "the historian" (Josephus), and combining elements from Matt 24:19–21 and Luke 19:42–44; 21:23–24, Eusebius, the fourth-century church historian, regards the Discourse as Jesus' prophetic expansion of the Roman destruction of Jerusalem under Vespasian.[11] Similarly, while Cyril of Alexandria could take the "end" in Matt 24:14 as the "last day of all"[12] or spiritualize the "flight" in 24:20, or in fact interpret 24:29–31 in terms of the "recapitulation of creation," he has no difficulty applying the Discourse to the destruction of Jerusalem and claiming that the disciples erroneously supposed that the teachings concerned the consummation of the age.[13] Augustine represents what might be considered a proto-historicist interpretation in his view that the Discourse addresses

---

6. Balabanski, *Eschatology*, 195.

7. Irenaeus, *Ad. Haer.* 5:25.

8. Origen, *Cels.* 2:13.

9. Hillary, *Comm. Matt.* 248.

10. Strauss claims that Irenaeus and Hillary "referred the entire prediction . . . to the still future return of Christ to judgment (*Life of Jesus*, 585).

11. Eusebius, *Hist. eccl.* 3:7; in his view, Christ finally abandoned Israel for the gentiles (cf. *Dem. ev.* 4:16).

12. Cyril of Alexandria, *Ths.*, in Kraszewski, *Gospel*, 353.

13. Cyril of Alexandria, *Frag.* 266, 269 and 271, in Reuss, *Matthaeus-Kommentare*, 153–269.

all things which were to come to pass from that time forward, whether relating to the destruction of Jerusalem, which had given occasion to their inquiry; or to His coming through the Church, in which He ceases not to come to the end of time; for He is acknowledged as coming among His own, while new members are daily born to Him; or relating to the end itself when He shall appear to judge the quick and the dead.[14]

The most important patristic treatments are the works of John Chrysostom[15] and Jerome.[16]

First, following a more literal interpretation, Chrysostom finds the disciples' inquiry to be twofold—concerning the destruction of the temple and the second coming. Chrysostom is of the view that Jesus corrects the disciples' suspicion that the world will end immediately after the destruction of the temple. His first answer (24:4–5) neither concerns the temple nor the second coming, but rather the evils which the disciples were to immediately experience. Chrysostom takes 24:6–22, including the preaching of the Gospel throughout the world, as fulfilled in the time before (24:6–14) and in the destruction of Jerusalem (24:15–22). Thus, for him, the "end" equals the destruction of Jerusalem; only from 24:23 does Jesus begin to focus strictly on the signs of his future second coming.[17] Consequently, Chrysostom interprets the sign of the Son of Man in 24:31 as the appearance of a bright cross in the sky heralding Christ's coming.[18] The expression "this generation" in 24:34 refers not to Jesus' contemporaries but to the age of the faithful. Chrysostom bases this on the claim that scriptures usually do not speak of "generation" chronologically only but also qualitatively in terms of kind of service and practice.[19]

Second, Jerome breaks the disciples' question into three—the time of Jerusalem's destruction, the second coming, and the consummation of the age.[20] Jerome leaves room for first-century fulfillments, but he clearly prefers futuristic interpretations, sometimes with significant doses of figurative connotations. For example, writing on 24:7–8, he states, "I do not call into question that these things that are written down are indeed predictions of

---

14. Augustine, *Ep.* 199. 25; Aquinas, *Commentary*, 803.

15. Chrysostom, *Hom. Matt.* 75–79.

16. Jerome, *Comm. Matt.*

17. Contra Carson who suggests Chrysostom took the second coming or *parousia* to begin at v. 36 ("Matthew," 552–53).

18. Chrysostom, *Hom. Matt.* 76.3.

19. Chrysostom, *Hom. Matt.* 77.1; cf. Gundry, *Matthew*, 490–91.

20. Jerome, *Comm. Matt.* 269.

future things ... but it seems to me that 'kingdom against kingdom' and 'pestilence' can be understood more of those [heretics] whose words creep in like cancer," adding, "The famine is the one for hearing the word of God."[21] For Jerome, the abomination of desolation may be interpreted literally in relation to the antichrist, but it can also be the image placed by Pilate in the temple or the statue of Hadrian "which stands to the present day in the holy of holies";[22] the spread of the gospel is either already completed or will be completed in a short time;[23] and "this generation" (24:34) refers to either the entire human race or the race of the Jews in particular."[24] Thus, Jerome is often imprecise. Unlike Chrysostom, his interpretation seems structurally amorphous because while first-century fulfillments are always in the background, he seems more driven by a futuristic schema.

During the Middle Ages, the interpretation of the Eschatological Discourse remained as diverse as commentators on it as Thomas Aquinas's *Catena Aurea* suggests. Aquinas records the view of two influential ninth-century medieval interpreters, Rabanus Maurus and Remigius of Auxerre. Their comments are fragmentary, but they held the Discourse to refer partly to the destruction of Jerusalem and partly to the end of the world in a literal sense. For Remigius, the "end" in 24:14 means the "end of life" but it could also mean the "end of the world" following the time of the Antichrist.[25] Remigius even takes 24:31 as a reference to the literal resurrection of the dead,[26] but he is not immune to allegorization as his view on vv. 40–41 shows. These verses, he claims, indicate three orders in the church: the two men in the field represent the order of preachers, the two grinding at the mill represent the order of married priests, and the two in bed represent the order of continence or repose of the righteous and the unrighteous.[27]

More could be said about many other medieval interpreters, but suffice it to say that during this period, emphasis on the *sensus literalis* appears to be on the upswing. Turning to the Reformation era, we observe that most interpreters from then up to the eighteenth century espoused the historicist view in general. That is, they correlated apocalyptic symbols with events in

---

21. Jerome, *Comm. Matt.* 270, 274.
22. Jerome, *Comm. Matt.* 272.
23. Jerome, *Comm. Matt.* 271.
24. Jerome, *Comm. Matt.* 277.
25. Aquinas, *Commentary*, 807, 808.
26. Aquinas, *Commentary*, 827.
27. Aquinas, *Commentary*, 835.

church history.[28] This applies especially to Martin Luther and John Calvin, although their views are more nuanced than just barefaced historicism.

On the one hand, Luther in a sermon on Matt 24:15–28, declares that Jesus in this passage, predicts the destruction of Jerusalem as well as the end of the world. However, while Luke (chs. 17 and 21) more clearly separates these events, Matthew (and Mark) has blended them together, focusing more on the end of the world than the destruction of Jerusalem.[29]

According to Luther, the first part (Matt 24:15–21) deals with the Jews. Here, Christ cites Daniel's prophecy of the abomination of desolation (Dan 9:27) to signal how Jerusalem and the Jewish kingdom would be destroyed forever. Luther claims that the abomination occurred during the reign of "Caius Caligula" [sic] who ordered his image to be set up in the temple at Jerusalem. The Jews vehemently protested and attempted to remove the image, but Pilate replaced it by night, causing great public uproar. Christ meant that this was to portend the destruction of Jerusalem as well as the fact that God would no longer dwell there.[30]

In the second part of the passage—from Matt 24:22[31]—Matthew leaves off the demise of the Jewish kingdom and focuses on the end of the world through the rest of the Discourse.[32] Luther then takes ample time to demonstrate how v. 23 has unfolded throughout the history of the Christian church up to his time, with the theme of false prophecy ultimately fulfilled in the false claims of the Papacy. The remainder of the sermon represents Luther's polemic against what he regards as papal abomination which fulfills the "abomination-of-desolation" prophecy of Daniel.

Calvin, on the other hand, believes that the disciples' question shows that they erroneously imagined that the temple could not fall without the entire world falling with it and the fullness of Christ's kingdom beginning immediately.[33] Thus, they confused the beginning of Christ's reign (the end of Judaism in the destruction of the temple) with the consummation of it. However, as Calvin believes, Jesus' response distinguishes the two events and exhorts them to patience.

---

28. Keener, *Revelation*, 27; Ice and Gentry, *Great Tribulation*, 6.

29. See "Sermon on Matt 24:15–28" in Luther, *Luthers Werke*, 3:192.

30. See "Sermon on Matt 24:15–28" in Luther, *Luthers Werke*, 3:193.

31. The view that a major shift occurs at 24:22 has been reinvented; see Carson, "Matthew," 564.

32. See "Sermon on Matt 24:15–28" in Luther, *Luthers Werke*, 195. Luther's interpretation of the Olivet Discourse ends with another Sermon on Matt 25:31–46 which he takes as the judgment of the last day when Christ visibly returns; see Lenker, *Sermons of Martin Luther*, 5:379–95.

33. Calvin, *Harmony*, 3:75.

Without going into many details, Calvin sees past events, the continuing experience of the church, and the future advent of Christ in Matt 24. The major elements of his interpretation may be summarized in six points: (1) Matt 24:4–14 strictly refers to events in Judea. While holding this view, Calvin does not hesitate to make contemporary as well as global applications. On 24:14, he comments that the preaching of the Gospel is "to the furthest ends of the earth," rejecting the idea of some who he says, "wrongly restrict to the destruction of the temple and the abolition of legal worship what should be understood of the end and renewal of the world." In other words, for Calvin, the word "end" refers not to the temple's destruction, but to the end of the world as it is. As Calvin argues, Jesus meant that "the end of the age will not come until I have long tested my Church with hard and wearisome temptations."[34] Obviously, Calvin is anything but a pretribulationist.[35] (2) Matthew 24:15–28 refers to the destruction of the temple/Judaism. Within this section, vv. 26–27 represents a contrast between the secrecy of Christ's appearance as claimed by first-century false prophets and the sudden and unexpected speed with which the kingdom of Christ spreads throughout the entire world.[36] (3) The enigmatic saying of 24:28 is understood ecclesiologically and polemically as a reference to the gathering of the saints in Christ as the bond of their unity as opposed to the Papal See. As Calvin opines, Christ employs an *argumentum a fortiori* (from the lesser to the greater): If the birds are so wise that many come together from distant regions over one corpse, it would be shameful for the faithful not to be drawn to the Author of life, from whom alone they take true nourishment."[37] (4) Verse 29 introduces a shift from reference to Jerusalem to the general recapitulation of the evils as Christ had stated earlier and the subsequent physical appearance of Christ at his last coming (24:30–31). Calvin does not take the fall of stars and angelic gathering of saints literally but as hyperbolic expressions indicating cosmic disturbances and the certainty of the saints' convergence to Christ respectively. (5) The phrase "this generation" in 24:34 is Christ's way of saying "in one generation," by which he means his own contemporaries who will experience every aspect of what he has predicted. However, it does not exclude future generations from the same kind of experience: "The Lord heaps on one generation calamities of every

---

34. Calvin, *Harmony*, 83.

35. Contra prominent Calvinists such as John F. MacArthur who espouse pretribulational rapture views although this runs counter to Calvinism. See MacArthur, *Second Coming*; MacArthur, *Matthew 24–28*, 15, 23, 65, 70–72.

36. Calvin, *Harmony*, 91 (influenced much here by Luke 17:20–24).

37. Calvin, *Harmony*, 92.

description," Calvin says, "although He does not spare later generations."[38] And 6) vv. 36–51 deals with the uncertain timing and suddenness of Christ's coming and the need to be alert.[39]

Finally, the interpretation of Johann Albrecht Bengel (1687–1752) deserves attention for its significant contribution during the period just before the rise of modern criticism.[40] A pietist and one of the most important exegetes of the era, Bengel begins his interpretation of the Discourse based on an alternating outline. He notes that the disciples ask two questions (1) concerning the *time* of the destruction of the temple, and (2) concerning the *sign* of the coming of Christ and the end of the world. Like Calvin, Bengel alleges that they did this without distinguishing the two concerns but rather conflated them as the same event. In response, Jesus separates these two events each with its own preceding signs in the order: (1) the destruction of the temple and its signs (Matt 24:4–5, 15–16); (2) the coming of Christ and the end of the world and its signs (24:29–31); (3) the time of the temple's destruction (24:32–33); and (4) the time of the end of the world (24:36). It is unclear why Bengel does not account for the omitted verses in this outline, but he seems to imply an A-B-A-B arrangement.[41]

Perhaps the most significant part of Bengel's interpretation is his handling of 24:29. He makes four observations: (1) Jesus speaks literally in the verse; (2) the tribulation in question deals specifically with a single generation of Jews; (3) what is said is neither "after that tribulation" nor "after those days" but "after the tribulation of those days"; and (4) the expression "immediately" implies a very short delay. To meet the challenge of why this verse should be transferred into the distant future end of the world disconnected from the temple's destruction, Bengel invents a hermeneutical principle that would prove influential for the interpretation of prophetic discourses in general. He describes this principle as follows:

> A prophecy resembles a landscape painting, which represents distinctly the houses, paths, and bridges in the foreground, but brings together, into a narrow space, most widely severed valleys and mountains in the distance. Such a view should they who study prophecy have of the future to which the prophecy refers. And the eyes of the disciples, who in their question had connected the end of the temple with that of the world, are left somewhat in the dark (for it was not yet time to know; ver. 36),

---

38. Calvin, *Harmony*, 98.
39. Calvin, *Harmony*, 98–109.
40. See Beasley-Murray, *Jesus and the Last Days*, 127–28.
41. Bengel, *New Testament Commentary*, 1:268.

hence they afterward, with entire harmony, imitated the Lord's language, and declared that the end was at hand. By advancing, however, both the prophecy and the prospect continually reveal a further and still further distance.[42]

In other words, this principle describes the way Seers viewed prophetic events as occurring in close connection to each other, even though they may be long intervals apart in reality. Applying this perspective helps to explain predictive prophecies. In this case, it helps to explain how the destruction of Jerusalem and Christ's *parousia* in the distant future can exist in immediate connection. Bengel's landscape-painting analogy attracted a heavy assault by the rationalists of the following century[43] as it has in recent times as well.[44] However, known by different names,[45] it has remained a popular hermeneutical key for interpreters of biblical prophecy.

Historical-Critical Currents and Interpretations

As already noted above, the most comprehensive documentation of the history of modern critical investigation on the Eschatological Discourse remains Beasley-Murray's *Jesus and the Last Days*.[46] In this work, Beasley-Murray critiques what is now a largely abandoned theory—the Little Apocalypse theory[47]—as well as provides an extensive commentary on the Markan version of the Olivet Discourse. However, by its absolute assumption of Markan priority, this work also aptly demonstrates the prevailing bias in Gospel scholarship. Although the direction of the synoptic relationship is out of the question in the present study, it is important to keep in

---

42. Bengel, *New Testament Commentary*, 274.

43. Strauss regards the interpretation as an ingenious attempt to absolve Jesus of error, citing Paulus who compares it to one laboring "under an optical delusion" (*Life of Jesus*, 591).

44. For a recent critique of the prophetic perspective, see Otto, "Prophets," 219–40.

45. See Otto, "Prophets," 219.

46. Beasley-Murray, *Jesus and the Last Days*.

47. Colani postulated this theory in his work, *Jèsus Christ*, in which he dismissed the synoptic Eschatological Discourse in Mark 13 (and parr.) as having no link to Jesus, contending instead that it derives from a Jewish apocalyptic tract originally "composed before the destruction of Jerusalem and interwoven with a short exhortation Jesus gave on the occasion when he predicted the destruction of the temple" (cited in Schweitzer, *Quest*, 224). Beasley-Murray shows the difficulty of isolating interpolations from the original apocalypse, arguing that the Discourse is Mark's eschatological exposition of Jesus' prophecy most likely composed during or around the Roman-Jewish war and drawing from various available sources (*Jesus and the Last Days*, 32–349; 354, 363). Cf. Gaston, *No Stone on Another*, 47; Burnett, *Testament*, 11–12.

mind that before the rise of modern critical scholarship, and indeed, well into the nineteenth century, "the eschatology of Jesus meant consideration of the Eschatological discourse of Matt. 24–25."[48]

David F. Strauss is perhaps the most influential and controversial figure of the modern era. Albert Schweitzer describes his *Life of Jesus* as "one of the most perfect things in the whole range of learned literature."[49] Rejecting the theory of Markan priority,[50] Strauss takes Matt 24–25 as the axiomatic starting point for examining the eschatology of Jesus.[51] However, he criticizes all contemporary attempts to find a long gap between the destruction of Jerusalem and Jesus' return, as borne out of hopeless desperation.[52] "It is impossible to evade the acknowledgment," he argues, "that in this discourse, if we do not mutilate it to suit our own views, Jesus at first speaks of the destruction of Jerusalem, and further on and until the close, of his return at the end of all things, and that he places the two events in immediate connexion."[53] Therefore, since it has been 1800 years and Jesus has not visibly returned, he must be mistaken in this particular regard.[54]

Although Strauss considers Jesus to be in error regarding his *parousia*, he nevertheless concedes that the Discourse represents Jesus' prediction of the destruction of Jerusalem and his visible return. However, such concession was soon overrun by rationalist anti-supernaturalistic objections inspired by Samuel Reimarus about a century earlier.[55] Many rationalists of the day regarded the notion of a second coming as a misinterpretation of Jesus by his disciples. F. C. Baur rejects both "the orthodox" view that

---

48. Beasley-Murray, *Jesus and the Last Days*, 2.

49. Schweitzer, *Quest*, 78.

50. C. H. Weisse and C. G. Wilke proposed the priority of Mark in 1838, just after the first edition of Strauss' *Life of Jesus* appeared in 1835–36. But Strauss did not accept the hypothesis in the subsequent editions of his *Life of Jesus*, informing Schweitzer's description of him as "the passionate opponent of Marcan hypothesis," Schweitzer, *Quest*, 203 (cf. 88, 128, and 195).

51. Strauss, *Life of Jesus*, 334.

52. Strauss, *Life of Jesus*, 582–89.

53. Strauss, *Life of Jesus*, 589.

54. Strauss, *Life of Jesus*, 591.

55. According to Reimarus (*Aims of Jesus and His Disciples*, based on Matt 10:23, Jesus aimed to provoke popular acclaim of himself as the political-eschatological messiah and thus to bring about an earthly kingdom in which he would be the ruler. Distinguishing between this political eschatology and apocalyptic eschatology, he ascribes the latter to the disciples. Schweitzer praises Reimarus as the first of the rationalists to grasp the eschatological consciousness of Jesus but critiques the assumption that Jesus' eschatology was earthly and political (non-apocalyptic) as his "sole mistake." See Schweitzer, *Quest*, 13–26, esp. 23–24; cf. Strauss, *Life of Jesus*, 4–5.

sought to dissociate the destruction of Jerusalem and the return of Christ and the "not orthodox" view of Strauss, his student.[56] Baur takes the lack of mention of the destruction of Jerusalem in the book of Revelation to indicate that Jesus neither predicted the event nor spoke of his *parousia*.[57] Thus, the Discourse must be regarded as *vaticinum post eventum*.[58] Further, Baur argues that the author of Matt 24 wrote around 130–34 CE during the Jewish revolt instigated by Hadrian's assault on the holy place.[59] Baur's interpretation is built on faulty Hegelian assumptions,[60] and his claim of late dates for the Gospels did not survive long after.[61]

During the last half of the nineteenth century, the view of an eschatological Jesus who imagined a future second coming came under even heavier assault,[62] resulting in an anti-eschatological climate that endured until it met its challenge in Johannes Weiss and ultimately in Albert Schweitzer's consistent eschatology.[63] Drawing from Weiss, Schweitzer argues that Jesus is more properly understood in light of Jewish apocalyptic tradition as thoroughly eschatological. Unfortunately, Schweitzer's interpretation of the synoptic apocalyptic material would prove even more devastating to eschatology. Based on his reading of Matt 10:23, Jesus expected the imminent coming of the Son of Man and the end of the world preceded by suffering for his followers. By claiming that this prediction of tribulation for his disciples failed to materialize,[64] Schweitzer contends it was Jesus' understanding that God "had eliminated it [general tribulation] from the series of the eschatological events and appointed to Him . . . to bring it about instead in his own person."[65] Schweitzer's infamous caricature of Jesus' "failure" is etched in these words:

---

56. See Baur, *Lectures*, 139.
57. Baur, *Lectures*, 139.
58. Baur, *Lectures*, 140.
59. See Baur, *Lectures*, 299–306.
60. See Zetterholm, *Approaches to Paul*, 33–40; Baur embraced Hegelian philosophy through the influence of Strauss, "the apostle of Hegel" as Schweitzer, *Quest*, 68–71, describes him.
61. Lightfoot's early dating of the *Epistles of Clement of Rome, Ignatius, and Didache*, all of which show Matthean influence contributed to the demise of Baur's theory (see Lightfoot, *Apostolic Fathers*, 3–40, 97–134, 215–25).
62. Colani, *Jèsus Christ*, was a major impetus to this effect.
63. Weiss, *Prediqt* (1892); Schweitzer, *Quest*, 328–96.
64. The "non-fulfillment of Matt 10:23 is [for Schweitzer] the first postponement [or delay] of the parousia" (*Quest*, 358).
65. Schweitzer, *Quest*, 387.

> Jesus . . . in the knowledge that he is the coming Son of Man lays hold of the wheel of the world to set it moving on that last revolution which is to bring all ordinary history to a close. It refuses to turn, and he throws himself upon it. Then it does turn and crushes him. Instead of bringing in the eschatological conditions, he has destroyed them. The wheel rolls onward, and the mangled body of the one immeasurably great man, who was strong enough to think of himself as the spiritual ruler of mankind and to bend history to his purpose, is hanging upon it still. That is his victory and his reign.[66]

Based on this claim, Schweitzer concludes that "the predictions of suffering and tribulation in the Synoptic Apocalypse in Mark 13 [and in Matt 24] cannot be derived from Jesus."[67] In other words, the future second coming idea was a conspiracy created by the evangelists to cover up Jesus' failure.[68]

After Schweitzer, credit for the decline of future eschatology goes especially to Rudolph Bultmann and C. H. Dodd. Like Schweitzer, they are skeptical of the Apocalyptic Discourse, but in opposition to his notion of thoroughgoing eschatology in Jesus' mindset and teaching, they favor non-futuristic interpretations of the existential and realized forms respectively. Bultmann's understanding of the Eschatological Discourse is based not on an analysis of the passage in whole (as is the case with many of the critical scholars discussed here), but on an existential conception of the kingdom of God. The kingdom of God, says Bultmann, is not something that is to come in the course of time, somewhere or sometime, but rather as "a power which, *although it is entirely future, wholly determines the present*" and constrains man to decision.[69] Thus, although Bultmann thinks that "the predictions of the *parousia* are old and are probably original words of Jesus,"[70] he considers most of the apocalyptic predictions of the return of the Son of Man as inauthentic.[71] As Bultmann argues, "The synoptic tradition contains no saying in which Jesus says he will some time (or soon) return. Nor was

---

66. Schweitzer, *Quest*, 368–69.

67. Schweitzer, *Quest*, 387n1.

68. Ladd, *Presence of the Future*, 4 notes that "Schweitzer did not arrive at his interpretation by an inductive study of the Gospels, but by assuming that Jesus must be interpreted in terms of his environment—Jewish apocalyptic," adding, "the result was a historical figure who belonged only to the first century."

69. Bultmann, *Jesus and the World*, 51 (italics original). For more on Bultmann's existential eschatology, see his *History and Eschatology*, 138–55; and *Interpreting Faith*, 118–20.

70. Bultmann, *Theology*, 30.

71. Bultmann, *Theology*, 27–30, 42; cf. Bultmann, *History of the Synoptic Tradition*, 122.

the word *parousia*, which denotes the 'coming' of the Son of Man, ever understood in the earliest period of Christianity as 'return,' but correctly as 'arrival, advent.'"⁷² In Matt 24:27, 37, 44 (and parr.), Bultmann observes that "Jesus speaks of the Son of Man in the third person without identifying himself with him," concluding that the identification of Jesus with Son of Man owes itself to the church *ex-eventu*.⁷³

On his part, Dodd is famous for his realized eschatology—a conception of the kingdom of God formulated on the basis of his claim that the term ἐγγίζω ("to come near"; Mark 1:14–15) is equivalent to φθάνω ("to arrive"; Matt 12:28//Luke 11:20).⁷⁴ To this effect, Dodd contends that "Jesus intended to proclaim the Kingdom of God not as something to come in the near future, but as a matter of present experience."⁷⁵ Dodd believes that some of the predictive sayings in the Gospels cannot be regarded as *vaticinia ex eventu*, but he allows the possibility that these predictions reflect the experience of the church by which they have been colored.⁷⁶ Dodd prefers Matt 24:37–39 (par. Luke 17:26–27) as more consistent and earlier than Mark 13:14–25. However, he finds the term *parousia* in Matt 24 inauthentic, preferring the phrase "the Day of the Son of Man" derived from Luke 17:24, 26.⁷⁷ In this way, Dodd is able not only to exclude the notion of a second coming, but also to claim that the "Coming of the Son of Man" sayings originally referred to "three aspects of one idea"—resurrection, ascension, and *parousia*. Dodd concludes that the church has reinterpreted the sayings in light of its own experience post-Easter.⁷⁸ Thus, where Jesus "had referred to one single event, they made distinction between two events, one past,

---

72. Bultmann, *Theology*, 29–31.

73. Bultmann, *Theology*, 29.

74. Dodd, *Parables*, 44.

75. Dodd, *Parables*, 46.

76. Dodd, *Parables*, 51.

77. Dodd, *Parables*, 83n1. Dodd takes the "Little Apocalypse" theory for granted and considers the predictive discourse in Mark 13 (elaborated in Matthew) as lying "under the suspicion of being a secondary composition; though it no doubt incorporates genuine sayings of Jesus, we cannot use it as it stands for evidence of his own forecast of the future" (52–53, 133); cf. Dodd, "Fall of Jerusalem," 47–54. Dodd makes no mention of Matt 24–25 at all.

78. Dodd, *Parables*, 98–101; cf. Glasson, *Second Advent*; Robinson, *Jesus and His Coming*. Both argue that the notion of second coming is a later invention, although they did not originate this view. Weiffenbach had earlier contended for the simultaneity of resurrection and *parousia* based on Matt 16:13–28 and *par*. (*Wiederkunftsgedanke Jesu*, 373–424). For a counter argument against this view, see Allison, *End of the Ages*, 160–62; he demonstrates that although the early Christians interpreted the passion and resurrection in terms of realized eschatology (an "already" view), they held a "not yet" view that was continuous with their pre-Easter expectation.

his resurrection from the dead, and one future, his coming on the clouds."[79] For Dodd's realized eschatological schema to work, he must further deny authenticity to the parables that indicate a future coming of Jesus for judgment, such as Matt 25:31–46.[80]

Some scholars who remain persuaded about Matthew's emphasis on future eschatology interpret it only as a window into the life and times of the Matthean church. Two significant figures in this regard are H. B. Streeter[81] and Günther Bornkamm.[82]

In his influential work on the Synoptic Gospels, Streeter primarily aims to resolve the synoptic problem by establishing Matthew's use of Mark and other sources. In doing this, Matthew's Gospel must be placed after 70 CE according to his reading of Matt 24. Streeter begins by asserting that the fall of Jerusalem produced intense apocalyptic speculation among both Jews and Christians alike.[83] "When Mark wrote (c. 65)," he claims, "it seemed possible that the prophecies of the appearance of the anti-Christ and the Return of Christ within the lifetime of the first generation might be fulfilled. But with every year after AD 75, the non-fulfillment of these prophecies became a more grievous difficulty to the early church."[84]

According to Streeter, Matthew resolves this problem in two ways, first, by omitting Mark's veiled reference (ὅπου οὐ δεῖ [Mark 13:14]) to the temple, and second, by detaching the Anti-Christ expectation from its local connection to Jerusalem. In this latter move, Matthew opens the door for interpreting the abomination of desolation in relation to the *Nero-redivivus* myth which flourished at Antioch where, as Streeter claims, Matthew wrote in 85 CE, and where intense apocalyptic expectation had been inspired by the Jewish war of 70 CE.[85] The problem with this is that Matthew's ἐν τόπῳ ἁγίῳ (24:15) appears to more explicitly reference a yet-standing temple than Mark's ὅπου οὐ δεῖ. Indeed, Matthew's connection of Christ's *parousia* with a supposedly past event from a post-75 standpoint appears irreconcilable with Streeter's claims. Yet Streeter curiously maintains that Matthew does not desire to tone down passages that imply the immediacy of Christ's *parousia*. "No Gospel," he asserts, "makes so much as does Matthew of the

79. Dodd, *Parables*, 101; cf. Beasley-Murray, *Jesus and Last Days*, 96–97; Smalley, "Delay," 42–43.
80. Dodd, *Parables*, 85n1; cf. Wilson, *When Will These Things Happen?*, 23–24.
81. Streeter, *Four Gospels*.
82. Bornkamm, "End Expectation."
83. Streeter, *Four Gospels*, 517.
84. Streeter, *Four Gospels*, 518.
85. Streeter, *Four Gospels*, 520–23.

expectation that the visible return of Christ will be within the lifetime of those who saw and heard him (cf. Matt 10:23)."[86]

For Bornkamm, the central emphasis of Matthew consists in the link between eschatology and ecclesiology—the coming judgment and the need for strict discipleship within the church. Bornkamm seeks to demonstrate how Matthew has redacted Mark to make this connection throughout the Gospel. Matthew does this with the view to combat antinomianism by promoting radical adherence to the law in the form of a new righteousness by which standard the members of the Church should expect to be judged at the return of the Son of Man.[87] Bornkamm maintains that Matthew's Gospel is dominated by end-of-the-world apocalyptic expectation. He considers Matt 24–25 to be typical for the end-expectation schema. Thus, broadly dividing the Discourse into two parts—*apocalyptic discourse* (Matt 24) and *eschatological parables*—he contends that "in these parables [including 24:45–51] the thought of judgment is solely directed to the Church,"[88] concluding:

> It would be difficult to maintain that the description of the judgment of the world, with which—no longer in parabolic form—the whole construction of the discourse concludes, refers only to the judgment that is to come upon the Gentiles in distinction from the members of the community of Jesus. Rather it is typical for the end-expectation of Matthew that by means of a great picture already current among Jews the judgment of the world is announced as applying to 'all nations', but now in such a way that no distinction is made between Jews and Gentiles, nor even between believers and unbelievers. All are gathered before the tribunal of the judge of the world and are judged by the 'one' standard, namely that of the love they have shown towards or withheld from, the humblest.[89]

O. L. Cope once complained that Bornkamm's insights have been paid little attention. He considers two reasons for this to be (1) that "Bornkamm's argument is, for the most part, persuasive," and (2) that he may have understated his case.[90] Yet because of his redaction-critical approach, what Bornkamm has done is make eschatology subservient to ecclesiology, with the former only intended for a parenetic function in service of the latter. Later, many interpreters, such as Georg Strecker and Wolfgang Trilling,

---

86. Streeter, *Four Gospels*, 520.
87. Bornkamm, "End Expectation," 24.
88. Bornkamm, "End Expectation," 23.
89. Bornkamm, "End Expectation," 23–24.
90. Cope, "Close of the Age," 113.

further marginalized eschatology and Christology in Matthew, placing greater emphasis on salvation-history and ecclesiology.[91]

One of the controlling presuppositions of the historical-critical exegesis is the view that Matt 24–25 is simply a reconstructed version of Mark 13. Burnett's 1979 *Testament of Jesus-Sophia* appears to be the most extensive monograph on Matt 24 following the redaction-critical approach.[92] I will discuss Burnett's work and contribution later in this study, but the redaction-critical methodology has become so deeply and firmly entrenched within Gospel scholarship that by 1992, Ben Witherington III could claim that "the redactional character in Matthew 24 must be considered virtually certain."[93] In that case, Matthew's unique materials can be considered suspect for inauthenticity. N. T. Wright re-enacts the view of the realized eschatological school, which denies the authenticity of the term *parousia* in Matthew. For Wright, the absence of the term in Mark 13 and Luke 21 (assumed more historical) makes its occurrence in Matthew least historically plausible.[94]

In this brief survey of historical-critical currents and interpretations, several issues are evident. The approach is not only fragmentary in nature with its focus on bits and pieces of texts, but also rooted in skepticism and suspicion regarding the historical authenticity of the Discourse. Often, whether or not a particular tradition is authentic or not depends on the presuppositions and conjectural reconstructions of the interpreter. Also, many of these interpretations depend on the absolute assumption of the Markan hypothesis as well as a post-70 composition of Matthew's Gospel. If the scholarly consensus is correct, then Matt 24–25 is secondary to Mark 13 and represents an after-the-fact reconstruction by some unknown scribe.[95] However, it is important to keep in mind at least three significant caveats.

First, most of the evidence for deciding synoptic relationship—internal or external—are capable of alternative interpretations.[96] In fact, the en-

91. For more on Trilling and Strecker, see Kingsbury, *Matthew*, 25–36; Bauer, *Structure*, 45–49.

92. See Burnett, Testament, esp. 11–12.

93. Witherington, *Jesus, Paul, and the End*, 171.

94. Wright, *Jesus and the Victory*, 345–46, 635 (cf. Wright, *New Testament and the People*, 461–63); Dodd, *Parables*, 83n1.

95. Note that the view that the Gospels were compiled by people other than the evangelists whose names became appended on them has been persuasively challenged; see Bauckham, *Eyewitnesses*.

96. Cope, for example, challenges Bornkamm's uncritical assumption of Markan priority. He raises two objections: (1) "Several judgments about Matthew's work based on that premise [of Matthew's use of Mark] may be more understandable if the reverse is true." (2) As to the claim that "Matthew is re-Judaizing the Hellenistic tradition found in Mark (or Q), it is much more likely that the early tradition was already Judaized and that Mark and Luke have Hellenized it" ("Close of the Age," 114).

tire Markan priority edifice rests on a hypothetical foundation upon which many advocates are now reluctant to build.[97] If the fundamental Q element of the theory has become so doubtful, why should one give absolute credence to it as the solution to the synoptic problem?[98] Moreover, the available data is complex and limited, and therefore, does not warrant the absolute adoption of any solution or particular direction of redaction.[99]

Second, while redaction critics do not necessarily reject Matt 24–25 as originating from Jesus, and indeed, while redaction criticism yields significant theological insight, the "Matthew-copied-Mark" hermeneutic often appears petty and exaggerated in attributing every single variation in the Discourse to Matthew's alteration of Mark.[100] It certainly hinders a text-focused interpretation of Matthew's Discourse on its own terms.

Third, although a large majority of scholars now date Matthew around the 80s CE, such dating is clearly uncertain.[101] In fact, there has been compelling evidence in favor of a pre-70 dating of Matthew as a whole,[102] and the Eschatological Discourse in particular.[103] However, even if Matthew was written as late as most scholars presume, one must be careful to differentiate between "date of composition" and "age of tradition."[104] Irrespective of when Matthew was penned, it is not impossible that it represents the

---

97. E.g., Wright believes some form of the hypothesis should remain fruitful, "but it does seem to me," he says, "that the more speculation there is about Q, the less plausible the hypothesis appears overall. . . . Supporters of Q should beware; if first-century editors were allowed to omit as well as to add material, the case for saying that Luke simply used Matthew looks more and more plausible" (*New Testament and the People*, 441). In another work, he writes, "I am not even sure whether to believe in Q or not and, if so, in what version of it" (*Resurrection*, 403). Cf. France, who maintains: "As for a unitary document 'Q,' I am among the growing number of scholars who find it an improbably simple hypothesis" (*Matthew*, 21).

98. Some have, indeed, maintained Markan priority without the necessity of Q, a view pioneered by Farrer, "On Dispensing with Q," 55–88.

99. See France, *Matthew*, 20–22.

100. E.g., Gundry, *Matthew*, 474–75.

101. See Mwangomo, "Critique." For how shaky the post-70 dating is, see Keener, *Matthew*, 44. Von Harnack asserts that the dating of Matthew's Gospel [in particular] cannot be proven with absolute certainty (*Date*, 134).

102. See Gundry, *Matthew*, 475, 599–609; France, *Matthew*, 18–19; Carson, "Matthew," 43–45; Keener, *Matthew*, 562. Hare argues that "sabbath" in 24:20 would be inappropriate and meaningless if Matthew is writing the Discourse as a fulfilled prophecy. Although, it seems curious that he also both concurs with the post-70 date consensus and advocates an entirely futuristic view of the whole Discourse (*Theme*, 177–78; *Matthew*, 277).

103. See Reicke, "Synoptic Prophecies," 121–34.

104. See Catchpole, "Poor on Earth," 379.

tradition more faithfully. The possibility of the Matthean Olivet tradition being earlier than those of Mark and Luke is well-documented.[105] In any case, for many interpreters, Matt 24–25 retains its prominence as the most comprehensive explication of Jesus' eschatology. There is hardly any reason why it cannot be the starting point for NT eschatology in general.

Synopsis of Evangelical Positions on Matt 24–25

Most evangelical interpreters of Matt 24–25, irrespective of their dating of the Gospel or what editorial changes Matthew is alleged to have made, recognize its predictive character. However, there remains no consensus on the issue of referent—Jerusalem's fall, Jesus' second coming, or both—and, if both, where the line(s) should be drawn. In deciding this issue, interpreters must first determine how many questions the disciples ask and how many Jesus answers, the order in which he addresses them, or in fact, whether or not he answers the question(s) at all.[106]

Based on the combination of these matters, evangelical interpretations fall into one of at least three schools according to Stanley D. Toussaint:[107] (1) "Past fulfillment"—the view that much of Matt 24 refers to the destruction of Jerusalem;[108] (2) "Fulfillment in the church age"—the view that the passage describes general conditions between Christ's first and second advents; and (3) "Fulfillment in the tribulation"—a view which gives the whole Discourse an entirely future referent and to which many premillennialists and Toussaint himself subscribe.

While this threefold categorization has remained standard for most part of the history of interpretation, David L. Turner has sought to update the classification based on what he considers to be the four generally agreed structural transitions (24:4–14, 15–28, 29–31, 32–41).[109] What follows is a

---

105. For instance, although David Wenham maintains the two-source hypothesis as the solution for the synoptic problem, he also argues that a pre-synoptic form known and used independently by Matthew, Mark, and Luke, lay behind the Eschatological Discourse, and that "Matthew appears from our study as the evangelist who most often and most fully reproduces the pre-synoptic form of the tradition," adding, "Mark abbreviates it substantially; Luke is the most free, so far as order is concerned" (*Rediscovery*, 365, 369–70).

106. For a helpful survey of views on these issues, see Christian, "Questionable Inversion," 45–46.

107. Toussaint, *Behold the King*, 266–67.

108. Toussaint, *Behold the King*, 266, notes, "There are none who actually believe the entire Discourse has already been fulfilled."

109. Turner, "Structure," 3–27; Turner, *Matthew*, 566–67.

reappraisal of the resulting four main evangelical positions. I will conclude with a brief mention of one view that has fallen out of favor and/or been just simply neglected.

Futurist Interpretation

The futurist interpretation has for a long time been the dominant view within evangelicalism.[110] It is often traced back to some of the church fathers and held by dispensational pretribulational premillennialists.[111] These interpreters find nothing in the Discourse that addresses the historical past. Based on their distinction between two comings of Christ—the coming for the rapture of the church and the second coming, they argue that the Discourse concerns only a future great tribulation, which will afterward be followed by the second coming of Jesus. According to Walvoord, "those who believe that the rapture, or translation of the church, occurs before the time of trouble at the end of the age usually do not believe that the rapture [pretribulational or posttribulational] is in view at all in this discourse."[112]

This view is challenged by only a minority of futurist interpreters.[113] But perhaps the most significant element is the claim that "Matthew does not answer the first question, which relates to the destruction of Jerusalem in AD 70,"[114] although it is admitted that Luke does.[115] By implication, according to the dispensational schema, the Discourse has "nothing to do with the church."[116]

In response, although this futuristic interpretation has retained hegemony in popular literature, one does not need a lot of hard thinking to see its numerous and serious problems. First, the futurist view violates the common exegetical rule of literary and historical context. Given the build-up

---

110. Ice and Gentry, *Great Tribulation*, 5–7.

111. E.g., Walvoord, *Kingdom Come*, 179–204; Barbieri, "Matthew," 76–81. See also Rand, "Survey," 162–73; Price, *Jesus' Prophetic Sermon*. For an expanded list, see Hart, "Should Pretribulationists Reconsider the Rapture?," 1:51–75, here 52n7.

112. Walvoord, *Kingdom Come*, 181.

113. For instance, Hart, himself a futurist, argues for a rather curious chiastic structure of Matt 24 that makes it possible for vv. 36–44 to refer to a pretribulation rapture. He lists more futurists who also see the rapture in these verses ("Should Pretribulationists Reconsider the Rapture?," 53n8).

114. Walvoord, *Kingdom Come*, 182.

115. Barbieri, "Matthew," 76.

116. Barbieri, "Matthew," 76; cf. Ware, "Is the Church in View?," 158–72. Note that an entirely futurist view does not necessitate the exclusion of the church, e.g., Hare, *Theme of Jewish Persecution*, 177–79; Hare, *Matthew*, 273–91.

of the theme of judgment from Matt 21, leading up to Jesus' desertion of the temple in 23:38-39, and culminating in the exchange in 24:1-3 and the emphatic warnings that follow (vv. 4, 15-18, 20, 23-25), it is grossly unlikely that Jesus' response lacks any connection both to the very temple about which an inquiry is made and to the ones directly addressed. Nor is it likely that the expression "this generation" (24:34) could have meant to the disciples something other than the natural meaning—their own time.

Second, the futurist view is based on an argument from supposed silence. Thomas Ice and Darrel L. Bock contend that while Luke emphasizes 70 CE, Matthew and Mark deal with a different future temple.[117] This amounts to the erroneous notion, "if emphases are different, then there must be different referents." Such a notion is hardly tenable for other synoptic traditions. While the admission that Luke records Jesus' answer regarding the first-century temple and the denial of the same to Matthew has the appearance of hermeneutical caution—an attempt to avoid harmonizing Matthew with Luke—it is indeed quite telling. The very fact that Luke connects Jesus' response to the first-century temple undercuts the dispensational futurist view since both accounts are of the same Discourse. To assume that Matthew is unconcerned about or does not record something, and then proceed to construct a theological schema on the assumption is, mildly put, hermeneutically invalid. Also, the notion of a rebuilt future temple to which 24:15 may refer is only a fantastic assumption that lacks any iota of exegetical warrant in Matt 24-25 or Matthew as a whole.[118] Moreover, the dispensational pretribulational rapture schema at the root of the futurist interpretation has largely been discredited, and rightly so since it is hardly biblically well-grounded.[119]

Third, futurists' claim that the Olivet Discourse addresses only Israel and not the Church is inaccurate. Gundry designates the view as hyper-dispensationalism, persuasively arguing that contextual evidence suggests that the Discourse addresses the church and not Israel.[120] However, Bruce A. Ware rejects Gundry's view and maintains the Israel-only view.[121] The present study contends that both the church-only and the Israel-only views should be rejected. There is no unambiguous reason in Matthew why the disciples whom Jesus addresses in Matt 24-25 should exclusively represent

117. See Ice and Gentry, *Great Tribulation*, 96-97; Bock, *Luke*, 1675-77.

118. Matt 23:39 cannot be co-opted into giving a hint of future temple restoration as YongHan Chung weakly attempts to do ("Temple in Matthew's eschatology," 191.

119. See, e.g., Ladd, *Blessed Hope*; Hoekema, *Bible and the Future*, 194-222; Walvoord's critique of Ladd's work in his "Review," 289-307 is largely unsuccessful.

120. Gundry, *Church and the Tribulation*, 129-39.

121. Ware, "Is the Church in View?," 158-72.

either Israel or the church. These either/or views are based on too radical a distinction between Israel and Church. The status of the disciples, as Matthew presents it, admits both/and representation. The disciples constitute a nuclear nation and foundation of the church, to whom Jesus promises the "keys of the Kingdom" (Matt 16:18-19, cf. 18:17). This promise is implied in Matt 21:43 where the expression, ἔθνει ποιοῦντι τοὺς καρποὺς αὐτῆς ("a nation yielding the fruits of it") designates the disciples as opposed to the Jewish leaders who fail to produce such fruits.[122]

Two significant observations support this claim. First, the announcement in Matt 21:41-45 exists in a logical connection with the elaboration of the failure of the Jewish leaders in chapter 23, including their "missional" failure in vv. 13-15.[123] Second, when Jesus implies in Matt 23:13 that the Jewish leaders hold the keys but have shut the [door of the] Kingdom (κλείετε τὴν βασιλείαν), he alludes back to the promise of κλεῖδας τῆς βασιλείας in Matt 16:19.

In view of these connections, it is plausible to read καρποὺς αὐτῆς in Matt 21:43 not only in the ethical sense, but also in the missional sense, embracing the role of calling the lost sheep of Israel (10:6)[124] and the nations

---

122. The designation "a nation" is quite significant. Of the 15 occurrences of the term ἔθνος in Matthew, it is plural and articular in 12 places (Matt 4:15; 6:32; 10:5, 18; 12:18, 21; 20:19, 25; 24:9, 14; 25:32; 28:19) and technically refers to gentile nations not Israel, although the use in 24:9; 25:32; 28:19 should be taken to include Israel; and the two instances in 24:7 are generic. However, it is singular and non-articular in 21:43, suggesting an entity other than gentile nations; cf. Meier, "Nations or Gentiles," 97-98; he argues that "a nation" in 21:43 is Matthew's way of conceiving "the church as a *tertia gens* which cannot be neatly categorized as Jewish or gentile. Stanton prefers to think that "a nation" designates Matthew's "own community" (*New People*, 151-52).

123. In three crucial passages in Matthew (3:7-9; 12:33-36; and 23:1-33), the Jewish leaders are particularly addressed as γεννήματα ἐχιδνῶν (brood of vipers) in connection with either being charged or accused of failing to produce καρπός (fruit). If we take 3:7-9 and 12:33-36 as abbreviated forms of the charge/accusation, then ch. 23 is the fullest explication of the failure of these Jewish leaders to produce fruit. If this is right, and if 23:1-33 relates to the parable of the wicked tenants in ch. 21 (esp. vv. 33-45), it becomes legitimate to expand the significance of the theme of "fruit" to embrace two categories: ethical (right acts based on right understanding of the law) and missional (leading the lost sheep of Israel and the converts of the nations into the Kingdom). On this second category, notice how the fruit-bearing theme in 12:33 is echoed in missional terms in 23:15; cf. Wilk, *Jesus und die Volker*, 117-19, who also sees a connection between Matt 21:43 and 23:13, although he is more open to the ethical sense (117n262).

124. Although the context leading up to Matt 24-25 is fraught with judgment motifs (see Walker, *Jesus and the Holy City*, 41-42), it is important to maintain that Jesus' commitment to the lost sheep of Israel (cf. 9:36; 12:11;15:24;18:12) cannot be said to be abandoned when he pronounced judgment on Jerusalem and the temple in Matt 23:38; 24:2. For a compelling case against the rejection of Israel, see Matthias, *Israel, Church, and Gentiles*.

(28:19, cf. 25:32) into the kingdom.¹²⁵ Thus, the disciples are rightly taken as the husbandmen to whom the King rents out his vineyard in Matt 21:41 (cf. 19:28). They replace the failed Jewish leadership, constituting in themselves the nucleus of a new Israelite nation through whom Jews and gentiles are brought into the Kingdom.¹²⁶ This interplay of "being the foundation of the Church," of "possessing the keys of the Kingdom," and of "constituting a nation producing the fruit of the Kingdom" (Matt 16:18-19; 21:41-43; cf. 23:13-15) forbids the simple pigeonholing of the disciples into either a church-only or Israel-only mold.

Preterist Interpretation

Broadly, preterism is the view that places the fulfillment of most Bible prophecies in the past. However, preterist interpreters are diverse in their applications of the view.¹²⁷ Thus, one must be careful not to lump the various forms together. In relation to the Olivet Discourse in particular, three shades of preterism may be differentiated: thoroughgoing preterism, hyper-preterism, and partial preterism.

First, some interpreters hold what I have called thoroughgoing preterism in which all of Matt 24-25 and the entirety of NT eschatological hope was fulfilled in the destruction of Jerusalem. Nineteenth-century scholar, J. Stuart Russell, is perhaps the most influential advocate of this view.¹²⁸ Russell rejects the distinction between the destruction of Jerusalem and the *parousia* and end of the world. He contends not only that the disciples' question in Matt 24:3 concerns only the fate of Jerusalem to which Jesus gave a plain answer, but also that the phrase "'all the nations [Matt 25:30] is equivalent to 'all the tribes of the land.'"¹²⁹ He, therefore, goes on to conclude that all of Matt 24-25—the "parousia [second coming], the resurrection,

---

125. Contrast Matt 23:13-15. The use of καρπός to describe the result of missionary activity is not unprecedented (cf. Rom 1:13; Phil 1:11; Col 1:6).

126. Cf. Matthias, *Israel, Church, and Gentiles*, 172-93; see Talbert, *Matthew*, 252; he takes "a people producing its fruit" as the twelve disciples and links Matt 21:43 to 19:28 and Ezek 34:10. Wilk argues that Matt 21:43 signals the transfer of the role of fulfilling the Abrahamic promise of Gen 12:2 to the disciples (*Jesus und die Völker*, 117-20). See also Clark, "Role of the Apostles," 173-75.

127. Ice identifies three kinds of preterism namely: (1) mild, (2) moderate, and (3) extreme (Ice and Gentry, *Great Tribulation*, 7). We should note that the remark by Toussaint, *Behold the King*, 266 that "there are none who actually believe the entire Discourse has already been fulfilled" is inaccurate at best.

128. Russell, *Parousia*; so also Feuillet, "Sens du Mot Parousie," 261-80.

129. Russell, *Parousia*, 57-58, 104-5.

the judgment, and the last day, all belong to the period of the destruction of Jerusalem."[130] This view became known as the 70 CE theory.[131]

Second, Russell's contemporary, Milton S. Terry, maintains a similar view on Matt 24–25, differing only by holding a future eternal reward and punishment based on Rev 20:11–15 rather than on Matt 25:31–46. The scene in the latter, he argues, is neither the single event of 70 CE nor the final assize at the end of human history but a parabolic picture of the age-long administration of Jesus Christ from the overthrow of Jerusalem until he hands over the kingdom to the Father (1 Cor 15:24).[132] Terry's form of preterism has been reinvented in recent times by a few interpreters, prominent among whom are Gary DeMar,[133] John L. Bray,[134] and N. T. Wright.[135] I categorize these as hyper-preterists based on the fact that while they all regard the entirety of Matt 24–25 as fulfilled in 70 CE, they, however, echo Terry's view, in contrast to Russell, that the judgment scene in Matt 25:31–46 represents not a one-time event but a process transpiring throughout history, beginning from the first century.[136]

To be clear, Bray's work focuses only on Matt 24, about which he declares, "Our interpretation sees only past events in this passage, there is no double fulfillment. There is no double reference. There is [sic] no mixed-up passages that change the time factor. There is no 'transition' verse separating the destruction of Jerusalem from another event 2,000 years or so in the future."[137] Yet he maintains what he calls a future "final coming of our Lord in resurrection and judgment" including reward and punishment based on Rev 20:11–15.[138] Similarly, Wright contends that the disciples' question in

---

130. Russell, *Parousia*, 121–22, 126; cf. MacArthur, *Second Coming*, 9–13.

131. See Bray, "Critique," 6–11; cf. Varner, *Studies in Biblical Eschatology*, ix.

132. Terry, *Biblical Apocalypse*, 251. Notice also that for Terry, the notion of a final resurrection (based on John 5:28–29) is metaphorical (458–59) and there is no one instantaneous event of second coming, only a long-continuing process of comings until 1 Cor 15:24–25 is fulfilled (480–81); Russell equates Matt 25:31–46 with Rev 20:11–15 (*Parousia*, 523–25).

133. DeMar, *Last Days Madness*.

134. Bray, *Matthew 24 Fulfilled*.

135. Wright, *Jesus and the Victory*.

136. DeMar, *Last Days Madness*, 200; "How Many Comings?" 1; Wright, *Matthew*, 143. For Russell (*Parousia*, 104–8), Matt 25:31–46 "is not the final judgment of the whole human race, but that of the guilty nation or nations [tribes] of Palestine, who rejected their King.

137. Bray, *Matthew 24 Fulfilled*, 108.

138. Bray, *Matthew 24 Fulfilled*, 108, 273–75. I cannot ascertain if by this he means a literal second coming, except that he appears to differ here from Terry, for whom the final resurrection is only a metaphorical concept.

Matt 24:3 (also Mark 13:4 and Luke 21:7) is "not a question about ... the 'parousia', [as traditionally understood] but a question about Jesus' 'coming' or 'arriving' in the sense of his actual enthronement as king," by which he means Jesus' vindication in the destruction of Jerusalem.[139] Yet, Wright is vocal about the second coming of Christ, the denial of which he describes as bizarre.[140] Likewise, DeMar manages to sneak in his belief in a future return of Christ for final judgment.[141] In other words, what Bray, DeMar, and Wright protest is the view that *parousia*, understood as Christ's second coming, is in view in any portion of Matt 24–25.[142]

These two forms of preterism are together textually challenged and therefore unacceptable. Russell's thoroughgoing preterism is too realized and too minimalist to fit the Matthean data. For example, his equation of πάντα τὰ ἔθνη (Matt 25:32) with "tribes of the land of Israel" appears seriously misguided[143] since Matthew consistently uses the plural, articular form of ἔθνος to refer to gentile nations.[144] It is unlikely that the final judgment, i.e., the consignment of some to eternal fire and others to eternal life, which is the concern of 25:31–46, could have taken place in the destruction of Jerusalem. Similarly, hyper-preterists' claim that the judgment scene in Matt 25:31–46 represents a process continuing throughout history is a concession, at least, to the potential that the Eschatological Discourse is not simply synonymous with the 70 CE event. If 25:31–46 refers to all of history, how legitimate is it to deny that 24:1—25:30 might refer to more than the destruction of Jerusalem? Matthew 24 and 25 together represent one inseparable Discourse. Moreover, these scholars do not agree on what point the "process" of judgment begins.[145] In light of Matt 25:46 (cf. 13:40–43; 16:27), vv. 31–46 clearly indicates a one-time event marked with finality; there is no evidence that it represents an ongoing or continuing process.

Third, most preterists today advocate a rather partial or moderate preterism. While consigning most of Matt 24 to the past as already fulfilled

---

139. Wright, *Jesus and the Victory*, 345–46; Wright, *New Testament and the People*, 459–64.

140. See Wright, *Surprised by Hope*, 127.

141. DeMar, *Last Days Madness*, 158–59.

142. See, e.g., Wright, *Matthew*, 111–44. On Wright's idea of what *parousia* means, see his *Paul*, 1082–83.

143. See Russell, *Parousia*, 104.

144. Although, I shall argue that πάντα τὰ ἔθνη in Matt 25:32 is universal; see note 122 above; cf. Stanton, *New People*, 214.

145. For Terry, it began at 70 CE (*Biblical Apocalypse*, 251) while Wright fixes it at "the resurrection and ascension till the present" (*Matthew*, 143).

in the 70 CE destruction of the temple, they take Christ's second coming as the subject of 24:36—25:46 based especially on the view that περὶ δέ in 24:36 marks the introduction of a new section dealing with the *parousia*. This version of preterism, often traced to Reformed scholar, J. Marcellus Kik,[146] has found able advocates in a growing number of scholars, including R. V. G. Tasker, Harold Fowler, R. T. France, J. A. Gibbs, and more recently D. R. Bauer.[147] In general, these scholars place 24:15–35 in the past and see a major transition in v. 36. However, they differ in their views on 24:1–14. For example, Kik and Fowler place 24:1–14 entirely in the time preceding 70 CE, with the "end" (v. 14) meaning the end of the temple/Judaism.[148] France also takes this view, although he could still consider 24:4–8 as "routine events within world history."[149] In contrast, Gibbs argues that "in light of the obvious connections between 24:14 and 28:19–20, . . . it is certain that 'the end' at both 24:6 and 24:14 refers to the consummation of the age."[150]

The strength of this partial preterism consists in its natural understanding of "this generation" as well as the fact that "Jesus does [indeed] emphasize that these events are not signs of the end."[151] But the most important contribution of preterists, in general, is their handling of Matt 24:29–31 which is taken to mean the judgment of Jerusalem and the missionary gathering of the elect.[152] Edward Adams has mounted a significant pushback against this interpretation in seeking to maintain the traditional view of actual second coming.[153] I shall undertake to evaluate the two views later on. In the meantime, I only note that while taking περὶ δέ in Matt 24:36

---

146. Kik, "Matthew Twenty-Four," 53–173.

147. Tasker, *Matthew*, 223–40; Fowler, *Matthew*, 4:389; France, *Gospel according to Matthew*, 333–58; *Matthew*, 885–967; Gibbs, *Jerusalem and Parousia*. Others include Wilson, *When Will These Things Happen?*; Gentry in Ice and Gentry, *Great Tribulation*, 11–66; Bauer, *Gospel*, 209–17. As I have shown above, the inclusion of Wright in this group by Carson ("Matthew," 552) is inaccurate.

148. Kik makes a distinction between witnessing to the nations in 24:14 and making disciples of all the nations in 28:19–20 ("Matthew Twenty-Four," 88, 101); cf. Fowler, *Gospel*, 433–34; Ice and Gentry, *Great Tribulation*, 44–45.

149. France, *Matthew*, 902; see discussion in 903, 907–10.

150. Gibbs, *Jerusalem and Parousia*, 182n93; cf. Tasker, *Matthew*, 224.

151. Turner, "Structure," 8–9.

152. See Gibbs, *Jerusalem and Parousia*, 187–204; France, *Matthew*, 919–28; cf. Wright, *Jesus and the Victory*, 343–65. I should note here that if this interpretation is correct, then the missionary activity anticipates a time of eschatological reward (Matt 24:45–51; 25:14–46; cf. Matt 16:27). Consequently, it would immediately argue against the thoroughgoing and hyper-preterist views outlined above since the missionary activity/work cannot, at the same time, be equated with the reward it anticipates.

153. See Adams, *Stars Will Fall*, 133–81.

as indicating a shift in focus,[154] the basic two-part structure that results is less accurate. As will be shown later, it makes it difficult to access the structural significance as well as the nature of the *parousia* theme within the Discourse.[155]

Traditional Preterist-Futurist Interpretation

Turner identifies his third category of interpretations as the "traditional preterist-futurist" view.[156] It represents a *via media* approach developed during the 1970s and championed especially by post-tribulation premillennialist scholar, George E. Ladd among others.[157] Ladd observes that "in the original discourse, the historical event of the fall of Jerusalem and the eschatological consummation were blended in a form impossible for us to recover, and the traditions preserved in Mark-Matthew and in Luke have emphasized the two elements in different ways."[158] He goes on to cite Cranfield: "Neither an exclusively historical nor an exclusively eschatological interpretation is satisfactory.... We must allow for a double reference, for a mingling of historical and eschatological." In other words, "the Olivet Discourse [holds] in dynamic tension the anticipation of certain historical events and the eschatological consummation"[159] which means that the text resists dissection into neat chronological patterns.[160]

However, Ladd appears to minimize the temple's fate by giving greater weight to the eschatological over against the historical. For example, in an earlier work, the passage is outlined as follows: 24:4–14 (the entire course of the church age), 24:15–25 (Great Tribulation and the Antichrist, called

---

154. Regardless of use elsewhere, περὶ δέ in Matthew does not signal a change in topic; rather, it marks a development of a presumed or already known topic (cf. Matt 22:31; 20:6; 27:46); contra Christian, "Questionable Inversion," 51n28.

155. The occurrence of *parousia* in Matt 24:27, though recognized as second coming, does not play a structural role in the partial preterist schema since it is taken simply as an "aside"; so France, *Matthew*, 917; Wilson, *When Will These Things Happen?*, 153; Gibbs, *Jerusalem and Parousia*, 187.

156. Turner, "Structure," 4.

157. Ladd developed the concept of "inaugurated eschatology"—a term apparently used first by A. M. Hunter in 1957; see Ladd, *Presence*, 33, and his discussion on the Olivet Discourse (309–15); Ladd, *Blessed Hope*, 72–73. Other advocates of the view include Hendriksen, *Matthew*, 846–92; Hoekema, *Bible and Future*, 109–72; Gundry, *Handbook*, 474–516.

158. Ladd, *Presence*, 310.

159. Ladd, *Presence*, 311.

160. Ladd, *Presence*, 324.

the abomination of desolation),[161] 24:26–31 (the glorious second coming of Christ);[162] with 24:32–46 usually understood as stressing the urgency of Christ's warning about alertness.[163]

Gundry is even less restrained in his minimization of the historical. The "abandonment [of Israel], rather than the building of the temple as such, he claims, "is the focus of Matthew's attention. . . . Jerusalem's destruction remains unidentified and emphasis falls instead on the Son of Man's coming, after the tribulation."[164] Taking 24:4–14 as describing non-eschatological characteristics of the church age closed off with the statement that the end will come only after the universal preaching of the gospel,[165] he contends that the abomination of desolation (24:15) is best understood as a reference to the image of some evil deified figure such as the Antichrist, and represents the actual specific eschatological sign that the end has drawn near.[166] Gundry then reasons that since the destruction of the temple would have made the command to flee impossible, therefore, in 24:16–18, "we are dealing . . . not with a flight from military attack, but with flight from a persecution signaled by a religious abomination."[167] In other words, although one should accept a double fulfillment of prophecy as a fact not to be objected to on literary grounds,[168] the second fulfillment looms larger than—almost to the exclusion of—the first and must drive interpretation.

Although this interpretation is, in Turner view, the most promising of all the interpretations,[169] it remains problematic in several ways. First, the minimization of the historical destruction of the temple is inconsistent with the view's underlying principle of "prophetic perspective" in which distant events are simultaneous and equally in view. It stretches credulity to say that Matthew is not interested in the temple. Otherwise, if Gundry is correct in both this claim and his absolute assumption of Markan priority, it raises the question why Matthew would "turn the vague reference [to the temple] in

---

161. Notice the muting of reference to the 70 CE temple destruction in this section.
162. Ladd, *Blessed Hope*, 72–73.
163. Turner, "Structure," 4–5.
164. Gundry, *Matthew*, 475–76; Kingsbury also claims, "the Eschatological Discourse is related not to the destruction of the temple . . . but to the parousia of Jesus and the consummation of the age" (*Matthew*, 29).
165. Gundry, *Matthew*, 481.
166. Gundry, *Matthew*, 481–82.
167. Gundry, *Matthew*, 482.
168. Gundry, *Matthew*, 491.
169. Turner, "Structure," 24–25.

Mark into a specific indication of a place of worship," since "'the holy place' [24:15] almost certainly means the Temple" as Gundry also contends.[170]

Second, Gundry's contention that "Matthew seemingly shifts direction . . . by dwelling on the qualitative rather than the chronological sense of γενεά" in 24:34,[171] is questionable. The claim of chronological openness in the phrase "this generation" sits awkwardly in context and remains quite unsupported within Matthew as preterists maintain. Moreover, except for its posttribulational stance, this interpretation appears more "futurist"[172] than Turner realizes. It certainly leans more towards the futurist than to the preterist of Turner's preterist-futurist category.

Revised Preterist-Futurist Interpretation

Turner describes a second *via media* interpretation he calls "revised preterist-futurist" view in which references to the church age, the destruction of the temple, and the second coming occur in an alternating fashion.[173] This view arose in the 1980s through the works of David Wenham and D. A. Carson.[174] As Carson himself describes it, in Matt 24 "Jesus warns that there will be delay before the End—a delay characterized by persecution and tribulation for his followers (vv. 4-28) but with one particularly violent judgment in the destruction of Jerusalem [in] vv. 15-21."[175] That is, after the 70 CE event, 24:22-28 continues with the same general period as does 24:4-14, while 24:29-31 refers to the second coming of Christ. Carson then argues that "the warning in 24:32-35 [again] describes the whole tribulation period, from ascension to the second coming"; the phrase "the generation" refers to Jesus' contemporaries who will experience all of the features of this general distress, including the fall of Jerusalem, which all point to the Lord's return;[176] and the last segment (24:36-44) deals with the time of the second advent as unknown.[177]

---

170. Gundry, *Matthew*, 482.
171. Gundry, *Matthew*, 491; cf. Nelson, "This Generation," 369-85.
172. Cf. Ridderbos, *Coming of the Kingdom*, 500-502; Ridderbos, *Matthew*, 450-51; Hendriksen, *Matthew*, 868-69.
173. Turner, "Structure," 3-4.
174. Wenham, "This Generation," 127-50; Carson, "Matthew," 548-74.
175. Carson, "Matthew," 557.
176. Carson, "Matthew," 557, 569.
177. Carson, "Matthew," 557. For a comparable interpretation, see Lambrecht, "Line of Thought," 519-28; Davies and Allison, *Matthew*, 3:331.

While this revised preterist-futurist view should be commended for its handling of "this generation,"[178] the structural basis is not solid for several related reasons. First, it incorrectly assumes that the "general period" is suspended in 24:15–21 (70 CE) and resumed shortly after. Second, the split between 24:21 and 24:22 is quite unlikely. These two verses amount to one complex γάρ sentence held together by a simple καί conjunction. In fact, Carson himself admits that none of his six arguments justifying the division is decisive.[179] However, I must note that Turner's description of the interpretation as "seemingly novel,"[180] and "dubious,"[181] especially for restricting the 70 CE event to 24:15–21 is based on the inaccurate notion that the indivisibility of 24:15–28 must be held sacrosanct. Carson may have made an incision at the wrong point, but as I shall argue, an alternating pattern—one that properly delineates reference to Christ's description of his second coming within 24:15–28—more accurately defines the structure of the Discourse.

Third, Carson's contention that "those days" in 24:22 refers neither to the period described in 24:15–21 nor to the eschatological period of 24:29, but to the same general period described in 24:4–14[182] is curious for the same structural flaw noted above. If 24:4–14 and 24:15–21 are both subsets of the general period (24:4–28), and since 24:15–21 is only a particularly violent moment within that general period, as Carson's analysis indicates, it becomes counterintuitive to say that "those days" in 24:22 applies to the first subset (vv. 4–14) and not to the second (vv. 15–21).[183] Moreover, Carson's assumption that the terms "elect" and "all flesh" in 24:22 mean all true believers and all mankind respectively, has the appearance of overinterpretation, again because of the strong unity between 24:22 and 24:21.

Ryan P. Juza has recently proposed what might be identified as a "Second Revised Preterist-Futurist Interpretation." Juza argues that for the disciples to ask about when the temple will be destroyed is also to ask about when the *parousia*/end of the age will happen. Similarly, for them to ask about the signs of the *parousia*/end of the age is to ask about the signs of the temple's destruction. These claims are based on the consideration that one

---

178. Turner concurs ("Structure," 25), although one might argue that the language of Matt 24:34, in terms of the aorist subjunctive (γένηται) suggests that the contemporaries of Jesus will see "all these things" completed in time rather than just "features" of a long-drawn time of distress that progresses beyond them as Carson's view suggests; cf. Carson, "Matthew," 557.

179. Carson, "Matthew," 564.

180. Turner, "Structure," 4n4.

181. Turner, "Structure," 21.

182. Turner, "Structure," 25; Carson, "Matthew," 564.

183. See my diagrammatical representation of Carson's structure in Appendix 1

must explain how Jesus' response reveals and answers the disciples' specific questions. Accordingly, surmising that Jesus' address concerns the timing and signs each of the temple's destruction and the *parousia*, Juza concludes that the disciples' question is better construed as fourfold: (1) When will the destruction of the temple happen? (2) When will the *parousia* and the end of the age happen? (3) What will be the sign of the destruction of the temple? And (4) what will be the sign of your *parousia* and the end of the age?[184]

In the structure of the Discourse that emerges from this proposal, Jesus first corrects the disciples' conflation of the temple's destruction and *parousia*/end, and second, inverts the order of the questions ([1] when? [2] sign?) in his further response. Thus, in 24:4–14, Jesus clarifies eschatological timetable, in 24:15–31 he takes on question 2, and in 24:32—25:46 he answers question 1. The passage further breaks down as follows: (1) "They end is not yet" (24:4–8), (2) "The end follows suffering and witness" (24:9–14), (3) "The sign of the temple's ruin" (24:15–28), (4) "The sign of the *parousia* and end" (24:29–31); (5) "When the temple will be destroyed" (24:32–35), and (6) "When the *parousia* will occur" (24:36—25:46).[185]

Juza's structural proposition and the resulting interpretation are quite helpful in several ways. However, his fourfold question view remains an assumption. Questions 2 and 3 in his reconstruction better reflects Mark 13:4b than the Matthew's plain statement in Matt 24:3. While it is possible to infer the number of questions from the response provided, it is not uncommon for responders to answer more questions than they are asked. This does not necessitate the attribution of more questions to the enquirer or the reconstruction of the question itself. Thus, it is better to make do with the disciples' question as stated and not multiply it by factors of our interpretation of Jesus' response. Moreover, in my view, Juza misplaces 24:26–28 by including it under "the sign of the temple's ruin."

Historicist Interpretation

The historicist view finds the fulfillment of apocalyptic events within Church history. This view is more pronounced in the scholarship of Revelation, but it also draws on the Olivet Discourse, where it devolves into a form of preterism.[186] A typical historicist interpretation sees both the fall of Jerusalem and the *parousia* in the Discourse but locates the fulfillment of 24:21–22

---

184. Juza, *New Testament*, 24–25.
185. Juza, *New Testament*, 26; cf. Moore, *Parousia*, 134.
186. Ice and Gentry, *Great Tribulation*, 6.

in Medieval tribulations.[187] Apart from this, the historicist view makes no other significant contribution to our study. Moreover, the view has receded from mainstream eschatological discussion, domiciled almost exclusively within the Seventh Day Adventist denomination.[188]

The survey above represents the major historical and current trends in the interpretation of the Olivet Discourse. The next chapter articulates the methodological framework for the present study.

---

187. See Charlesworth, "Historicist Interpretation," 1:112; Charlesworth, "Historicist Interpretation," 2:240–54.

188. Ice and Gentry, *Great Tribulation*, 6.

2

Statement of Problem, Purpose, and Methodology

The Problem

THE GENERAL HISTORICAL OVERVIEW in chapter 1 has shown that no consensus currently exists on the interpretation of the Olivet Discourse. Much debate persists regarding both the structure and the interpretation of the Discourse. One finds a cacophony of voices ranging from thoroughgoing preterism to dispensational futurist views with different shades of interpretations in-between. None of these interpretations adequately satisfies the sweep of discourse data. As such, the Discourse remains in need of cogent and holistic interpretation.

This reality is very surprising given Matt 24–25's significance for NT eschatology. But what is even more surprising is the limited amount of attention that the Discourse in its entirety has attracted. For the most part, the reason for this is the presumption that Matthew is simply a redaction of Mark. While the redaction-critical approach has yielded significant theological insights, the obvious problem is that such treatments often tend to be belabored or bogged down by claims of Matthew's editorial changes. Some lump synoptic parallels together.[1] Others focus only on Matt 24.[2] The

---

1. E.g., Fuller, "Structure."

2. Burnett, *Testament*, 30–355. Other treatments limited to Matt 24 or sections of it include Hart, "Chronology"; Lassman, "Matthew 24"; Buzzard, "Olivet Discourse"; Longstreth, "Matthew 24." Beare, "Synoptic Apocalypse," distinguishes the apocalypse (24:1–42) from the parables of the *parousia* and last judgment.

important work by Burnett follows a redaction-critical approach and seeks to interpret the Matthean Discourse in light of the wisdom Christology of the Gospel as a whole. However, Burnett's work is limited to Matt 24:1–31.

Although the number of commentaries and articles on various elements of the passage continues to grow, recent studies focusing primarily and completely on Matt 24–25 have been anything but significant, with the most important being the works of Viktor K. Agbanou, J. A. Gibbs, and A. I. Wilson.[3] While Agbanou's interpretation relies on tradition and redaction-critical assumptions, Gibbs and Wilson employ narrative-critical and composition-critical approaches respectively. The latter two offset the problems of the older form of redaction criticism by focusing squarely on the final form as well as seeking to interpret the Discourse largely in light of the Gospel as a whole.

Gibbs' and Wilson's approaches result in, perhaps, the strongest analyses supporting the partial preterist view, in which case Matt 24:36 is taken as the hinge verse beginning Jesus' focus on the second part of the disciples' question—the *parousia*. However, the essentially two-part structure is not decisive since it fails to discern any structural value to the first reference to the *parousia* in Matt 24:27. A more nuanced structure will yield greater insight into the overall interpretation of the Discourse than has been offered.

In addition, the significance of the apocalyptic language in relation to eschatology is central to the interpretation of such a passage as Matt 24–25. While discussions on this have not been wanting,[4] the dispute regarding the significance of apocalyptic and cosmic imagery within the Discourse remains unabated, with several scholars taking the metaphorical view and others maintaining the literal interpretation.[5] The current stalemate obviously demonstrates the need to re-evaluate the language and overall character and form of the Discourse.

Furthermore, most interpreters approach the passage from established presuppositions, which often lead to forcing the text into some broad theological system against its own will. While presuppositions are not completely avoidable, one must attempt to read the passage from the author's point

---

3. See Agbanou, *Le Discours*; Gibbs, *Jerusalem and Parousia*; Wilson, *When Will These Things Happen?*

4. Wilson, *When Will These Things Happen?*, 110–32, makes this a crucial part of his methodology. For discussions on various apocalyptic motifs from the lenses of Jewish apocalyptic literature, see, e.g., Hartman, *Prophecy Interpreted*, 71–101; Lunde, "Salvation-Historical Implication"; Kon, "Signs of the Parousia"; cf. Sabourin, "Apocalyptic Traits," 19–36.

5. Gibbs, *Jerusalem and Parousia*, 187–204; France, *Matthew*, 919–28; Wright, *Jesus and the Victory*, 343–65; cf. Adams, *Stars Will Fall*, 133–81.

of view as codified in the text, aided by a thorough examination of literary structure, grammatical and linguistic clues, as well as how the passage functions conceptually and structurally within the larger whole.

Key Questions

Considering the problems noted above, this study will be based on the core belief that literary structure and genre are indispensable hermeneutical foundations for adequate interpretation. To this effect, this study will be undergirded by four broad questions:

1. What is the nature or form of the language in Matt 24–25? In asking this question, I am interested in (a) highlighting relevant sources and/or motifs that help illuminate the Discourse and (b) evaluating current approaches to its linguistic form.
2. What is the structure or organizing principle of Matt 24–25. The answer to this question will facilitate the main objective of elucidating the meaning and eschatology of the Discourse.
3. What is the relationship of this passage to the rest of the Gospel and what structural and conceptual role does it play in Matthew's overall communication?
4. How does the eschatology of the Discourse, as interpreted, cohere or correlate with NT eschatology in general?

The Purpose of This Study

This study is an investigation into the meaning and eschatology of Matt 24–25. I intend to show that the Discourse neither supports thoroughgoing preterism and hyper-preterism—the views that the Discourse in its entirety concerns the destruction of Jerusalem and has nothing to do with the second coming—nor does the dispensational futurist view have any cogent basis in the text. These two broad views are extreme and bother on too opinionated either/or hermeneutic. While leaning towards the views that see both past and future events in the Discourse, I will seek to demonstrate why the extant views on the passage, including the partial preterist two-part structure and what Turner has labeled the "traditional preterist-futurist" and "revised preterist-futurist" views, do not accurately reflect the structure and meaning of the Discourse.

In pursuit of this goal, I will demonstrate that the organizing principle of the Discourse reflects the alternation or interchange of materials within an *inclusio* and a "problem-solution" structural framework. This structural schema includes "generalization" and "particularization"—categories which will be further explicated at the appropriate juncture in this study. Analysis of the organizing principle or structure that is set forth will serve to flesh out the meaning and eschatology of the Discourse.

In connection with these, I will explore how the Discourse functions within Matthew's Gospel, arguing that it complements Matthew's overall Christological goal. Finally, I will carry out an exercise in inductive correlation, relating the eschatological schema reflected in the Discourse with what is taught in the NT in general. I will make the case that the views are in broad agreement despite apparent diversities.

Methodology, Scope, Design, and Thesis of Study

Methodology

In pursuit of the goals set forth above, I will employ a literary-critical exegetical method that integrates the inductive approach as articulated by David R. Bauer and Robert A. Traina[6] with insights from the Discourse grammatical studies by Stephen H. Levinsohn, Steven E. Runge, Randall Buth, Stephanie L. Black, and many others.[7]

The Inductive Approach

According to Bauer and Traina, the inductive approach involves:

> *a comprehensive, holistic study of the Bible that takes into account every aspect of the existence of the biblical text and that is intentional in allowing the Bible in its final canonical shape to speak to*

---

6. Bauer and Traina, *Inductive Bible Study*.

7. Levinsohn, *Discourse Features*; Levinsohn, "'Therefore' or 'Wherefore'"; Levinsohn, *Textual Connections*; Runge, *Discourse Grammar*. Other relevant studies include Dooley and Levinsohn, *Analyzing Discourse*; Black, *Sentence Conjunctions*; Buth, "Οὐν, Δέ, Καί and Asyndeton"; Buth, "On Levinsohn's 'Development Units'"; Buth, "Semitic Καί and Greek Δέ"; Poythress, "Use of the Intersentence Conjunctions"; Bestgen, "Segmentation Markers"; Schiffrin, *Discourse Markers*; Westfall, "Οὖν in the New Testament." Cf. Wallace, *Greek Grammar*, 666–78.

us on its own terms, thus leading to accurate, original, compelling, and profound interpretation and contemporary appropriation.[8]

This definition may further be elaborated by considering essential aspects, principles, general features, and analytical concepts of the inductive approach.

First, two aspects of the inductive study are *inductive spirit* and *inductive process*. By inductive spirit is meant the attitude of radical openness or willingness to go with whatever conclusion the biblical evidence leads to. As Bauer and Traina explain, such openness welcomes discussion and challenge in contrast to the dogmatic, authoritarian character of the deductive approach that does not entertain the possibility of error, depends on proof texts, controls the outcome of the study in order to maintain cherished traditions.[9] The inductive process involves the application of inferential reasoning, that is, drawing conclusions from one or more premises about the meaning of the text.[10] Related to these, the inductive approach is based on two broad principles: (1) The principle of *probability*. This entails acknowledging that sometimes evidence can be ambiguous or conflicting, leading to no specific conclusion. (2) The principle of *realism*. Here one must acknowledge that pure and absolute induction does not exist, and that we all come to the text with certain presuppositions. Therefore, we must subject our presuppositions to the text and be willing to change as the evidence demands.[11] This principle is further explicated in terms of "transjectivity" by which Bauer and Trainer mean that the inductive approach is neither purely objective nor exclusively subjective but rather combines both dimensions in a dynamic manner.[12] Thus, the inductive approach embraces the critical-realist hermeneutics espoused by several scholars.[13]

Second, the inductive approach is characterized by at least three intricately related features:

1. The communication model: The inductive approach aims at "the objective dimensions of the communicative act," following the conviction that the goal of interpretation is the intention of the author as it has

---

8. Bauer and Traina, *Inductive Bible Study*, 6 (italics original).

9. Bauer and Traina, *Inductive Bible Study*, 18–19.

10. Bauer and Traina, *Inductive Bible Study*, 20–25.

11. See Bauer and Traina, *Inductive Bible Study*, 20–25, 34–36; cf. Wilson, *When Will These Things Happen?*, 46n4.

12. Bauer and Traina, *Inductive Bible Study*, 26, 28.

13. E.g., Wright, *New Testament and the People*, 3–46; Meyer, *Reality and Illusion*, 3–4.

been encoded in and can be inferred from the text.[14] This hermeneutical *via-media* avoids two common extremes—the death of the author on the one hand,[15] and the appeal to the intention or consciousness of the historical author on the other.[16] Consequently, it emphasizes what literary critics refer to as *the implied author*—the author as may be inferred from the text—and its corollary, the *implied reader*—the reader that the text envisions and that one can infer from it.[17]

2. Focus on the final form of the text: The inductive approach is a text-based interpretation. Nonetheless, in keeping with its emphasis on the *implied author* and *implied reader*, it incorporates all historical data relevant to understanding the text, although only as required by the text itself in its final form as a literary entity.[18]

3. Holistic and integrative study: The inductive approach acknowledges the value of all other critical approaches. However, in contrast to the application of each approach in isolation, it seeks to integrate evidence from all critical approaches relevant for understanding the text. In doing this, it maintains the final form of the text in its literary as well as canonical context as the coherent center instead of using it merely as a window to what lies behind or as a mirror for what is before it.[19]

Third, the inductive approach employs a set of analytical or compositional categories for determining the literary arrangement of either whole books or book segments, as well as how units are related to one another both structurally and semantically. Bauer and Traina identify several structural or compositional relationships defined as "*organizational systems* that pertain to the dynamic arrangement of various thoughts and themes throughout the book."[20] They are categorized into three, namely: recurrence, semantic, and rhetorical structures. Recurrence involves the repetition of the same or similar terms, phrases, or other elements.[21] Semantic structures are binary concepts indicating sense connection in terms of movement from one thing to another. These are contrast, comparison, climax, particularization,

---

14. Bauer and Traina, *Inductive Bible Study*, 34, 42.
15. French literary critic Roland Barthes advocates this in a 1967 essay, *La mort de L'auteur*.
16. Hirsch, *Validity of Interpretation* (cf. Hirsch, *Aims of Interpretation*).
17. Bauer and Traina, *Inductive Bible Study*, 42–49.
18. Bauer and Traina, *Inductive Bible Study*, 48.
19. Bauer and Traina, *Inductive Bible Study*, 53–56.
20. Bauer and Traina, *Inductive Bible Study*, 94.
21. Bauer and Traina, *Inductive Bible Study*, 95.

generalization, causation, substantiation, cruciality, summarization, interrogation, preparation, and instrumentation. Rhetorical structures deal with the placement or arrangement of elements within the text which serves to strengthen semantic relationships. These are interchange (A-B-A-B arrangement), inclusio (A . . . A¹ arrangement), chiasm (A-B-B¹-A¹ arrangement), and intercalation (A-B-A arrangement).[22]

Discourse Grammar Approach

Discourse Grammar as described by Levinsohn and Runge represents a descriptive and functional approach to linguistics.[23] It is defined as "an attempt to discover and describe what linguistic structures are used for: the functions they serve, the factors that condition their use."[24] Essentially, discourse grammar seeks to answer the question of why an author would use a certain feature—form, structure, or device instead of the alternatives. In contrast to traditional approaches where variation in these features is simply said to be stylistic, discourse grammar is based on three core principles articulated by Runge:[25] (1) Choice implies meaning. (2) Semantic or inherent meaning should be differentiated from pragmatic effect (i.e., effect achieved by use in context).[26] (3) Default (considered unmarked) patterns of use should be distinguished from marked ones.

Among the many elements of discourse grammar, the pragmatic effect of sentence "connectives"[27] or "conjunctions"[28] will be of particular interest for this study. In what follows, I review five important discourse markers used throughout Matthew and, for our more specific purpose, in the Eschatological Discourse. These are καί, δέ, τότε, οὖν, and asyndeton.

---

22. For detailed discussions on these concepts, see Bauer and Traina, *Inductive Bible Study*, 94–122; Bauer, *Structure*, 13–20.

23. Runge, *Discourse Grammar*, xviii, identifies two focal aspects: *cross-linguistic* (i.e., focus on how languages tend to operate as opposed to just Greek) and *function-based* approach (i.e., attention to the description of discourse features).

24. Dooley, cited by Levinsohn, *Discourse Features*, vii; Runge, *Discourse Grammar*, 3n1.

25. Runge, *Discourse Grammar*, 5–16.

26. Levinsohn, *Discourse Features*, viiin3, understands "meaning" as loosely denoting any semantic or pragmatic distinction."

27. Runge, *Discourse Grammar*, 17–57.

28. Levinsohn, *Discourse Features*, 69–126 (cf. 271–80).

Καί

Καί is the single most prevalent particle in Matthew and the NT.[29] Traditionally, it is simply viewed as connecting additional discourse elements (clauses, phrases, or words), hence the common translation "and."[30] In terms of discourse pragmatics, the element introduced by a connective καί is meant to be processed as an addition to and in association with the preceding material.[31] This means that materials on both sides of καί are of equal status, "regardless of whether there is semantic continuity or not."[32]

As Stephanie Black's study has demonstrated, καί is the default connective in Matthew.[33] She argues that καί signals unmarked [narrative] continuity—a characterization which contrasts it with discourse discontinuity markers like δέ.[34] This assessment generally holds and would imply that the implied author's choice to use a different conjunction at a given time may signal a new development or topical transition.[35] However, certain καί-initial discontinuities are arguable, especially in formulaic constructs.[36] In the Eschatological Discourse, καί functions almost exclusively as an unmarked connective.[37] This corresponds to its use in the narrative sections of Matthew as well.

---

29. Καί occurs 1178 times in Matthew out of 9018 times in the NT.

30. Exceptions include cases in which καί is adverbial (translated in the emphatic sense as "indeed," "even," or "also") or adversative ("but") depending on context; for various nuances of these two broad categories, see BDAG, "Καί," 494–96.

31. Levinsohn, *Discourse Features*, 125; Runge, *Discourse Grammar*, 26; this strict additive or associative connection remains even when the sense of καί is adversative.

32. Levinsohn, *Discourse Features*, 124; Runge, *Discourse Grammar*, 26; Porter, *Idioms*, 211.

33. Black, *Sentence Conjunction*, 111n11. In contrast, asyndeton is the unmarked default conjunction in John's Gospel, see Levinsohn, *Discourse Features*, 81–82; Poythress, "Intersentence Conjunctions," 324; Buth, "Ουν, Δέ, Καί and Asyndeton," 145, 154.

34. Black, *Sentence Conjunction*, 112; Levinsohn and others regard δέ as a new development marker, discussed below.

35. See Runge, *Discourse Grammar*, 26.

36. E.g., καί signals more discontinuity than continuity in 11:1 and 26:1. In these instances, there is greater connection with what follows than with what precedes. For similar functional variations with the English "and," see Bestgen, "Segmentation Markers," 753–63.

37. Exceptions are in Matt 24:24, 33, [39].

Δέ

Outnumbered only by καί of all the conjunctives, δέ is one of the most common particles in the Greek NT. Traditional Grammarians regard δέ as a mere connective for clauses, expressing "contrast or simple continuation, . . . [which] may be left untranslated."[38] However, this common notion is unsupported by several instances of the particle. Many years ago, G. B. Winer observed that δέ is used when the author "subjoins something new, different and distinct from what precedes, but on that account not sharply opposed to it."[39] This view has been largely corroborated by contemporary linguistic and discourse studies. Levinsohn specifically cites Winer's view with approval, although he complains that Winer's description misses an important factor—the author's communicative intent. Levinsohn contends that "if δέ is to be used, not only must the sentence contain something distinctive,[40] . . . it must also represent *a new step or development in the author's story or argument.*" Matthew 1:18–25 provides a typical example of not only the use of δέ to signal changes in subject but also a change in circumstance from the genealogy of vv. 1–17.[41] Accordingly, δέ "is used [in both narrative and non-narrative] to mark new development in the sense that the information it introduces builds on what has gone before and makes a distinct contribution to the argument."[42]

Runge maintains "new-development" as the function or constraint of δέ.[43] According to him, "the use of δέ represents the writer's choice to explicitly signal that what follows is a new, distinct development in the story or argument, based on how the writer conceived of it."[44] In other words, as a development marker, δέ breaks "the discourse into meaningful chunks"[45] that provides the reader with what C. J. Fresch has called "cognitive breathing space." Fresch states that δέ "organizes and structures the discourse by

---

38. BDAG lists several other nuances based on five broad uses namely: a marker connecting a series of closely related data or lines of narrative (*and, as for*), a marker linking narrative segments (*now, then, and so, that is*), a marker with an additive relation, with possible suggestion of contrast (*at the same time*), a marker of contrast (*but, on the other hand*), and a marker of heightened emphasis, in combination with καί (*but also*); Porter claims that the most common use is adversative (*Idioms*, 208).

39. Winer, *Treatise*, 551–52 (cf. 566–67).

40. Since καί may also be used when something distinctive is added.

41. Levinsohn, *Discourse Features*, 72 (emphasis original); cf. Wallace who also considers Matt 1:18–25 as a typical example of δέ signaling a new topic (*Grammar*, 674).

42. Levinsohn, *Discourse Features*, 112.

43. Runge, *Discourse Grammar*, 31–33; cf. Long, *Koine Greek Grammar*, 83–84.

44. Runge, *Discourse Grammar*, 31.

45. Runge, *Discourse Grammar*, 29.

signaling the beginning or (less typically) the end of a distinct information unit," adding, "It often segments material that corresponds with a new development within the discourse, such as a new scene or topic to be discussed."[46]

However, Randall Buth and Stephanie Black take exception to this developmental view. Buth prefers the label "thematic shift" as the more adequate description of the function of δέ that reflects its backward, as well as forward-looking character.[47] Elsewhere, Buth describes the discourse constraint of δέ as "+DIFFERENCE or +CHANGE" in order to emphasize the notion of distinctiveness in the change that δέ introduces, including change of participant, paragraph or episode unit, theme line, tense, and binary changes or contrasts.[48]

Stephanie Black whose work extensively focuses on Matthew's Gospel similarly takes exception to Levinsohn's developmental view of δέ. "Unless 'development' can be shown unequivocally to be present in all cases of δέ in the Synoptic Gospels and Acts," she argues, "Levinsohn's claim that 'development is what δέ itself adds to the discourse cannot be sustained."[49] In line with Buth,[50] and citing both classicists and traditional grammarians, Black claims that δέ marks low- to mid-level discontinuity.[51] In her view, a change in mental representation using δέ to bring into focus a different subject would constitute discontinuity. She analyzes Matt 14:26–31 as a typical example but takes Matt 1:2–16 to be the "most obvious example of this dynamic in Matthew's Gospel."[52]

This whole discussion appears to bother much on semantics. Taking the *introduction of something distinct* as the pragmatic bottom-line for δέ, the terms, "new development," "thematic shift," and "low- to mid-level discontinuity" arguably do not appear to be mutually exclusive.[53] A New development or thematic shift implies discontinuity in a sense. Similarly,

---

46. Fresch, "Discourse Markers," 314.

47. Buth, "On Levinsohn's 'Development Units,'" 54.

48. Buth, "Semitic Καί and Greek Δέ," 13; cf. Buth, "On Levinsohn's 'Development Units,'" 55.

49. Black, *Sentence Conjunction*, 147.

50. According to Black, Buth is the first to integrate the traditional understanding of δέ as contrastive or adversative with its function as a marker of discontinuity in discourse" (*Sentence Conjunction*, 149).

51. Black, *Sentence Conjunction*, 146–53, 153n53.

52. Black, *Sentence Conjunction*, 157–58.

53. Buth could also use 'development' and 'thematic shift' interchangeably while noting, "after all any change of topic could also be a development" ("On Levinsohn's 'Development Units," 55); he describes δέ as a development connector ("Ουν, Δέ, Καί, and Asyndeton," 145).

STATEMENT OF PROBLEM, PURPOSE, AND METHODOLOGY 43

a low- to mid-level discontinuity in Black's determination invariably implies development within the flow of the discourse. Whether a particular instance of δέ will be more developmental or more discontinuous becomes a matter of context, but to take a minimalist approach that associates δέ with a singular and invariable constraint will be to ignore the actual data. For example, the use of δέ in Matt 3:1 signals a high-level discontinuity with the preceding material both in terms of the introduction of a new subject (John) and change in theme. Although development is not entirely lacking, this instance of δέ is clearly more discontinuous than the 9 instances in 3:4–16.[54] In other words, while the foregoing discussions focus on internal sentence-to paragraph-level texts or units of argument, δέ may also be used to mark higher-level breaks.[55] This confirms Black's assertion that the fact that δέ marks low- to mid-level discontinuity (or new development as Levinsohn and others argue) "does not mean that it cannot be used to signal higher-level breaks elsewhere."[56]

Moreover, against Buth's claim that the span of the thematic shift marked by δέ would be thought of as "supra-units" rather than "surface-structure units,"[57] the example above suggests that δέ may be used for discontinuities at or near the surface-structure level, especially in combination with other circumstantial factors. I should point out that Levinsohn himself notes that "δέ cannot be described as an exclusively developmental conjunction, since it also introduces background material, which can be viewed as a new step in a narrative, but scarcely as a new development."[58] Therefore, barring any contextual constraints, δέ is more accurately a +discontinuity +development marker.

Τότε

More than half of all instances of τότε in the Greek NT occurs in Matthew's Gospel (90/160). Τότε (often translated "then") is a temporal adverb when occurring with other conjunctions (Matt 24:21; 26:16). But when occurring alone it takes up the function of a connective particle without necessarily losing its adverbial characteristics.[59] According to Levinsohn, in Mat-

---

54. Notice also that the contrastive use in Matt 25:29 lacks the same discourse status as that in 24:36.
55. Cf. Matt 5:1; 8:1; 24:3; 28:1.
56. Black, *Sentence Conjunction*, 153n53.
57. Buth, "On Levinsohn's 'Development Units,'" 54.
58. Levinsohn, *Discourse Features*, 76n4 (cf. *Textual Connections*, 86–120).
59. Levinsohn, *Discourse Features*, 94–95; cf. Runge, *Discourse Grammar*, 37.

thew's Gospel, the conjunctive τότε provides cohesion or continuity within the same episode while also signaling development in subsections.[60] Such development occurs between (1) units that deal with the same *topic* but involves a *modified* cast [Matt 2:16; 13:43; 13:36; 16:20], (2) sets of events that involve the same cast of participants [Matt 4:5; 26:31], (3) units in which the same major participants successively interact with different participants [Matt 2:7; 11:20; 23:1]. Furthermore, τότε is used to introduce (4) a new participant into an existing scene [Matt 3:13; 19:13], (5) a scripture fulfilled at the time congruent to the event described [2:17; 27:9], and (6) the concluding event or speech to which an episode has been building up, often in such a way as to highlight that conclusion [15:21–28; 26:74].[61]

Black's analysis of Matthew's narrative corroborates these observations.[62] Black further emphasizes that τότε, unlike καί, signals marked continuity with "some measure of emphasis or prominence."[63] On his part, Runge argues that narrative τότε segments the text into developments. "Since it is assumed that one narrative event follows the next in sequence, the pragmatic effect of using it in a context of relative continuity is to instruct the reader to segment the text into a new chunk." He further adds that "τότε indicates that the primary basis for relating what follows to what precedes is as the next discrete step or development in the discourse."[64] Commenting on Matt 18:2, Runge takes τότε as signaling "a low-level break in the text, yet not so great as to make the reader think that a whole new topic follows." Also, he views Matt 18:21 and other instances such as Matt 2:7, 16; 4:1, 5; 15:12; 16:24 as "paragraph-initial instances of τότε" all of which indicate the next development of the discourse.[65]

One question arises from this analysis. What is the difference between τότε and δέ? As it appears, in segmenting episodes into developments, τότε functionally resembles δέ. But why does an author choose to use one instead of the other? Levinsohn claims that τότε may be viewed as a marked form of δέ.[66] Runge comments,

> Since both δέ and τότε mark new developments, the question arises of how they differ from one another. Based on the idea of default versus marked, δέ should be viewed as the default

60. Levinsohn, *Discourse Features*, 96.
61. Levinsohn, *Discourse Features*, 96–97.
62. Black, *Sentence Conjunction*, 218–54.
63. Black, *Sentence Conjunctions*, 221, 248–49.
64. Runge, *Discourse Grammar*, 37–38.
65. Runge, *Discourse Grammar*, 38.
66. Levinsohn, *Discourse Features*, 73n1.

development marker, the one used when there is no desire to specify the exact nature of the development. Due to the semantic nature of τότε, it makes explicit that the development that follows is *temporal* in nature.[67]

Apparently, in none of the treatments is τότε identified as a discontinuity marker but δέ does mark discontinuity regardless of its preponderance and many instances in which it merely moves the discourse forward developmentally. Taking all the details (temporal character and markedness) into account, it is justified to conclude that τότε is indicated for +continuity +development in contrast to δέ which, as we have observed above, more properly indicates +discontinuity +development. In the Eschatological Discourse, τότε occurs 12 times as a conjunctive and tends to signal continuity while segmenting the Discourse into developments of a temporal kind.[68]

Οὖν

The conjunction οὖν is recognized to have a range of senses. According to BDAG, οὖν "is an inferential and then mainly a transitional conjunction." As an inferential conjunction, it denotes that what it introduces is the deduction from, result, conclusion, or summary of what precedes.[69] As a transitional particle, it functions as a "marker of continuation in a narrative" serving to resume the main subject after a digression or interruption or "to indicate a transition to something new." Οὖν may also be emphatic or even adversative.[70]

These characterizations have been nuanced in a variety of ways. Levinsohn associates οὖν with δέ as both "development markers in that both are used to introduce information that represents a significant development as far as the author's purpose is concerned." However, οὖν, he believes, is more marked than δέ.[71] Also, "οὖν marks a return to the same topic as before, whereas δέ permits a change of topic."[72] Levinsohn goes further to claim

---

67. Runge, *Discourse Grammar*, 38.

68. Matt 24:9, 16, 23, 40; 25:1, 7, 31, 34, 37, 41, 44, 45; the remaining 5 (24:10, 14, 21, 30) are adverbial.

69. BDAG, "Οὖν," 736; Westfall, "Οὖν in the New Testament," 284.

70. BDAG, "Οὖν," 737, identifies a potential adversative use in Acts 23:21; 25:4; 28:5; Rom 10:14.

71. Levinsohn, *Discourse Features*, 85, 126; Buth, "Οὖν, Δέ, Καί, and Asyndeton," also links οὖν with δέ as development connectors in John's Gospel (145); Westfall describes οὖν as "a moderately marked conjunction" ("Οὖν in the New Testament," 300).

72. Levinsohn, *Discourse Features*, 85n16.

that "the presence of οὖν *only* constrains what follows to be interpreted as further development of the topic that has been resumed."[73] By implication, as Levinsohn sums up in a later work, "οὖν constrains what follows to be interpreted as a distinct point that advances an argument in an inferential way." Consequently, he characterizes οὖν as "+Inferential +Distinctive."[74] Runge expatiates on Levinsohn's view by stating,

> If the event line of a narrative is interrupted by background material, it is common to find the resumption of the mainline marked by οὖν. The +development signals the transition from the background material; the +continuity indicates that the same event line will be resumed. In contrast, resumption marked using δέ would indicate a new line of development.[75]

As it appears, these claims do not differ much from the traditional inferential, resumptive, or continuative view of οὖν. Put simply, in Levinsohn's and Runge's view, οὖν introduces something "distinctive or developmental but still continuous and inferential."

However, as already noted from BDAG, οὖν does not only or always indicate an inferential relationship or continuity in terms of resuming an interrupted discourse or narrative mainline, it can also "indicate a transition to something new." In his now dated but classic study on Greek particles, J. D. Denniston describes the function of οὖν in terms of "proceeding to a new point, or a new stage in the march of thought." Denniston notes that "the inferential use of οὖν is too common to need illustration" and observes "passages in which the sequence of thought is not at first obvious."[76] More recently, Black accords more weight to the "distinctive" constraint, contending that οὖν indicates a type of discontinuity similar to γάρ and δέ.[77] She claims that, in Matthew's narrative, οὖν is used to help the audience integrate into their mental representation of the discourse an additional material which is off-line with respect to the main narrative events.[78] Such added material

---

73. Levinsohn, *Discourse Features*, 128 [emphasis mine].

74. Levinsohn, "'Therefore' or 'Wherefore,'" 327 (cf. *Discourse Features*, 127–28).

75. Runge, *Discourse Grammar*, 45.

76. Denniston, *Greek Particles*, 426; cf. Poythress, "Intersentence Conjunctions," 330.

77. In Black's view, δέ signals discontinuity within the narrated event while γάρ and οὖν signal discontinuity involving the sequential flow of the narrative (*Sentence Conjunction*, 260).

78. Black, *Sentence Conjunction*, 261–63.

represents "a new conceptualization" rather than mere "explicitly logical operations" or "summary statement" of preceding material.⁷⁹

While Black's main example (Matt 1:17) may seem precarious since it represents the only narrative use of οὖν in Matthew apart from 27:17, the view that οὖν does more than mark inference, summaries, conclusions, or even resumption has been argued in a recent study by Cynthia L. Westfall.⁸⁰ Westfall complains that despite "suggestions that οὖν has other rather unusual functions that require additional categories, most of the discussion has revolved around the seemingly idiosyncratic use of οὖν in the Gospel of John."⁸¹ Her investigation deals with both sentence level and discourse level uses of οὖν in the NT as a whole. She argues that at the sentence level, οὖν in collocation with prominence phenomena, such as commands, questions, responses, and conditionals does not always mark inference, conclusion, or summaries. In such collocations, they function to engage the audience more rhetorically and emphatically than propositional statements.⁸² At discourse levels, her study found that οὖν

> occurs with introductions and frameshifts, with inferences, summaries, and conclusions, and with discourse peaks and mainline material. *The occurrence at the boundaries of discourse draws attention to the shifts in the discourse*, while summaries, conclusions, and peaks indicate mainline material. Therefore, οὖν collocates with material that is relatively prominent in terms of at least two different functions: the *horizontal discontinuity* in the discourse in the creation of *transitions at various levels: frames, paragraphs, or sections, and vertical discontinuity in the creation of emphasis.*⁸³

The important thing to note in this conclusion is that οὖν can mark not only inferences or summaries but also discontinuities in the form of transitions or frames. Westfall gives Matt 7:24 as an example of the discourse use of οὖν to introduce a frame shift, in this case, the beginning of a new, discrete, and illustrative unit.⁸⁴

---

79. Black, *Sentence Conjunction*, 263.

80. Westfall, "Οὖν in the New Testament," 297, regards Matt 1:17 as "one of the most classic examples of inferential summaries."

81. Westfall, "Οὖν in the New Testament," 284–85.

82. Westfall, "Οὖν in the New Testament," 292; although she notes that οὖν with conditionals functions majorly as summaries and conclusions (291, 297).

83. Westfall, "Οὖν in the New Testament," 300 (italics mine).

84. Wallace, *Grammar*, 294–95; although she also notes that Matt 7:24 introduces the conclusion of the whole Sermon on the Mount.

Wallace corroborates the transitional view of οὖν, categorizing it, along with δέ, under "transitional conjunctions" which are translated "now" and "then" and used when "change to a new topic of discussion" is involved, although he maintains the limitation of this use to "narrative materials, especially John."[85] Wallace hesitates to dabble into discourse analysis,[86] but he is in accord with recent advances in discourse-analytical studies when he states: "the transitional force of οὖν sometimes comes close to the inferential force. . . . But to label a conjunction as transitional is to regard the conjunction to be more chronological [or sequential] than logical."[87] In other words, to use Black's words cited above, "explicit logical operation" is not necessary to οὖν.

As it appears, it may be too restrictive to maintain that οὖν signals transition, discontinuity, and or new development only in narrative materials and mostly in John. For example, although Matthew generally uses οὖν to mark inference or logical conclusions in discourses,[88] in some instances, the nuance is arguably less inferential but more of a new unit of thought within the discourse progression.[89] Thus, as with other connectives, consideration of specific discourse contexts will help determine the nuance of a particular use of οὖν.

Asyndeton (Ø)

The term asyndeton defines the absence of sentence conjunction where one would normally be expected.[90] In the NT, asyndeton performs a variety of functions including rhetorical amplification and discourse marking.[91] In

85. Wallace, *Grammar*, 674.

86. For his fourfold reason, see Wallace, *Grammar*, xv.

87. Wallace, *Grammar*, 674; cf. Denniston, *Greek Particles*, 426.

88. Discourse (Matt 3:8, 10; 5:19, 23, 48; 6:2, 8, 9, 22; 23, 31, 34; 7:11; 9:38; 10:16, 26, 31, 32; 12:12, 26; 13:18, 27, 28, 40, 56; 17:10; 18:4, 26, 29, 31; 19:6, 7; 21:25, 40; 22:9, 17, 21, 28, 43, 45; 23:3, 20; 24:26, 42; 25:13, 27, 28; 26:54; 27:22, 64; 28:19); narrative (1:17; 27:17).

89. E.g., Matt 7:12, 24; 13:18; 24:15.

90. As Aristotle suggested, Greeks may have considered this undesirable in written discourses, preferring to use it specifically in public speeches for dramatic effect; he reasoned that a connective make many things one, conversely asyndeton makes it appear as if many things are being said when in fact one point is being amplified (*Rhet.* 3.12); cf. Winer, *Treatise*, 673.

91. For a helpful summary of the uses of asyndeton, see Long, *Koine Greek Grammar*, 68, 280–81; cf. Winer, *Treatise*, 673–74; Wallace defines asyndeton as "a vivid stylistic feature that occurs often for emphasis, solemnity, or rhetorical value (staccato effect), or when there is an abrupt change in topic" (*Grammar*, 658).

terms of discourse marking, Levinsohn argues that "asyndeton tends to imply *not* strengthening, *not* developmental, *not* associative, *not* inferential, etc." However, he also notes that it may indicate close connection or no direct connection in non-narrative text.[92] According to Runge, asyndeton may be used to signal topical discontinuity or at the beginning of a new thought or topic or simply where the writer chose not to make a relation explicit. "The choice to use asyndeton," he claims, represents the choice not to specify a relation."[93] Runge is silent on whether this claim applies to narratives or discourses. However, in the two examples he offers (John 1:1–8 and Matt 6:24–26, both discourses), asyndeton is arguably used for rhetorical effect and to create cohesion between the main clauses. The asyndetic connection of the beatitudes in Matt 5:3–12 also seems to have this effect.[94]

Asyndeton occurs more frequently than any single connective in Matthew's Gospel. Here, Black argues that it signals "either tight continuity in conversation [discourse] or mid-to-higher level breaks in the narrative."[95] She also finds that in the narratives, asyndeton is more frequently used to signal continuity in "speech margins,"[96] but somewhat less frequently with the "aorist (or occasionally with imperfect but never present) tense-forms" to indicate discontinuity.[97] Moreover, she argues that asyndeton often combines with formulaic phrases at points where discontinuities occur in Matthew's narrative. For example, seven instances of formulaic "Ø + ἐν ἐκείνῳ" phrases and two instances of "Ø + ἀπο τότε" formulaic phrases appear to signal narrative breaks.[98]

This brief survey indicates that Matthew in particular uses asyndeton to signal topical breaks in narratives, whereas, in discourses, he uses it to

---

92. Levinsohn, *Discourse Features*, 118; he finds asyndeton used for both continuity and discontinuity in John's Gospel (82).

93. Runge, *Discourse Grammar*, 20.

94. Notice that there is no change of topic necessarily in the beatitudes. In other words, they are mutually reinforcing and emphasize the same or similar conditions of the one who is blessed.

95. Black, *Sentence Conjunction*, 179, 182–83.

96. Black, *Sentence Conjunction*, 183; speech margins are clauses or phrases that introduce an indirect or reported speeches (*he said . . . she said*); Levinsohn refers to them as "speech orienters" (*Discourse Features*, 216).

97. Black, *Sentence Conjunction*, 204.

98. Matt 11:25; 12:1; 13:1; 14:1; 18:1; 22:23; 26:55 (cf. 3:1), and 4:17; 16:21 respectively. We should note that Black's claim of a Subject-Verb (SV) constituent order as supporting a narrative break in 4:17 is mistaken (see Black, *Sentence Conjunction*, 210); what we have in 4:17 is "Ø + ἀπο τότε . + VS" constituent order. Also, Black's case for "Ø + genitive-absolute-participial" construction indicating narrative breaks in 1:18b; 9:18; 12:46; and 17:5 is less persuasive (see Black, *Sentence Conjunction*, 205–13).

signal continuity, sometimes with the added effect of rhetorical iteration or emphasis or even to conclude a unit of thought within a discourse (cf. Matt 24:28, 34–35, 46–47). This conclusion should be taken as a general rather than static rule. In other words, it is necessary to consider the context when trying to determine the kind of relation or effect signaled by a given instance of asyndeton.[99] As with οὖν and, indeed, other discourse markers discussed above, careful consideration of the discourse connective values of neighboring conjunctions or other discourse elements in context is one way to do this.

Scope and Presupposition of Study

The scope of this study is Matthew and his version of the Eschatological Discourse throughout. In other words, this study will not delve into redaction or source criticisms; the assumption that Matt 24–25 is a redaction of Mark's version of the Discourse will not form the basis of interpretation. Regardless of the current consensus on the synoptic relationships—that Matthew simply redacted Mark—there are more reasons to doubt such redactional activity than many scholars are willing to concede.[100] As such, I will simply take the Synoptics as witnesses to the same tradition without considerations of the direction of relationship.[101] And as a presupposition, I am inclined to the possibility that Matthew may have been written prior to 70 CE although this will have little or no effect on the interpretation. Also, in attempting to correlate the eschatology of Matt 24–25 to what is taught elsewhere in the NT, the focus will be general observations in those other NT passages rather than detailed exegesis.

Design

Based on the four key questions undergirding this study as stated above, I will proceed first by considering the general literary character and form of Matt 24–25 in relation to the Gospel of Matthew as a whole (chapter 3). The second part will deal with the structure of the Eschatological Discourse. Then, following the inductive methodological principle that the whole informs the part and vice versa, I will consider the structure of the Discourse

---

99. See Runge, *Discourse Grammar*, 22.

100. Despite all its logical strength, the so-called two-source solution remains a hypothesis.

101. For a similar approach, see France, *Evangelist and Teacher*, 48; France, *Matthew*, 22.

in relation to the structure of Matthew as a whole (chapter 4). This second part will form the interpretive framework for the entire study. The third part will engage the Discourse proper, providing an interpretation of the meaning and eschatology of the Discourse based on the structure proposed (chapter 5). Following this, the fourth part (chapter 6) will focus on the place of Matt 24–25 within the broader sweep of Matthew's Gospel in terms of its role in the overall communication goal. Finally, I will draw together the conclusions of the entire study showing how it coheres with the eschatology of the NT in general (chapter 7).

Thesis of Study

Matthew 24–25 is a prophetic-apocalyptic organized to reflect the alternation or interchange between two distinct events—the destruction of the temple and the parousia or second coming. A close reading of the passage following this structural schema, shows that although closely linked in the Discourse, these two events are, in reality, separated by an indefinite period of tribulations. The resulting interpretation, as compelled by the data, is at variance with much of the current views from thoroughgoing preterism to exclusive futurism. It also refutes both ideas of rapture to heaven and a future earthly millennial reign. Against these two popular eschatological views, the Discourse only shows that Jesus' awaited coming (i.e., his second coming) is for final judgment/salvation and the immediate commencement of the eternal age. This understanding is largely in accord with the rest of the NT's eschatological outlook. Moreover, the Discourse in its literary and structural location, functions to complement Matthew's overarching Christological goal: to depict Jesus as Universal Judge-King.

3

Matthew 24–25: Form and Hermeneutics

Introduction

THE INTERPRETATION OF ANY literary document depends directly on its genre or form. Any attempt to ignore this consideration sets the interpretive venture up to fail. Therefore, this chapter will focus on a descriptive overview of the literary form of Matt 24–25 that directs interpretation relative to the Gospel as a whole. First, I will review scholarly studies related to the form of Matthew's Gospel, stressing its apocalyptic worldview in general and as epitomized by the Discourse. Second, I will deal with the issue of interpretation by highlighting and evaluating competing approaches to the language of the Eschatological Discourse. And third, I will develop a set of hermeneutical criteria for engaging the apocalyptic language of the Discourse. These three considerations combined will set the stage for the interpretation that will be offered later.

Form of Matthew's Gospel in General and chs. 24–25 in Particular

The search for the genre of the Gospels (Matthew in this case) has yielded many proposals with no specific consensus.[1] However, the current state of affairs seems to have settled with the recognition that the Gospels compare

---

1. For these proposals, see Dulling, "Gospel of Matthew," 300–301.

most favorably with ancient biographies (*Bios* or *Lives*).² As Aune defines it, "Greco-Roman biography is a type of independent literary composition which typically focused on the character, achievements, and lasting significance of a memorable and exemplary individual from birth to death, emphasizing his public career."³ Richard A. Burridge's comprehensive study further demonstrates that while ancient biographies show both variety and flexibility, they all exhibit a common set of generic features. These include, among other things, narrativity, positive characterization of the subject, and didactic motive.⁴ Matthew exhibits similar characteristics and is therefore properly read as a biographical account of the life of Jesus.⁵

As I shall discuss later, the case for the biographical reading of Matthew has been demonstrated structurally and hermeneutically. However, to identify Matthew's Gospel as a biography is only one step in the interpretive process. One must also seek to understand the conceptual framework of the implied author or biographic subject since "form" or genre is to be distinguished from "content."⁶ In terms of "content" (worldview and language), Matthew's Gospel expresses an apocalyptic flavor most evident in chs. 24–25. Reacting to the identification of Mark 13 as a "little apocalypse," by modern critics, N. T. Wright contends that this chapter (parr. Matt 24) cannot "come away clean from its context, leaving a non-apocalyptic Mark, and perhaps, a non-apocalyptic Jesus." He goes further to describe Mark as a sort of "meta-apocalypse."⁷ This assessment applies no less to Matt 24–25 in relation to Matthew in general. Put succinctly, while Matthew's Gospel approximates the biographic form, its content or message is largely apocalyptic; its

---

2. See Talbert, *What Are the Gospels?*; Shuler, *Genre for the Gospels*; Aune, *New Testament*, 46–76; Aune, "Greco-Roman Biography," 107–26; Burridge, *What Are the Gospels?*; Licona, *Why Are There Differences?*

3. Aune, "Greco-Roman Biography," 107.

4. See Burridge, *What Are the Gospels?*, 124–84.

5. Here, the work of Kingsbury (*Matthew*) is particularly of interest. Kingsbury argues that Matthew centrally deals with the ultimate significance of Jesus (his life, ministry, and death and resurrection) as Messiah for both Jews and gentiles within a salvation-historical frame of two epochs—the time of Israel (OT) and the time of Jesus (his birth to his *parousia*). Stanton notes that "the evangelist [Matthew] does not intend to tell us about his own community, but to set out both his story of the origins, life and ultimate fate of Jesus of Nazareth and also his convictions about the significance of Jesus" (*New People*, 147). For more on the biographical character of Matthew and its implication for interpretation, see Bauer, *Gospel*, 9–24.

6. See, Aune, "Apocalypse of John," 13–96; cf. Kreitzer, "Apocalyptic, Apocalypticism," 57–58.

7. Wright, *New Testament and the People*, 393–94; by "meta-apocalypse" he means that the Gospel writers tell the story of Jesus' use of apocalyptic imagery to tell the story of Israel.

biographic center is an apocalyptic figure. Therefore, to properly interpret Matt 24-25, it is important to understand this character or aspect of the form of Matthew's Gospel as a whole.

Apocalyptic in Matthew

The adjectival term "apocalyptic" derives from the Greek word, ἀποκάλυψις, which means "revelation" or "disclosure."[8] In the noun form, it occurs as a description of a book only in Rev 1:1, never in Matthew,[9] but used to describe both apocalyptic and non-apocalyptic phenomenon in other NT writings.[10] So in what sense is Matthew's content apocalyptic?

Critical research on "apocalyptic" dates as far back as the 1800s with the primary focus on the question of literary form or genre.[11] This state of affairs continued until "apocalyptic" emerged as a theological conception in the consistent eschatological school of Weiss and Schweitzer. Both men challenged the prevailing rejection of an apocalyptic Jesus by modern critics. They argued that Jesus is understood properly only against the backdrop of the Jewish apocalyptic worldview in relation to the coming of the kingdom of God. Weiss argued that Jesus' proclamation and messianic consciousness consisted of the impending but wholly future kingdom.[12] Furthering this view, Schweitzer interprets Matt 10:20-23 as the key to Jesus' imminent eschatological expectation.[13] Since Weiss and Schweitzer, much advance has been made in the study of "apocalyptic" in terms of its historical development and as a hermeneutical grid for NT interpretation.[14] In what follows, I set forth some of the important studies and views on "apocalyptic" in Matthew's Gospel.

---

8. BDAG, "Ἀποκάλυψις," 112.

9. Verbal forms occur in Matt 10:26; 11:25, 27; 16:17.

10. Luke 2:32; Rom 2:5; 8:19; 16:25; 1 Cor 1:7; 14:6, 26; 2 Cor 12:1, 7; Gal 1:12; 2:2; Eph 1:17; 3:3; 2 Thess 1:7; 1 Pet 1:7, 13; 4:13.

11. E.g., Lucke, *Versuch einer vollständigen*.

12. Weiss, *Predigt Jesu*, 11-13, 50-52.

13. See discussion in Schweitzer, *Quest*, 357-64.

14. See Rowley, *Relevance of Apocalyptic*; Russell, *Method and Message*; Koch, *Rediscovery*; Rollins, "New Testament and Apocalyptic," 454-76; Beardslee, "New Testament Apocalyptic," 419-35; Hanson, *Dawn of Apocalyptic*; Hanson, "Apocalypticism," 28-34; Hanson, *Visionaries and Their Apocalypses*, 28-34; Bauckham, "Rise of Apocalyptic" 10-23; Collins, *Apocalyptic*; Collins, *Apocalyptic Imagination*; Hellholm, *Apocalypticism*; Sturm, "Defining the Word 'Apocalyptic,'" 17-48; Rowland, *Open Heaven*; Murphy, *Apocalypticism*; Greg, *Apocalyptic Literature*; Reynolds and Stuckenbruck, *Jewish Apocalyptic Tradition*.

From Streeter to Käsemann

Streeter and Bornkamm

I have already reviewed the views of Streeter and Bornkamm in chapter 1. Here, I highlight their claims regarding Matthew's apocalyptic character and intention. Streeter argues that in contrast to the progressive minimization of the apocalyptic from Mark to Luke and to John,[15] Matthew represents a development in the opposite direction with a predilection towards an apocalyptic eschatology involving a visible *parousia* of Jesus.[16] Matthew 24, in particular, is recognized as an apocalyptic chapter derived from Mark 13 and "ingeniously expanded with material from Q."[17] Apart from the unique notion of the "immediacy of [the] parousia," Streeter notes several other instances indicating Matthew's heightened apocalyptic interest compared to Q and Mark. For example, Matthew, he claims, fills out Matt 24:29–31 (cf. Mark 13:25–27) with details such as "trumpet . . . derived from conventional scenery of Jewish eschatology." The unique phrases, συντελεία τοῦ αἰῶνος (occurring 5 times in Matthew) and "weeping and gnashing of teeth" (occurring six times and only once in Luke out of the entire NT), and the interpretation of the parables of the Tears and the Dragnet in terms of "catastrophic eschatology," all betray Matthew's apocalyptic interest.[18] These, in addition to Matthew's sense of urgency regarding the second coming of Christ, suggested to Streeter that the Gospel "must have been written during a period of intense apocalyptic expectation."[19]

But Streeter also regards Matthew's apocalyptic as "subservient to a moral purpose." Thus, for him, "the Gospel of Matthew is a call for moral reformation" in view of imminent eschatological judgment.[20] Here, one finds the apparent root of the view later developed by Bornkamm in his essay, "End Expectation and the Church in Matthew" in which he consigns Matthew's use of the apocalyptic language of judgment to a paraenetic goal. For both Bornkamm and Streeter, Matthew's apocalypticizing of his sources

---

15. Streeter, however, concedes that John does not absolutely deny apocalyptic judgment but has substituted the coming of the Comforter for the Return of Christ (Streeter, *Four Gospels*, 468).

16. Streeter, *Four Gospels*, 172, 394, 425. "In the Appendix to the *Oxford Studies*," Streeter writes, "I argued that Q, Mark, and Matthew show an ascending scale in the tendency to emphasize and conventionalize our Lord's Apocalyptic teaching" (521).

17. Streeter, *Four Gospels*, 264.

18. Streeter, *Four Gospels*, 521–22.

19. Streeter, *Four Gospels*, 522–23.

20. Streeter, *Four Gospels*, 522.

essentially provides entry into the life setting and moral exigency of the Matthean community.

Hadfield

A similar view of Matthew's apocalyptic character is espoused by P. Hadfield in a short article written in 1959.[21] Hadfield observes certain apocalyptic motifs which he claims derive from Matthew's alteration of Mark and Q, and use of other sources. These motifs, he posits, uniquely parallel ideas in Jewish apocalyptic literature and Iranian sources. In particular, Hadfield notes Matthew's idea of "guardian angel,"[22] the themes of "final judgment," "reward for the righteous,"[23] and punishment of the wicked in the outer darkness.[24] He observes that the Matthean theme of "righteousness"[25] and some elements of the judgment scene of Matt 25:31–46 are also found in other apocalyptic literature.[26]

Consequently, Hadfield concludes that the author or final editor of Matthew's Gospel belonged to an apocalyptic school of thought. Hadfield's discussion is brief, but it is enough to betray assumptions that appear too optimistic, particularly his suggestion that Matthew represents an apocalyptic redaction of "the original version," i.e., Mark, Q, or both.[27] Not only is Q hypothetical, but also, the question of which source is the original version is potentially uncertain.

Käsemann

Only a year after Hadfield's article, Ernst Käsemann wrote a famous essay, "Die Anfange Christlicher Theologie" (1960).[28] This essay is based "almost exclusively on the Gospel of Matthew" which is considered "nearer than the other synoptics to the primitive age."[29] Käsemann's goal in this essay

---

21. Hadfield, "Apocalyptic Editor," 128–32.
22. See Matt 18:6–9 (cf. Mark 9:42–48; Tob 5:4; Jub. 35:17; T. Jud. 3:10).
23. Said to probably derive from Isa 62:11.
24. Matt 25:30; cf. Q (Luke 19:27); 1 En. 48:9; 10:4.
25. Matt 6:33; the term is not present in Q (Luke 12:31) and is said to have "apocalyptic significance" (cf. Matt 3:15; 5:6,10,20; 6:33; 21:32, and 1 En. 94:1; 46:3).
26. Matt 25:35–36 compares to and must therefore have been derived from T. Jos. 1:5–20.
27. Hadfield, "Apocalyptic Editor," 128.
28. Short abbreviation for translated version: Käsemann, "Beginnings," 17–46.
29. Käsemann, "Beginnings," 18; he apparently held the Matthean priority view (cf. 36).

is to reconstruct the rise of Christian theology. He argues that there existed within the earliest Christian community opposing theological camps. Matthew's camp was part of a rigorous Jewish Christian sect located in the region between Palestine and Syria.[30] This sect gave the teaching of Jesus its apocalyptic flavor. While taking the apocalyptically oriented message of the Baptist as the starting point, Jesus' own proclamation, contends Käsemann, "was not constitutively stamped by apocalyptic," rather Jesus "proclaimed the immediate nearness of God." Therefore, it was "the Easter and the reception of the Spirit [that] caused the primitive Christianity to resort again to apocalyptic as a means of responding, and in a certain sense, supplanting Jesus' preaching of the nearness of God."[31]

Based on the saying in Matt 10:41, Käsemann claims that the Matthean community was characterized by a Spirit-inspired prophetic enthusiasm. To this community "the possession of the Spirit was a pledge of the imminent *parousia* and the authority for its mission that accordingly [prophetic] enthusiasm and apocalyptic theology are here united by inner necessity."[32] As Käsemann understands it, much of the eschatological sayings are to be attributed to this post-Easter Spirit of prophecy. In terms of its form, this prophetic enthusiasm re-appropriates OT traditions and gnomic or proverbial sayings, transforming them apocalyptically into sacred eschatological laws.[33] Käsemann thus concludes with the well-known dictum: "apocalyptic—since the preaching of Jesus cannot really be described as theology—was the mother of all Christian theology."[34]

Käsemann's "risky experiment" in historical reconstruction, as he himself considers the venture,[35] and his central thesis, did not prove convincing to many critics.[36] Part of the problem is his ambiguous use of the term "apocalyptic."[37] As Koch later complained, Käsemann's interpretation took

---

30. Käsemann, "Beginnings," 18; this view is signaled to Käsemann by several passages such as Matt 7:22–23; 23:8–10; 5:17–20; 10:5, 41; 11:20–24.

31. Käsemann, "Beginnings," 40.

32. Käsemann, "Beginnings," 29.

33. E.g., Matt 10:15; 11:20–24; 12:41; 24:37; 7:2; 13:12; 25:29; 10:26–27; 23:12.

34. Käsemann, "Beginnings," 40.

35. Käsemann, "Beginnings," 18.

36. See two responses to Käsemann's essay by Gerhard Ebeling and Ernst Fuchs in Funk, *Journal*, 47–98; Rollins, "New Testament and Apocalyptic," 471, argues, "it appears that a post-Easter apocalyptic if it existed at all, represented only one of several theological options in the primitive church, developed by a group of Christians who felt that the pendulum had swung too far from popular Jewish piety. This 'post-Easter apocalyptic' was not the mother of all Christian theology, but at best one of many brothers."

37. In a subsequent publication, Käsemann makes clear that by "apocalyptic" he refers to "the expectation of an imminent Parousia" ("Primitive Christian Apocalyptic," 108n1).

"the theory of the non-apocalyptic Jesus and his apocalyptic church to a new and almost unparalleled extreme."[38] Yet, Käsemann successfully moved apocalyptic from the periphery to the mainstream of biblical scholarship.[39] Much of NT interpretation has, ever since, proceeded with "apocalyptic" close to its center. The critical point to keep in mind, however, is Käsemann's fundamental assumption of the apocalyptic character of Matthew's Gospel.

From Sabourin to Sim

Leopold Sabourin

In his 1983 essay, Leopold Sabourin wonders why the apocalyptic phenomenon could have been missed by many previous Matthean commentators, although he draws from the earlier works of Hadfield and Käsemann.[40] Sabourin claims that Matthew's apocalyptic character depends on his proximity to the Jewish context of the earliest Christian generation. "At the dawn of the New Testament," he notes, "apocalyptic had become in the Jewish world the ordinary vehicle of religious thought," adding, "Jesus himself and the authors of the New Testament have used this mode of thought and of speech to express the advent of the eschatological salvation."[41]

Many will challenge the assertion linking Matthew to the earliest Christian tradition and even implying an earlier date of writing relative to the other Gospels. Indeed, apocalyptic character hardly should imply primitivity since several apocalyptic writings originated much later than the earliest Christian movement. However, Sabourin's assertion that "it is not at all doubtful that Matthew is the most apocalyptic of the evangelists,"[42] corroborates what some before him had found.

Sabourin takes for granted the apocalyptic traits shared in common by Matthew 24–25 and Mark 13,[43] but he enumerates several apocalyp-

---

38. Koch, *Rediscovery*, 78.

39. Koch, *Rediscovery*, 14. Cope, "Close of the Age," 121, affirms Käsemann's dictum as "largely correct"; Allison, "Apocalyptic," 19, considers it as "exaggerated," although he grants that "the influence of apocalyptic eschatology in significant portions of the NT is clear"; and Kreitzer, "Apocalyptic, Apocalypticism," 56, describes it as "a veritable Archimedean point within NT studies," while linking the "potential confusion" of terms to Weiss and Schweitzer.

40. Sabourin, "Apocalyptic Traits," 19.

41. Sabourin, "Apocalyptic Traits," 19–20.

42. Sabourin, "Apocalyptic Traits," 19.

43. Mark 13 is referred to as "the prophetic discourse Jesus pronounced," and along with Matt 24–25, as an Eschatological Discourse (Sabourin, "Apocalyptic Traits," 19, 22).

tic motifs which are unique to Matthew or "which he has modified in an apocalyptic sense."[44] In each instance, he identifies OT as well as Jewish apocalyptic texts that may have influenced Matthew's rendition.[45] He is of the view that a comparison between Matt 24–25 and Mark 13 will most evidently reveal Matthew's apocalyptic interest, concluding that readers would recognize Matthew's presentation of Jesus as the apocalyptic Son of Man of the *parousia* and the coming universal Judge.[46] In all, while Sabourin offers no extended analysis on particular apocalyptic parallels in the Synoptics, this essay is a model exercise in intertextuality.

G. N. Stanton

Stanton, in a 1984 article entitled "The Gospel of Matthew and Judaism," argues that Matthew uses heightened apocalyptic language in chs. 24–25 to intensify his anti-Jewish polemic. Stanton takes this as crucial support for his historical and sociological judgment regarding Matthew's setting. As he argues, the Matthean community had recently parted ways with Judaism, resulting in present hostility from the Jews in particular and the gentile world in general.[47] Stanton does not, however, deal extensively with the apocalyptic character of Matthew's Gospel which he takes as a biography of Jesus.[48]

O. Lamar Cope

Cope picks up on Bornkamm's view on the significance of apocalyptic in Matthew. Based on his assessment that Bornkamm's argument is both "persuasive" and "understated,"[49] he sets out to determine (1) how pervasive, indeed, apocalyptic/judgment is in Matthew's Gospel, (2) what role(s) it plays, and (3) what these reveal about the setting of Matthew's church.[50]

---

44. These unique passages are Matt 6:33; 7:13–14; 8:12, 24; 9:6; 10:21; 11:23; 12:32; 13:11, 32, 35, 36–43; 16:19, 21, 27, 28; 17:1–9; 18:10; 19:28; 21:10; 22:14; 24:3, 27, 37, 39, 4–8, 10–12, 30a, 31; 25:30, 31–46; 26:39, 51b–53; 28:2–3, 18–20.
45. Sabourin, "Apocalyptic Traits," 22–32.
46. Sabourin, "Apocalyptic Traits, 33.
47. The article in question is reprinted in Stanton, *New People*, 146–68.
48. Stanton, *New People*, 62–70.
49. Ch. 2 of this study.
50. Cope, "Close of the Age," 114.

First, Cope argues that Matthew employs a heavy dose of apocalyptic/judgment language. Throughout, "Matthew keeps the readers' attention fixed upon the apocalyptic consequence of discipleship," and each of the discourses closes with a judgment scene.[51]

Second, as to the role of apocalyptic, Cope notes the presence of the notions of hope, assurance, and warning of coming judgment in Matthew. However, he argues that the dominant role of apocalyptic in Matthew concerns "avoiding punishment for misdeeds and receiving rewards for good deeds." Echoing Bornkamm, he further claims that Matthew is concerned far more with judgment coming to test the followers of Christ than he is with judgment for the unbelievers.[52] Thus, although Matt 23 and 25:31–46, for example, suggest more extended applications, Matthew's use of apocalyptic/judgment language serves the discipleship need of the Matthean congregation.

Third, Cope surmises that something must account for how Matthew could combine a conservative view on Torah and Christocentric emphasis. He finds the answer in the Matthean community's recent experiences—their experience of the fall of Jerusalem (Matt 21:41; 22:7) and persecution (Matt 10:34–38) which have given rise to an apocalyptic hope in the return of Christ, as well as their discipleship struggles (Matt 5:21; 7:21–23). These lead Cope to hypothesize that the Gospel must have been written in Syria/Palestine following the destruction of Jerusalem.[53]

D. A. Hagner

Like others before him, Hagner recognizes the apocalyptic perspective as more dominant in Matthew than any other Gospel, describing it categorically as "the Apocalyptic Gospel."[54] Hagner views Matthew as standing in continuity with contemporary apocalyptic thought while at the same time remaining in discontinuity with it because of the new perspective introduced by Christ.[55] He further identifies materials that are "not quite apocalyptic" but "apocalyptic-like," namely: "apocalyptic-like material describing the past" (birth, baptism, temptation, crucifixion narratives) and "apocalyptic-like material describing the future" (John the Baptist's preaching and

---

51. Cope, "Close of the Age," 116–17.
52. Cope, "Close of the Age," 118.
53. Cope, "Close of the Age," 120.
54. Hagner, "Apocalyptic Motifs," 53, 68.
55. Hagner, "Apocalyptic Motifs," 54.

the five discourses which are all permeated by an apocalyptic perspective, especially the fifth).[56]

Following Sabourin and Hanson, Hagner argues that Matthew "is a complex mixture of traits, similar, on the one hand, to the characteristics of apocalypses and apocalypticism, but on the other, and to a greater degree, to apocalyptic eschatology" by which he means that "Mt's eschatology has an apocalyptic orientation."[57] The last part of Hagner's essay identifies four functions of apocalyptic in Matthew namely: instruction, encouragement, paraenesis, and readiness.[58]

David C. Sim

Sim begins by providing a helpful survey of the history of scholarship on Matthew's apocalyptic eschatology, noting that with the works of Stanton, Hagner, and Cope, emphasis on Matthew's apocalyptic eschatology turned full circle in reasserting Streeter's sociological approach.[59] Further, Sim identifies eight major characteristics of apocalyptic eschatology, namely: dualism, determinism, eschatological woes, the arrival of a savior figure, the judgment, the fate of the wicked, the faith of the righteous, and the imminence of the end, all of which he finds expressed in Matthew.[60]

According to Sim, Matthew constructs his apocalyptic eschatology by drawing from his Christian sources (Mark, Q, and others) the doctrine of the return in glory of the Son of Man while adopting these eight characteristics of the apocalyptic worldview as found in the Qumran community and the book of Revelation.[61] Based on this view, Sim moves to reconstruct the social setting of Matthew's community, arguing that Matthew wrote to encourage his sectarian and alienated community during the crisis of the post-Jewish war era.[62] He concludes: "Matthew lends authority to his apocalyptic-eschatological scheme by placing it in the mouth of an authoritative

---

56. Hagner, "Apocalyptic Motifs," 60–68.
57. Hagner, "Apocalyptic Motifs," 56.
58. Hagner, "Apocalyptic Motifs," 73–76.
59. Sim, *Apocalyptic Eschatology*, 10.
60. Sim, *Apocalyptic Eschatology*, 35–175.
61. Sim, *Apocalyptic Eschatology*, 73–177; he defines apocalyptic eschatology as "an all-embracing religious perspective which considers the past, present and, future within a dualistic and deterministic framework" (1).
62. Sim, *Apocalyptic Eschatology*, 179–221.

figure, namely, Jesus the Son of Man who will return in the eschaton and preside over the judgment."[63]

Of all the studies highlighted above, Sim's work is the most comprehensive and, perhaps, most illuminating treatment of Matthew's apocalyptic eschatology. However, this comprehensive and illuminating quality does not make up for the serious issues with the work's approach. First, much of Sim's reconstruction borders on sheer conjecture, as does that of Streeter himself—a conjecture rooted in the discredited form-critical assumption that each Gospel was written to one community.[64] Second, Sim does not attempt to reconstruct Jesus' own life to demonstrate the validity of dissociating him from Matthew's apocalyptic. Thus, the claim that Matthew constructed and placed his apocalyptic schema in Jesus' mouth is too simplistic, more so by its assumption of a necessary connection between "apocalyptic" and *ex eventu* prophecy.[65] Also, while it is commonly assumed that apocalyptic phenomena arise from situations of crisis among marginalized people, such a condition and connection are unnecessary.[66] No necessary correlation between literary form and *sitz im leben* can be maintained.[67] Nor, indeed, is it possible to neatly circumscribe the purpose(s) which a given tradition serves within a community.[68] Moreover, attempts at reconstructing the sociological contexts of apocalyptic visionaries and their audience are often marred by their circularity (reconstruction of sociological context based on text and interpretation of the text based on the reconstruction) and speculative nature.[69]

In light of this brief survey, it is clear, as many scholars have recognized, that Matthew's Gospel is significantly apocalyptic in character and content. The next important question has to do with what sort of apocalyptic this

---

63. Sim, *Apocalyptic Eschatology*, 248. Allison also makes a similar claim (*Jesus of Nazareth*, 1). For a persuasive counter argument, see Bauckham, *Eyewitnesses*, 246.

64. See Bauckham, *Gospel for All Christians*, 9–48; Gurtner, "Interpreting Apocalyptic Symbolism," 529.

65. In other words, not all apocalyptic materials present after-the-fact prophecies; see table in Collins, *Apocalyptic Imagination*, 8.

66. E.g., Kreitzer, "Apocalyptic, Apocalypticism," 59; see also Rowland, "Apocalyptic Literature," 184. And as Wilson, *When Will These Things Happen?*, 119, argues, "we must be wary . . . of accepting 'apocalyptic' literature in the Bible as no more than a literary mirror of the political events of the writer's day."

67. See Koch, *Rediscovery*, 21–22; Bauckham, *Eyewitnesses*, 246.

68. See Vansina, *Oral Tradition as History*, 101.

69. So Hanson, *Dawn of Apocalyptic*, 33; cf. Gurtner, "Interpreting Apocalyptic Symbolism," 528–30. Hanson's own reconstruction of the sociological context of the emergent apocalyptic phenomenon is also critiqued by Bauckham as speculative ("Rise of Apocalyptic," 11).

Gospel is. This question will be taken up below in connection with a clarification regarding the term "apocalyptic" and its use in this study.

Clarifying Terminology

Discussions on the apocalyptic phenomenon have long been associated with terminological confusion.[70] The term "apocalyptic" is adjectival. However, it came to be used, confusedly so, as a noun. To bring some clarity, Hanson proposed a threefold distinction within the term "apocalyptic," namely: apocalypse, apocalypticism, and apocalyptic eschatology.[71] First, "apocalypse designates a literary genre." By genre is meant the media or literary form used by apocalyptic writers to communicate their messages, including not only apocalypses but also forms such as testaments, salvation-judgment oracles, and parables.[72] Second, Hanson defines "apocalypticism" as "the symbolic universe in which an apocalyptic movement codifies its identity and interpretation of reality. This symbolic universe crystallizes around the perspective of apocalyptic eschatology which the movement adopts."[73] The key here is "association" with a particular social movement. Third, "apocalyptic eschatology" describes "neither a genre nor a socio-religious movement, nor a system of thought but rather a religious perspective, a way of viewing divine plans in relation to mundane realities . . . a perspective which individuals or groups can embrace in varying degrees at different times."[74] In other words, apocalyptic eschatology is not tied to a particular genre but may be expressed by works other than those describable as "apocalyptic genre." But Hanson earlier defined "apocalyptic eschatology" as

> the disclosure (usually esoteric in nature) to the elect of the cosmic vision of Yahweh's sovereignty—especially as it relates to his acting to deliver his faithful—which disclosure the visionaries have *largely ceased to translate into the terms of plain history, real politics and human instrumentality* due to a pessimistic view of reality growing out of the bleak post-exilic conditions.

This definition may appear to contradict the idea that apocalyptic eschatology views "divine plans in relation to mundane realities" as seen above. Hanson offers it to distinguish "apocalyptic eschatology" from "prophetic

---

70. See Sim, *Apocalyptic Eschatology*, 23–31.
71. Hanson, "Apocalypticism," 29; Hanson, "Apocalyptic Literature," 470.
72. Hanson, "Apocalypticism," 29.
73. Hanson, "Apocalypticism," 30.
74. Hanson, "Apocalypticism," 29.

eschatology." In the latter, an announcement regarding God's plan for Israel and the world is translated into the realms "of plain history, real politics, and human instrumentality."[75]

Many scholars consider Hanson's threefold terminological distinction a significant and helpful contribution. However, it still does not beam with much clarity, leading some to urge the abandonment of the terms "apocalyptic" and "apocalypticism" altogether.[76] Robert L. Webb regards the term "apocalypticism" as "too simplistic."[77]

Another issue is the relationship between "apocalyptic" and "eschatology." It is traditional to associate these two terms—an association assumed in Hanson's threefold categorization and in the term "apocalyptic eschatology" in particular. The association is also reflected in the commonly accepted definition for the apocalyptic genre later offered by J. J. Collins and his group of Society of Biblical Literature scholars: "An apocalypse," the definition goes,

> is a genre of revelatory literature with a narrative framework in which a revelation is mediated by an otherworldly being to a human recipient, disclosing a transcendental reality which is both temporal, insofar as it envisages eschatological salvation, and spatial, insofar as it involves another supernatural world.[78]

Notice the theme, "eschatological salvation." As Hanson would later claim, "it has grown increasingly clear that at the heart of apocalyptic is its eschatological orientation."[79]

However, some have pointed out that apocalyptic and eschatology are not necessarily synonymous.[80] Indeed, some apocalyptic writings such as 1

---

75. Hanson, *Dawn of Apocalyptic*, 11 (italics mine). Isaiah 7 is said to reflect prophetic eschatology while Isa 65:17 reflects apocalyptic eschatology ("Apocalypticism," 30).

76. See Stone, "List of Revealed Things," 443. Glasson, "What Is Apocalyptic?," 105, claims the adjectival term is "a useless word which no one can define, and which produces nothing but confusion and acres of verbiage."

77. Webb, "Apocalyptic," 116–17; he rejects the equation of the term with a social movement, arguing that as an ideology which an individual, group, or movement may express, "apocalypticism" is nonetheless a literary category inseparably linked with the apocalyptic genre.

78. Collins, *Apocalyptic*, 9; Collins, *Apocalyptic Imagination*, 5. For a succinct discussion on the development of this definition, see Yarbro Collins, "Apocalypse Now," 448–57.

79. Hanson, "Apocalyptic Literature," 469. The tradition of treating "apocalyptic" and "eschatology" as synonymous goes back to Weiss, Schweitzer, and importantly, Käsemann.

80. Carmignac does not include eschatology in his definition of the apocalyptic genre ("Qu'est-ce que L'apocalyptique?"). See Stone, "List of Revealed Things," 415–52;

En. 1–36 (Book of the Watchers) and 1 En. (72–82) (Astronomical Book) do not deal with eschatology *per se*; that is, not with eschatology as their central feature. Accordingly, Christopher Rowland argues that "to speak of apocalyptic, therefore, is to concentrate on the theme of the direct communication of the heavenly mysteries in all their diversity." He goes on to insist that while the term "apocalyptic" should not be defined in too restricted a manner, it "should . . . be confined to those works which purport to offer disclosures of the heavenly mysteries [through] dreams, visions, heavenly ascent or verbal [angelic] revelations."[81] Webb considers this position as an overreaction to the traditional preoccupation with eschatology when dealing with apocalyptic.[82] Similarly, Collins points out that "the common equation of apocalyptic with the scenario of the end of history [eschatology] is based on the 'historical' type [of apocalypses] like Daniel." Collins, however, maintains, "all the apocalypses involve a transcendent eschatology that looks for retribution beyond the bounds of history."[83]

It is true that Matthew's Gospel can hardly be described as apocalyptic if we follow Rowland's recommendation. However, the adjectival term can describe a wide range of literary expression and/or phenomenon in its "extended sense."[84] Thus, while Hanson's threefold terminology of apocalyptic is far from perfect—Hanson regards the definitional system itself as "flexible"[85]—for many scholars, it remains the starting point for any meaningful discussion on the topic.[86] The Gospel of Matthew is "apocalyptic" not in form but in content, that is, insofar as its conceptual framework, its worldview, is encoded in language or motif similar to that found in formal

---

Rowland, *Open Heaven*, 9–48; Aune takes "eschatology" as a feature which occurs "often" (i.e., rather than "necessarily") in apocalyptic literature ("Apocalypse of John," 87); Bauckham even suggests a distinction between "eschatological apocalypses" and "cosmological apocalypses" in light of 1 En. ("Rise of Apocalyptic," 17); Kreitzer states that "the substance of the heavenly revelation might be knowledge about astronomy, or the creation, or celestial worlds, or matters concerning the heavenly Jerusalem, for example, and not knowledge of eschatological matters or what is going to happen in the future" ("Apocalyptic, Apocalypticism," 57).

81. Rowland, *Open Heaven*, 70–71.
82. Webb, "Apocalyptic," 120.
83. Collins, *Apocalyptic Imagination*, 15.
84. Collins, *Apocalyptic Imagination*, 15.
85. Hanson, "Apocalypticism," 29.
86. See Aune, *New Testament*, 227–28; Collins, *Apocalyptic Imagination*, 3–17; Rowland, *Open Heaven*, 9–72; Sim, *Apocalyptic Eschatology*, 23–31; Reynold and Stuckenbruck note that the failure to differentiate between Hanson's threefold distinction has hampered consensus regarding the term "apocalyptic" (*Jewish Apocalyptic Tradition*, 5).

apocalypses.[87] In the extended sense, therefore, it may be said of Matthew's Gospel, as of other NT writers, that it is characterized by "apocalyptic eschatology," which among other things, consists in the expectation of future divine intervention in judgment and vindication.[88] This futurity is not exclusive, but as Sim says, "apocalyptic eschatology" in Matthew is "an all-embracing religious perspective which considers the past, present, and future within a dualistic and deterministic framework."[89] It embraces the past in present and future fulfillments.

With respect to Hanson's second definition of apocalyptic eschatology as seen above, it must be maintained that while the apocalyptic eschatological vision in Matthew's Gospel is no doubt cosmic, it reflects no discernible pessimism regarding "plain history" or present reality. To this extent, the apocalyptic eschatology in Matthew's Gospel is not opposed to prophetic eschatology. Matthew's or Jesus' apocalyptic eschatology is prophetic-apocalyptic eschatology.[90]

Matthew 24–25 as Prophetic-Apocalyptic

According to P. F. Ellis, interpreters are agreed that Matt 24–25 is apocalyptic in character.[91] Although Ellis himself argues that the Discourse fits the

---

87. See Collins, *Apocalyptic Imagination*, 16.

88. In some treatments of Matthew's Gospel, the term, "apocalypticism" appears to be used instead of "apocalyptic eschatology; see Murphy (*Apocalypticism*, 5, 227–377) and Kristian Bendoraitis ("Apocalypticism, Angels, and Matthew").

89. Sim, *Apocalyptic Eschatology*, 1, 175; cf. Hanson, "Apocalypticism," 31.

90. In contrast to Gerhard von Rad's view that the apocalyptic view of history is impossible to reconcile with that of the prophetic (*Message of the Prophets*, 272), there has been a shift in recent times away from a strict distinction between prophecy and apocalyptic. E.g., Hanson himself admits both continuity and discontinuity between prophecy and apocalyptic ("Apocalyptic Literature," 469); Aune notes that this continuity/discontinuity view has become increasingly evident since the end of the last century (*Apocalypticism, Prophecy, and Magic*, 6); Stein maintains that since the book of Revelation refers to itself as both apocalypse (1:1) and prophecy (1:3; 22:7, 10, 18–19, cf. 22:6) and since "the same rules apply to interpreting the cosmic, exaggerated, and metaphorical language found in both," there is "no clear distinction between the genre of prophecy and that of apocalyptic" (*Commentary on Mark* 13, 42–43); Collins argues that the distinctive character of apocalyptic in contrast to prophecy is the hope of individual "transcendence of death" ("Apocalyptic Eschatology," 30).

91. So Ellis, *Matthew*, 86.

farewell address genre,[92] he still concludes it leans heavily on the apocalyptic genre,[93] summarizing its nature (esp. vv. 4–31) by noting that it

> has all the major, and most of the minor, characteristics of apocalyptic literature. It is eschatological and transcendental. It is relatively deterministic. And it smacks faintly of a mitigated dualism. It is pseudonymous in as much as Matthew speaks through the mouth of Jesus. It envisages future events such as the destruction of Jerusalem, the end of the world, and the coming of the Son of Man in judgment. It describes these events in terms of cosmological catastrophes. It has a cast of angels and the customary apocalyptic trumpets.[94]

There is much truth in this, except, perhaps, in its claim of pseudonymity. While no claim can be made about Matt 24–25 (or any other logia of Jesus for that matter) being *ippssisima verba* of Jesus, the view that Matthew retrojects a prophecy of his own making into the mouth of Jesus, as also espoused by Sim and others, is weakened by its highly speculative nature.[95] Matthew 24–25 is best taken as a re-presentation of Jesus' apocalyptic prophecy. It needs to be kept in mind that Matthew's Jesus is in a unique sense both a prophetic,[96] and an apocalyptic figure[97]—a fact supported by his "almost indisputable" association with John the Baptist.[98]

A cogent case for understanding Jesus' message in the prophetic-apocalyptic perspective has been made by G. E. Ladd. In reaction against liberal

92. Ellis, *Matthew*, 82–85; he compares it to other biblical (e.g., Gen 47:29—49:33; Josh 23–24; 1 Chr 28–29; John 13–17) and non-biblical farewell addresses (e.g., Socrates in Plato's *Crito* and *Phaedo*) or testaments. Others who regard the Discourse as a farewell address include Michaels, "Apostolic Hardships," 28; Burnett, *Testament*, 28–29; cf. Balabanski, *Eschatology*, 70–71; Dyer, *Prophecy on the Mount*, 233. For a brief introduction to testaments, see Charlesworth, *Old Testament Pseudepigrapha*, 1:773.

93. Ellis, *Matthew*, 85.

94. Ellis, *Matthew*, 85.

95. Sim, *Apocalyptic Eschatology*, 248.

96. See Matt 13:57; 16:21; 17:22–23; 20:18–19, 23; 21:11, 46; 22:7; 26:21–25, 34; cf. Turner, *Israel's Last Prophet*, 151–75.

97. As many scholars note, Jesus had revelatory experiences of apocalyptic nature; see Rowland, *Open Heaven*, 358–68; Witherington, *Christology of Jesus*, 148–55. Of course, there remain a few dissidents regarding Jesus' apocalyptic character, particularly Crossan (*Historical Jesus*). However, many affirm this characterization, including agnostic Ehrman; see his *Jesus*. Allison, "Apocalyptic," 19, remarks that no direct influence from any of the apocalypses can be traced in Jesus' teaching, yet he concludes that the influence of apocalyptic eschatology on him "cannot be denied" (cf. *Jesus of Nazareth*, 34–39); cf. Murphy, *Apocalypticism*, 281–305.

98. Sanders, *Jesus and Judaism*, 11, 326; cf. Allison, "Plea for Thoroughgoing Eschatology," 655; Koester, "Jesus the Victim," 4, 14.

views that denied Jesus either or both of the characterizations—prophetic and apocalyptic, Ladd describes Jesus' teaching as prophetic-apocalyptic.[99] Ladd acknowledges the widely held differences between these two perspectives,[100] but he furthers the suggestion that prophetic and apocalyptic eschatologies are not mutually exclusive.[101] Ladd contends that (1) the OT prophets share basic elements of apocalyptic eschatology such as the apocalyptic upheaval and radical transformation of the physical world (cf. Amos 8:8–9; 9:5–6); (2) prophetic-apocalyptic as is represented in the teachings of Jesus, "is to be contrasted with a non-prophetic apocalyptic which largely characterizes the "eschatology" of Jewish apocalyptic literature," especially by differing from their ethical passivity and pessimism regarding present history; and (3) in Jesus' "prophetic-apocalyptic" eschatology, "the kingdom of God has a twofold manifestation: in the apocalyptic consummation, and in the historical mission of Jesus and the church."[102]

Ladd's view makes it clear that while Jesus transcends the prophets and apocalypticists, he nonetheless stood in continuity with them, a view shared by many scholars. The Eschatological Discourse in Matt 24–25 is properly seen through this prophetic-apocalyptic lens. It combines a prophetic reality specific to Israel and an apocalyptic expectation of cosmic consummation. Such a view is fundamental to any adequate interpretation. One must begin by considering the significance of apocalyptic language. This is the concern of the next section.

Competing Approaches to Apocalyptic Language

Scholars are divided on how to interpret apocalyptic language in the Gospels. One approach is to take such language literally as many traditional interpreters do. However, a growing number of scholars advocate metaphorical interpretations.[103] Notable scholars have made significant contributions in both the literal and metaphorical directions.

99. Ladd, "Why Not Prophetic-Apocalyptic?"

100. Ladd, "Why Not Prophetic-Apocalyptic?," 193.

101. Ladd, "Why Not Prophetic-Apocalyptic?," 196; see Bowman, *Religion of Maturity*. Rowley once declared: "That apocalyptic is the child of prophecy, yet diverse from prophecy, can hardly be disputed" (*Relevance*, 15). For a recent argument challenging the strict dichotomy between the prophetic and apocalyptic, see Grabbe, "Prophetic and Apocalyptic," 107–33.

102. Ladd, "Why Not Prophetic-Apocalyptic?," 196–200; see Matt 12:28.

103. To say that something is literal is to take it in its plain or primary sense. By contrast, metaphor (Gk. μεταφορά) "is a trope in which a word, group of words or a sentence is used to stand for something different from the literal reference but is linked to it by some perceived similarity" (Aune, *Dictionary*, 301).

G. B. Caird

Caird's approach to apocalyptic language, as articulated in two of his works, hinges on two key issues.[104] The first issue deals with the question of the definition of "eschatology." On this, Caird complains that the term has come to be used without careful differentiation.[105] In particular, two types of eschatologies—individual (death, judgment, heaven, and hell) and national/historical eschatologies—are often confused as the same, leading to the "baseless assumption that the finality which attaches to death, judgment, heaven and hell must be characteristic also of the national eschatology, and therefore to an intolerable kind of literalism in the interpretation of the imagery used by the prophets and the apocalypticists to describe the Day of the Lord.'"[106] Caird sets the stage for his approach to eschatological language with this dual framework—individual versus national eschatology.

The second issue then deals with what Caird describes as "transferred metaphor" by which he means the use of language already metaphorical in one situation in several other situations. In his words, "We should think of eschatological language as capable of being adapted to many purposes." He further claims that "90 percent of what we have come to call 'eschatology' in the Bible has nothing to do with the *eschaton* in the strict sense; it is rather the use of eschatological language to describe something quite different," precisely past and contemporary events of history.[107]

Based on these two considerations, Caird summarizes his view in three propositions: (1) The biblical writers believed literally that the world had a beginning in the past and would have an end in the future. (2) They regularly used end-of-the-world language metaphorically to refer to that which they well knew was not the end of the world. (3) As with all other uses of metaphor, we must allow for the likelihood of some literalist

---

104. See Caird, *Language and Imagery*, 243–71; Caird, *New Testament Theology*, 243–50.

105. Caird identifies different senses of the term "eschatology:" EI (Individual eschatology: the doctrinal themes of death, Judgment, heaven and hell), EH (Historical eschatology: the Jewish understanding of the goal of history in terms of Israel's destiny vis-à-vis the world), EK (*Konsequente* eschatology: the view of Weiss and Schweitzer that Jesus expected an imminent end of the world), ER (Realized eschatology: Dodd's view that in Christ the eschaton has fully entered into the present), EE (Existential eschatology: a more philosophical rationalization of EK by Weiss's student, Bultmann, in which Jesus' eschatology simply consists in a present encounter with God leading to self-understanding and existential decision), and EN/P (Eschatology understood not in terms of "finality" or "imminence" but in terms of "Newness" or "Purpose"); for details, see Caird, *Language and Imagery*, 243–56.

106. Caird, *New Testament Theology*, 243–44.

107. Caird, *New Testament Theology*, 246–47, 265.

misinterpretation on the part of the hearer, and for the possibility of some blurring of the edges between vehicle and tenor on the part of the speaker."[108]

The first proposition is supported both implicitly and explicitly by several OT texts.[109] In the second proposition, Caird uses the recurring prophetic phrase, the "Day of the Lord," and its context, to show that the language of cosmic disaster was not intended literally for the end of the world, but metaphorically for the judgment and victory of God over nations.[110] Yet Caird is aware that the prophetic vision of the future was not unifocal. Rather, in what he describes as "prophetic camera technique,"

> the prophets looked to the future with bifocal vision. With their near sight, they foresaw imminent historical events which would be brought about by familiar human causes; for example, disaster was near for Babylon because Yahweh was stirring up the Medes against them (Is 13:17). With their long sight, they saw the day of the Lord; and it was in the nature of the prophetic experience that they were able to adjust their focus so as to impose the one image on the other and produce a synthetic picture. Yet they did not thereby lose the ability to distinguish between the two types of vision, any more than the writer of Ps 23 lost the ability to distinguish between himself and a sheep.[111]

This camera technique is evident in the prophecy of Joel (1:15; 2:1–2; 3:14, 21), showing that the focus is not the final destiny of individuals in the end-of-the-world form of *Konsequente* Eschatology (EK), but the reversal of the fortunes of Israel.[112] In contrast to Weiss and Schweitzer, Caird suggests that except for its "intense nationalism" in the context of struggle for survival, the apocalyptic worldview is not drastically different from that of the prophetic.[113] Thus, apocalyptic writings such as Daniel and 4 Ezra, employ

---

108. Caird, *Language and Imagery*, 256 (cf. 152). The concepts of "tenor" and "vehicle" were invented by I. A. Richards to describe the two parts of a metaphor—the principal subject and the figure respectively (*Philosophy of Rhetoric*, 96–97).

109. Gen 8:22; Ps 72:7; 103:25–26 (cf. Isa 51:6; 54:10).

110. Caird believes that the phrase, "the day of the Lord" was first used by Amos in the eight-century BC but preceded by a long history of development; see Amos 5:18–20; Isa 13:9; Joel 1:15; 2:1–31; 3:14; Zeph 1:7–14; Jer 46:10; Ezek 13:5; 30:3; Obad 15; Zech 14:1; Mal 4:5. A similar phrase, "the latter end of the days" (Gen 49:1; Num 24:14; Deut 4:30; 31:29; Hos 3:5; Isa 2:2; Jer 23:20; 30:24; 48:47; 49:39; Ezek 38:16; Dan 2:28; 10:14) is the English equivalent of "in the end'" or "ultimately" but it has some vagueness to it that lends it to such literalist misunderstanding as referred to in proposition 3 (*Language and Imagery*, 257n19–20, 258).

111. Caird, *Language and Imagery*, 258–59.

112. Caird, *Language and Imagery*, 260.

113. Caird, *Language and Imagery*, 261; also n24.

coded and symbolic eschatological language for contemporary historical events rather than for the literal end of the world.[114]

This understanding is then applied to the Markan version of the Eschatological Discourse. Caird argues that Mark 13 aims to show that Jerusalem was to be destroyed and, in that destruction/judgment, the disciples are to see the coming of the Son of Man.[115] In his view, even Matthew—writing after the fall of Jerusalem, and modifying Mark with the addition of *parousia* and the "end of the world"—is "far from being committed to a literalist eschatology." On the contrary, "Matthew's emphasis on the final judgment [e.g., Matt 25:31–46] does not arise out of any preoccupation with the end of the world, but rather from a recognition that the final judgment is forever pressing upon the present with both offer and demand."[116] This interpretation is suggested to Caird by Matt 26:64 (cf. Mark 14:62) where the adverbial phrase ἀπ' ἄρτι ("from now") is taken to indicate progressive or continuous experience throughout history.

Caird's metaphorical interpretation of eschatological language in the Gospels takes seriously the close connection and continuity between OT prophetic tradition and apocalyptic. He is of course averse to crass literalism, and rightly so. However, in several ways, Caird does seem to overstate his case. First, concerning how prophets envisioned the future, one would expect that the use of the eschatological language of the "Day of the Lord" to describe an impending contemporary crisis as Caird contends, does not abolish the distinctness of "that Day" itself, but indicates the complex referential nature of such language. It may therefore be questioned whether Caird is right in simply resolving Jesus' complex prophetic words in Mark 13 (parr. Matt 24–25) exclusively in favor of the imminent contemporary crisis.[117]

Second, in discussing the Eschatological Discourse, Caird so blends Matthew's thought into Luke and Mark that one must wonder whether he has been faithful to his own rule: "it is not enough for us to show that a certain locution is a figure of speech by the standards of modern grammar; we must also be satisfied that the author intended it."[118] If we follow

---

114. Caird, *Language and Imagery*, 262–63.

115. Caird, *Language and Imagery*, 266.

116. Caird, *Language and Imagery*, 268, 271 (cf. *New Testament Theology*, 263). Here, Caird echoes Bultmann's EschatologyE which he characterizes as inadequate but "very near to expressing Matthew's thought," as well as affirms Dodd's EschatologyR as a correct description of early Christian eschatology.

117. See Caird, *Language and Imagery*, 266; for a similar critique, see Allison, *End of the Ages*, 88–89; a summary of Allison's case is presented below.

118. Caird, *Language and Imagery*, 183.

this criterion, it requires that we must consider Matthew on its own terms whatever Luke's or Mark's version entails. Therefore, Caird's diachronic interpretation, following the order: Luke-Mark-Matthew, is hardly a sound hermeneutical procedure for arriving at what Matthew intended.[119] One evidence of this is that Caird fails to see that in Matthew's Eschatological Discourse, the destruction/judgment of the temple in the Great Tribulation is clearly distinguished from the apocalyptic "coming of the Son of Man" by the temporal expression εὐθέως δὲ μετά in Matt 24:29.

Third, with respect to Caird's third proposition, it is indeed possible that hearers may misinterpret metaphors in a literalistic manner, and that speakers may blur the distinction between a figure ("vehicle") and the subject ("tenor") it describes.[120] But there is in this a hidden assumption of static hermeneutic. We must wonder, for example, whether NT writers were bound to always replicate meanings implied by their OT counterparts when they use eschatological language. Wilson similarly questions whether present commentators understand Jewish metaphorical language better than first-century Jews.[121] As it appears, Caird's view leaves no room for imagination and development,[122] and therefore does not take into account how speakers/writers may direct hearers/readers to an understanding of how they may be re-appropriating metaphoric language.

N. T. Wright

In Wright, we find the most extensive advocacy for the metaphorical interpretation of apocalyptic language in the Gospels following Caird, his mentor. Wright's view is based on, at least, a twofold complaint. First, he argues that interpreters have erroneously attributed to Jewish apocalyptic a "cosmological dualism in which the present space-time universe is inherently evil, and so must be destroyed in order that a different and better world

---

119. See Caird, *Language and Imagery*, 266–68.

120. For Caird, in metaphor, two things are not compared as in simile; rather, "the name of one is substituted for the name of the other." A metaphor is said to be "living" (when speakers and hearers are aware that the vehicle and tenor are two entities but grasps them as one, in which case it is a lens through which something else is observed, with the lens itself ignored) or "stock" (when after repeated use, "speakers and hearers are unaware of the duality of vehicle and tenor and treat the word as a new literalism" (*Language and Imagery*, 152–53).

121. Wilson, however, ends up favoring Caird's approach (*When Will These Things Happen?*, 119, cf. 132).

122. See Allison, *Jesus of Nazareth*, 157 (cf. *End of the Ages*, 89, where he suggests such a development).

may take its place."[123] As a result of this rather platonic conception, "hugely figurative language of apocalyptic must be interpreted literally, and the clear dualities inherent in apocalyptic is taken to indicate a radical dualism which sought the destruction of the present world altogether."[124] Second, Wright shares Caird's frustration about the misuse of the term eschatology.[125]

In reaction to these issues, Wright contends that the Jewish hope did not consist in the end of the space-time universe but rather in the restoration of Israel.[126] This hope was expressed using apocalyptic language in which "complex and highly colored metaphors ... describe one event in terms of the other, thus bringing out the perceived meaning of the first."[127] Wright further claims, "there is virtually no evidence that Jews were expecting the end of the space-time universe. There is abundant evidence that they ... knew a good metaphor when they saw one and used cosmic [apocalyptic] imagery to bring out the full significance of cataclysmic socio-political events." In this socio-political upheaval, Israel will be vindicated, the exile will finally be ended, and YHWH will become king.[128] Wright thus conceives of eschatology in a more historical sense as "the climax of Israel's history"—a sense which, as he argues, is supported by (1) the prevalent notion of imminence in Jesus' teaching, and (2) the referent of OT 'apocalyptic' language which Jesus seems to have shared (e.g., Isa 13).[129] Wright further contends that a threefold scriptural background provides the clue to the story of Jesus as apocalyptically and subversively told by Mark.[130] These are (1) allusions in Mark 13 of previous destructions of YHWH's people,[131] (2) passages aligning coming destruction with the Maccabean crisis,[132] and (3) OT allusions evoked in Mark 13.[133]

---

123. Wright, *New Testament and the People*, 297.

124. Wright, *New Testament and the People*, 299.

125. See Wright's own list of various options (*Jesus and the Victory*, 208).

126. Wright, *New Testament and the People*, 280–338, esp. 299.

127. Wright, *New Testament and the People*, 282.

128. Wright, *New Testament and the People*, 333; cf. Caird; *New Testament Theology*, 249; Borg, *Conflict*, 227–29.

129. Wright, *Jesus and the Victory*, 208–9.

130. On Mark's Gospel as a meta-apocalypse and ch. 13 as subversive, see Wright, *New Testament and the People*, 394–96.

131. Mark 13:5 (cf. Mic 3:12; Jer 7:14; 46:8; Ezek 24:21); Mark 13:17 (cf. Hos 13:16); Mark 13:20 (cf. Isa 65:8); Mark 13:22 (cf. Deut 13; Jer 6:13–14); Mark 13:14 (cf. Ezek 7:12–16).

132. Dan 9:26–27; 11:31–35; 12:10–11 (cf. 1 Macc 1:54–56, 62–64; 2 Macc 8:17; Josephus, *Ant.* 18.257–309); Mark 13:14–16 (cf. 1 Macc 2:7–12; 15–28; 3:45, 50–53).

133. Isa 13:6, 9–11 (cf. T. Mos. 10:1–10); Isa 14:4, 12–15; 34:3–4; Ezek 32:5–8; Joel

More importantly, the apocalyptic "Son of Man" tradition in Dan 7:13–14 provides the crucial foundation for Wright's interpretation of Mark 13 and parallels. Considering this tradition, he argues that the "coming of the Son of Man" does not refer to the *parousia* in the sense of the descent to earth of a human figure in literal clouds. Rather, the "'coming of the son of man' is good first-century metaphorical language for the defeat of the enemies of the true people of God, and the vindication of the true people of God."[134]

In broad terms, Wright's discussion of the story of Jesus and its apocalyptic significance is replete with imaginative insights, often leaving the feel of persuasiveness. However, much of the details are far from convincing,[135] although Wright has attempted to clarify some aspects of his views.[136] On the fate of the universe, the possibility that some Jews believed in the physical end of the world cannot be ruled out as Wright himself concedes.[137] In other words, the complex nature of Judaism,[138] cautions against broad sweeping claims. But Wright's view harbors even more telling weaknesses.

First, Wright's contention that "ascent to heaven" rather than "descent to earth" of the "one like the Son of Man" in Dan 7:13, and his assumption that this is determinative for the meaning of the "coming-of-the-son-of-man" theme in Mark 13 (and parr.),[139] is made difficult by the plausible allusion in Dan 7:9 to Jerusalem (not heaven) as the place where "thrones for judgment

---

2:10–11, 30–32; 3:14–15 (cf. Amos 8:9; Zeph 1:15); Isa 48:20; 52:11–12. The theme of "fleeing" in Mark 13:17–20 alludes to Jer 50:6, 8, 28; 51:6–10, 45–46, 50–51, 57; Zech 2:6–8; 14:2a, 3–5, 9 with Jerusalem now the new Babylon and the escapees the renewed Israel (Wright, *Jesus and the Victory*, 349–60). According to Wright, "When Jerusalem is destroyed, and Jesus' people escape from the ruin just in time, *that will be* YHWH becoming king, bringing about the liberation of his true covenant people, the true return from exile, the beginning of the new world order" (*Jesus and the Victory*, 364 [italics original], cf. Wright, *New Testament and the People*, 395–96).

134. Wright, *Jesus and the Victory*, 361–62.

135. See, e.g., Casey, "Where Wright Is Wrong," 95–103; Stein, "N. T. Wright's *Jesus*," 207–18.

136. E.g., if one accuses Wright of denying the "second coming" as he appears to do in his two earlier works (Wright, *New Testament and the People*, 462; Wright, *Jesus and the Victory*, 517, 635), he denies this in his later works where "second coming" is a sort of intensified active presence of Jesus in a fusion of heaven and earth (Wright, *Surprised by Hope*, 127–35; Wright, *Paul*, 1082–83).

137. Wright, *New Testament and the People*, 333; cf. Caird's proposition 1 above.

138. Neusner, "Defining Judaism," 6–7, reminds us of the need to speak of "Judaisms" instead of "Judaism."

139. Wright, *Jesus and the Victory*, 361; Wright, *Matthew*, 122; so also France, *Matthew*, 396.

were set up" (Ps 122:3–5).¹⁴⁰ In fact, an equally plausible allusion is 1 En. 90:13–20 where, after the beasts oppressing God's sheep are judged, "a throne was set up in a *pleasant land* [not heaven] and the Lord of the sheep sat upon it" (v. 23). These suggest descent from rather than ascent to heaven.

Second, Wright's interpretation of the Danielic "Son of Man" as a nonmessianic corporate symbol for Israel is also made difficult by the individual and messianic understanding of the figure in 1 En. 37–71 and 4 Ezra.¹⁴¹ In the Gospels, Jesus uses the phrase, "Son of Man," not as a corporate designation but clearly as a self-identification. Even Wilson, who endorses the metaphoric approach of Caird and Wright, questions whether Jesus could not have adapted the phrase "Son of Man" to his own purpose, even if one admits the corporate significance in Dan 7.¹⁴² This objection to Wright's view does not mean that the shorter phrase, "coming of the Son of Man," or the longer phrase, "Son of Man coming in the cloud,"¹⁴³ does not require interpretation. One must approach apocalyptic language with caution and on a case-by-case basis. In any case, the triumph of the wholesale metaphorical view remains understandably farfetched for many interpreters.

Dale C. Allison

Allison does not see eye to eye with Wright on the nature of apocalyptic language.¹⁴⁴ He favors the Schweitzerian view that Jesus expected the imminent end of the world,¹⁴⁵ considering those who oppose Schweitzer's *Konsequente*

---

140. See Evans, *Matthew*, 348; cf. Witherington and Ice, *Shadow*, 79. As Davies and Allison argue, that "Dan 7 is a theophany which issues in the *earthly* rule of the one like the son of man (v. 14) and v. 22 speaks of the Ancient of Days coming (to earth) for judgment" imply a descent to earth (*Matthew*, 1:531); so also Beasley-Murray, *Jesus and the Kingdom*, 28–29. Collins, *Daniel*, 311, notes that "the text does not indicate whether the figure is ascending or descending or moving horizontally . . . [it] does not provide a warrant for concluding that the figure in Daniel is being lifted up to heaven in the clouds."

141. Wright himself comes close to conceding this point: "there is no evidence to suppose that a messianic interpretation would have taken a first-century Jew by surprise" (Wright, *Jesus and the Victory*, 590, 598; cf. Wright, *New Testament and the People*, 317); see Witherington and Ice, *Shadow*, 75–88.

142. Wilson, *When Will These Things Happen?*, 122, supports his adoption of the metaphoric approach by showing how Peter interprets Joel 3:1–5 (LXX 2:28–32) in Acts 2:16–21, indicating that cosmological signs are referenced intentionally but not literally (130–31).

143. Matt 24:30; 26:24; Mark 13:26; 14:62; Luke 21:27.

144. See Allison, "Jesus and the Victory," 126.

145. His view on what sort of "end" Jesus expected is "not literal termination" of

Eschatology (Dodd, Glasson, but especially Caird and Wright) as hoping to rescue Jesus from "eschatological fallacy."[146] To be sure, Allison concedes that "the New Testament does [indeed] attach the language of eschatology to what is for us today the non-eschatological, the passion and resurrection of Jesus."[147] However, he argues that "when a document depicts the present or immediate past in apparently eschatological terms, talks of metaphor is appropriate only if the redemption remains distant." In the NT, the notion of *Naherwartung* ("immediate expectation" of final redemption or the end) is prevalent. Therefore, "the present is seen as the time immediately before the redemption and hence naturally draws on itself the language of eschatology." "This" Allison thinks, "has nothing to do with metaphor."[148]

Allison challenges the view that Mark 13:24–25 is to be understood as metaphor. "Other dramatic events prophesied in Mark 13—wars, famines, earthquakes—are intended as literally as Exodus intends the plagues or as literal as the list of portents Josephus associates with the Jewish war [6.288–300].... In Joshua 10, the sun really stands still, and in the Synoptic passion narratives the sun literally goes dark."[149] As Allison argues, if Mark 15:33 is an actual fulfillment of Amos 8:9 as seems likely,[150] then it cannot be taken as metaphor.[151]

Allison also demonstrates that a wide variety of evidence (millenarian movements, stoicism, and first-century Jewish traditions) points to the use of apocalyptic language in quite literal manner.[152] In some of the instances, the 'end' does not mean the cessation of the space-time universe, but, as Allison maintains, "that possibility should not be excluded."[153] Even in the Qumran War Scrolls, the prophecy of eschatological battle involves the literal combat of angels.[154] But of all the instances adduced, the most

---

space-time but radical "transformation" of the world; see his "Thoroughgoing Eschatology," 651n2. He also questions whether any scholar really thinks of the "end" in terms of end-of-space-time-universe as Wright alleges; see Allison, "Jesus and the Victory," 128–30 (cf. 134).

146. Allison, *Jesus of Nazareth*, 153.
147. Allison, *End of the Ages*, 88.
148. Allison, *End of the Ages*, 88; Wright, *Jesus and the Victory*, 209n38, 321n2; 322n3 questions Allison's understanding of Caird's use of the term metaphor.
149. Allison, "Jesus and the Victory," 131.
150. See Irenaeus, *Ad. Haer.* 4.33.12.
151. Allison, *End of the Ages*, 89 (see 26–30); cf. "Jesus and the Victory," 131–34.
152. Allison, *Jesus of Nazareth*, 152–69; see 1 En. 91:16; cf. 45:4–5; 69:29; 72:1; 2 En. 65:7; cf. 65:10; 2 Pet 3:10–13; Syb. Or. 2:196–210; 3:75–90; 4:171–92.
153. Allison, *Jesus of Nazareth*, 154.
154. Allison, *Jesus of Nazareth*, 157.

determinative for Allison is the literal interpretation of Exod 19:16–18 by Aristobulus.[155] It is on the weight of this singular instance, most of all, that Allison is happy to recant his metaphorical interpretation of three passages (*Bib. Ant.* 11:3; 4 Ezra 3:18–19, and *b. Zebahim* 116a) which, as he once noted, tended to support Caird's proposition 2.[156]

Several scholars welcome Allison's rejection of the metaphorical interpretation of apocalyptic language.[157] However, Wilson argues that evidence of the literal use of eschatological language in the first century "does not demonstrate that Jesus and the writers of the Gospels took the same hermeneutical approach."[158] This objection is, to say the least, too weak to stand since one could also argue that there is no certainty that Jesus and NT writers simply replicated OT metaphoric use of eschatological language. Other grounds must be found as to why an apocalyptic or eschatological language may be considered metaphorical.

Edward Adams

In what may be the most extensive discussion of a monograph size, Edward Adams takes a most direct aim at the symbolic view espoused by Wright. While endorsing Wright's reading of the NT within the Jewish cultural context, he maintains the relevance of the Greco-Roman context too. Adams contends that Wright's two major claims—that the end of the physical world was alien to Jewish eschatology and that catastrophic cosmic language is metaphor in light of Isa 13 and 34—are based on little or no analysis of post-biblical apocalyptic writings.[159] Adams does not deny that Jewish apocalyptists envisioned eschatological bliss in this-worldly terms.[160] Rather, he is of the view that historical eschatology is not mutually exclusive with belief in the destruction of the present cosmos: "To argue, as Wright does, that the 'this-worldly' character of Jesus' vision of the new age rules out the possibility of belief in the destruction of the present world is to employ a fallacious line of reasoning."[161]

---

155. See Eusebius, *Praep. ev.* 10:8.
156. Allison, *End of the Ages*, 89 (cf. *Jesus of Nazareth*, 158–59n236).
157. E.g., Meyer, *Christus Faber*, 14; Pitre, *Jesus*, 336–37.
158. Wilson, *When Will These Things Happen?*, 123.
159. Adams, *Stars Will Fall*, 10–11.
160. Adams, *Stars Will Fall*, 12; cf. Rowland, *Open Heaven*, 160–76.
161. Adams, *Stars Will Fall*, 12–13.

Adams explores a comparative OT,[162] Jewish apocalyptic,[163] Greco-Roman,[164] and NT[165] literary evidence in a bid to disprove Wright's claims. According to Adam's reading, the Jewish apocalyptic writings show "a very widely attested" evidence of belief in the catastrophic end of the cosmos. He thus rejects Wright's claim that such beliefs were either "unJewish," marginal, or "unattributable to the New Testament writers."[166] Adams argues that "New Testament cosmic catastrophe language cannot be regarded as symbolism for socio-political change; writers who use this language have in view real catastrophe on a universal scale." Moreover, "it is plausible," he insists, "to interpret Mark 13:24-27 (+ par.) in terms of catastrophic event that leads to the end of the created cosmos."[167]

In opposition to Wright and France, Adams says it is unclear that the movement of the one like the Son of Man in Daniel 7:13 is upward. He also notes that Dan 7:13 is applied in Rev 1:7 to Jesus' return to earth not ascent to heaven.[168] But more importantly, he argues that the conventional interpretation of the "coming of the Son of Man" in Mark 13:26-27 (and parr.) as a descent to earth from heaven (i.e., *parousia*) "can be securely established from Mark alone"; Mark 8:38 already establishes the notion of *parousia* as a descent to earth. It adapts Dan 7:13 and alludes to the coming of God for judgment in Zech 14:5.[169] This is perhaps the central and strongest point in Adams' analysis. However, one particular issue stands out as troubling: Adams's use of language such as "real calamity" and "total cosmic

---

162. Texts implying cessation of earth or return to primeval chaos (Gen 8:22; Ps 46:1-3; 102:25-27; Isa 51:6); texts implying enduring earth (Ps 93:1; 148:6; Eccl 1:4 etc.); oracles envisioning renewed world (Isa 65:17; Zech 14:6-8, etc.), global catastrophe (Isa 13:9-13; 34:4; Jer 4:23-28; Joel 2:1-11, etc.), and eschatological catastrophe (Isa 24:19-20; cf. Joel 2:30-31; 3:14-16, etc.).

163. Text employing language of cosmic catastrophe (1 En. 1:3b-9; 83:2b-5; 91:11-17; 102:1-3; Ps. Soph. fr. 2; T. Mos. 10:3-6; 1QH 11:19-36; 2 Bar. 32:1; 59:3; Apoc. Zeph. 12:5-8; Sib. Or. 3:80-92; 3:675-81; 4:175-92; 5:155-61; 5:211-13; 5:477-78; 5:512-31), and celestial disturbances (1 En. 80:4-8; Ps.-Philo, *Bib. Ant.* 3:10; 4 Ezra 5:4b-5; Sib. Or. 3:796-804; 5:346-49); texts implying dissolution of created order (1 En. 72:1; 91:16; T. Job. 33:3-9; Ps.-Philo, *Bib. Ant.* 3:10; 4 Ezra 5:5-55; 7:30-42; 14:18; 2 Bar. 85:10; 2 En. 65:6-11), and non-catastrophic cosmic renewal (1 En. 45:4-5; Jub. 1:29; 4:26; 1QS 4:2; 4Q225 1:6-7).

164. Esp. in the Epicurean and Stoic philosophies, see a helpful summary in Adams, *Stars Will Fall*, 127-28.

165. Mark 13:24-25 and *par.*; Heb 12:25-29; 2 Pet 3:5-13; Rev 12-17.

166. Adams, *Stars Will Fall*, 100.

167. Adams, *Stars Will Fall*, 3, 253; see 133-81 for his detailed discussion on Mark 13:24-27.

168. Adams, *Stars Will Fall*, 147n82, 148n86.

169. Adams, *Stars Will Fall*, 147-53.

destruction" or "dissolution" in his interpretation seems overhyped.[170] Such expressions strike one as the dictionary definition of a literal interpretation of apocalyptic language. Even so, since Adams also agrees with others who claim the literal end of the world,[171] it is somewhat surprising that he denies the "intention to argue for a literal interpretation of New Testament language of cosmic catastrophe over against a metaphorical or figurative one." Adams thinks that what we have in Mark 13:24–25 and its parallels is "linguistic *imagery*" rather than "language of literal or prosaic exactitude."[172] Matthew does not intend "the cosmic images" in 24:29, "to be taken literally, but he expects them to cash out into real cosmic disaster."[173]

Whatever this means, most scholars would probably agree that catastrophic apocalyptic language is more than just a metaphorical cipher for socio-political upheaval; but these comments by Adams may seem confusing if not outrightly contradictory. This is the reason Richard J. Middleton thinks that if Adams's "absolute-sounding rhetoric" is overlooked, he significantly agrees with Wright.[174] Similarly, Juza observes that Adams claims to interpret apocalyptic catastrophic language metaphorically but in essence reads it literally while ignoring texts that suggest cosmic renewal.[175] Perhaps a fair assessment of Adams's view of catastrophic apocalyptic language would place it somewhere within a literal-metaphor continuum, certainly closer to the literal than the metaphorical end. In any case, whether Adams's interpretation is successful or not, the evidence appears to reflect a complex use of catastrophic apocalyptic language, which cautions against dogmatic claims or generalizations.

Towards an Integrative Hermeneutic of Apocalyptic Language

Like all literary ambiguities, apocalyptic language does not lend itself to some infallible deciphering criteria.[176] However, certain considerations are necessary for adequate interpretation. To this important matter I now turn.

---

170. Adams, *Stars Will Fall*, 3, 17 (cf. 20).

171. See Adams, *Stars Will Fall*, 170; cf. Davies and Allison, *Matthew*, 3:368; Sim, *Apocalyptic Eschatology*, 104.

172. Adams, *Stars Will Fall*, 17.

173. Adams, *Stars Will Fall*, 170.

174. Middleton, *New Heaven*, 196–97.

175. Juza, *New Testament*, 6.

176. See Black, "More about Metaphor," 34.

General Considerations

Rhetorical Quality

When approaching apocalyptic literature, it is important to consider the rhetorical and/or poetic quality of the language. Characteristically, the apocalyptic worldview employs extraordinary and evocative language that summons imaginative hearing/reading. Thus, one should expect hyperboles and/or symbols. Indeed, much apocalyptic language or imagery aims "to appeal to the eye of the imagination,"[177] sometimes to the "deepest emotions, fears, and desires" of the hearers."[178]

However, this understanding ought not to imply that apocalyptic language is simply rhetoric or poetic and nothing more. Apocalyptic imageries do point to literal realities. Thus, Murphy can go as far as asserting that "apocalyptic language is simultaneously literal and figurative"; it points to historical referents in terms of "real places, creatures, and events." Murphy also warns: "to push every detail for its referent in the 'real' world is to reduce the entirety to allegory. Similarly, an overly literalistic reading can push their referentiality too far. It can miss their mythological, even poetic nature."[179]

Literal vs. Metaphorical

Our second consideration concerns how to determine what needs to be taken literally and what needs to be understood metaphorically. Even if we subscribe to the view expressed by Keith D. Dyer that the binary distinction between literal and metaphor "betray[s] an underlying modernist duality that can no longer be sustained,"[180] or to Murphy's remark above regarding the simultaneity of the literal and the metaphoric within apocalyptic language as we should, this question remains inevitable, although not an easy one. Dyer himself goes on to interpret the falling stars in Mark 13:24–30 as representing "falling leaders and powers immediately preceding Mark's day," and the coming of the Son of Man as "the vindication and exaltation of the 'human one' before God in heaven" based on Dan 7 rather than as a messianic second coming or earthly *parousia*.[181] In this, he echoes Wright

---

177. Bauer and Traina, *Inductive Bible Study*, 149.
178. Murphy, *Apocalypticism*, 13.
179. Murphy, *Apocalypticism*, 12.
180. Dyer, "When Is the End Not the End?," 51.
181. Dyer, "When Is the End Not the End?," 52.

and others. The question is how one determines whether and when an apocalyptic language is to be taken literally or metaphorically.

Ellis suggests that affinity with apocalyptic language should imply symbolic meaning. This, however, appears too simplistic.[182] According to Max Black, when faced with the choice between a metaphorical reading and a literal reading, a metaphorical reading is preferred if the literal alternative is patently false, pointless, or contextually incongruent.[183] Similarly, Bauer and Traina compare apocalyptic language to poetry.[184] Therefore, "the default assumption" they conclude, "is that the language is figurative unless the plain sense of the passage or literary clues indicate that in a given apocalyptic passage, the language is to be understood literally."[185] As already noted above, this tendency of apocalyptic language to lean towards poetry than prose is well-taken as long as long as one is careful not to think of this poetic tendency in the modern sense of mere ornamental or fanciful rhetoric.[186]

Prophetic Perspective

We have already encountered the phenomenon of "prophetic perspective" as articulated by Bengel and Caird. It involves the merging of distant events in the Seer's vision.[187] While some have challenged this idea, it remains an important consideration to keep in mind as one approaches apocalyptic literature or discourse. The assumption undergirding the present study is that Matt 24–25, for example, lends itself to this perspective. In other words, while involving two events in close connection, one can delineate these events by paying attention to discourse clues and themes. Even short apocalyptic sayings or pronouncements can weave together events not temporally and/or closely connected in reality (e.g., Matt 16:27–28).

---

182. Ellis, *Matthew*, 86, makes this point particularly with respect to Matt 24:31. Thus, granting that Matt 24:31 shares the characteristics of the apocalyptic genre "it follows that [it] should be interpreted in the same way as other apocalyptic writings. As with all other figurative language, the symbolic and cosmological language should be demythologized." He further states: "Historical events clearly 'predicted' by the author should be identified with events which preceded the time of the author, since the form allows the author to speak in the name of the one who preceded him and to 'predict' what has happened in the interim."

183. See Black, "More about Metaphor," 34.

184. Bauer and Traina, *Inductive Bible Study*, 149, although they also note that apocalyptic language tends to be more esoteric, strange, and bizarre.

185. Bauer and Traina, *Inductive Bible Study*, 149.

186. Cf. Murphy, *Apocalypticism*, 12.

187. See discussion on Bengel (ch. 1 of this study); and Caird (above).

Apocalyptic Dynamism

Apocalyptic language often exhibits a dynamic quality. An apocalyptic imagery may be applied to a variety of analogous phenomena or realities. One should be aware and open to "apocalyptic multivalence" as Collins describes it.[188] For example, the expression, "kingdom of God/heaven" in the Gospels, is apocalyptic and dynamic. It describes Jesus' defeat of sickness, demons, and death in his earthly ministry;[189] but it also refers to a future reality.[190] In this sense, the "kingdom of God" may be described as a "tensive symbol" (many referents) as opposed to a "steno symbol" (single referent) to use Norman Perrin's terms.[191]

Another way to describe the dynamic nature of apocalyptic language is what Tom Thatcher has referred to as "linguistic emptiness" or "empty metaphor"—"the use of language [by apocalyptic authors] that intentionally lacks external referents and therefore lacks one absolute meaning."[192] Following Richards's metaphor theory in which meaning is created by the interaction of the tenor and the vehicle,[193] Thatcher notes that often in apocalyptic rhetoric, the tenor space of a metaphoric construct may be empty, creating an ambiguity. This suggests that the author wishes to invite the reader to understand the language by textualizing aspects of known history (as contained in sacred literature, particularly the Hebrew Bible) as well as the reader's own historical experience.[194] Of course, the danger of this consideration is that apocalyptic language becomes construed as lacking semantic content or meaning until the reader constructs one, or that it has endless meanings depending on the reader's own exigencies. Contemporary metaphor theories lean in this direction.[195] However, in so far as the concept

---

188. See Collins, *Apocalyptic Imagination*, 63; also, Murphy, *Apocalypticism*, 12.

189. Matt 12:28; Luke 11:20.

190. Matt 6:10; 13:43; 25:34. For more on this, see Bauer, *Gospel*, 297.

191. Perrin, *Jesus*, 32, 194–98; certain aspects of Perrin's thesis are questionable, such as the downplaying of time reference and the assumption that the interpretation of the kingdom of God in terms of the coming of the Son of Man was a later development (esp. 197).

192. Thatcher, "Empty Metaphor," 550.

193. Again, see Richards, *Philosophy*, 96–97.

194. Thatcher, "Empty Metaphor," 554.

195. Scholarly discussions on metaphor theory usually begin with Aristotle (*Poet.* 21.7–9; cf. *Rhet.* 3.10.7) for whom metaphor was comparative and ornamental. However, with Richards (*Philosophy of Rhetoric*), metaphor began to be conceived not merely as a rhetorical embellishment but in terms of cognition and the creation of meaning; see also Richards and Ogden, *Meaning of Meaning*; Black, "Metaphor," 273–94; Black, *Models and Metaphor*; Black, "More about Metaphor," 19–41; Funk, *Language*, 124–62;

of linguistic emptiness, multivalence, tensivity, or dynamism (preferred in this work), is confined within the framework of specific considerations, it can help shed light on difficult apocalyptic expressions or images. These specific considerations are structure, intertextuality, and context. These considerations are discussed below.

Specific Considerations

Structure

The arrangement or placement of materials is a critical factor for interpreting apocalyptic discourses. According to Grant R. Osborne, one should not only consider the type of literature and its perspective, but also the structure of the passage or book.[196] In this regard, it should be borne in mind that apocalyptic materials do not necessarily follow linear or chronological sequence; they are often topical in arrangement.[197] Apocalyptic materials may be adapted in different iterations and/or recapitulations.[198] This adaptation has direct relevance to structure.[199] Milton S. Terry complains that although repetition "is a very noticeable formality of biblical apocalyptic, it has been strangely ignored by many expositors."[200]

Moreover, discourses in general can exhibit alternations or back-and-forth topical movement of materials or ideas, apocalyptic literature even more so. Thus, in relation to the tendency of recapitulation or repetition, one should not assume strict logical continuity in thought development within an apocalyptic discourse. As Robert H. Mounce puts it: "It is helpful to remember that apocalyptic literature is a genre that does not share our Western concern for orderly continuity . . . it is not uncommon for prophetic material to move between type and antitype without calling attention to

---

Ricoeur, *Rule of Metaphor*; Lakoff and Johnson, *Metaphor*; Soskice, *Metaphor*; Liebenberg, *Language*, 75–80. Witherington, *Jesus the Sage*, 149–50, regards the application of modern metaphor theory to the sayings of Jesus as an "anachronistic enterprise" in service of the post-structuralist notion of semantic polyvalence; here Witherington deals with parables in particular, but he favors seeking a single historical or authorial meaning in general.

196. Osborne, *Hermeneutical Spiral*, 285–87; cf. Taylor, *Interpreting Apocalyptic Language*.

197. Bauer and Traina, *Inductive Bible Study*, 149.

198. Such iterations do not represent chronologically "next" events but the re-imagining or re-imaging of data.

199. See Murphy, *Apocalypticism*, 12 (cf. Murphy, *Fallen Is Babylon*, 51–53).

200. Terry, *Biblical Apocalyptics*, 21.

exactly what is happening."²⁰¹ Where alternations exist, certain grammatical clues may help discern the movement and thus facilitate the interpretive process. This awareness will play a pivotal role in the analysis of the structure of Matt 24–25.

Intertextuality

Intertextuality deals with the interconnectedness of texts—the discernment of meaning in one text by reference to other texts. While it remains critical to let a literary work interpret itself, it should be kept in mind that apocalyptic imageries lend themselves to intertextual cross-referencing. Their meanings may be illuminated by other texts which the implied author directly cites, alludes to, or echoes, and which the implied reader is assumed to be familiar with. Apocalyptic writers or seers are immersed in OT prophetic literature and ancient mythology. Much of the apocalyptic imageries in the NT derives from OT and Jewish apocalyptic literature; they are drawn from already existing imageries within the cultural and literary milieu. These provide important clues for interpretation.

One caution is, however, in order. The tendency in interpretation, as noted earlier, is the static or mechanistic transfer of meaning from one literary expression to another. It is critical to remember that later writers may re-appropriate existing or earlier traditions in ways not originally intended. Old Testament texts may be "filtered through later Jewish uses"—what Witherington calls "layered intertextuality."²⁰² The Synoptics themselves re-apply inherited traditions to different situations producing different applications or interpretive nuances. Therefore, there is no reason apocalyptic symbols, imageries, or metaphors could not exhibit such re-appropriations. Caird's concept of metaphor transfer,²⁰³ and the practice of "recycling parables"²⁰⁴ corroborate this.

Context

Witherington's cliché, "a text taken without context is just a pretext for whatever we want it to mean," represents a necessary critique against the

---

201. Mounce, *Matthew*, 222.
202. Witherington, *Torah Old and New*, 397; cf. Beale, *Handbook*, 1–13.
203. Again, see Caird, *New Testament Theology*, 246–47.
204. McArthur and Johnston, *They Also Taught in Parables*, 156–64; cf. Witherington, *Jesus the Sage*, 149.

mishandling of texts. Apocalyptic texts lend themselves even more to such mishandling. By context, Witherington means "historical, rhetorical, literary, social, and religious contexts."[205] One should be aware of this broader perspective and draw relevant and evidential insights from these aspects of context. However, since authors are free to re-use themes or symbols in different ways, it is crucial to prioritize the literary context of an apocalyptic expression.[206] Of course, this does not mean that all ambiguities will be settled simply by investigating texts and their literary contexts. Sometimes it simply means that we can arrive at an interpretation that may be judged preferable to the alternatives. The literary context should determine the preferability or plausibility of any interpretation, helping to show how the implied author could intend or the implied readers could grasp such an interpretation.

Space will not permit testing out these criteria (structure, intertextuality, and context), especially using the critical "coming of the Son of Man" motif in Matthew. Suffice it to say that the phrase may refer to various things: Jesus' resurrection/exaltation (10:23b; 16:28), the *parousia* (16:27), or, as is the case with 26:64, an apocalyptic rendition of Jesus' vindication perceived by Jews in the judgment and destruction of the temple. In other words, only in light of structural, intertextual, and contextual considerations can one discern the more likely meaning or referent in each instance, including the one in 24:30, which I will explore later.

Conclusion

The purpose of this chapter has been to identify the form and character of Matthew's Gospel in general and chs. 24–25 in particular, as a necessary foundation for interpretation. While Matthew is biographical in form (at least closer to the genre), it reflects an apocalyptic character in worldview, content, and tone. Most scholars agree with this assessment, and it has significant implications for interpretation. In addition, I developed a set of specific considerations (structure, intertextuality, and context) that, when applied to Matt 24–25, helps elucidate the meaning of the Discourse. I will demonstrate how this is indeed the case in the chapters that follow.

---

205. Witherington, *Indelible Image*, 1:41.
206. Cf. Wilson, *When Will These Things Happen?*, 119.

4

Structures of Matthew and the Eschatological Discourse

Introduction

MATTHEW 24–25 IS NOT a self-contained unit to be read in isolation from its whole-book context. Therefore, to adequately interpret the discourse, it is important to understand where it belongs within the broader structural context of Matthew as a whole.[1] This consideration will play a significant role in fulfilling one of the goals of this study—to relate the Eschatological Discourse to Matthew's overall communication goal.

The Structure of Matthew

Matthew is widely recognized as one of the most artistic and structurally organized books of the New Testament. P. F. Ellis entitles part two of his work on the Gospel, "meticulous Matthew," noting that "the author put together his gospel with the precision of a Swiss watch."[2] John P. Meier describes Matthew as "a superb 'verbal architect,' building his literary basilica with many finely fitted, interlocking stones."[3] This assessment notwithstanding,

---

1. The importance of this whole-book consideration is underscored by Bauer and Traina, *Inductive Bible Study*, 79–81.

2. Ellis, *Matthew*, 27.

3. Meier, "Matthew," 4:627.

a consensus regarding the actual structure of the Gospel remains far from reached, as different historical surveys have shown.[4]

This lack of consensus has become so frustrating that some have cautioned against the need to seek to understand Matthew's structure. Gundry, for example, warns that "we should avoid imposing an outline on Matthew. It is doubtful [he says] that the first evangelist thought in terms of one." After a brief foray into the major proposals, Gundry concludes that "the Gospel of Matthew is structurally mixed."[5] Davies and Allison concur with this conclusion: "Matthew's architectonic grandeur does not appear to derive from a clear blueprint (so rightly Gundry). We, in any case, cannot claim to have found the blueprint, and we cannot credit anyone else with the discovery. The claimants just do not persuade."[6] Similarly, according to Allan J. Nichole, "at present, we are in no position to give a resounding 'yes' in response" to the question: "Did the author of Matthew have a clear overarching structural arrangement in mind when producing his gospel?" Nicole thinks that "the issue may prove to be insoluble."[7]

Given these skepticisms, one could as well give up completely on the quest to understand how Matthew has structured his Gospel. However, as well-intentioned as these skepticisms or criticisms are, the position of the current study is that it is unlikely that Matthew wrote with no discernible overall plan at all. As it appears, a lack of structure in this Gospel would make Matthew a scribal *sui generis* within his literary milieu. That such a lack of structure is unlikely is corroborated by Keener's finding that "Matthew's arrangement coheres with the practice of ancient rhetoric and biography." Keener also notes the "penchant for arrangement" among the rabbis.[8]

Moreover, in response to Gundry, a mixed structure is quite different from no structure at all. The very attempt to outline a book, as Gundry and Nicole themselves do, betrays the presumption of structure, and just because one has not found an adequate, if not, the correct structure does not

---

4. See Thompson, "Structure of Matthew," 195–238; Bauer has expanded his earlier threefold categorization (geographical-chronological structures, topical structures) to seven categories of structures namely: geographical-chronological structures, conceptual structures, enumeration structures, alternating narrative-discourse pattern, concentric structure, biographical threefold structures, and other unclassified structures (Bauer, *Structure*, 21–55; cf. Bauer, *Gospel*, 95–128).

5. Gundry, *Matthew*, 10–11; Mullins, *Matthew*, 46–47, describes Matthew as "poly-structural."

6. Davies and Allison, *Matthew*, 1:61; cf. France, *Evangelist and Teacher*, 153; Senior, *Matthew*, 30–31; Senior, *What Are They Saying?*, 34–37.

7. Nichole, *Jesus' Direction*, 71.

8. Keener, *Matthew*, 36n103.

mean that it is not there. In what follows, I highlight the prominent proposals that have been made over the years under three major trajectories.

Geographical-Chronological Trajectory

The first trajectory of structural proposals is characterized by geographical-chronological considerations. Those who espouse this approach consider the structure of Matthew as a replication of the geographical outline of Mark framed in terms of the chronology of the life of Jesus and his movement from Galilee to Jerusalem. A typical example of this approach is the structure argued by Willoughby C. Allen and L. W. Grensted. In their view, Matthew is only structurally unique in the birth and infancy stories (Matt 1–2), while the rest breaks down into Mark's chronological-geographical shape: preparation for ministry (Matt 3:1—9:11//Mark 1:1-13), ministry in Galilee (Matt 4:12—15:20//Mark 1:14—7:23), ministry outside Galilee (Matt 15:20—18:35//Mark 7:24—9:50), journey to Jerusalem (Matt 19:1—20:34//Mark 10), and last days of Jesus (Matt 21-28//Mark 11—16:8).[9]

Those who follow this trajectory vary in specific details, and some combine geographical-chronological and Christological interests.[10] However, the notion that Mark is a chronological life of Jesus has been jettisoned.[11] Moreover, although it may still be possible to structure Matthew geographically without recourse to Mark, as William R. Farmer, for example, has argued,[12] developments in literary criticism have led many to question the propriety of determining Matthew's structure by recourse to Mark's.[13]

---

9. Allen and Grensted, *Introduction*, 23.

10. See Evans, *Matthew*, 9–10; Mullooparambil, *Macrostructure*.

11. Even some who maintain Markan priority do not associate Matthew's alleged changes with chronological arrangement; see Beare, *Matthew*, 15; cf. France, who takes Mark's outline as a systemization rather than actual chronological movement (*Matthew*, 3).

12. A key advocate of Matthean priority, Farmer, contends that Matthew's use of Isa 9:1-2 in Matt 4:12-13 is "the structural backbone or organizing principle governing the theological and geographical framework of Jesus' ministry" which is structured based on the geographical turns in Matt 4:18, 23; 13:1; 15:29; and 19:1 (Farmer, *Jesus and the Gospels*, 138–39).

13. E.g., Kingsbury, *Matthew*, 17; Bauer, *Structure*, 25; cf. Weren, who regards the claim of Matthew's use of Mark's outline as "not entirely convincing" (Weren, "Macrostructure," 183; Weren, *Studies in Matthew's Gospel*, 25). Patrick, "Matthew's *Pesher* Gospel," 81, describes the attempt to derive Matthew's structure from Mark's as a "simplistic redaction-critical over-reliance on supposed literary derivation from Mark's Gospel." Patrick's proposal is highlighted in n67 below.

Alternating Narrative-Discourse Trajectory

The second trajectory is based on the alternating narrative-discourse structure first advocated by Benjamin W. Bacon.[14] According to Bacon, Matthew's Gospel consists of five books. Each book begins with a narrative, setting the stage for a discourse of Jesus, and is linked to the next by the stereotypical formula, καὶ ἐγένετο ὅτε ἐτέλεσεν ὁ Ἰησοῦς τοὺς λόγους τούτους ("And it happened when Jesus had finished these things" [Matt 7:28; 11:1; 13:53; 19:1; 26:1]).[15]

Thus, as Bacon describes it, Matthew constructs "a five-fold *Torah* of Jesus preceded by a prologue describing his Davidic birth and infancy and closed by an epilogue relating the passion and resurrection."[16] The resulting structure is as follows:

The Preamble (1:1—2:23)

Book First: Discipleship

    Division A. Introductory Narrative (3:1—4:25)

    Division B. The Discourse (5:1—7:28)

Book Second: Apostleship

    Division A. Introductory Narrative (8:1—9:38)

    Division B. The Discourse (10:1—11:1)

Book Third: The Hiding of the Revelation

    Division A. Introductory Narrative (11:2—12:50)

    Discourse B. The Discourse (13:1-53)

Book Fourth: Church Administration

    Division A. Introductory Narrative (13:54—17:21)

    Discourse B. The Discourse (17:22—19:1a)

Book Fifth: The Judgment

    Division A. Introductory Narrative (19:1b—22:45)

    Discourse B. The Discourse (23:1—26:2)

Epilogue (26:3—28:20).[17]

---

14. See Bacon, "Five Books," 56-66.
15. Bacon, *Studies in Matthew*, 81.
16. Bacon, "Five Books," 66.
17. Bacon, *Studies in Matthew*, xxii–xxiii; 264–326.

One reason Bacon came to this understanding was that he considered Papias's famous statement regarding Mark's lack of order as a correct divination of Matthew's intention—to revise (not replicate) Mark's Gospel in order to emphasize all that Jesus had commanded in light of Matt 28:19.[18] Based on this he concludes that Matthew was a "'converted rabbi,' a Christian legalist" who revered the law of Moses and intended to present the teachings of Jesus (viewed as the new Moses) in a manner typically Jewish and particularly equivalent to the Pentateuch.[19]

Bacon's proposition is not lightly described by Bauer as "a watershed in the history of investigation into Matthew's structure."[20] According to Dan O. Via, "the five-fold structure is too obvious and unmistakable, and the motif of the law, too prominent in Matthew for this structure not to be a—if not the—organizing principle."[21] Meier asserts that "it is the most traditional and remains the most likely" solution to Matthew's structure.[22] However, Bacon's fivefold structure is sadly riddled with many problems. First, that the supposed fivefold narrative-discourse arrangement particularly reflects the Pentateuch is a false assumption. As many have noted, five-book arrangements are a commonplace among Jewish and Christian writers.[23] None of the individual books of the Pentateuch even reflects a fivefold structure. Second, not only does there exist the plausibility of more than five discourses in Matthew,[24] there is also uncertainty regarding the relationship and order of

---

18. Bacon, *Studies in Matthew*, 81. For Papias's comment regarding Mark's lack of order, see Eusebius, *Hist. eccl.* 3.39.14–16.

19. Bacon, "Five Books," 62, 66; Bacon, *Studies in Matthew*, 81.

20. Bauer, *Gospel*, 102.

21. Via, "Structure," 200.

22. Meier, "Matthew," 628.

23. Streeter writes, "There are five books of the Law and of the Psalms, five *Megilloth*, and five original divisions in the Rabbinic work the *Pirqe Aboth*; so also, Papias wrote 'Interpretations of the sayings of the Lord,' divided into five books" (*Four Gospels*, 262). According to Meier, "Matthew," 692, "the five-book division rests on data internal to the gospel and has nothing to do with any Pentateuch hypothesis"; cf. Meier, *Matthew*.

24. Ellis, *Matthew*, 12–13, identifies seven: five traditional and two minor discourses—the Baptist's discourse (3:8–12) and Jesus' final discourse (28:18–20). Without endorsing Bacon's Pentateuch theory, Davies and Allison regard the narrative-discourse alternation and the fivefold discourses as "two ['firmly established'] certainties [that] constitute the foundation stone upon which all further discussion must build," yet they cannot avoid describing ch. 23 as "a discourse addressed to disciples and crowds" (*Matthew*, 1:61 and 3:308). Similarly, Stendahl can defend Bacon's fivefold structure and still hold ch. 23 to be "one long and distinct discourse which lacks the concluding remark [but represents] an enlarged edition of debate material, considered as preparatory to the concluding discourse of the fifth part of the gospel" while labeling chs. 24–25 as "Eschatology and Farewell address" (*School of St Matthew*, 25–26); Witherington,

Bacon's five books—narrative-discourse or discourse-narrative.[25] Third, the bracketing out of the infancy and passion stories (Matt 1–2; 26–28) as mere preamble and epilogue respectively, appears to minimize their significance to Matthew's communicative goal. Such a move leaves greater (perhaps undue) weight on Jesus' teaching activity in favor of ecclesiological concerns presumed to be central to the Gospel's aim.[26]

Because of these and other issues, some have sought to adapt the narrative-discourse framework. One way they have done this is to posit a whole-book chiastic structure for Matthew's Gospel. These scholars usually take the parable discourse in Matt 13 (esp. v. 36) to be the central or pivotal point of the Gospel.[27] To the extent that these chiastic structures integrate Matt 1–2 and chs. 26–28 into the mainstream of the book, they represent a marked shift away from or improvement on Bacon's structure.[28] Others, including Terence J. Keegan, Tyler J. VanderWeele, and C. R. Smith, have also found more literary bases for either the chiastic structure or the underlying Baconian narrative-discourse schema.[29] If one, for example, has any reason to doubt the structural value of the concluding καὶ ἐγένετο …

Matthew, 15–16, takes ch. 23 as a "stand-alone discourse" arguing that, constituting the sixth discourse, it shows that "Jesus is one greater than Moses or David or Solomon, to each of whom was attributed a five-fold collection of sacred writings (Law, Psalm, Proverbs)"; Hendriksen, *Matthew*, 818, 846, maintains ch. 23 as the fifth discourse and ch. 25 as the sixth; so also Hagner, *Matthew*, 653–54.

25. Smith defends Bacon's narrative-discourse direction by seeking to show how each of the five discourses develops a/the major theme in the narrative that precedes it ("Literary Evidence," 540–51). Many Matthean scholars maintain this view, e.g., Turner, *Matthew*, 10; cf. Talbert, *Matthew*, 8. Some have argued for a discourse-narrative direction, i.e., that the discourses relate instead to the narratives that follow, e.g., Philippe, "From Genesis," 155–76.

26. Bauer, *Structure*, 131, even rejects Bacon's alternating structure categorically: "there is no alternation" he declares, "between narrative and discourse material in Matthew," although this alternation in my view may be defensible. See further critiques in his *Gospel*, 106–10; Kingsbury, *Matthew*, 2–7.

27. See Lohr, "Oral Techniques." Lohr does not mention Bacon in this work, but he rejects his fivefold structure (427–28); Ellis, *Matthew*, 12–13; Green maintains the Pentateuch hypothesis for the first part (Matt chs. 1–10) as presenting the figure of Jesus; the second part (chs. 12–28) mimics the historical books that follow the Pentateuch and deals with Israel's rejection of Jesus; and ch. 11 represents the chiastic center ("Structure," 50–53); Crosby, *House of Disciples*, 54–55; see discussion in Bauer, *Gospel*, 111–14.

28. Although Meier thinks that the assumption that the Infancy and Passion narratives are mere prologue and epilogue respectively derives from a misconception of the fivefold structure ("Matthew," 629).

29. Keegan, "Introductory Formulae"; cf. Smith, "Literary Evidence," 540–51. VanderWeele defends Lohr's chiasm in his "Some Observations," 669–73.

formulaic markers, Keegan argues that Matthew makes the fivefold structure certain by using "an array of distinctive terminology found at the beginning of each of the five discourses" (i.e., 4:25—5:2; 9:36–37; 13:1–3; 18:1–3; and 24:3–4).[30] But the distinctive terminology occurs also in the middle of the third discourse (13:36–37). Keegan curiously surmises that this is related to the chiastic arrangement of the Gospel. Thus, he claims that Jesus' entrance into a house in 13:36 represents "the great turning point of the Gospel"—the point "signaling a new beginning, from which Jesus addresses his major discourses to the disciples alone."[31] Consequently, he concludes that "neither chaps 11 or 23 nor any other section is to be included among the major discourse."[32]

More recently, Smith defends a slightly modified version of the fivefold structure. Against some forms of literary- and narrative-critical approaches,[33] he argues that more literary boundary markers, other than just the concluding καὶ ἐγένετο formula, evidence the validity of the fivefold structure of Matthew's Gospel.[34] Despite Smith's endorsement of Keegan's argument as compelling, he objects to his array of multiple discourse introductory terminology.[35] In contrast, he suggests "the simpler possibility that a single recurring formula [προσῆλθον οἱ μαθηταὶ . . .] signals the beginning of each of the structurally significant discourses in Matthew" even though this formula occurs in only four of the five discourses.[36]

---

30. Keegan, "Introductory Formulae," 418–30; the distinctive terminology includes verbs of "sitting" that present Jesus as a teacher (καθέζομαι, κάθημαι, καθίζω), Matthew's use of aorist indicative of προσέρχομαι in the formulaic phrase προσῆλθον οἱ μαθηταὶ . . . for the "coming" of the disciples to Jesus, and references to the "crowd" (ὄχλος) following Jesus, or Jesus "seeing" (ἰδών) them.

31. Keegan, "Introductory Formulae," 423–24; see also Ellis, *Matthew*, 13. It is not clear on what basis Kingsbury describes παραβολή in Matthew as signaling the "'great turning point'" (*Parables*, 13).

32. Keegan, "Introductory Formulae," 429–30.

33. Here, Smith has in mind especially the analysis of Warren Carter, but also the threefold narrative structure supported by Bauer. He claims that "the Gospel does not present any episodes, or 'incidents' a great deal of the time" as Carter's plot structure assumes, and that "Bauer's analysis, on the other hand, is not able to account, by literary critical means, for the presence of discourses that keep interrupting this three-stage narrative" ("Literary Evidence," 541, 551). The views advocated by Carter and Bauer are discussed below.

34. Smith, "Literary Evidence," 541–42.

35. Smith, "Literary Evidence," 542–43.

36. Smith, "Literary Evidence," 543–44; it is not clear which passages Smith finds these formulaic phrases; presumably he means 5:1; 13:10; 18:1, and 24:1. If so, then the occurrence of the formulaic phrase in 13:10 which is not the beginning of the parable discourse, as well as in 24:3 makes this view difficult to sustain.

Keegan's and Smith's contributions are helpful; it is not unlikely that certain terms or themes may help discern the opening and closing of discourse units. However, the introductory terminologies are far from accurate, especially since Matthew can deploy the same introductory terminology at structurally insignificant points *per* their judgment.[37] France is therefore right when he states: "Compared with the concluding formula, Keegan's 'precise and distinctive' opening formulae are hardly impressive. The form is very variable, and the elements he mentions variously distributed."[38] Apart from this, to argue that Jesus, from 13:36, addresses his major discourses to the disciples alone adds nothing to the structural equation if he continues to freely address both the crowd and the disciples in significant teaching moments (cf.15:10-21; 23:1). Matthew 23 where Jesus addresses his most scathing speech to both the crowd and his disciples can hardly be denied the status of a major discourse simply because it is not bracketed by or closed off with a formulaic phrase.[39]

Moreover, Matt 13:36 cannot be taken as the center of the Gospel; it is simply a shift in setting and audience that sets the stage for the explanation of a parable. In terms of connectivity, the use of conjunctive τότε instead of a simple καί in 13:36 indicates a marked cohesion or continuity as well as development within the same episode. Some have sought to demonstrate the theological significance of the household motif in Matthew.[40] Given the preponderance of οἰκία/οἶκος in Matthew, one must admit that there is significant truth in this.[41] However, the household motif remains secondary. It is unlikely that the mere movement into a house in 13:36, the disciples-only composition of Jesus' audience, and/or the disciples' curiosity about a parable will signal to the implied reader that here we have reached a pivotal moment or turning point in the Gospel.

To further clarify this last point, the view that Matt 13:36 is "the high point of the Gospel,"[42] or "the great turning point of the Gospel"[43] is incon-

---

37. In particular, προσελθόντες οἱ μαθηταὶ . . . occurs in 13:10; 13:36-37; 14:15; 24:1; 26:17. Keegan's rationalization of these extra occurrences is unsatisfactory ("Introductory Formulae," 422-23); cf. Smith, "Literary Evidence," 543-44.

38. France, *Evangelist and Teacher*, 142.

39. Contra Keegan, "Introductory Formulae," 429-30; Smith, "Literary Evidence," 549.

40. Crosby, *House of Disciples*, 49-75; Hood, "Extent of Fifth Discourse," 531.

41. Οἰκία (Matt 2:11; 5:15; 7:24-27; 8:6, 14; 9:10, 23, 28; 10:12-14; 12:25, 29; 13:1, 36, 57; 17:25; 19:29; 24:17, 43; 26:6); οἶκος (Matt 9:6-7; 10:6; 11:8; 12:4, 44; 15:24; 21:13; 23:38).

42. Lohr, "Oral Techniques," 427. Ellis, *Matthew*, 13, calls it "the highpoint and turning point of the gospel."

43. Keegan, "Introductory Formulae," 423.

sistent with Matthew's goal as suggested by its biographic tenor or rhetorical bracket. In other words, since the divine identity of Jesus, as indicated by the whole-book *inclusio* (especially in terms of the *God-with-us* theme in Matt 1:23//28:20), is the "the spirit of the whole work" as Lohr also argues,[44] one would expect that the central or high point should in some way repeat or at least reflect the burden or theme of the Gospel's *inclusio*.[45] Neither Keegan nor Smith shows how their proposals verify and illuminate Matthew's pervasive and defining Christological burden. This is, in my view, a significant problem, and it certainly compels the conclusion that Davies and Allison have reached, i.e., that "the chiastic analyses are too uncertain."[46]

Regardless of what modifications scholars make of the alternating narrative-discourse model, the question of how the fivefold (whole-book) structure relates to the main concern or theme of Matthew's Gospel remains unaddressed. While the discourses of Jesus are prominent and may even be structurally significant in Matthew, it remains the case that as Gibbs asserts, "if the simple question 'what is Matthew's Gospel about' is presented, the answer 'the great discourses of Jesus" fails to satisfy."[47]

Narratival Trajectory

The third trajectory of structural propositions is broadly narratival in character. Those within this trajectory all view Matthew as a story, and they seek to interpret the book based on its plot. This emphasis on narrativity has produced at least three structural propositions.[48]

The first and most influential proposition is the topical-biographical structure based on the formulaic expression, ἀπὸ τότε ἤρξατο ὁ Ἰησοῦς ("from that time on Jesus began") in Matt 4:17 and 16:21. Edgar Krentz was the first

---

44. Lohr, "Oral Techniques," 410 (cf. 412–13); see also Burnett, "Prolegomenon."

45. Blomberg, "Structure," 4–7, has shown that this kind of repetition is typical for determining the presence of chiasmus, esp. number 8 of the 9 criteria he offers.

46. Davies and Allison, *Matthew*, 1:61.

47. Gibbs, *Matthew*, 39.

48. Combrink may argue that his proposed structure belongs here as well and thus count as the fourth. But we do not need to discuss it more than simply noting that he only modifies the alternating concentric or chiastic model, taking Matt 13:1–53 as the pivotal and emphasized point ("Structure," 70–90); he is too unspecific in taking a section as broad as 11:1—16:20 as the "main turning area" (82). Moreover, in seeking to force a narrative plot upon the alternating concentric structure, Combrink, as Bauer argues, "seeks to have it both ways . . . but in the end the reader is left wondering how the alternating structural pattern relates to the flow of the narrative toward its climax in the passion and resurrection" (Bauer, *Gospel*, 108n43).

to make the structural proposition,[49] but J. D. Kingsbury has been more vocal and extensive in its defense.[50] According to Kingsbury, Matthew divides into the following threefold sections: (I) The Person of Jesus Messiah (1:1—4:16); (II) The Proclamation of Jesus Messiah (4:17—16:20); and (III) The Suffering, Death, and Resurrection of Jesus Messiah (16:21—28:20). This structure suggests to Kingsbury, as it did to Krentz,[51] that Matt 1:1 functions not as a title for the entire Gospel but as a "superscription" analogical to 4:17 and 16:21, with each of these verses representing the broad themes elaborated in their respective sections, altogether leading to the climax in Matt 28:18-20.[52] In essence, Kingsbury's proposal emphasizes the centrality of Christology in Matthew's plotline. But for this structure to hold, Kingsbury must challenge the more traditional beginning of Jesus' ministry in 4:12. In his view, the subject, "Jesus" in 4:12 is left to be inferred from 4:1-11. Kingsbury takes this to indicate that 4:12-16 belongs to the preceding pericope and concludes the divinely ordained travels of Jesus from ch. 2.[53]

Several scholars have defended this threefold Christological structure, prominent among them being Bauer,[54] and Gibbs.[55] Others find it unsatisfactory, questioning the structural strength and priority of the ἀπὸ τότε formula (4:17 and 16:21) over against the fivefold καὶ ἐγένετο formula (7:28; 11:1; 13:53; 19:1; and 26:1). Although not necessarily so, a similar ἀπὸ τότε phrase in Matt 26:16 may appear to compromise the uniqueness of Matt 4:17 and 16:21 for structural purposes. Davies and Allison describe the tripartite structure as "too precarious."[56] Warren Carter considers it helpfully broad but argues that attention to the one formula and "the neglect of others seems somewhat arbitrary."[57] In defense of the traditional demarcation in

49. Krentz, "Prologue," 409-14.

50. See Kingsbury, *Matthew*, 2-7; Kingsbury, *Matthew as Story*; Kingsbury, "Plot of Matthew," 347-56.

51. Krentz, "Prologue," 411.

52. Kingsbury, *Matthew*, 8-10; cf. Krentz, "Prologue," 411-12.

53. See Kingsbury, *Matthew*, 15-16.

54. See Bauer, *Structure*, 57-134. He argues that Matthew is structured according to four compositional relationships namely: repetition of comparison; repetition of contrast, repetition of particularization and climax; and climax with *inclusio*.

55. Gibbs, *Matthew 1:1—11:1*, 38-47; cf. Stock, *Method and Message* and Garland, *Reading Matthew*, 9. Some maintain major divisions at 4:17 and 16:21 but do not structure the entire book according to the threefold format, e.g., Gardner, *Matthew*, 23. Blomberg adopts the threefold structure with subdivisions informed by the Bacon's outline (*Matthew*, 22-25, 49); see also Sabourin, *L'Évangile Selon Saint Matthieu*, 15. For more entries, see Bauer, *Gospel*, 123n77.

56. Davies and Allison, *Matthew*, 1:61.

57. Carter, *Matthew*, 133-34.

4:12 as the beginning of Jesus' ministry, Frans Neirynck appeals to Mark 1:1–15.[58] However, this dependence on Mark for the structure of Matthew is methodologically weak. On literary grounds, Matthew can simply not be tied to the structural apron strings of Mark.

The defect in Kingsbury's structure is arguably not where he takes as the beginning of Jesus' ministry (4:17) but where he takes as its end (16:20). Demonstrably, the proclamation of Jesus Messiah does not end in Matt 16:20. We should note that the formulaic expression, ἀμὴν λέγω ὑμῖν ("truly I say to you"), which marks or, at least, is closely associated with Jesus' didactic and prophetic proclamation continues to occur within the entire range of Matt 5–26:34.[59] The last three occurrences (26:13, 21, 34) understandably take a different character, being embedded within the passion narrative, but the continuing recurrence of the formula argues against limiting Jesus' proclamation to 16:20. As France contends, "a division of the gospel which does not allow these sections [Matt 16:17–19 and 16:22–23] to be read in direct sequence is surely not going to do justice to Matthew's dramatic purpose."[60] More critically, the loss of the proclamative as well as structural and central Christological significance of the Eschatological Discourse (Matt 24–25) is a considerable problem with the Kingsbury's threefold structure.

The second proposal within the narratival approach may be called kernel-block structure. It is conversed by Frank J. Matera and others working within the same or similar conceptual framework. Frustrated by the lack of consensus and borrowing from S. Chatman's literary concepts of *kernel* and *satellite*,[61] Matera proposes a plot-driven analysis as an alternative to the formula-driven approaches to Matthew's structure. He argues that Matthew's plot consists of six kernels or hinge passages: the birth of Jesus (2:1a), the beginning of Jesus' ministry (4:12–17), the question of John the Baptist (11:2–6), Jesus' conversation at Caesarea Philippi (16:13–28), the cleansing of the temple (21:1–17), and the Great Commission (28:16–20).[62] Based on

---

58. Neirynck, "ΑΠΟ ΤΟΤΕ ΗΡΞΑΤΟ."

59. See 16:28; 17:20; 18:3, 13, 18–19; 19:23, 28; 21:21, 31; 23:36; 24:2, 34, 47; 25:12, 40, 45; 26:13, 21, 34. Note that Kingsbury also affirms his structural decision based on the verb "proclaim" (*Matthew*, 20).

60. France, *Evangelist and Teacher*, 152, although he himself begins a new section in 16:21 (*Matthew*, xii).

61. Chatman identifies kernels as logically essential or major events while satellites are non-essential or minor events that fill out the narrative (*Story and Discourse*, 32, 53–56).

62. Matera, "Plot," 244–46.

these kernels, Matera concludes that Matthew is structured according to six narrative blocks:

1:1—4:11	The Coming of the Messiah
4:12—11:1	The Messiah's ministry to Israel of preaching, teaching, and healing
11:2—16:12	The crisis in the Messiah's ministry
16:13—20:34	The Messiah's journey to Jerusalem
21:1—28:15	The Messiah's death and resurrection
28:16–20	The great commission.[63]

Table 1: Matera's Narrative Blocks of Matthew

In Matera's view, "the great commission is a kernel without satellites"; it climaxes and begins a new open future of proclamation and discipleship of the nations.[64] This idea of openness alone makes this structure unsustainable. An open future cannot be part of literary work. It is also difficult to accept Matt 28:16–20 as a kernel over against the resurrection event that forms the basis for the commission. The resurrection, in Matera's view, essentially turns out to be a satellite which, following Chatman's theory, functions merely aesthetically and thus "can be deleted without disturbing the logic of the plot."[65] Clearly, this poses a major problem and reveals the subjective nature of Matera's determination of what constitutes a kernel or satellite.

Consequently, Warren Carter has reviewed Matera's proposal. He offers what he calls "an alternative reading," rejecting three of Matera's kernels (1, 2, 6), shrinking one (4), expanding another (5), and retaining just one (3):[66]

---

63. Matera, "Plot," 238, 246–52.
64. Matera, "Plot," 245 (cf. 252).
65. Chatman, *Story and Discourse*, 54.
66. Carter, "Kernels," 473–81.

	Kernel 1 (Block)	**Kernel 2** (Block)	**Kernel 3** (Block)	**Kernel 4** (Block)	**Kernel 5** (Block)	**Kernel 6** (Block)
Matera	2:1a (1:1—4:11)	4:12–17 (4:12—11:1)	11:2–6 (11:2—16:12)	16:13–28 (16:13—20:34)	21:1–17 (21:1—28:15)	28:16–20 (28:16—20)
Carter	1:18–25 (1:1—4:16)	4:17–25 (4:17—11:1)	11:2–6 (11:2—16:20)	16:21–28 (16:21—20:34)	21:1–27 (21:1—27:66)	28:1–10 (28:1–20)

Table 2: Comparing Matera's and Carter's Structures of Matthew

Carter's revision appears valid. Unlike Matera's proposal, it accords some structural significance to the repeated formulas used by Kingsbury and Bacon by incorporating some of them into his sixfold kernel-block structure. Yet Carter's version is unsatisfactory; the whole kernel-block schema emphasizes events over the discourses or teachings of Jesus. In Matthew's Gospel, both events and discourses are linked together in revealing the identity of Jesus. Thus, the structure of Matthew cannot be discerned by the subjective delineation of kernel and satellite events or materials.[67] One must consider discourse clues within the entire material of Matthew as well.

Wilhelmus J. C. Weren has recently offered a new proposal drawing from Matera and Carter.[68] Weren argues that some cardinal passages or hinge texts perform double functions, determining subsequent pericopes as well as pointing back to preceding blocks. Matthew 4:12–17 and 26:1–16 constitute the hinge texts of the book, with the material in-between (4:18—25:46) representing a *corpus* in which a continuous story of Jesus' ministry is presented.[69] The resulting structure is as follows:[70]

overture	hinge	*corpus*	hinge	finale
1:1—4:11	4:12–17	4:18—25:46	26:1–16	26:17—28:20

Table 3: Weren's New Proposal on Matthew's Structure

Weren then takes Matt 16:13–28 as the hinge text within the central corpus.[71] This new proposal is commendable and should form the basis for more

---

67. This problem of subjectivity is also the issue with the recent attempt to organize Matthew based on Isaiah quotations by Patrick ("Matthew's *Pesher* Gospel," 43–81). He argues that Matthew organized his Gospel in ten *pesher* units, each consisting of a "kernel" of Isaiah citation around which "satellite" materials are clustered.

68. Weren, "Macrostructure," 172–200; Weren, *Studies in Matthew's Gospel*, 13–41.

69. Weren, "Macrostructure," 188.

70. Weren, "Macrostructure," 189.

71. Weren, "Macrostructure," 190.

nuanced structural specificity. The implied author may indeed intend certain passages to serve as hinges. However, the problem with Weren's proposal is that the hinges are too extensive and topically varied to constitute hinges. A hinge must be as concise and thematically monolithic as possible. It must also be remarkable and memorable. Weren's central and framing hinges fail to satisfy these conditions.

The third offering under the narratival trajectory is the approach advanced by France. Like Matera, France rejects all attempts at the formulaic and symmetrical diagraming of Matthew. His proposal incorporates narrative plot development and geography. On the one hand, he contends that Matthew is "designed to build up towards a dramatic climax of the confrontation of Jesus with the authorities in Jerusalem."[72] Thus, the principle of Matthew's structure is to be found not in the symmetry of sections but in the narrative plot; "the plot," he says, "*is* the structure."[73] Yet on the other hand, France argues that "Matthew shares Mark's view of the contrast between Jesus' ministry in Galilee and that in Jerusalem."[74] Matthew expands Mark's "conscious [geographical] structuring of the story," emphasizing movement from Galilee to Jerusalem, and differing only in "a dramatic return to Galilee (28:16-20)."[75] France's outline follows a sixfold movement:

I. Introducing the Messiah (1:1—4:11)

II. Galilee: The Messiah revealed in Word and in Deed (4:12—16:20)

III. From Galilee to Jerusalem: The Messiah and his Followers Prepare for the Confrontation (16:21—20:34)

IV. Jerusalem: The Messiah in Confrontation with the Religious Authorities (21:1—25:46)

V. Jerusalem: The Messiah Rejected, Killed, and Vindicated (26:1—28:15)

VI. Galilee: The Messianic Mission is Launched (28:16-20).[76]

This outline is clearly eclectic insofar as it combines a geographical/Christological approach within a narratival framework. One problem, however, is that just like the six-part structures proposed by Matera and Carter, it is not broad enough. While the cyclic Galilee-Jerusalem-Galilee movement may

---

72. France, *Evangelist and Teacher*, 149.

73. Weren, "Macrostructure," 153. Bauer, *Gospel*, 125, argues that "a distinction must be made between plot and structure," taking structure as "both broader and deeper than plot."

74. France, *Evangelist and Teacher*, 149.

75. France, *Matthew*, 3, 4.

76. France, *Matthew*, vii–xv.

be significant, this problem stems from the redaction-critical penchant that seeks to perpetuate the largely abandoned geographical model.[77] Importantly, section 6 is too limited to be regarded as a major section in the book.

Proposed Structure of Matthew

Of the views reviewed above, it is the opinion of this study that Weren's proposal comes closest to resolving the structural issue in Matthew's Gospel. However, as already noted, the hinges are too broad. By paying attention to discourse markers as articulated in chapter 2 of this study, it is possible to be more specific than Weren. The broad structure proposed in this study breaks the Gospel of Matthew into three movements as follows:

I. Introductory Movement: The Identity of Jesus Introduced and Tested (1:1—4:16)

II. Revelatory Movement: The Identity of Jesus Demonstrated in Deed and Proclamation (4:17—25:46)

III. Vindicatory Movement: The Identity of Jesus Vindicated through Passion and Resurrection (26:1—28:20).

This threefold movement eliminates Weren's first and third hinges, shrinks the central hinge, and simplifies Matthew into a Christologically shaped Gospel by showing what is the central burden of Matthew—Jesus. In what follows, I provide justifications for this structural decision.

First, the introductory movement culminates in 4:16 rather than in 4:11. In other words, the ministry of Jesus begins in 4:17 rather than 4:12. The opening of 4:12 does not provide strong support for the beginning of a new segment or section there. The conjunctive δὲ indicates development in a new and distinct direction but within the ongoing storyline. Moreover, given the lack of explicit subject (inferred only by reference to 4:10), as Kingsbury argues,[78] and the aorist participle + δὲ initial,[79] 4:12 resists strict

---

77. We should also note that the fact that France is reluctant to apply the "Matthew-copied-Mark" redaction-critical approach when it comes to actual interpretation would seem to call to question his Mark-based geographical outline; see France, *Matthew*, 22.

78. Again, see Kingsbury, *Matthew*, 15–16.

79. Most aorist participle + δὲ initials in Matthew develop an ongoing storyline often in a new and distinct direction (cf. 2:22; 3:7; 8:5, 10, 18; 9:8, 28; 36; 13:46; 14:13, 28; 16:8, 16; 17:17; 18:27, 28; 19:22, 26; 20:2, 11, 22, 34; 21:15, 21, 24, 30; 22:11, 18, 29; 25:22, 24, 26; 26:8, 10; 27:21, 24, 35; 28:5. In few instances, a low-medium break may be indicated especially in combination with an explicit subject of the main verb and/or major other factors such as change in location, audience, and topic (cf. 5:1; 8:1; 16:13).

discontinuity from the preceding material. Regarding 4:17 as the beginning of Jesus' ministry, one can argue by the same token that the construct, ∅ + ἀπὸ τότε, is referential and requires a temporal frame of reference in the preceding material (4:13) to be meaningful. That is, the implied reader gets the sense that Jesus began to proclaim his message *from* the time he began to dwell in Capernaum. In other words, the asyndeton in 4:17 may be taken to signal cohesion or continuity.

However, the location of the beginning of Jesus' ministry in 4:17 is supported by several important considerations: (1) The phrase "from then on" corresponds to what linguists recognize as "point of departure." Levinsohn defines "point of departure" as a *bi-directional* element placed at the beginning of a sentence to represent the starting point of a communication as well as to anchor the subsequent clause(s) to something which is already in the context or accessible to the hearer's mental representation.[80] In this case, Jesus' settlement at Capernaum (4:13) remains accessible to the hearer's mental representation while a new section is initiated. (2) While points of departures involve sentence-level discontinuities *per* Levinsohn's examples, the use of asyndetic conjunction in 4:17 suggests a significant discontinuity.[81] Consistent with our finding on pages 48–50, the fact that this instance is not only within a narrative but also formulaic in association supports a topical break here, even if a temporal link to v. 16 remains.[82] But perhaps, more importantly, the combination of asyndeton with the *commencement* verb ἄρχω, and the explicit mention of Jesus as the subject of the main verb (in contrast to 4:12) makes 4:17 a marked and recognizable point at which the implied reader makes a major shift in the mental representation of the narrative.[83] (3) In light of Matt 26:16, if the implied author wanted to indicate a strict cohesion or continuity between 4:17 and the preceding material, he is capable of making this explicitly clear by using καὶ + ἀπὸ τότε. That he does not do this suggests the intention to begin a new segment in 4:17. And (5) the use of δὲ in combination with a change in scene and the introduction of new participants may argue for a major break in 4:18 instead. However, δὲ at this point more properly functions to develop the proclamation theme

---

80. Levinsohn, *Discourse Features*, 8–11. Other examples of point of departure would be expressions like, "not long after" (Luke 15:13) and "in those days" (Matt 3:1).

81. Asyndeton, as all discourse markers, can be both anaphoric and cataphoric; it can "look simultaneously forward and backward," so that "the beginning of one unit is the end of another and vice versa" (Schiffrin, *Discourse Markers*, 37).

82. Cf. 16:21.

83. We should note the claim of Moulton: "Asyndeton makes the beginning of a new long section conspicuous, e.g., Rom 9:1; 10:1; 13:1; 1 Pet 5:1; 2 Pet 3:1" (*Grammar*, 3:341).

in 4:17 (cf. v. 23). Moreover, the lack of an explicit subject in 4:18 will also suggest to the implied reader to strictly maintain a link with 4:17.[84] Based on these observations, it is appropriate to take 4:17 as the beginning of Jesus' ministry.

Second, if the analysis above is correct, and the proclamation of Jesus begins at 4:17, then we should proceed to further ask where that proclamation ends. That end is clearly not in Matt 16:20, as Kingsbury and others have argued, but Matt 25:46. The Eschatological Discourse cannot be excluded from Jesus' proclamation as Kingsbury does. Rather, it is the conclusion of Jesus' proclamation, which raises the question of why the implied author has placed it in the present location and what role it is playing. This question will be fully addressed in chapter 6 of this study. In the meantime, we should note two factors that support our claim. The first factor is that the Eschatological Discourse ends with a depiction of the final realization of the kingdom in Matt 25:31–46. The kingdom theme in this passage forms an *inclusio* with the topical kingdom proclamation in Matt 4:17.[85] The second factor is that the phrase, καὶ ἐγένετο ὅτε ἐτέλεσεν ὁ Ἰησοῦς πάντας τοὺς λόγους τούτους ("and it happened when Jesus had finished *all* these words") in Matt 26:1, not only looks forward to what follows as I have argued above but also indicates that Matt 25:46 is the proper end of Jesus' proclamation.[86] The idea of *completion* in Matt 26:1 complements that of *commencement* in 4:17 and the inclusion of the indefinite adjective, πᾶς (*all*)—a unique element compared to the other καὶ ἐγένετο phrases[87]—represents what I would describe as "πᾶς cumulative." That is, it comprehends not merely the Eschatological Discourse but also *all* that Jesus has proclaimed from the time he began his ministry. Joachim Gnilka makes a similar point, "The summary remark in 26:1 implies that all the Discourses belong together in one comprehensive sense, and in the final analysis are to be understood as complementing one another as a unity."[88] Moreover, the combination of πᾶς with the *completion*

---

84. Although this is not a necessary criterion (cf. Matt 5:1; 24:3). The beginning of the sermon on the Mount can hardly be placed at Matt 4:17 rather than 5:1 simply because the subject "Jesus" is inexplicit in the latter. For further analysis on the demarcation in 4:17, see Appendix 2.

85. Gaechter rightly affirms that 25:31–46 not only concludes the Eschatological Discourse but also all of Jesus' discourses (*Literarische Kunst im Matthäus-Evangelium*, 47).

86. Although καί usually marks continuity, the use in Matt 26:1 is more properly taken as discontinuous since the verse is inextricably linked to what follows rather than to what precedes.

87. Cf. Matt 7:28; 11:1; 13:53; 19:1.

88. My translation. In German, "Die zusammenfassende Bemerkung in 26:1, deutet an, dass alle Reden in einem übergreifenden Sinn zusammengehören, einander

verb τελέω in the formulaic phrase makes it more memorable to the implied reader whether or not the phrase has been recognized from previous uses to be a structurally important formula.

In summary, the structure proposed here is a limited synchronization (of the key formulaic phrases) in which a Christological superstructure retains subsuming priority.[89] The revelatory movement (4:17—25:46) comprises of proclamations, teachings, deeds, and symbolic acts that reveal the identity of Jesus. It has two extended parts (4:17—16:12 and 16:21—25:45) each consisting of three discourses.[90] Matthew 16:13–20 represents a hinge passage with a point of cruciality in 16:16.[91] The revelatory movement ends with the Eschatological Discourse completing the superstructure of Jesus' identity that Matthew is driving at.[92] How all this fits together into the broader structure of Matthew will be worked out in chapter 6. But before that, I will turn my attention now to Matt 24–25. Since I have reviewed the major structural proposals for this Discourse in relation to the various interpretations (ch. 1), I will proceed here to offer my own structural proposition. This will form the basis for the interpretation that will follow in the next chapter.

Delimitation and Structure of the Eschatological Discourse

Delimitation of the Eschatological Discourse

To properly interpret the Eschatological Discourse, it is critical to answer a twofold question: (1) at what point does the Discourse begin? And (2) at what point does it end? None of these questions has been answered definitively.

---

ergänzen und letztlich als Einheit aufzufassen sind" (Gnilka, *Matthäusevangelium*, 2:522).

89. The validity of such synchronization is not at all inconceivable. E.g., Via provisionally claims that "Matthew foregrounds the three-fold Christological structure and backgrounds the five-fold legal one" ("Structure," 201); even Krentz, whose view Kingsbury expounds, recognizes this synchrony when he states that "into this scheme [the three-fold Christological structure] Matthew inserts his five great discourses" ("Prologue," 411).

90. A double triadic discourse arrangement (i.e., six main discourses) is consistent with Matthew's structural disposition; see Allison, "Structure."

91. For "cruciality," see Bauer and Traina, *Inductive Bible Study*, 108–10; Hagner describes Matt 16:16 as a sort of climax before the climax—"the climax of the narrative, short of the passion itself" (*New Testament*, 202).

92. For a further breakdown of the structure described, see Appendix 3.

Beginning of the Eschatological Discourse

Commentators have taken different positions on the beginning point of the Eschatological Discourse. As observed earlier, Bacon takes the limits of the Discourse—what he calls "Discourse on Judgment"—to be from 23:1 to 26:2. For Bacon, chs. 23—26:2 is part of the entire fifth book beginning in ch. 19:1b which he entitles, "concerning judgment."[93] Many commentators link the Eschatological Discourse with ch. 23 whether or not they follow Bacon's fivefold structure.[94] For some who subscribe to the Baconian structure, the major reason for this view is the absence of the formulaic expression, "when Jesus had finished these things" between chs. 23 and 24 (cf. 7:28; 13:58; 19:1; 26:1), which is taken to mean that chs. 23–25 constitute a single unit of discourse.[95] This view also makes sense from redactional and thematic points of view. It is argued that Matthew's deletion of Mark's *pericope* on the widow's mite (Mark 12:41–44, cf. Luke 21:1–4) indicates that chs. 23 and 24 are intended to be held together as a continuous discourse.[96] Perhaps the most cogent support for the view is that there is a thematic continuity from chs. 23 to 24. Within the immediate connection point between these two chapters, the movement from Jesus' declaration that the temple is abandoned (23:38) to his actual departure from the temple (24:1), and finally to the prophecy about the temple's destruction (24:2) appears seamless. More broadly, the themes of woes and judgment in ch. 23 go even further into ch. 24 with a striking resonance between two similar declarations in 23:36[97] and 24:34.[98] Some have argued for the unity of chs. 23–25 as constituting the fifth and final discourse based on the similarities between 24:1–3 and 13:34–37.[99] I shall consider this shortly. In the meantime, Jason

---

93. Bacon, *Studies in Matthew*, 308–25.

94. E.g., Lohr, "Oral Techniques", 427; Ellis, *Matthew*, 12; Gundry, *Matthew*, 453; Guthrie, *New Testament*, 59; most scholars connect ch. 23 to the preceding material instead, while some consider it as a distinct discourse; see n24 above. For more entries on these, see Bauer, *Gospel*, 105n29.

95. Although some like Gundry take Matt 23–25 as Jesus' fifth discourse without subscribing to any overall structure (*Matthew*, 453, cf. 10–11).

96. Hummel, *Auseinandersetzung*, 85–86; Burnett makes the same observation (*Testament*, 21), although he argues that the Eschatological Discourse begins in 24:4 (23); so also Lambrecht, "Parousia Discourse," 313, 317.

97. Ἀμὴν λέγω ὑμῖν, ἥξει ταῦτα πάντα ἐπὶ τὴν γενεὰν ταύτην.

98. Ἀμὴν λέγω ὑμῖν ὅτι οὐ μὴ παρέλθῃ ἡ γενεὰ αὕτη ἕως ἂν πάντα ταῦτα γένηται.

99. See Balabanski, *Eschatology*, 135–37; Hood, "Extent of Fifth Discourse," 530–31, 540–42; Stanton takes chs. 24–25 as the final discourse, yet he argues that ch. 23 belongs to it on the basis that "polemic and apocalyptic are both the responses of a minority community very much at odds with the world at large" (*New People*, 165).

Hood further finds literary and intertextual correlations between chs. 5 and 23 (mostly contrasting themes) that imply, in his view, that Matthew likely intended chs. 23–25 to be read as a unit in light of ch. 5–7.[100]

On similar thematic grounds, some have also argued for taking chs. 21–25 as a single unit. Wilson, for example, has sought to demonstrate that this unit represents "a coherent portrayal of Jesus as an agent of judgment."[101] He argues that the mention of Mt Olives in 21:1 and the placement of chs. 24–25 on Mt. Olives in conjunction with the theme of "the coming king in 21:1–11 and 25:31–46" constitute an *inclusio* indicating this extended unit. In contending that "there is a great advantage for interpretation in taking chapters 21 to 25 as a wider, over-arching unit," Wilson is certainly right. But the same could also be said of the broader Baconian section (i.e., 19:1b—26:2). Bauer rightly notes that the Matthean discourses are closely related to their context as well as "integrated into the [overall] narrative framework."[102] There is no question that chs. 24–25 stands in close thematic connection with chs. 23, 21, or even 19. Taking this extended connection into account certainly pays hermeneutical dividends.

However, this does not imply that chs. 24–25 is indistinguishable from these preceding chapters. The contention by some, like Balabanski and Hood, that the similarities between 24:1–3 and 13:34–37 compel us to take chs. 23–25 as a single discourse, is worth consideration. The two transitional passages are strikingly similar. There are in both instances a change in location, a change from public to private audience, as well as thematic continuity with both preceding and subsequent materials. Should we, therefore, conclude that since ch. 13 is a single discourse, chs. 23–25 must equally be so treated? Hardly.

Several factors support the unity and distinctness of ch. 23 and provide warrants for separating it from chs. 24–25: (1) The conjunctive τότε in 13:36 is a very weak link for adjoining a completely new discourse—the same reason a new discourse cannot begin in 18:21 or 25:1.[103] In contrast to the use of δέ in 24:3, it indicates strict continuity with the same frame of parabolic discourse rather than discontinuity, although both τότε and δέ are developmental in function. In other words, the implied author's use of τότε in 13:36 suggests that what follows from here should be processed in

---

100. Hood, "Extent of Fifth Discourse," 530–31, 540–42; although after considering this matter, Davies and Allison declare: "we find no evidence that our author intended the reader to juxtapose the [Sermon on the Mount] and chapter 23" (*Matthew*, 3:309).

101. Wilson, *When Will These Things Happen?*, 66.

102. See Bauer, *Structure*, 131.

103. Hagner, *Matthew*, 654, argues that the break in 24:1 is "a far more significant break than that of 13:36) but fails to identify why.

tandem with or as a continuation of the preceding parable material. Commenting on Matt 13:36, Levinsohn states: "τότε links Jesus' telling of a series of parables with the disciples' request that he interprets one of the parables. No point of departure occurs, so τότε signals the commencement of a new subsection of the overall episode. Nevertheless, there is continuity of time and of other factors between the subsections."[104] Such continuity is not necessary with the use of δέ in 24:3.[105] (2) Although Jesus may have taken a seat in 13:36, that the implied author does not mention another "sitting" here, after 13:1-2, may suggest that he does not see this relocation as indicating a different discourse. (3) The alternating crowd-disciple focus in ch. 13—(crowd [vv. 1-9]-disciple [vv. 10-23]; crowd [vv. 24-35]-disciple [vv. 36-52])—strengthens its unity and distinctness. (4) In 13:53, the concluding formula, . . . ὅτε ἐτέλεσεν ὁ Ἰησοῦς τὰς παραβολὰς ταύτας is 'particular,'[106] specifically groups all the parables in the entire chapter into one discourse envelop regardless of the brief interspersing narrative breaks. (5) While 13:24-30 must be tied to its interpretation in 13:36-43, chs. 24-25 (cf. Mark 13) can be hermeneutically independent of ch. 23 despite the fluid boundary.

Moreover, ch. 23 is stylistically different from chs. 24-25. The former is a denunciatory polemic, but the latter is an apocalyptic-eschatological discourse.[107] Shirley Jackson Case even suggests that the purposes and settings to which the early church would apply ch. 23 and 24-25 will differ.[108] Wilson, himself, is aware of chs. 24-25 being "a subunit" and he treats it so structurally.[109] Thus, we must agree with Hagner's conclusion: "Chap. 23 can . . . be seen as the formal indictment for the judgment that is described in chaps. 24-25. Yet this function of chap. 23 and its natural relatedness to chaps. 24-25 can be affirmed without the insistence that structurally the three chapters should be thought of as forming a single discourse."[110]

---

104. Levinsohn, *Discourse Features*, 96.

105. I shall argue below that 24:3 is the proper beginning of the Eschatological Discourse.

106. Cf. 26:1 where the formula is 'general,' comprehending *all* that Jesus has said from the beginning.

107. Cf. Garland, *Reading Matthew*, 232; Senior, *Matthew*, 256-66.

108. Case, "Origin and Purpose," 391.

109. Wilson, *When Will These Things Happen?*, 67-69; 133-34; so also many who think chs. 21-25 belong together, e.g., Gardner, *Matthew*, 308-9; Osborne, *Matthew*, 46; even Meier who holds to Bacon's five-book structure strictly and structurally demarcates chs. 24-25 as the eschatological discourse (*Matthew*, 276).

110. Hagner, *Matthew*, 654.

Accordingly, the overwhelming majority of commentators take Matt 24 as the beginning of the Eschatological Discourse.[111] Gnilka argues that Matthew distinguishes the woe speech (ch. 23) and end-time speech (ch. 24–25) by giving them each a different audience and setting.[112] However, views vary as to the exact point at which the Discourse begins in ch. 24. Some maintain a strict demarcation in 24:1.[113] Others, including Lambrecht,[114] Edward Schweizer,[115] Burnett,[116] and Keegan,[117] have sought to more finely delineate the Eschatological Discourse by positing a beginning in 24:3/4.

Burnett questions the Baconian formulaic rationale, claiming that in the context of judgment on Israel (19:3—22:46) as further highlighted by the woes of ch. 23, the formula, "when Jesus had finished these sayings" is no longer necessary. "Jesus' action of permanently abandoning the temple in 24:1," he believes, "shows as clearly as a formula would that this discourse (chapter 23) has ended." Burnett goes on to argue that Matthew creates a caesura between 24:2 and 24:3 by structurally connecting Jesus' announcement of judgment (23:38) with its fulfillment when Jesus actually leaves the temple (24:1) and the consummation of the judgment in the prophecy of 24:2. He concludes that "24:2 ends the theme of judgment against Israel" and that "23:3 begins a new theme, the Parousia of Jesus, which constitutes a new introduction for the eschatological discourse which begins in 24:4."[118]

---

111. Hood, "Extent of Fifth Discourse," 529n10.

112. Gnilka, *Matthäusevangelium*, 2:522; cf. France, *Gospel according to Matthew*, 333.

113. See Beare, *Matthew*, 461; Morris, *Matthew*, 594; Witherington, *Matthew*, 443; Osborne, *Matthew*, 864–67; Senior, *Matthew*, 266; Patte, *Matthew*, 333; Nolland, *Matthew*, 956; Brown, *Introduction*, 198.

114. Lambrecht thinks that 24:1-4a is an introduction to the eschatological discourse which starts in 24:4b; although he also argues that "Matt 24:1-3 must be read in light of 23:29-39 and vice versa," taking Matthew's deletion of Mark widow's mite episode as making this certain ("Parousia Discourse," 313, 317).

115. Schweizer, on the same basis as Lambrecht, takes 24:1-3 as concluding God's judgment on Israel, with v. 3 introducing v. 4, the beginning of the coming judgment on the world (*Good News*, 448–49).

116. Burnett, *Testament*, 23, 29.

117. Keegan, "Introductory Formulae," 415–30; cf. Luz, who (like Wilson) takes 21:1—25:46 as a new stage dealing with the final reckoning with Israel and judgment of the community, gives chs. 24–25 the distinctive title "Matthean Eschatology" (*Theology*, 117, 125); however, he begins the Discourse proper in 24:3; see also his *Matthew 21–28*, 178–79. France identifies 24:1—25:46 as "Jesus' teaching about the future" (*Gospel according to Matthew*, 333) but in a later work delineates the discourse as 24:3—25:46 (*Matthew*, xiii, 889); Talbert, *Matthew*, 264.

118. Burnett, *Testament*, 23; he thinks that 23:32—24:1-2 constitutes a transitional passage leading to the new discourse taken as 24:3-31 (29).

On his part, Keegan bases his demarcation in 24:3 on what he considers to be consistent use of introductory terminology (here, Jesus' taking of a *sitting position* and the disciples' *coming to him*) at the beginning of the Matthean discourses (cf. 5:1; 10:1; 13:1-2; 18:1; 24:3).[119]

Regarding the beginning, the present study advocates the strict demarcation of the eschatological discourse in 24:3 without necessarily dissociating it from 24:1-2. On the one hand, while 24:1 may signal the beginning of a new segment with the re-entrance of Jesus by name,[120] the use of the καί initial (+ aorist participle) conjunction in 24:1 signals that 24:1-2 should be processed in association with ch. 23 thematically.[121] The implied reader will more readily than not associate the announcement of the temple being abandoned in 23:38 with Jesus' actual departure in 24:1 as the announcement's symbolic fulfillment, and the prediction in 24:2 as its further reiteration. Thus, the motif of judgment on the temple is progressively heightened from 23:38 to 24:2. Given this thematic continuity, the καί-initial connection in 24:1 is a weak beginning of an entirely new segment.

On the other hand, the use of δέ conjunction in 24:3 not only signals a new and distinct development but also a change in circumstance. One may compare this change to the distinction between the genealogy of Matt 1:1-17 and the birth narrative which is signaled by δέ in Matt 1:18.[122] In both instances, there is significant degree of discontinuity. Along with this δέ conjunction, three other factors converge to substantiate this judgment: (1) In 24:3, we have a definitive shift to a new geographical location. The relocation to Mt Olives itself is eschatologically significant.[123] In contrast, there is no change of scene in 24:1, nor should the possibility of a mixed multitude be entirely excluded at this point. (2) In 24:3, the privacy between Jesus and his disciples (made explicit by the word ἴδιος) and Jesus' taking of a sitting position sharply contrast the transitory and public nature of 24:1 (cf. 5:1). (3) The introduction of a new concept παρουσία strengthens the beginning of a new discourse segment in 24:3.[124] (4) Although not necessary, the use of a genitive absolute construction in the present tense which is far less common compared to the aorist participle, may also serve to strengthen

---

119. See Keegan, "Introductory Formulae," 422.

120. So also 9:35; 26:1.

121. See Levinsohn, *Discourse Features*, 125; Runge, *Discourse Grammar*, 26; Black, *Sentence Conjunction*, 112; cf. Buth, "Ουν, Δέ, Καί and Asyndeton," 145, 52.

122. Levinsohn, *Discourse Features*, 72; Runge, *Discourse Grammar*, 31-33; Black, *Sentence Conjunction*, 146-48, 153n53.

123. Note the eschatological significance of this location (cf. Zech 14:4).

124. The term παρουσία occurs first here while συντελείας τοῦ αἰῶνος has already been used in association with the final events of history (13:38-42, 49-50; cf. 28:20).

this demarcation.¹²⁵ Moreover, that Matthew intends to signal a significant structural break using δέ in Matt 24:3 is supported by the fact that Mark, in contrast, uses καὶ in 13:1–3.

None of this means that 24:1–2 is unrelated to the Eschatological Discourse; but taking these observations together, we can conclude that 24:3 properly represents the *terminus a quo* of the Eschatological Discourse. While constituting the backdrop against which the Discourse is set, 24:1–2 is properly described as a short transitional narrative that completes the polemical and denunciatory course of ch. 23.¹²⁶

Extent of the Eschatological Discourse

As noted earlier, apart from commentaries, the few studies on the Matthean Eschatological Discourse only focus on Matt 24.¹²⁷ However, to correctly interpret the Discourse as the implied author intended, Matt 24–25 must always be held together as a continuous coherent discourse unit. The use of τότε in 25:1 points to the unity of these two chapters. Here, τότε functions to further highlight the event of the *parousia* using additional parables that develop the motifs of unknownness, suddenness, and watchfulness already initiated from 24:36.¹²⁸ In order words, this τότε does not signal "next development" in a temporal sequence of events. Rather it serves to introduce further explications of the same event. The idea is that *at the time of* the *parousia*, things will play out in ways similar to the parabolic "events" in Matt 25. Thus, the discourse connective value of this τότε is more properly characterized as + continuity/cohesion. Black's argument that τότε signals marked continuity with "some measure of emphasis or prominence" is likely valid here as well.¹²⁹

Apart from the use of τότε in 25:1 to signal cohesion and continuity, chs. 24 and 25 are also connected thematically. This study claims that the expression, παρουσίας καὶ συντελείας τοῦ αἰῶνος (24:3) finds its ultimate fulfillment in 25:31–46. As such the latter represents the appropriate end of the Discourse. However, while most commentators take 25:46 as the end of

---

125. Cf. 9:32; 17:22, 24; 18:25; 26:26; 27:19; 28:11.

126. In inductive Bible Study terminology, 24:1–2 (by extension, chapter 23 as a whole) *may be* thought of as "preparation" and 24:3—25:46 as "realization"; see discussion on these terms in Bauer and Traina, *Inductive Bible Study*, 114–15. I maintain a demarcation at v. 3 because, in a sense, to say that x is "preparation" for y is to imply a differentiation—x does not structurally belong to y.

127. See chapter 2, n2.

128. Black, *Sentence Conjunctions*, 221, 248–49.

129. Cf. Levinsohn, *Discourse Features*, 96; Runge, *Discourse Grammar*, 37–38.

the Discourse, some have called this end-limit to question. First, recall that Bacon extends the Eschatological Discourse to 26:2.[130] Second, following Lambrecht's rather curious claim that the saying, "you shall not see me from now" in 23:39 is fulfilled not only in Jesus' departure from the temple in 24:1 but preferably in his death,[131] Mlungisi P. Dlungwana has surmised that the Discourse must include Jesus' prediction about his crucifixion in 26:2.[132] He argues that the entire portion of 24:4b up to 25:46 represents an interruption, so that, in his words, "Jesus' response [to the disciples' question] which appears vaguely scattered all over the speech (24:4b—25:46), is clearly and definitively given in 26:1–2."[133] Based on this, Dlungwana proposes a tripartite structure of the discourse comprising of three levels: The first level consists of the dialogues in 24:1–4a and 26:1–2; the second level consists of the monologues in 24:4b–31 and 25:31–46, and the third level consists of the parable monologue in 24:32—25:30.[134]

While Dlungwana's study helps strengthen the unity of Matt 24–25, his case is quite unconvincing. First, as already argued above, 24:1–2 is transitional but more properly concludes ch. 23. Thus, to include it in the eschatological discourse would compel the taking along also of ch. 23. Second, Dlungwana's claim that a supposed parallel between 24:1–4a and 26:1–2 implies that the whole speech from 24:4b—25:46 is an insertion and therefore an interruption[135] appears inexplicable. Even supposing that 24:1–4a and 26:1–2 constitute an *inclusio* (which is not evident), the main body of a text so enclosed can hardly be regarded as an interruption. Verse 4b is inseparable from v. 4a; Jesus' response in v. 4 directly takes on the disciples' question via a general introduction that then leads into specifics with parabolic illustrations, and the implied reader could hardly discern that the answer to the disciples' question is only to be found in the Passover and crucifixion of Jesus hinted at in 26:1–2. While it is possible to conceive of the coming of the Son of Man in terms of his resurrection, his crucifixion could hardly be thought of in the same way, and there is no mention of resurrection in 26:1–2.

Third, one may argue that the καί-initial conjunction in 26:1 signals continuity with ch. 25. However, an exception is appropriate here, as is also

---

130. Bacon, *Studies in Matthew*, 325; see also Turner, *Matthew*, 565.
131. Lambrecht, "Parousia Discourse," 317.
132. Dlungwana, "Jesus' Parousia."
133. Dlungwana, "Jesus' Parousia," 1, 24–26.
134. Dlungwana, "Jesus' Parousia," 47–49.
135. See Dlungwana, "Jesus' Parousia," 1–2, 44.

likely in a few other instances.[136] Of the five occurrences of the formulaic καὶ ἐγένετο phrase, here, in particular, Streeter's view is correct that the emphasis of the formula is "not on the 'Here endeth' but on the 'Here begineth;' it is a formula of transition from *discourse to narrative*."[137] This is verified not only by the fact that the themes of Passover and crucifixion in 26:1-2 are clearly extraneous to the subject of chs. 24–25, but also that the only thematic resonance and continuity that exists is between 26:1-2 and what follows.[138] Jesus' passion is predicted in 26:2 and the plot to kill him follows in 26:4, with the mediating τότε in 26:3 providing cohesion and continuity.[139] Even Ernst Lohmeyer who groups chs. 24–28 as one doublet of "ende und vollendung" still maintains the distinctness of chs 24–25.[140] In light of these observations, I conclude that 26:1-2 does not belong to the Eschatological Discourse but rather represents the beginning of the passion narrative. In this study, the limits of the Eschatological Discourse are taken to be 24:3 and 25:46.

Structure of the Eschatological Discourse

Having located the Eschatological Discourse within the context of Matthew as a whole, and having delineated its boundaries, I turn to the structure of the Discourse itself. This study claims that the organizing principle of the Discourse broadly reflects *generalization and particularization with interchange and inclusio within a problem-solution structural binary*. The broad outline thus described is set forth as follows:

Problem	Solution	
24:3	Generalization	Particularization
	vv. 4–14	vv. 15—25:46

Table 4: Preliminary Structure of the Eschatological Discourse

As I have already been indicating, the discussion on discourse connectives will again be brought to bear on the passage.

---

136. Cf. 11:1; 13:53; 16:1; 19:1; 21:1.

137. Streeter, *Four Gospels*, 262; cf. Philippe, "From Genesis," 156.

138. This contrasts 24:1 where a thematic connection exists in both ways.

139. See Levinsohn, *Discourse Features*, 96–97; Runge, *Discourse Grammar*, 37–38; Black, *Sentence Conjunction*, 218–54.

140. Lohmeyer, *Evangelium des Matthäus*, 346.

Problem-Solution Binary

The Eschatological Discourse is, at its broadest level, a problem-solution Discourse. It consists of the disciples' questions (24:3) on the one hand and a long-intertwined response from Jesus (24:4—25:46) on the other. First, as already argued above, 24:3 begins with the conjunction δέ, signaling discontinuity/new development. With Jesus in a sitting position (cf. 5:1), v. 3a sets the stage for the disciples' questions (the problem) in v. 3b and these together prepare for what follows. Second, the response (solution) that Jesus provides runs intricately from 24:4 to 25:46 and consists of generalization (24:4–14) and particularization (24:15—25:46) with interchange and *inclusio*.

I begin with the first part of the solution representing generalization (24:4–14). Bauer and Traina define generalization as "the movement from particular to general." A generalization may be "identificational" involving "a general description of the essential character of the material that precedes this general description," "ideological" encapsulating in a general way the message of a material either at the beginning or at the end of that material, "historical" representing a general description of a historical period, "geographical" involving an expanded area from a particular point, or "biographical" moving from a particular description of an individual to a larger group of people.[141] If we think of the disciples' question in 24:3 as consisting of particulars, then 24:4–14 fits the description "generalization" with ideological and historical elements. Precisely, 24:4–14 is a panoramic view of eschatological history that broadly sketches the experience of Jesus' followers, including his immediate disciples in relation to the proximal fate of Jerusalem and the temple as well as all disciples from then on in relation to the *parousia* of the Son of Man and the end.[142]

The second part of the solution (24:15—25:46) involves "particularization" with "interchange." Bauer and Traina define particularization as "the movement from general to particular." In other words, particularization is the reverse of generalization and it takes the same forms as identified above. It isolates and highlights individual elements of the general material. In connection with particularization, an interchange is the "exchanging or alternation of certain elements in an a-b-a-b arrangement."[143] I will argue in the next two subdivisions that two elements in the disciples' questions in 24:3 (temple destruction/aftermath and *parousia*) are particularized in this

---

141. Bauer and Traina, *Inductive Bible Study*, 103–4.

142. The tradition, ὃ δὲ ὑμῖν λέγω πᾶσιν λέγω ... ("what I say to you, I say to *all*" [Mark 13:37]) may provide a clue that Jesus had in mind disciples other than the immediate ones in his audience.

143. Bauer and Traina, *Inductive Bible Study*, 100, 116.

alternating manner in Jesus' response, and that this pattern is discerned by taking into account discourse markers used by Matthew, aided by contextual and thematic considerations.

Finally, the problem and solution parts of the Eschatological Discourse combined is framed within an *inclusio*. As Bauer and Traina define it, "inclusio is the repetition of words or phrases at the beginning and end of a unit, thus creating a bracket effect" of the form A. . . . . A^1.[144] In this case, what we have is an extended *inclusio* in which several thematic correspondences bracket Matt 24:3—25:46 into an indivisible unity within its broader setting: (1) The "sitting" terminology (καθημένου) in 24:3 bears an eschatological significance and anticipates Matt 25:31 where the Son of Man again "shall sit [καθίσει] on his throne of glory" to judge the nations. Here we have a little window into the essence of the Discourse—the Son of Man who sits in the latter is the Jesus who sits in the former. (2) The phrase πάντα τὰ ἔθνη (or the like) occurs in 24:9, 14 (cf. v. 7) as well as in 25:32. (3) Both ends also end with the theme or notion of finality (24:14; 25:32); the term αἰῶνος (24:3) is echoed by an almost synonymous term αἰώνιος (25:46). Moreover, the materials depict a reversal of fortune. Thus, the faithful disciples (brothers) of Jesus are hated and persecuted by all nations in 24:4–14, but they are rewarded with eternal life in 25:31–46 while the wicked nations are condemned.[145] The following diagram represents this extended *inclusio*:

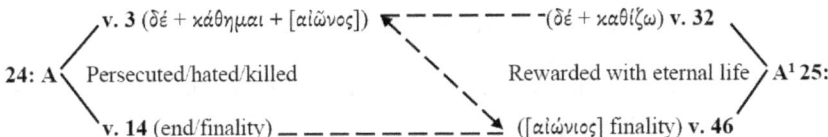

Extended *Inclusio* Framing the Eschatological Discourse.

Particulars of the Disciples' Question in 24:3

Before proceeding with the case for an alternation of two "particulars" in Jesus' response, it is important first to demonstrate that there are, in fact, two "particulars" in the disciples' question in 24:3. Understanding this question is critical for both the structure and interpretation of the Discourse.

144. Bauer and Traina, *Inductive Bible Study*, 117–18.

145. See Gray, *Least of My Brothers*, 358. She contends that the "least of my brothers" are Christians in general as opposed to the nations, and not any specific group of Christians.

Yet there is no consensus on the matter.[146] Most scholars maintain two questions, but some contend for three[147] or four,[148] while others argue for just one, including hyper-preterists for whom the question concerns only the destruction of Jerusalem[149] and some futurists for whom the question concerns only the future coming of Jesus.[150]

On this impasse, at least three considerations are key to arriving at a resolution. The first consideration is *synoptic*. Although the disciples' question in Mark and Luke appears to be singular and temple-specific, an examination of Jesus' response in these two evangelists still appears to reference two separate events (temple destruction and *parousia*), at least, in the judgment of the majority of exegetes, including Beasley-Murray.[151] In a sense, from a text-critical point of view, the clear singularity of Mark's and Luke's versions of the question would seem to make Matthew's more complex version the difficult reading with explanatory power for the former two. Moreover, allowing a degree of tentativeness regarding the current dating of the Gospels, the referential singularity of the question in Mark in particular, may reflect a post-70 effort to correct a presumed problem of the non-occurrence of the *parousia* at the same time as the destruction of the temple.[152]

The second consideration is *contextual*. As already noted above, the disciples' question in Matt 24:3 begins a new segment. Yet the question itself presupposes not only v. 2 but also 23:38–39 where the themes of "temple desolation" and "coming in the name of the Lord" are separated by the

---

146. Again, see Christian, "Questionable Inversion," 45–46.

147. E.g., Walvoord identifies three questions: (1) when shall these things be? (2) what shall be the sign of thy coming? and (3) what shall be the sign 'of the end of the world'? (*Kingdom Come*, 182); so also Ellis, for whom 24:4–14 answers question three, 24:15–22 answers question one, and 24:23–31 question two (*Matthew*, 87–88).

148. See Juza, *New Testament*, 25.

149. So, Wright, *Jesus and the Victory*, 345–46; Wright, *New Testament and the People*, 459–64.

150. Burnett (following Rolf Walker) takes the first καὶ in the disciples' question to be epexegetical, such that the second part explains the meaning of the first part. He claims that Matthew has reworked Mark in 24:3 so that "the discourse deals only with the parousia and the consummation of the age" (*Testament*, 207, 224–25).

151. See Beasley-Murray, *Jesus and the Last Days*, 350–75.

152. Against Wright's claims that there is no real need to imagine that Mark 13 was written in light of the events of 70 CE (*Jesus and the Victory*, 340), "perhaps the majority" of scholars, as Kloppenborg, "Evocatio Deorum," 420n3, suggests, dates Mark in the period after 70 CE. Kloppenborg argues that Mark 13:1–2 is a retrospective account of the fate of the temple (428). Similarly, Zeichmann has recently argued that based on the geopolitical administration, coinage, and tax policies reflected in the taxation episode (Mark 12:13–17), Mark was written not earlier than 29 August 71 CE ("Date of Mark's Gospel").

temporal phrase ἕως ἄν. Although not absolutely necessary, given a certain understanding of what Jesus means (treated below), the saying in 23:39 may evoke Jesus' *coming again*, hence the disciples' second question.[153] Even if we set aside such an evocative connection between 23:39 and 24:3c, the disciples already have a basis in 16:27 for assuming that the destruction of the temple will be one thing and the *parousia* and end of the age another, since, in this verse, no notion of temple destruction is conceivable.

The third consideration is *grammatical*. That is, how does the organization of 24:3 indicate how many questions there are? On this, we should note that the question consists of two clauses—the *when* (πότε) and the *what* (τί) clauses:

24:3
- A: πότε ταῦτα ἔσται (→ 24:2 ──────────→ 23:38)
- καί
- B: τί τὸ σημεῖον τῆς σῆς παρουσίας καὶ συντελείας τοῦ αἰῶνος; (------→ 23:39)

Grammatical Arrangement and Connections of 24:3.

In this arrangement, the two instances of καί are similar in the sense that they connect additional material. However, the first instance connects the two clauses in such a way as to strengthen the differentiation indicated by πότε and τί. Clauses A and B are of equal status but not semantically continuous. In light of Matt 17:17, for example,[154] if the implied author intended these parts to be understood as the same event, it would have been possible to, at least, suggest it by the exclusion of this first καί thereby implying a restatement or an apposition of some sort.[155] As shown, the demonstrative ταῦτα in clause A mimics the same phrase ταῦτα πάντα in v. 2 referring to the temple's fate as hinted in 23:38, but παρουσίας and συντελείας τοῦ αἰῶνος in clause B are likely evoked (but not necessarily) by 23:39, certainly by 16:27.[156]

Furthermore, in clause B, the second instance of καί binds two substantives of the same case (παρουσίας and συντελείας) in an

---

153. Cf. Lambrecht, "Parousia Discourse," 317; Brown, *Introduction*, 198.

154. Notice that without an intervening καί, the two parts of Jesus' question are in apposition and mean the same thing. In Mark 13:4 and Luke 21:7, the question of the disciples is undifferentiated because the repetition of ταῦτα in both parts of the πότε . . . καί . . . τί construction cancels out such differentiation.

155. Contra Wright, who ignores the καί in 24:3 and reads the question appositionally (*Jesus and the Victory*, 346).

156. I will discuss 23:39 in more detail in chapter 5.

article-substantive-καί-substantive construction. This construction substantially fits the Granville Sharp well-known rule:

> When the copulative καί connects two nouns of the same case, [viz. nouns (either substantive or adjective, or participle) of personal description reflecting office, dignity, affinity, or connection, and attributes, properties, or qualities, good or ill,] if the article ὁ or any of its cases, precedes the first of the said nouns or participles, and is not repeated before the second noun or participle, the latter always relates to the same person that is expressed or described by the first noun or participle: i.e., it denotes a farther description of the first-named person.[157]

Sharp restricts this rule to singular, personal descriptive, and non-proper nouns, specifically in texts where Christ's deity is the subject.[158] As such, παρουσίας and συντελείας being impersonal nouns, do not meet the rule's requirement. However, it is justifiable to apply this rule here.[159] First, not only is there a singular governing article (τῆς), but there is also a singular governing "sign" (τὸ σημεῖον). Second, Sharp's rule may indeed admit of impersonal substantives. For example, the article-substantive-καί-substantive construction is employed in 24:36 (περὶ δὲ τῆς ἡμέρας ἐκείνης καὶ ὥρας) where it is clear that ἡμέρας and ὥρας (both impersonal) refer to the same event. In the same way, παρουσίας and συντελείας are most likely related as identical, simultaneous, or complementary in the sense that the second further describes the first.[160] Thus, the breaking of clause B into two, making three questions, is unwarranted.[161]

Based on these three factors, it seems legitimate to conclude that the disciples' question consists of two particulars—temple destruction and *parousia*/end of the age—as two distinct events that Jesus goes ahead to address. Thus, we must dismiss the claims of a single and triple question by hyper-preterists and some futurists respectively. Juza's claim of four questions

---

157. Sharp, *Remarks*, 3.

158. For the validity of and nuanced discussion on Granville Sharp's Rule, see Wallace, *Grammar*, 270–90.

159. So also Christian, "Questionable Inversion," 48, although he provides no cogent justification.

160. See Porter, *Idioms*, 110. In Wallace's description of the article-substantive-καί-substantive construction (TSKS), "that connection always indicates at least some sort of *unity*. At a higher level, it may connote *equality*. At the highest level it may indicate *identity*" (*Grammar*, 270). Although he takes the instance in Matt 24:3 as a "theologically significant" and "ambiguous impersonal TSKS construction" (288n87), he does not discuss it.

161. Contra Walvoord, *Kingdom Come*, 182; Ellis, *Matthew*, 87–88.

based on the response of Jesus is unnecessary,[162] as is also the assumption that the disciples' question constitutes a mistaken conflation of the temple destruction with παρουσία and συντελεία which Jesus then goes on to correct—an assumption that has become axiomatic in many interpretations.[163] As I will argue later, such an assumption remains unsupported in the text.

Particularization and Discourse Structure of Matt 24:15—25:46

So far, I have argued that Matt 24:3 sets the stage for the Eschatological Discourse with the session of Jesus, and the question of the disciples consisting of two "particulars." I have also argued that 24:4-14 represents all eschatological history, hence a generalization. A further claim of this study is that the two elements of the disciples' question in 24:3 are taken up and particularized in an alternating manner in 24:15—25:46. Despite the intricate and closely interwoven nature of this segment, the implied reader can still discern distinctions by paying attention to the interchange of discourse connectives in addition to thematic associations.

Before getting into the details, I set forth the broad structural movement of this segment as follows: the conjunction οὖν in 24:15 marks the transition from Jesus' initial general remarks to his response to the first of the two "particulars" of the disciples' question (the fate of the temple) ending in v. 25. Again, the conjunction οὖν is used in v. 26 to mark a discourse transition to the second of the two "particulars" of the question (the *parousia*) ending in v. 31. With these two topical "particulars" established, Jesus answers the disciples' two questions. However, he proceeds to develop/clarify each "particulars" in the form of an analogy(ies) signaled by δέ. Within this segment as a unity, δέ is both discontinuous and developmental. Thus, vv. 32-35 opens with δέ, signaling discontinuity with v. 31 while introducing a developing/clarifying analogy in respect to the destruction of the temple. But δέ occurs also in v. 29, which raises the question as to what vv. 29-31 develops—the temple's fate (vv. 15-25) or the parousia (vv. 26-28).

The δέ in v. 29 indeed occasions a disconnect, but there is strong evidence that the development it introduces relates to the *parousia* already explicitly mentioned in v. 27. The implied reader would most readily connect the "sign" in the disciples' second question and the "sign" in v. 29.[164] Thus, vv. 29-31 must be held together with vv. 26-28 as concerning the *parousia*. As to which of the two topics vv. 32-35 develops or clarifies in view of the

---

162. Juza, *New Testament*, 25.
163. Juza, *New Testament*, 24n30; note his discussion in 28-33.
164. Cf. Lunde, "Salvation-Historical Implication," 176-77.

opening δέ in v. 32, we should observe that the phrase ὅταν ἴδητε ("when you see") in v. 33 is already used v. 15 to introduce the first temple-specific topic. Both "when-you-see" phrases properly relate to the disciples' "when-will-the-temple-destroyed" question in v. 3. Therefore, it must be concluded that v. 33 (hence vv. 32–35) concerns the temple's destruction rather than the *parousia*.

Finally, δέ is used in v. 36 to indicate discontinuity from v. 35 and to begin an extended development (in the form of analogies) of the nature of the *parousia* going all the way to 25:46, hence the reappearance of the term in vv. 37 and 39. This gives an alternating movement of the form: a(T^1)-b(P^1)-a(T^2)-b(P^2), where a-b-a-b represents interchange; T^1 = 24:15–25; P^1 = 24:26–31; T^2 = 24:32–35; and P^2 = 24:36—25:46.[165] I will proceed to show the validity of this movement by focusing on the discourse values of the conjunctions as articulated in chapter 2.

First, the conjunction οὖν at the beginning of a(T^1), i.e., 24:15, signals a shift to the first concern of the disciples' question—when will these things be? There is neither digression at v. 15 nor strict logical continuity with vv. 4–14. While Matthew generally employs οὖν to signal inference,[166] there is virtually no inference here. It certainly does not indicate a conclusion or summary of the preceding section.[167] On the contrary, οὖν in v. 15 signals (a) discontinuity from the general period sketched in vv. 4–14 and (b) transition to new material, initiating response to the first specific topic in the disciples' question in v. 3. Denniston's characterization of οὖν as initiating "a new point, or a new stage in the march of thought"[168] fits the use of οὖν here, as do Levinsohn's "distinctive development"[169] and Black's idea of "new conceptualization."[170] Moreover, in line with Westfall's study, the collocation of οὖν in v. 15 with an imperative (νοείτω) plausibly affirms here not only a "horizontal discontinuity" but also a "vertical discontinuity in the [rhetorical] creation of emphasis."[171]

Three observations appear to validate or strengthen this discontinuity: (1) The reader/hearer will more readily hear a connection between "therefore, when you see" (v. 15) and "when will these things be" in v. 3. (2) The description of "tribulation" in v. 21 (θλῖψις μεγάλη οἵα οὐ γέγονεν ἀπ' ἀρχῆς

---

165. T = reference to the destruction of the temple, and P = reference to the *parousia*.
166. E.g., Matt 5:19, 23; 6:31, 34, etc.
167. Cf. Matt 7:12, 24; 13:18.
168. Denniston, *Greek Particles*, 426.
169. Levinsohn, "'Therefore' or 'Wherefore,'" 325.
170. Black, *Sentence Conjunction*, 263.
171. Westfall, "Οὖν in the New Testament," 300.

κόσμου ἕως τοῦ νῦν οὐδ' οὐ μὴ γένηται) of vv. 15-25 is unique and local as opposed to the more global and generic description (θλῖψις) in v. 9 of vv. 4-14. (2) In relation to this, there appears to exist a certain disconnect between the fact that the disciples are to expect to be betrayed, killed, and hated "by all nations" (ὑπὸ πάντων τῶν ἐθνῶν) in v. 9 of vv. 4-14, but must flee in vv. 16-20 of vv. 15-25. The warning to flee in order to avoid death in the latter seems inconsistent with the notion that endurance amid adversity is the key to being saved in the former (v. 13 of vv. 4-14).

Second, the use of οὖν at the beginning of b(P¹), i.e., 24:26 signals another transition to a new topic, this time, the *parousia* and consummation—the second concern of the disciples' question. This may seem difficult at first, but only until we consider several supporting facts: (1) There exists a clear notion of conclusion in the clause, ἰδοὺ προείρηκα ὑμῖν (24:25). (2) Verse 26 is linked with v. 27 using the substantiating conjunction γάρ. Since v. 27 is a supportive description of the *parousia* and thus cannot stand alone, it implies that both verses must be held together, and both together concern the *parousia*. Consequently, the occurrence of *parousia* in v. 27 cannot be taken as just a parenthetical aside.[172] (3) In light of Westfall's conclusion, the collocation of οὖν with a conditional particle in v. 26 serves to re-engage the audience or implied reader "in a more rhetorical and emphatic way than propositional statements."[173] While Westfall also notes that οὖν with conditionals functions majorly as summaries and conclusions,[174] the fact that v. 25 is already a concluding statement, permits οὖν to signal a transition in v. 26 to the second of the two particulars of the disciples' question—the *parousia*. That v. 26 is somewhat a repetition of v. 23 should not deceive us into maintaining a seamless reading here, disregarding the transitional role of the conjunction οὖν. What the repetition shows is that the warning against deception by messianic pretenders applies to the question of the impending eschatological catastrophe in Jerusalem as well as to that of the *parousia* of Christ. (4) A division within vv. 15-28 is not unthinkable. As noted in chapter 2, Chrysostom begins the *parousia* of Christ in v. 23. Carson argues for demarcation in v. 22 and regards vv. 22-28 as a continuation of the general period in vv. 4-14.[175] The view that the objective point of demarcation is v. 26 instead is supported by Ladd.[176]

172. Contra France, *Matthew*, 917; Wilson, *When Will These Things Happen?*, 153; cf. Gibbs, *Jerusalem and Parousia*, 187.

173. Westfall, "Οὖν in the New Testament," 292.

174. Westfall, "Οὖν in the New Testament, 291, 297.

175. Carson, "Matthew," 557; although Davies and Allison find a division at v. 22 unpersuasive (*Matthew*, 3:357n192).

176. See Ladd, *Blessed Hope*, 72-73.

Third, having made initial entries of the two "particulars," the Discourse proceeds with the re-entry of these "particulars" in the same order. Each topic is re-introduced using δέ connective and further developed using an analogy(ies). Taking together the discourse-analytical studies conducted by Levinsohn, Black, Runge, and many others, the only reasonable conclusion is that δέ is marked for +discontinuity +development.[177] Some Grammarians also ascribe similar functions to δέ. For example, we have already noted Levinsohn's use of Winer's view that δέ "subjoins something new, different, and distinct from what proceeds, but . . . not sharply opposed to it."[178] Winer also shows that δέ is used "when after a parenthesis or digression, the interrupted train of thought is taken up again."[179] Thus, he could further claim that the δέ and οὖν "most readily approximate in meaning."[180] Wallace also shares this view when he categorizes δέ, together with οὖν, as transitional conjunctions used when a change to a new topic is involved.[181]

This study contends that at certain points within the Eschatological Discourse, the conjunction δέ is used in a similar discontinuous or transitional manner as οὖν but with the added nuance of development. While δέ is commonplace in the Eschatological Discourse,[182] the instances in 24:32 and 24:36 appear structurally significant in helping to switch topics and complete the interchange a(T^2)-b(P^2). First, δέ is used at the beginning of a(T^2), i.e., v. 32 to signal discontinuity with v. 31 which belongs to the *parousia* passage.[183] I will show later that vv. 32–33 thematically supports the uniqueness of this δέ as introducing a reference to the temple topic.[184] Second, δέ at the beginning of b(P^2), i.e., v. 36, signals discontinuity with v. 35 and the re-entry of the *parousia* topic which remains the focus until 25:46. Accordingly, the instances of δέ after v. 36 relate to matters subordinate and explicatory to the theme of "unknownness-of-the-time-of-*parousia*" (vv. 36–37), with most of the instances representing intraepisodic and/or intrasentential

---

177. See discussion in chapter 2, pp. 41–43.
178. Levinsohn, *Discourse Features*, 72; Winer, *Treatise*, 551–52.
179. Winer, *Treatise*, 553.
180. Winer, *Treatise*, 570.
181. Wallace, *Grammar*, 674.
182. Matt 24:2–3, 6, 8, 13, 19–20, 22, 29, 32, 35–36, 43, 48–49; 25:2, 4–6, 8–12, 15, 18–19, 22, 24, 26, 29, 31, 33, 38–39, 46.
183. While many interpreters begin a new section in v. 29, e.g., Davies and Allison, *Matthew*, 3:345, 357; Blomberg, *Matthew*, 361; Carter thinks it arbitrary to separate vv. 28 and 29 ("Are There Imperial Texts?," 468n5); *Matthew and the Margins*, 469, 476.
184. See pp. 210–12.

connections.[185] This structural analysis of the particularization segment takes the following form:

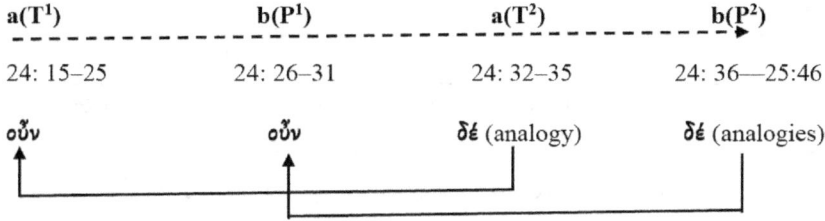

Interchange of Particulars within the Eschatological Discourse.

To conclude, the question may be raised as to why the Eschatological Discourse is structured in this fashion. What is the purpose of this alternating structure? There are several considerations in this regard. First, linguistic studies suggest that while readers in general tend to assume a maintained discourse continuity, they will likely discern patterns, structural disjunctions, and resumptions based on segmentation markers used by authors.[186] Second, the alternation of materials, like other forms of rhetorical structures, is not uncommon, especially with prophetic-apocalyptic writings as discussed in chapter 3. Third, in terms of purpose, and as I explained in chapter 2, such an arrangement strengthens semantic relationships and textual unity. In this case, the alternation of temple destruction and *parousia* strengthens the rhetorical and hermeneutical resonance between the two events. And fourth, the alternation between temple destruction and *parousia* is consistent with Matthew's literary tendency, especially in light of the broader narrative-discourse interchange which most Matthean scholars acknowledge. The alternating structure I have argued is consistent with what some have noted but have scarcely explored. Mounce rightly comments on Matt 24: "The essential problem is that Matthew seems to move back and forth between an impending crisis (the fall of Jerusalem) and the end of the age."[187]

The overall structure of the Eschatological Discourse proposed in this study may be represented as follows:

---

185. Matt 24:43, 48–49; 25:2, 4–6, 8–12, 15, 18–19, 22, 24, 26, 29.
186. E.g., Bestgen, "Temporal Adverbials."
187. Mounce, *Matthew*, 221; see also Witherington, *Matthew*, 453.

The Disciples' Question	Jesus' Response	
	Generalization: Overview of Eschatological History	Particularization: Temple-Parousia Interchange
24:3	vv. 4–14	vv. 15—25:46
		a(T^1)-b(P^1)-a(T^2)-b(P^2)

T = reference to the destruction of the Temple/aftermath; P = reference to the *Parousia*; T^1 = vv. 15–25; P^1 = vv. 26–31; T^2 = vv. 32–35; P^2 = vv. 36—25:46

Table 5: Proposed Structure of the Eschatological Discourse

5

An Interpretation of Matt 24:3—25:46

Introduction

HAVING LAID THE HERMENEUTICAL and structural groundwork in the preceding chapters, this chapter focuses squarely on the interpretation of the Eschatological Discourse. My goal here is not a deep and comprehensive commentary on the Discourse, but an extended engagement with pressing interpretive issues, which are many. I will begin by looking at the Discourse setting and then work my way through to the end, following the structure argued in the preceding chapter.

Discourse Setting (Matt 23:37—24:2)

The crisis that culminates in the Eschatological Discourse has been brewing throughout the Gospel of Matthew with the interweaving motifs of resistance and judgment.[1] In the immediate context, the Discourse flows directly from 23:1—24:2. Here, the judgment of Jerusalem comes to a chilling climax in Jesus' double prediction of the destruction of the temple. The arrangement of the material into a sandwich—prediction /exit/ prediction—is significant for interpretation.

---

1. Matt 3:7–12; 7:19, 26–28; 8:11–12; 10:14–15; 11:20–24; 12:41–42; 13:40–42, 47–50; 21:40–43; 22:4–7, 11–14; 23:1–39; cf. Wilson, *When Will These Things Happen?*, 66–73.

In the first half of the sandwich (23:37), Jesus accuses Jerusalem of frustrating his attempts "to gather your children" (ἐπισυναγαγεῖν τὰ τέκνα σου); therefore, in v. 38, he declares, "Your house is left to you desolate" (ἀφίεται ὑμῖν ὁ οἶκος ὑμῶν ἔρημος). This is a prediction of or, at least, a proleptic reference to the temple's destruction.[2] That which, on entrance, Jesus referred to as οἶκός μου ("my house" [21:13][3]) has now become οἶκος ὑμῶν ("your house" [23:38]).[4] Matthew 24:2 constitutes the second half of the sandwich. Thus, the declaration, οὐ μὴ ἀφεθῇ ὧδε λίθος ἐπὶ λίθον ὃς οὐ καταλυθήσεται ("no stone will be left here upon a stone which shall not be destroyed"), further reiterates the fate of the temple. As Matt 22:7 already hints, Jerusalem is steeped in rebellion; therefore, the temple will certainly be destroyed.[5]

Within the sandwich are two important developments. First, in 23:39 Jesus declares, οὐ μή με ἴδητε ἀπ᾽ ἄρτι ἕως ἂν εἴπητε εὐλογημένος ὁ ἐρχόμενος ἐν ὀνόματι κυρίου ("you will [certainly] not see me [again] until you say, 'Blessed is the one who comes in the name of the Lord'" [23:39]). Second, Jesus exits the temple (24:1) in an act reminiscent of the departure of the glory of God from the first temple.[6] Since Matthew believes Jesus to be "God with us" (1:23), this exit is an ominous sign of imminent destruction.

We should further probe into 23:39. What exactly does Jesus mean by this saying? The two broad interpretations are that it refers to the *parousia* or that it alludes to the destruction of the temple. The *parousia* interpretation breaks down into four views:[7] (1) Some interpret the saying positively as a promise or an indication that Israel will eventually be saved at the *parousia*.[8] Peter Fiedler claims that the saying, in light of Ps 117:26a (LXX) and

---

2. The association of ἀφίεται and ἔρημος will be important for the interpretation of 24:40–41.

3. Cf. 23:21; Walker, *Jesus and the Holy City*, 28, takes these verses to indicate Jesus' positive view of the temple.

4. Allison, "Matt. 23:39 = Luke 13:35b," 76, thinks that "your house" includes the city and temple ("Matt. 23:39 = Luke 13:35b as a conditional prophecy"). This is possible in light of Dan 9:26 (LXX) where a singular pronoun (αὐτοῦ) embraces "the city and the sanctuary." However, in view of 23:13, 24:1, and the fact that ἔρημος ("desolate") in 23:38 anticipates ἐρημώσεως ("desolation") in 24:15, it is better to take "your house" as a reference to the temple in particular; so Evans, *Matthew*, 399.

5. Matt 12:6 (cf. 26:61) suggests an imminent temple replacement. Walker, *Jesus and the Holy City*, 29–31, argues that Matthew presents the charge made against Jesus in 26:61 as "a true one," and given the repetition of the charge in 27:40, Matthew saw in it a reference to the resurrection which for him represents the rebuilt temple.

6. Cf. Ezek 10:18; 1 En. 89.56; 2 Bar. 8.2.

7. Luz, *Matthew*, 163 has it in three categories.

8. See Keener, *Matthew*, 58–59; Gundry, *Matthew*, 474; Blomberg, *Matthew*, 351;

Matt 21:9, indicates that the *parousia* of Christ is the "Heilsgeschehen für ganz Israel."[9] Such a view derives from an unlikely interpretation of Rom 11:25-27 (cf. Acts 3:19-21) than it does from the Matthean context. Reacting to the view, Luz rightly asserts:

> the announcement of a possibility or even the reality of Israel's conversion would be surprising, rhetorically awkward, and would go beyond the scope of the context. . . . such a statement would be completely isolated in the Gospel of Matthew. It would have no place in the eschatological statement of 24:29—25:46 . . . [and would be] internally illogical.[10]

(2) Most ancient and modern commentators take the saying negatively as a declaration of judgment. In this sense, the acclaim will be a forced acknowledgment of Jesus by Israel, but one made too late at the *parousia*.[11] Luz offers, perhaps, the strongest defense for this view by appealing to several passages in 1 En. (see 48:5; 55:4; 61:7-11; 62:6-16; 10; 63:1-12).[12] There is indeed a striking parallel between these passages and Matt 23:39. However, the Enochian passages speak of a forced acknowledgment of the Lord, specifically by pagan overlords—"the mighty kings and rulers of the earth" (cf. 1 En. 46:7)—not by Jerusalem and its religious leaders, the actual addressees in Matt 23:39. Moreover, whereas Jerusalem will not see Jesus *until* they say the acclaim, these mighty kings and rulers of the earth acknowledge and bless the Lord only after he sits on the throne and executes judgment, a scenario which clearly differs from what the Matthean saying demands. By using ἕως ἄν ("until"), it is implied that the acclaim is a condition for, not the result of seeing him again; the idea is not that they will see him and then make the acclaim.

(3) William Hendriksen advocates a sort of double *entendre* in which the "blessed" acclaim will be joyful proclamation for those who will have repented at the Lord's coming, but for others, remorseful rather than repentant proclamation.[13] Although this interpretation is a safe compromise

---

Talbert, *Matthew*, 260; Nolland, *Matthew*, 952–53; Harrington, *Matthew*, 329; Evans, *Matthew*, 399; Senior, *Matthew*, 264; Hill, *Matthew*, 316; Morris, *Matthew*, 592; Fiedler, *Matthäusevangelium*, 358.

9. Fiedler, *Matthäusevangelium*, 358.

10. Luz, *Matthew*, 163–64.

11. E.g., Calvin, *Harmony*, 3:71; Luz, *Matthew*, 164; Meier, *Matthew*, 275; Hare, *Matthew*, 272.

12. Luz, *Matthew*, 164.

13. Hendriksen, *Matthew*, 840–41.

that combines the positive view (1) and negative view (2), it remains a mere assumption with nothing to support it within the text.

(4) Allison takes a *via-media* approach by interpreting Matt 23:39 as a conditional prophecy.[14] First, he demonstrates that belief in the contingency of Israel's salvation on repentance is grounded in rabbinic sources. Second, he highlights the contingent function of ἕως in Greek. In his view, ἕως, commonly translated "until," is more properly conditional than temporal, and, therefore, close to the sense of "unless." Thus, "the text . . . means not, when the Messiah comes, his people will bless him, but rather, when his people bless him, the Messiah will come."[15] Third, Allison argues that the structure of Matt 23:39 supports the conditional interpretation. And fourth, he views this conditional interpretation as a middle ground that offsets the weaknesses of the positive (salvation at the *parousia*) and negative (Judgment at the *parousia*) interpretations.

Theophilos considers Allison's submission unconvincing, further noting that there is no indication that "Matthew intended to recall some sort of echo with the Jewish literary sources."[16] Luz also challenges this conditional interpretation by claiming that "'until' cannot introduce a condition" because "Jerusalem will greet the parousia-Christ with the words of Ps 118 only after they have seen him."[17] Luz's view here appears opposite to the saying. As already noted above, the conjunctive-particle phrase, ἕως ἄν, validly indicates conditionality.[18] The real problem with Allison's view is that it supposes that the *parousia* can take place only if Israel, as a whole, repents. In my view, this incorrectly attributes causality to ἕως ἄν. This conditional phrase does not require causal contingency between two events such that event 'B' happens immediately after, as a necessary sequel or consequence of event 'A'.[19] Allison's view, just as the ones above, has no support in the Eschatological Discourse, since, as I shall argue, the *parousia* is described in Matt 24:29–31 and further in 25:31–46 without any notion of Israel's repentance. Instead of any such repentance, the Discourse is concerned with the safety and salvation of only the elect of Israel and those of the nations (24:22, 24, 31).

The second interpretation of 23:39 relates it to the destruction of Jerusalem. In defending this interpretation, Theophilos appeals to the

---

14. Allison, "Matt. 23:39 = Luke 13:35b," esp. 77–80.
15. Allison, "Matt. 23:39 = Luke 13:35b," 77.
16. Theophilos, *Abomination*, 49–50.
17. Luz, *Matthew*, 164.
18. E.g., Matt 2:13; 5:26; 10:11, 23; 13:30.
19. Cf. Matt 5:18; 12:20; 16:28; 22:44; 24:34.

Greco-Roman tradition of entry processions. He contends that because Jesus was given an "unwelcome[ing] response" in Jerusalem, quite unlike the grand welcome accorded to victorious generals or kings when they entered cities, the acclaim will be made too late when the Son of Man comes to destroy the city.[20] There is some contextual awareness in this interpretation, especially with respect to the motif of judgment. But that is as far as it goes. Again, there is nothing in Matt 24–25 or even extra-biblical sources to indicate such acclaim in connection with the destruction of Jerusalem and the temple. The mourning in 24:30 is certainly not such acclaim.

Given the issues raised above, it is my considered opinion that these interpretations all miss the point. Several factors suggest that the "blessed" acclaim will, in fact, never be made by Jerusalem and its religious leaders.[21] First, as many interpreters avow, Matt 23:39 alludes to Ps 118:26 (117:26 LXX). There, the acclaim is to be said ἐξ οἴκου Κυρίου ("from the house of the Lord"). However, while the acclaim is made beginning from outside Jerusalem (21:9–11) until it fades into "Hosanna to the Son of David" in the lips of children (21:15), it is rejected by the house itself; and there is no guarantee that Jesus will be blessed *from that house* until judgment falls on it. The fact that Matthew knows nothing of a future rebuilt temple from which the acclaim may be expected does not help the association of the saying with the *parousia*.

Second, given the use of γὰρ conjunction, 23:39 substantiates 23:38 in a causal sense. This implies that the saying strictly relates to the temple. France is right in noting that the γὰρ-link indicates "the only condition on which the desertion of the house can be reversed or averted."[22] Thus, when Jesus says, "you will certainly not see me *from now*" (23:39a), he means that he will no longer return to the temple until, *from that house*, Jerusalem and its leaders acknowledge him as the one *coming* (i.e., "who has come") in the name of the Lord (v. 39b). As such, 23:39 does not refer to a future second coming, even though it might evoke it. This interpretation is supported by the fact that, in Matthew, Jesus never again appears in the temple from that point on.

Third, the surrounding context makes clear that Jerusalem would not, indeed, acknowledge their Messiah; instead, they would conspire to have him killed ((23:33–37; 26:3–4). All hope that they will bless him from that temple is lost when, under their judgment, Jesus declares, "From now on *you will see* the Son of Man sitting at the right hand of power and *coming* on

---

20. Theophilos, *Abomination*, 50–56.
21. Cf. France, *Matthew*, 888–89; Gardner, *Matthew*, 338.
22. France, *Matthew*, 884.

the clouds of heaven" (26:64). As it appears, this solemn declaration recalls and reverses the "*you will certainly not see* me from now until" of 23:39. The saying in 26:64, in context, alludes to the vindication of Jesus as the Christ. Against its wish, Jerusalem will "see" (perceive) this vindication in his resurrection (enthronement), a vindication re-enacted in the destruction of the temple and specifically implied here in 26:64 by the "coming on the cloud" motif.

When combined with the fact that, in the Eschatological Discourse, Jesus speaks not of the hope of Israel as a whole but only of the safety and salvation of the elect (24:22, 24, 31), these observations compel the conclusion that 23:39 is meant to accentuate the rebellion of Jerusalem and its leaders, indicating not what they will, but what they will not confess; hence it points to the eventual destruction of the temple.[23] In other words, the saying does not refer to the *parousia* even if it evokes it.

Problem and Solution

Problem: The Disciples' Question

In Matt 24:2, Jesus responds to the disciples' curiosity about the temple with an emphatic prediction of utter destruction. This prediction accentuates 23:38–39, leading to the problem expressed in 24:3—πότε ταῦτα ἔσται καὶ τί τὸ σημεῖον τῆς σῆς παρουσίας καὶ συντελείας τοῦ αἰῶνος; (when will *these things* be, and what is the sign of your *parousia* and consummation of the age?). Any interpretation of the ensuing Discourse rises or falls on the understanding of this question, hence the need to critically evaluate it. I will carry out this evaluation by addressing three related aspects of the matter: (1) How many questions are there in the disciples' question? (2) How legitimate is/are the question(s)? And (3) does Jesus reject or correct the disciples' question(s) in whole or in part? Parsing the matter in this threefold manner provides needed clarity for adequate interpretation.

Number of Questions

On this first issue, I have already argued in chapter 4 (pp. 114–18) that the disciples' question consists of two particulars—the fate of the temple and the sign of the *parousia* and the end of the age. There, I contended that

---

23. Luke also suggests this by having the saying brought forward (13:35) and later having the disciples make the acclaim while the Jewish leaders resist it, leading to the prophecy of impending destruction (19:37–44).

the plausibility of this twofold view of the question has three warrants: (1) synoptic warrant—on the assumption that Matthew used Mark, it is difficult to see any reason why Matthew has transformed the question other than to indicate that there are two events referenced, (2) contextual warrant—the second coming of Jesus may be evoked in 23:39; but even if we exclude such evocation here, Jesus had earlier in 16:27 spoken of his "second coming" completely without any reference to temple's desolation or destruction, and (3) grammatical warrant—the structure of the question indicates that two separate events are referenced.

Here, I consider a further reason for taking the disciples' question in 24:3 to be two rather than one, three, or four. The number of the disciples' question(s) ultimately depends on the term συντέλεια. We must be clear about what this term means and how it is used in Matt 24:3. In the first place, it must be recognized that συντέλεια is not an especially eschatological term. It is used to describe the "end," utter destruction of something, or when something is consummated or finished.[24] The instances in the apocalyptic section of Daniel reference the infamous acts of Antiochus IV Epiphanes. There, συντέλεια refers to the utter desecration or pollution of the temple;[25] the verbal συντελέω is used for the making an end of sin and fulfilling of vision/prophecy;[26] the desecration of the temple is described as ἡ συντέλεια αὐτοῦ ("its end");[27] and the end of the desolator himself is called his συντέλεια.[28] The term can be used in other ways too. For example, Jesus is said to appear once (ἅπαξ) to take away sin in the συντελείᾳ τῶν αἰώνων ("end of the ages").[29]

Thus, συντέλεια may be applied to different notions of "end." In Dan 8–12, it refers especially to the desecration of the temple not its destruction.[30] While the instance of συντέλεια in Matt 24:3 most likely alludes to

24. Cf. LXX Exod 23:16; Deut 11:12; Josh 4:8; Judg 20:40; 1 Sam 8:3; 20:41; 1 Kgs 6:22, 25; 2 Kgs 13:17, 19; 2 Chr 24:23; Ezra 9:14; Neh 9:31; Ps 58:13–14; 118:96; Job 26:10; 30:2; Amos 1:14; 8:8; 9:5; Nah 1:3, 8–9; Hab 1:9, 15; 3:19; Zeph 1:18; Jer 4:27; 5:10, 18; 26:28; Ezek 11:13; 13:13; 20:17; 21:33; 22:12; Dan 4:28, 31, 34; 11:6, 13.

25. LXX Dan 8:19 in light of context (vv. 9–27, esp. 11–14).

26. Dan 9:24; cf. MT.

27. Dan 9:26; this is so because (1) while the term φθείρω here can mean "to destroy," in context, it is more properly taken as "to corrupt," and (2) 9:24, 27 implies that the temple still stands. Cf. 11:27, 35–36, 40; 12:4, 6–7.

28. Dan 11:45 (cf. 9:27).

29. Heb 9:28; cf 1 Cor 10:11 where Paul refers to his time as already τὰ τέλη τῶν αἰώνων.

30. Although, see Evans, "Predictions," 98; he cites Liv. Pro. 12:10–12 where the "end" (συντέλεια) is used in reference to the destruction of the temple; cf. "The Lives of the Prophets," in Charlesworth, Old Testament Pseudepigrapha, 2:393.

the Danielic passages, we must keep in mind that biblical authors are wont to re-appropriate source materials.³¹ This clearly appears to be the case in Matthew. Thus, in association with *parousia* (24:3) and the final eschatological judgment (25:31–46), συντέλεια (24:3) is given a unique application. Moreover, in apparent anticipation of the Discourse, συντέλεια is already established in Matt 13 (vv. 39–40, 49–50) as that "end" when the wicked will be finally separated from the righteous and cursed to everlasting punishment.³² Nothing in Matthew suggests that this separation was fulfilled in the destruction of the temple. Therefore, Matthew's συντέλεια, it must be concluded, is a different "end"—the consummation of history—not the end of temple.³³ In other words, and based on the three warrants identified above, a distinction is to be maintained between the destruction of the temple on the one hand, and the *parousia* and συντελείας τοῦ αἰῶνος on the other.

Legitimacy of the Disciples' Question and Understanding

The second issue that needs to be considered concerns the legitimacy of the disciples' questions. By legitimacy, I mean whether the questions are valid and warranted or whether the disciples are mistaken or have confused the two events, unable to tell them apart. This latter view goes back, at least, to Calvin. The disciples, according to Calvin,

> had considered from childhood that the temple would stand to the end of time and had the idea deeply rooted in their minds, that they had not thought that the temple could fall down [*sic*] as long as the world's order stood. So as soon as Christ said the temple would perish, at once their minds turned to the consummation of the age. Because (one error leading to another) they were sure that immediately Christ began to reign they all would be very blessed, their minds fly to thoughts of triumph, overlooking warfare.³⁴

This assessment is echoed by several scholars today. Hagner states that the disciples "were unable to separate the two events in their minds, the

---

31. See discussion in chapter 3.

32. Cf. Kingsbury, *Matthew*, 29n119. Also, in both Matt 25:46 and 28:20, συντελείας τοῦ αἰῶνος implies the end of history.

33. Wright is probably correct that the συντελείας τοῦ αἰῶνος which the disciples expected, "was not the end of the space-time order, but the end of the present evil age" (*Jesus and the Victory*, 345–46; *New Testament and the People*, 299–301). But in saying this, he also implies that the "end" they expected was not merely the "end" of the temple.

34. Calvin, *Harmony*, 3:75.

destruction of the temple must entail the end of the age and the parousia of Jesus."[35] As Turner puts it, "in the disciples' thinking, the end of the temple would augur the end of the present world."[36] Davies and Allison think that the disciples' confusion derives from their assumption that ταῦτα πάντα in Matt 24:2 implies a complex of events: "The disciples' question seemingly presumes a close connexion between AD 70 and the end (cf. Mark 13), especially as 'these things' implies that the event prophesied in v. 2 belongs to a complex of eschatological events."[37] Likewise, although Juza is aware that "'these things'(ταῦτα [24:3]) most naturally refers to the events surrounding the temple's destruction," he claims that "the plural appears to carry the disciples' misunderstanding."[38] Juza thus concludes that "by juxtaposing multiple subjects (temple and parousia), *Matthew demonstrates that the disciples believed the destruction of the temple would accompany the parousia and the end of the age*."[39]

To both maintain this claim and still hold that the disciples ask two questions might appear contradictory. In any case, even granting that the disciples were thinking as these interpreters suppose, there is no literary basis for such a claim. Concerning whether the phrase "these things" in Matt 24:3 points to a complex of events (*per* Davies and Allison), the text also suggests the contrary. "These things" in 24:3 simply picks up from "all these things" (ταῦτα πάντα) in Matt 24:2 which explicitly refers to the *buildings* of the temple (τὰς οἰκοδομὰς τοῦ ἱεροῦ [24:1]).[40] In fact, since by their question the disciples imply that some sign will intervene between the destruction of the temple and the *parousia*/end of the age, it cannot be judged that they could not tell the events apart. Moreover, it is erroneous to suppose that if two events are juxtaposed or closely connected, then they must be thought to be simultaneous or accompany each other. The close linking of two different "comings" of Jesus without conflating them is already present in

35. Hagner, *Matthew*, 688.
36. Turner, *Matthew*, 569.
37. Davies and Allison, *Matthew*, 3:337.
38. Juza, *New Testament*, 25.
39. Juza, *New Testament*, 24–33 (esp. 24 [italics original]); see also Zahn, *Matthäus*, 664; Carson, "Matthew," 557; Blomberg, *Matthew*, 353; Gibbs, *Jerusalem and Parousia*, 178–81; France, *Matthew*, 895; Osborne, *Matthew*, 869.
40. See Gibbs, *Jerusalem and Parousia*, 179. Burnett's view (influenced by Mark's version) that ταῦτα points forward (cataphoric), so that the question is "when will these things be, i.e., what will be the sign of your advent and the consummation of the age" ("Prolegomenon," 100) is unlikely. A cataphoric view of ταῦτα in Matt 24:3 is made unlikely not only by the intervening καὶ, but also by the fact that a what-is-the-sign question (using τί) can hardly be synonymous or epexegetical to a when-will-these-things-be question (using πότε).

Matthew.[41] Often, events are juxtaposed for other effects, such as contrast or comparison, regardless of when such events occur in time. Accordingly, the best that can be said in Matt 24:3 is that the destruction of the temple and the *parousia* are placed closely together as comparable events.

Another way of supporting the notion that the disciples confused the temple destruction and the *parousia* in Matt 24:3 is by adducing their inadequate understanding elsewhere in Matthew and then extrapolating such in the Discourse.[42] Theodor Zahn notes Matt 16:22-23 and 20:21-22 as evidence that the disciples are both in error and impatient.[43] Gibbs goes further to categorize seventeen instances in which the disciples are portrayed by Matthew as showing a general lack of understanding (15:12, 15; 16:7; 17:4, 10), a failure to understand the nature of discipleship (8:21; 15:23; 16:22; 18:1, 21; 20:20), or a failure or weakness of faith (8:25; 14:15, 28; 15:33; 17:19).[44] Of these, the transfiguration episode (17:9-12) and the request of the mother of the sons of Zebedee (20:20-23) involve what he calls "eschatological misunderstanding." Based on these, Gibbs concludes that the awareness of these incidences of misunderstanding, in addition to the opening response of Jesus in 24:4, primes the implied reader to reject the point of view of the disciples' question in 24:3 as a mistaken conflation or joining together of the destruction of the temple and the consummation of the age.[45]

Of the instances of misunderstanding identified above, it should be noted that Jesus' reaction/response when the disciples are in error (esp. Matt 15:16-17; 16:7-12; 20:22) is completely different from his reaction/response in Matt 24. To be clear, I in no way suppose that the disciples had a perfect or even adequate understanding of all of Jesus' sayings. However, Gibbs' conclusion is inaccurate. Matthew also presents the disciples as capable of

---

41. Esp. 16:27-28.

42. Gibbs, *Jerusalem and Parousia*, 179-81; Patte, *Matthew*, 334, argues that Matt 24:1-2 warns the reader that the disciples "are still not trustworthy," their question confuses temple destruction and the coming of Jesus which are clearly separated in 23:37-39, therefore the reader is to expect that the entire discourse is "a polemical statement rejecting the disciples' question and their implications." Cf. Turner, *Matthew*, 569. See also Wright who caricatures the disciples by asserting that they "were not exactly at their sharpest in picking up redefinitions even of ideas with which they were already somewhat familiar," although he also feels confident that they would have understood that the destruction of the temple will be "the end of Israel's period of mourning and exile and the beginning of her freedom and vindication," and their own flight from Jerusalem as the "end of the exile" and YHWH becoming king (*Jesus and the Victory*, 345-46, 364).

43. Zahn, *Matthäus*, 664.

44. The number of instances amounts to fifteen times by my counting; 15:12 is not a valid case.

45. Gibbs, *Jerusalem and Parousia*, 81.

exhibiting both faith and understanding.⁴⁶ In 13:51, Matthew credits the disciples with or, at least, does not refute their claim of understanding regarding a matter of eschatology, even if this understanding happens after an explanation. Part of what they understand in that context is that the final "harvest" (θερισμός) will happen at the "end of the age" (συντέλεια αἰῶνός [13:39]), that the angels will separate the wicked from the righteous, and that the wicked will be judged by fire (13:40, 49). Thus, to summarily dismiss the disciples as lacking "eschatological understanding" is not only to deny any development in their thinking but also to distort the portrait of them that Matthew appears to paint.⁴⁷

Certainly, Gibbs' view that "if the disciples have 'gotten it wrong' so frequently, it is inherently likely that they are 'getting it wrong' once again"⁴⁸ is a mere assumption. The instances of misunderstanding do not necessarily prove that a misunderstanding is going on in 24:3. Such misunderstanding must be demonstrated by what Jesus or the implied author plainly states in the present text. It is instructive to note that the disciples do not ask a rationale (*why*) question. They also do not ask an explanatory (*what*) question in relation to the meaning of Jesus' prediction either in 23:38 or 24:1–3. They do not approach Jesus with a "what-did-you-mean" or "explain-it-to-us" question (cf. 13:36), but rather with a "when-will-these-things-happen" question.⁴⁹ The latter question implies, if not prove, an improvement rather than a deterioration of understanding.⁵⁰ The "when" and "what sign" questions together elevate the exchange to matters which Jesus had not yet specifically addressed.

One can possibly read Jesus' words, δεῖ γὰρ γενέσθαι, ἀλλ' οὔπω ἐστὶν τὸ τέλος ("it is necessary for [these things] to happen but the end is not yet" [24:6]) to mean a rebuke of the disciples' confusion. But this would amount to an overinterpretation or some sort of mirror-reading of the text that goes behind the plain text to hypothesize on "thought"—what or how the disciples and/or Jesus were thinking.⁵¹ Such mirror-reading is unwarranted for two reasons. First, unlike in many polemical responses to some unknown

46. Matt 4:20; 13:51; 16:16; 17:13.

47. See Gundry, *Matthew*, 476.

48. Gibbs, *Jerusalem and Parousia*, 179n61.

49. For similar questions in the apocalyptic tradition, see Dan 8:13; 12:6, 4 Ezra 4:33–37, 51–52; 6:7, 11–12; 8:63; 2 Bar. 3:4–9; 21:19.

50. Contra Patte, *Matthew*, 334. Gundry argues that Matthew has tailored the question to portray the disciples as already having some understanding about Jesus' coming and *parousia* (*Matthew*, 476–77).

51. For a discussion on mirror-reading involving a polemic between the implied author and unknown opponents, see Barclay, "Mirror-Reading"; Gupta, "Mirror-Reading Moral Issues."

parties whose actual position is not stated,[52] we have the disciples' question in which two elements (temple destruction and parousia/end of the age) are plainly distinguished. Second, the implied author gives no clear signal that he is interpreting the exchange in terms of Jesus correcting an error,[53] and the opening response of Jesus in 24:4 is cautionary (conveying warning) rather than corrective (indicating dissatisfaction with the disciples' question). The expression, βλέπετε μή τις ὑμᾶς πλανήσῃ ("be careful lest anyone deceive you"), in combination with v. 5, implies an external attempt to deceive the disciples in the future, not a deception that is already resident in them. As such, this opening verse is unlikely to alert the implied reader that the question to which it responds is erroneous or ill-conceived as Gibbs and others claim.

It may be possible to argue the disciples' conflation of temple destruction and the parousia/end of the world based on the view that Jews thought of the temple in cosmic terms as a microcosm or center of the world,[54] or that they shared the ancient worldview regarding "the relation between the destruction of divine beings or temples and the destruction of cities or the world."[55] There are also instances in the apocalyptic tradition where the destruction of the temple is described in terms of the "end of the age"[56] or along with the coming of God.[57] Some texts further appear to imply that the Messiah will rebuild the temple once it is destroyed.[58] However, neither these nor the Matthean text proves that the disciples supposed what these texts imply. One can equally appeal to the fact that the destruction or desolation of the temple or similar holy place is not unprecedented.[59] Earlier

---

52. Paul's letters such as Galatians present such scenarios.

53. More on this below.

54. Philo claims that the temple was "regarded like the sun which shines everywhere" (*Legat.* 29.191), probably thinking in terms of magnificence rather than cosmic centricity; he also believes that "the whole world is the highest and truest temple of God" (*Spec.* 1:66–67); cf. Josephus, *J.W.* 5.5.4–5 (212–18). It is not certain whether this was a standard universal Jewish belief, although it is often taken as such; see Levenson, "Temple and the World," 282–89; Montague, *Companion God*, 289; Arthur, *Jewish Spirituality*, 51–53.

55. Kolenkow, "Fall of the Temple," 243–50.

56. Esp. Dan 8:19; 9:26–27; 11:6, 13, 27, 35–36, 40; 12:4, 6–7, 13.

57. Zech 14:1–5.

58. 2 Sam 7:10–14 (4Q174); Zech 6:12–13, although, Juel, *Temple*, 204, contends: "nowhere do we find evidence of a tradition according to which the Messiah will destroy the present temple before rebuilding a new one."

59. Certainly, one can imagine their shock at the idea that God's temple will be destroyed, but the implied author does not highlight this. As Mitch and Sri argue, it remains the case that "the temple's destruction was not unimaginable" (*Matthew*, 302).

destructions live on in Jewish memory. Jeremiah points to the destruction of Shiloh as a model of coming destruction of the first temple (Jer 7:4, 12, 14; 26:6). His prophecy was fulfilled as narrated in 2 kings 25:8–10, but the end of world history did not ensue with it. Why must it be supposed that the disciples were thinking so in this context?

Since historical precedent does not permit the conflation of the destruction of the temple with the end of the age/world, and insofar as Matt 24:3—its grammatical structure and literary context—does not lead to an explicit diagnosis of confusion of two events in the disciples' mind, such a view remains only an assumption. Witherington seems right to insist that the view that "the early Christians couldn't separate the eschatological events surrounding the imminent demise of the temple from the imminent return of Christ," as expressed by Hagner, is "most unlikely."[60] Even if the disciples were confused in their thinking, such psychoanalytical basis for interpreting 24:3 and the Discourse as a whole is unnecessary and should be jettisoned.

On Whether Jesus Rejects or Corrects the Disciples' Question in Part or Whole

Some interpreters accept the twofold nature of the disciples' question, but they argue that Jesus either rejects or corrects the questions themselves. Those who interpret the entirety of the Discourse futuristically claim that Jesus (or Matthew) rejects or ignores the first question.[61] This view is an unsustainable overreaction against those for whom the Discourse is all history for Matthew.[62] As Luz points out, it requires the implied reader to ignore 23:37—24:2 and think only of the eschatological future.[63] But what Luz himself and others allege appears equally unsustainable: "Both of the questions the disciples asked—not just the first one-" Luz claims,

> are in a sense rejected by Jesus' discourse that follows. Jesus does not precisely answer the question about the time of the destruction of Jerusalem, even though he says much in vv. 15–22 about the destruction of Jerusalem and also often (vaguely) refers to time ("then" seven times). He also answers the question

---

60. Witherington, *Matthew*, 451.

61. E.g., Hare, *Theme of Jewish Persecution*, 177–79; Hare, *Matthew*, 275. See also Luz, *Matthew*, 190n71.

62. E.g., Feuillet, "Parousie," 261–80; cf. Hare, *Theme of Jewish Persecution*, 178–79.

63. Luz, *Matthew*, 190–91.

about the sign only by speaking in v. 30 of a sign that in reality is no sign.[64]

I will consider the second question on the sign of the *parousia* later. For now, I focus on Luz's judgment here regarding the first question, a view shared by many others.[65] There are three issues with Luz's claim: (1) It appears contradictory to claim that Jesus somehow rejects the disciples' question about the time of the destruction of Jerusalem and yet concede that he says much about it with ample time markers. (2) Luz, by this claim, demands more than the disciples' questions necessarily require—exact specific timing. In other words, in the absence of exact timing in the response, the question must be rejected by Jesus. (3) Such rejection is not in any way signaled either by Jesus or the implied author as we might expect if they perceived a problem with the question.

In a recent article, Timothy Christian is convinced that "Jesus does not correct the disciples' apparent distinguishing between the temple's destruction and the παρουσία and συντελεία" but rather affirms it.[66] However, he follows Luz in the view that Jesus rejects the questions as stated:

> there is hardly any timing language or themes about "when" these things will happen in 24:4–35. While "whenever" (ὅταν) appears twice in Section One (24:15, 33), this is not the same as "when" (πότε) from Question One (24:3). Moreover, both Question One and Section One have more to do with signs and instructions thereabout than they do with temporality. In addition, there is hardly any "sign" language describing the παρουσία and consummation in 24:36—25:46. . . . In some ways, then, Jesus rejects the questions of 24:3, particularly in that Section One does not possess much time language and Section Two does not have much sign language.[67]

Christian attempts to ground this view in a strict disconnect between πότε in 24:3 and ὅταν in 24:15. But this attempt appears somewhat dubious. The close correspondence between πότε (24:3) and ὅταν (24:15, [32], 33) strikes

---

64. Luz, *Matthew*, 191 (cf. 207).

65. E.g., Patte, *Matthew*, 334; Hagner thinks it remarkable that the first question concerning "when" is not answered in the Discourse (*Matthew*, 688); Gundry claims that "the time of Jerusalem's destruction remains unidentified" (*Matthew*, 476); Burnett says that "Jesus never explicitly answers the question, unless verses 14 and 29–30 could be indirect and ambiguous answers" ("Prolegomenon," 100).

66. Christian, "Questionable Inversion," 61.

67. Christian, "Questionable Inversion," 54.

one as undeniable.[68] Taking 24:4–14 as general material, which Christian fails to see, Jesus' answer to the first question ("when [πότε] will these things be?") corresponds to the response initiated with "when" (ὅταν) in 24:15. It is reiterated again with "when" (ὅταν) in 24:33, and climaxed with "this generation" in 24:34. Accordingly, "this generation" is when "these things" will happen.[69] Except one thinks of time language parochially in terms of minutes or seconds, this is a perfectly corresponding and sufficient response to the question, "when [πότε] will these things be?"[70]

Moreover, in addition to the numerous uses of temporal τότε,[71] 24:15–16 already implies that by the time the "abomination of desolation" is "set up" (or happens) in the temple, the destruction of the temple is almost a given and as such flight should immediately begin. As Keener avows, "the Sanctuary once desecrated, was doomed."[72] Thus, the discussion beginning in 24:15 affirms the validity of the first question in 24:3 by responding to, not rejecting it. This fact is not altered even with ὅταν taken in the indefinite ("whenever") form.

Regarding the second question, it is also claimed that Jesus rejects the disciples' assumption that a sign(s) will herald the *parousia* and consummation of the age. By following the bipartite structure advocated by France and others, Timothy Christian can thus also claim that "Section Two [i.e., 24:36—25:46] does not have much sign language."[73] Similarly, although Toussaint finds it significantly important that "Christ did not say their [disciples'] theology was incorrect," he goes on to add that "he [Christ] carefully distinguished his eschatological coming by denying signs."[74] Gibbs argues

---

68. Πότε and ὅταν (ὅτε + ἄν) may be synonymous temporal particles/adverbs both translated "when." However, while πότε is interrogative (Matt 17:17; 24:3; 25:37–39, 44), ὅταν often features in indicative statements, sometimes indefinite ("whenever"). Of the 19 occurrences in Matthew (5:11; 6:2, 5–6, 16; 9:15; 10:19, 23; 12:43; 13:32; 15:2; 19:28; 21:40; 23:15; 24:15, 32–33; 25:31; 26:29), ὅταν can only mean "when" rather than "whenever" in 9:15; 19:28; 26:29. Also, only "when" rather than "whenever" is appropriate in 10:19, 23 in view of vv. 17–18.

69. See France, *Matthew*, 899; Hagner, *Matthew*, 701; Gibbs, *Jerusalem and Parousia*, 184.

70. Compare the disciple's inquiry and Jesus' response with the apocalyptic dialogue between Ezra and the Lord in 4 Ezra 8:63—9:13. Without implying any dependence, the significant phraseological similarity between the dialogues lends support to the fact that when Jesus says "when you see" in Matt 24:15, 33 he means to answer the disciples' first question, not reject or change it.

71. Cf. Matt 24:16, 21, 23, 30.

72. Keener, *Matthew*, 575.

73. Christian, "Questionable Inversion," 54.

74. Toussaint, "Critique," 475–76.

that to the second question, Jesus' response is: "There will be no sign that shows my Parousia and the consummation of the age, Your only response until that day is to watch and to be faithful."[75]

According to France, the *parousia* "will come without any 'sign' or prior warning, so that one must always be ready for it." However, France's recognition that "Jesus does not know when it [the parousia] will be and so will offer no 'sign'"[76] would seem to dilute this claim. In other words, if Jesus will offer no sign because he does not know the time of the *parousia*, how does this lead to the conclusion that the *parousia* will, in fact, have no prior sign? The view that signs will precede the messianic age is a common feature in the apocalyptic tradition.[77] Thus, in relation to Matt 24, Hagner notes that "Jesus accepts the basic correctness of this viewpoint but plays down the notion of imminence."[78] We may indeed allow that the disciples' second question presupposes that the *parousia* will be imminent following the destruction of the temple. But to respond to the question, "what is the sign of your coming?" with the answer, "no one knows that day or hour," is to say something essentially different from the conclusion, "there is/will be no sign." Nor is it necessary to deny or reject the question as invalid or erroneous. An event may be preceded by a sign(s) that are not recognized as such, in which case the occurrence of the event retains its character of suddenness or unknownness. In other words, the *parousia* may be preceded by a sign and people fail to correctly recognize or interpret it as such. Such failure will impinge on readiness. But even these objections seem unnecessary once the structure of the Discourse is correctly discerned.

The major problem with the view espoused by Gibbs, France, and others is that they have chosen to ignore all literary and thematic clues in order to maintain a twofold structure in which 24:4–35 must be interpreted as all reference to the temple's destruction, while vv. 36–25:46 only refers to the *parousia*. Again, as noted above, Christian seeks to validate this twofold structure not only by claiming that Jesus rejects the disciples' questions but also that he inverts them to correct their "faulty assumptions and presuppositions about the temple" and the *parousia*. Christian argues that Jesus inverts the questions by replacing the "when-will-these-things-be" question with "what-will-be-the-signs-of-these-things (τί τὰ σημεῖα τούτων ἔσται)"

---

75. Gibbs, *Jerusalem and Parousia*, 207.

76. France, *Matthew*, 899.

77. E.g., 4 Ezra 5:1; 6:20; Sib. Or. 2:6–40, 154–214; 3:796–805; 8:169–210; 2 Bar. 25:2–4; Jub. 23:11–25.

78. Hagner, *Matthew*, 692.

question,[79] which is answered in 24:4-35, while vv. 36—25:46 answers something related to a "when-will-your-coming-and-consummation-of-the-age-happen" question, whose answer then is that the "when" is "unknown and unexpected."[80]

This argument fails to convince. First, as I demonstrated above, Jesus' response to the disciples' first question cannot be taken to concern signs rather than time. Second, within Matt 24:4-35, vv. 4-14 represents general eschatological events which Jesus describes as "the beginning of pangs" (ἀρχὴ ὠδίνων [v. 8]), leading to the consummation or "the end" (τὸ τέλος [v. 6]) rather than merely signaling when these things (that is, temple destruction) will be. Third, Christian's reconstruction of the questions to validate the twofold structure does not account for the explanation of *parousia* given, at least, in 24:26-28. Fourth, as I shall more fully argue later, the sign of the *parousia* is as stated in 24:29. In this verse, especially in connection with the "*sign* of the Son of Man" in v. 30, the implied author signals to the implied reader that Jesus responds to the disciples' question accordingly.

Earlier, I pointed out three issues with Luz's claim that Jesus rejects both questions of the disciples, a claim Christian also supports. But Luz appears to contradict himself by stating that Jesus "also answers the question about the sign only by speaking in v. 30 of a sign that in reality is no sign."[81] The reality is, irrespective of whether "sign" in v. 30 is a sign at all or not, the implied reader will find the connection between vv. 29-30 and the disciples' question about "sign" in v. 3b a most natural one. Thus, Christian's reconstructed questions must be rejected as deviations from the text. There is simply no evidence that Jesus ignores, rejects, corrects, or inverts the disciples' questions in the way Christian has proposed.

I will conclude this section by noting Anthony Buzzard's insistence that it is a "mistake to charge the disciples with ignorance or misunderstanding unless the text does this." Buzzard offers no argument at all on the matter but simply concludes that "the question (as in Acts 1:6), was a well-informed question which is nowhere corrected by Jesus."[82] Although Buzzard's view that the Discourse does not concern the events of 70 CE event is implausible, I concur with this conclusion. The disciples can only be guilty of error or confusion in Matt 24:3 if one makes an unlikely universal application of their dullness of understanding, veers into the uncertainties

---

79. Cf. Juza's third question (*Future of the Cosmos*, 25).
80. Christian, "Questionable Inversion," 54-57.
81. Luz, *Matthew*, 191.
82. Buzzard, "Olivet Discourse," 17; cf. Toussaint, "Critique," 475.

of psychoanalytical hermeneutic, or reconstructs the question against the plain text as Christian does.

Solution: Jesus' Response and Its Interpretation

Having taken such a long and hard look at the disciples' questions and whether or not Jesus answered them, this section deals more fully with how Jesus' response resolves the problem posed by the questions. Following the structure argued in chapter 4, I will consider the most salient matters within the Discourse, especially to show how the thought flow supports the structure argued. Jesus' response takes the form of movement from generalization to particularization.

Generalization (vv. 4–14)

The first section of Jesus' response (Matt 24:4–14) represents "generalization" in that it provides a panoramic view of history until the consummation. The general character of this section is recognized by interpreters across a broad spectrum of eschatological thought.[83] Gundry describes it as "general characteristics of the present age that do not signal the onset of the end." By "the present age," Gundry means "the church age" but with the destruction of the temple remaining unidentified.[84] Contrary to Gundry, in speaking of 24:4–14 as a generalization, I mean that it comprehends and characterizes all of history from Jesus' own generation (precisely, the disciples' ministry) to the *parousia*/end of the age. Within this stretch of history, the Great Tribulation introduced in 24:15 represents one explosive moment—the destruction of Jerusalem and the temple.[85] The initial layout is as follows:

---

83. See Ladd, *Blessed Hope*, 72n1; Walvoord, *Kingdom Come*, 182–84; Hagner, *Matthew*, 692–96; Keener, *Matthew*, 567; Turner, *Matthew*, 571–75; Gibbs, *Jerusalem and Parousia*, 181–83; recall France's view that vv. 4–8 refers to "routine events within world history" (*Matthew*, 902).

84. Gundry, *Matthew*, 476, 481; cf. Kingsbury, *Matthew*, 29.

85. Cf. Carson, "Matthew," 557, although I do not share Carson's structure of the Discourse.

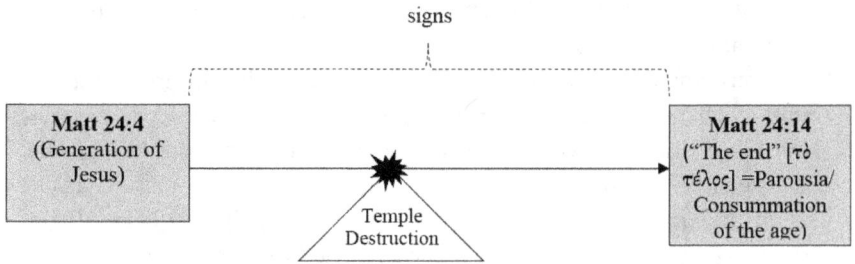

Matt 24:4-14 in Panoramic View.

The Signs

Jesus begins his response to the disciples' question by giving a general warning against misconstruing signs and being deceived by messianic pretenders. Of the twelve signs in Matt 24:4–14, eight are commonly attested and associated with the messianic age in Judaism[86]—wars and rumors of war,[87] nation rising against nation,[88] earthquakes,[89] famine,[90] tribulation,[91] betrayal, death, and hatred of one another,[92] false prophets deceiving many with signs,[93] and increased lawlessness.[94] Jesus appears to be unique with respect to three of these signs—false Christs, the hatred and killing of saints by all nations, and apostasy. As the use of δεῖ in 24:6 implies, Jesus regards these signs as necessities incorporated into God's eschatological plan.[95] Yet he cautions the disciples against reading into them the arrival of the end: these things will happen, "but the end is not yet" (ἀλλ' οὔπω ἐστὶν τὸ τέλος [24:6]). The reason the end is not yet is not that the end will not be preceded or

---

86. See discussion in Wright, *New Testament and the People*, 277–78; Wright, *Jesus and the Victory*, 577–84; Keener, *Matthew*, 566–70.

87. Sib Or. 2:155; Jub. 23:20; cf; 1QM 15:1.

88. 4 Ezra 6:13–15; 9:3; 13:31; 15:15; 2 Bar. 27:2–6; 48:34; 70:3, 7.

89. 4 Ezra 9:3; 2 Bar. 27:2–13; 70:8; Sib. Or. 2.5–9, 20–24.

90. 2 Bar. 27:2–13; 70:8; Sib. Or. 2:20–24, 155; Jub. 23:13.

91. 2 Bar. 25:2–4; Jub. 23:12–13; 1QM 1:11–14.

92. 2 Bar. 70:3.

93. Sib. Or. 2:165.

94. 4 Ezra 5:2, 10; 6:24–25.

95. Witherington, *Matthew*, 445.

even heralded by signs but because there is another necessity which, though technically not a sign, must happen before the end arrives—the universal proclamation of the gospel.

Jesus' answer hardly implies that he is distancing himself from the traditional belief that signs in form of messianic woes will precede the messianic age.[96] There is a certain tension between the statement in 24:6 that these signs will happen "but the end is not yet" (ἀλλ' οὔπω ἐστὶν τὸ τέλος) and the addendum in v. 8 that "all these" signs are only "the beginning of birth-pangs" (πάντα δὲ ταῦτα ἀρχὴ ὠδίνων). The former statement may imply that these signs will have nothing to do with the end or that they will be far removed from it. However, the later statement presupposes that the signs begin and continue until they come to a culmination at or just before "the end." In other words, the phrase "beginning of birth-pangs" implies progression.[97]

The point here is, if we take the disciples' question and the Discourse as addressing both the fate of the temple and the consummation as two separate events, there is no reason to suppose that all the signs mentioned in this section will only precede the destruction of the temple and cease thereafter.[98] Not even the rise of false Christs should be limited to the immediate pre-70 era leading to the fall of the temple.[99] In fact, we appear to have no evidence of false Christs in association with the destruction of the temple, only false prophets.[100] In any case, when Jesus warns the disciples

---

96. Recall Hagner's comment that Jesus accepts the correctness of the tradition but only rejects the notion of imminence (*Matthew*, 692).

97. In the OT, "pangs" or labor pain may refer to sufferings within history (e.g., Exod 15:14; Deut 2:25; Mic 4:9; Nah 2:11, etc.) but it can also refer to eschatological suffering leading to or near the end. This latter sense appears to be indicated in Isa 13:8. France, *Matthew*, 903–4, takes the instance in Isa 26:17–18 as "more eschatological," adding that later rabbinic use associated it with the time preceding the Messiah's coming, but that this use is not attested as early as the NT period. However, "pangs" are used in relation to eschatology in the apocalyptic tradition: 1 En. 62:3–4 states that on the day of judgment pain will come upon kings of the earth as birth-pangs; cf. 4 Ezra 4:40–42 where birth-pang is associated with the notion of resurrection prior to or leading into the new eschatological age.

98. Matthew 24:34 does not communicate such cessation, nor does it mean that these things will cease to happen at that point any more than it means that "this generation" will pass away immediately after these things take place.

99. Contra Witherington, *Matthew*, 445.

100. See Josephus, *J.W.* 6.5.2 (285–87); cf. 7.11.1 (437–39); *Ant.* 20.5.1 (97). Gundry, *Matthew*, 477, claims that no evidence of any messianic claimant exists prior to Barkokhba, a hundred years after Jesus [almost seventy years after 70 CE], arguing that "one did not have to claim messiahship to be a false prophet." This, for him, militates against the view that the Discourse is *vaticinum ex eventu*.

against misconstruing the signs as the arrival of the end, he does not by this suggest that "the end" itself (that is, the *parousia*/end of the age) will not be preceded by any such signs. Matthew 24:6 is not intended to mean that no sign(s) will precede the "end" itself. As I will argue later, vv. 29–31, as a reference to the *parousia*, belies such a view.

Furthermore, there have been attempts to partition the signs in 24:4–14. On a small scale, taking vv. 4–8 as "routine events within world history," France discusses it as a separate group of signs from those in vv. 9–14.[101] However, this is an unlikely dichotomy. The use of τότε in v. 9 signals continuity and development. Certainly, vv. 9–13 is "another aspect" associated with the signs in vv. 4–8,[102] but all of vv. 4–13 nonetheless constitutes general material. On a larger scale, Balabanski has argued an elaborate partitioning of 24:4–14. She advances a hypothesis in which the structure of the Discourse is discerned by allotting different parts of 24:4–14 to different times relative to the Matthean community. Thus, vv. 6–8 refers to the past from the Matthean community's perspective (66–74 CE), vv. 9–12, to the present (74 CE), and vv. 4–5, to the end.[103]

This hypothesis is unsuccessful because (1) it is based on an uncertain assumption of a post-70 date of Matthew's writing, and (2) the determination that 24:9–12 constitutes the present experience of Matthew's community is somewhat arbitrary. There is no evidence in the text as to which of the signs are past from the standpoint of the Matthean community or which ones are their current experience. The whole of 24:4–14 belongs together and is best taken as general eschatological signs. In other words, these signs will occur throughout the entire stretch of history until the *parousia* and consummation; the immediate disciples of Jesus will, in their generation, also hear about or witness these or such signs.

---

101. France, *Matthew*, 901–10.

102. France, *Matthew*, 900n26.

103. Balabanski, "Mission in Matthew," 163–65; Balabanski, *Eschatology*, 153–79. In more detail, the structure deals with only Matt 24:1–31 constructed in two sequences of what to Matthew's community is past (24:6–8//15–20), present (24:9–12//21–28 [suffering and false prophets]), and future (24:13–14//29–31); cf. Thompson, "Historical Perspective," 248–50; Sim, "Gospel of Matthew," 31–35; Keener also suggests that Matthew may be combatting "false prophetic reinterpretation of the parousia" now seen as delayed (*Matthew*, 564).

The ἔθνος/ἔθνη (nation/nations)

The term ἔθνος/ἔθνη, its referent and whether or not it embraces Israel in any sense, is crucial for the interpretation of the Eschatological Discourse. According to Gernot Garbe,

> The contrast of Israel and the Gentiles in 10:5 and 15:24, which is not explicitly withdrawn by Matthew in the course of the Gospel, weighs so heavy that Israel may not be included in the expression πάντα τὰ ἔθνη. Already, in Matt 10, Jesus announces to the disciples that in their mission among the Jews, they must suffer failure and persecution, which will not cease until the coming of the Son of Man (Matt 10:23). This statement is not required again in Matt 24, and it is not made explicitly.[104]

There is no question about the distinction between Israel and the nations in 10:5–6 (cf 15:24). But does this distinction extend to every instance of ἔθνη in Matthew? The answer to this question is not in the affirmative.

Garbe's claim is not based on an adequate consideration of the term ἔθνος/ἔθνη in Matthew, especially the Eschatological Discourse where 30 percent of all the uses occurs.[105] As I noted earlier, with the exception of Matt 21:43 where "a nation" is more likely a reference to the disciples of Jesus,[106] Matthew consistently uses the plural and articular form of ἔθνος to refer to peoples or nations other than Israel, that is, gentiles, whether they are distant lands or regions surrounding Jewish territory[107] or entities within it.[108] But ἔθνος is singular and non-articular in 24:7, implying a generic sense. This verse itself most likely alludes to the Jewish wars as well. Although 24:9 uses πάντων τῶν ἐθνῶν ("of/by all the nations"), which most commonly refers to gentile peoples/nations, it also embraces Jewish hatred and persecution. It is unlikely that Jesus means to exclude Jewish hatred and

---

104. My translation. In German, "Die Gegenüberstellung von Israel und den Weltvölkern in 10,5 und 15,24, die von Mt im Verlauf des Evangeliums nicht ausdrücklich zurückgenommen wurde, wiegt so schwer, dass Israel auch in den Ausdruck πάντα τὰ ἔθνη nicht eingeschlossen sein dürfte. Schon in Mt 10 kündigt Jesus den Jüngern an, dass sie unter den juden bei der Mission Misserfolge und Verfolgungen erleiden müssen, die bis zum Kommen des Menschensohnes nicht aufhören werden (10,23). Diese Aussage ist in Mt 24 nicht nochmals erforderlich, und sie erfolgt auch nicht ausdrücklich" (Garbe, *Hirte Israels*, 181).

105. Matt 4:15; 6:32; 10:5, 18; 12:18, 21; 20:19, 25; 24:7 (2x), 9, 14; 25:32; 28:19.

106. See chapter 1, n118.

107. Matt 4:15; 10:5, 18, etc.

108. Matt 20:19.

persecution of the disciples here.[109] In fact, if there might have arisen any doubt for the implied reader regarding the all-inclusive referent of 24:9, it is already cleared up in Jesus' rebuke of Jerusalem just before the Discourse:

> Therefore *I send* [ἀποστέλλω] to you prophets and wise men and scribes, some of them *you will kill and crucify*, and some *you will scourge in your synagogues and persecute from town to town*, that upon you may come all the righteous blood shed on earth, from the blood of innocent Abel to the blood of Zechariah the son of Barachiah, whom you murdered between the sanctuary and the altar" (Matt 23:34-35).

Clearly, this passage represents a second mission sending to the Jews and their persecution of the disciples after the one referred to in Matt 10. The phrase "I send"/"I am sending" is constrained by its futuristic co-texts to act as a "futuristic present."[110] Thus, it proleptically alludes to the post-resurrection mission sending (28:18-20) inextricably linked with and anticipates Jewish evangelization.[111]

While Matt 23:34-35 suggests that a great outcome is not guaranteed with respect to this Jewish evangelization, it should not necessarily imply a total failure. In connection with 24:9, it leads to the conclusion that Jews must now be considered as one of (certainly in league with) the ἔθνη.[112] In fact, for some of the disciples to whom the saying of 24:9 is addressed, Jewish persecution is the only one they will know, following the post-resurrection commission.[113] It is fascinating that most interpreters fail to see or ignore this contextual clue implying the Israel-inclusive referent of ἔθνη (i.e., the interpretive relationship between 23:34-35 and 24:9).[114]

What about the ἔθνη of 24:14? Might it be Israel-inclusive as well? D. R. A. Hare and D. J. Harrington reject the inclusive view here based on the claim that "the assumption underlying 24:14 (and Mark 13:10) is that the Jewish nation in Palestine has *already* heard the gospel." For them, the dictum, "'To the Jew first, and also to the Greek' is Matthew's order (cf. Matt 10:5,17-18) as well as Paul's (cf. Rom 1:16)."[115] There is certainly some truth

---

109. Cf. Matt 24:9 and Mark 13:8-10.
110. See Wallace, *Grammar*, 535-36.
111. Cf. Luke 24:47.
112. See Zahn, *Matthäus*, 666n7.
113. Cf. Matt 23:34 and the testimony of Paul in Acts 26:9-12.
114. Luz merely mentions 23:34, 37 but places more emphasis on the universality of mission than the inclusion of Jews in 24:9; his discussion on 28:18-20 appears undecided on the matter (*Matthew*, 192-93, 6329-31).
115. Hare and Harrington, "Make Disciples," 366.

in this. The tenor of 24:14 suggests a reference to "all nations" to whom the gospel has not yet been proclaimed. It may also appear unlikely that Jesus, just after departing from the temple (23:37—24:1), would mean in 24:14 that the gospel needs to be proclaimed to the nation of Israel in Palestine as *a testimony to them*, as though it has not already been so proclaimed.

Some have suggested that the expression εἰς μαρτύριον πᾶσιν τοῖς ἔθνεσιν can mean a testimony *to* or *against* the nations.[116] It would then become possible to include Israel by arguing that the gospel will be a testimony *to* gentiles who are yet to hear it but a testimony *against* Jews who have already heard it. Such double *entendre* or even a straight negative reading ("testimony against Jews and Gentile") would be both unnecessary and unlikely.[117] The expression, εὐαγγέλιον τῆς βασιλείας ("'gospel' of the kingdom") is already used positively in two instances (4:23; 9:35) to describe the gospel as preached by Jesus himself. However, in 24:14 (cf. 26:13), τοῦτο τὸ εὐαγγέλιον τῆς βασιλείας ("this gospel of the kingdom") ought to be understood in terms of the fuller expression of the gospel. It anticipates or alludes to *the gospel of Jesus' vindication through the resurrection as Son of God, Savior, and King*. It assumes the mission *statement* in 23:34 and anticipates the mission *sending* in 28:28-20.[118] This fuller gospel, as Jesus envisages, is to be addressed as a testimony in a positive sense to all nations—Jews and gentiles (cf. Luke 24:47).

As such, the problem with the interpretation of Hare and Harrington (as with Garbe) is that they not only miss the second mission sending (or *statement* to the effect) implied in 23:34-35 as part of the universal commission, but they also fail to consider the fuller gospel that Jews were yet to hear because the resurrection had not yet taken place at the time. Moreover, their view is symptomatic of the problem associated with interpreting Matthew using the lenses of Mark or Luke or Paul or someone else, rather than first in Matthew's own terms. While the implied reader knows Matt 10 well, the more accurate assumption in 24:14 is that, in light of Matt 21:43, those to whom the Discourse in general, and the mission saying of 24:14 in particular, are addressed, now constitute the true Israel-nation formed around Jesus.[119] And so all unbelieving Israelites have become "*ethnosized*"—that

---

116. See Davies and Allision, *Matthew*, 3:344.

117. Cf. 8:4; 10:18; see Trilling, *Wahre Israel*, 128.

118. Kingsbury, *Matthew*, 10, 128-31, rightly argues that the expression, "the Gospel of the Kingdom," enables Matthew "to summarize in the same terms both the pre-Easter message of Jesus and the post-Easter message of the Church"; cf. Konradt, *Israel, Church, and the Gentiles*, 318; Luz, *Matthew*, 194.

119. Cf. Bauer, *Gospel*, 291.

is, regarded as gentiles and therefore subject to the gospel of the kingdom.[120] This should not be surprising. Even members of Matthew's faith community in Jesus could themselves become regarded as ἐθνικός (gentiles) according to Matt 18:15–17. Thus, *ethno*sization *a fortiori* is plausible for unbelieving Israelites.[121]

Furthermore, the term ἔθνος/ἔθνη is directly tied to Matthew's emphasis on mission. Meier, following Zahn and Trilling, takes 24:7, 9, 14 as evidence that ἔθνος/ἔθνη in Matthew includes Israel. He describes the phrase πᾶσιν τοῖς ἔθνεσιν in 24:14 as "the most explicitly universalistic use of *ethnos* in Matt[hew]," concluding that Israel falls under the mandate of Matt 28:19.[122] Considering the Great Commission passage closely, it is clear that when Jesus stands on the mountain and claims "all authority in heaven and *on earth*" (28:18) and then commissions the disciples to go to *all the nations* (v. 19), the implication is that the expressions, "on earth" and "all the nations" are equivalent, representing all humanity in juxtaposition with the expression "in heaven."[123] Based on this, Catchpole states: "it would be damaging to the concerns of Matthew's gospel for the commission of the exalted one to extend to the Gentiles and exclude the Jews."[124] There is no evidence in Matthew that unsaved Jews can no longer be evangelized.[125] Nor is it likely that they will cease at any point to be answerable to the gospel, since the judgment in 25:31–46 must also include them as I shall argue later.[126]

---

120. Cf. Lunde, "Salvation-Historical Implication," iv, 305–10. According to him, "by virtue of its rejection of 'true Israel' [Jesus], the nation became 'non-Israel.' Now numbered among τὰ ἔθνη, the Jews continue to be among those to whom the disciples go in their universal mission."

121. Note that in the mission sending of Matt 10 (vv. 13–15), the disciples are to depart from any Israelite city once rejected. They are to shake off the dust of their feet as a sign of their decisive exit, implying that such cities are from then on "to be reckoned as Gentiles." So Borg (*Conflict*, 219); cf. 22:1–14, esp. 11–14.

122. Meier, "Nations or Gentiles," 98–99, 102. In the words of Trilling, *Wahre Israel*, 128, "Der Vers 24,14 ist das Seitenstuck zu 28, 19." Others who hold the inclusive view of 28:19 include France, *Gospel according to Matthew*, 413–14; Gundry, *Matthew*, 595; Hagner, *Matthew*, 887; Davies and Allison, *Matthew*, 3:684 (for more, see Konradt, *Israel, Church, and the Gentiles*, 311n252); contra Hare and Harrington, "Make Disciples," 359–69; Garbe, *Hirte Israel*, 180–81; Konradt, *Israel, Church, and the Gentiles*, 311–23; Burnett, *Testament*, 281–92.

123. In Mark 16:15, the subject of the mission is πάσῃ τῇ κτίσει ("to all the creation"). Hare and Harrington may be right that "Matthew does not envisage the conversion of Israel as a nation" but to maintain that in no case could πάντα τὰ ἔθνη in Matt 28:19 include Israel[ites] ("Make Disciples," 363, 366) is to go too far off the mark.

124. Catchpole, "Poor on Earth," 389.

125. Although several passages may be exploited to argue this, as, for example, famously done by Clark, "Gentile Bias," 166–68.

126. I shall discuss "nations" in Matt 25:31–46 at the right point.

Additionally, it should not be surprising that Matthew can use ἔθνος/ ἔθνη in a universal sense; the term φυλή ("tribe") specifically used for Israel (19:28)[127] is also most likely used in the same all-inclusive sense in 24:30.[128] All of the points made above lead to the conclusion that, for Matthew, especially beginning with the Eschatological Discourse, unbelieving Jews have become merged with the broader ἔθνη of the world and, therefore, subject to the mission mandate. I should also point out here that the use of ἔθνος/ ἔθνη, in addition to the recurrence of πολύς ("many") in 24:5, 10, 11, 12,[129] lends support to the characterization of Matt 24:4–14 as "generalization" as argued earlier.

Gospel in the ὅλῃ τῇ οἰκουμένῃ (24:14)

In light of the analysis on ἔθνος/ἔθνη above, it becomes easy to see how the saying, καὶ κηρυχθήσεται τοῦτο τὸ εὐαγγέλιον τῆς βασιλείας ἐν ὅλῃ τῇ οἰκουμένῃ εἰς μαρτύριον πᾶσιν τοῖς ἔθνεσιν, supports this study's claim of "generalization" as the best way to take 24:4–14. Because of the controversial nature of ὅλῃ τῇ οἰκουμένῃ, I will proceed to argue that this saying refers to the universal proclamation of the gospel before the *parousia*/end of the age.

Those who lean in full or in part to the preterist view of the Discourse consider ὅλῃ τῇ οἰκουμένῃ as a reference to the Roman empire rather than the whole world.[130] Consequently, these interpreters are led to advance the view that this mission was already fulfilled prior to the destruction of the temple in 70 CE—a view often supported by appeal to Pauline passages such as Rom 10:18; 16:26; Col 1:6, 23; and 2 Tim 4:17.[131] Although the hyperbolic character of Paul's sayings in these passages (especially in Col 1:6, 23) should not be missed, it is true that the gospel would have permeated most

---

127. Cf. Luke 2:36; 22:30; Acts 13:21; Rom 11:1; Phil 3:5; Heb 7:13–14; Jas 1:1; Rev 5:5; 7:4–8; 21:12.

128. Cf. Rev 1:7; 5:9; 7:9; 11:9; 13:7; 14:6.

129. Cf. Matt 7:13–14.

130. See Benoit, *Matthieu*, 147; Wright, *Matthew*, 115; France, *Matthew*, 907–9. Blomberg, *Matthew*, 356–57, thinks it means that "the gospel ... will be proclaimed widely throughout the known world (though *oikumene* in the first century often referred merely to the Roman Empire)."

131. Cf. 1 Clem. 5:5–7. Clement of Rome claims that Paul proclaimed the gospel in both the east and the west, taught the whole world (ὅλον τὸν κόσμον) righteousness and reached the farthest ends of the west. Alford, *Greek Testament*, 238, suggests a limited sense in which the gospel was already fully preached not only to the Gentiles but also to give Jews scattered in all the world opportunity to hear the gospel before the destruction of Jerusalem, and a broader sense of universal proclamation before the great and final end.

parts of the Roman empire before 70 CE. But is this what the Matthean Jesus means in the context of the Eschatological Discourse?

According to BDAG, οἰκουμένη has four nuances: (1) the earth as inhabited area, (2) the world as administrative unit (i.e., Roman Empire), (3) all inhabitants of the earth, and (4) an extraordinary use—the whole world including the realm of transcendent beings.[132] While many of the NT instances appear to support the limited (Roman Empire) sense,[133] there are also several which are more properly taken in the universal sense.[134] Allowing some degree of ambiguity, the meaning in the LXX also varies between limited[135] and universal senses.[136] Based on these, and given the fact that οἰκουμένη is a *hapax legomenon* in Matthew's Gospel, it cannot be assumed without question that Matthew uses it to refer narrowly to the Roman empire or to "the area surrounding the Mediterranean and the lesser known areas to the east, around which stretched mysterious regions (comprising much of our "old world") beyond the fringes of civilization," as France argues.[137] In fact, it is unlikely that the implied reader of Matthew would compare the synoptics, consider other occurrences in the NT or elsewhere, or consult a lexicon to see what the term means. Often this standard hermeneutical practice merely circumvents the difficulty of literary exegesis.

To understand the implied author's meaning, we should prioritize the immediate and broader literary context and co-texts of οἰκουμένη in Matt 24–25. First, within the immediate context, ὅλῃ τῇ οἰκουμένῃ is abutted to πᾶσιν τοῖς ἔθνεσιν. If the earlier analysis is correct, then this abutment suggests that the two expressions must be taken together as reference to all the nations of the world. Second, taken with the broader context, the mission to ὅλῃ τῇ οἰκουμένῃ and πᾶσιν τοῖς ἔθνεσιν in 24:14 requires a universal interpretation constrained by the universal judgment of the πάντα τὰ ἔθνη in 25:31–46. Πᾶσιν τοῖς ἔθνεσιν in 24:14 resonates with πάντα τὰ ἔθνη in 25:32, constituting an *inclusio* of universality in the sense that it is only fitting that all peoples who must have Jesus as their judge should also have the opportunity to either embrace or reject him as Lord.[138] Thus, it is inaccurate

---

132. BDAG, "οἰκουμένη," 699–70.

133. Esp. Luke 2:1 (cf. 21:26; Acts 11:28; 17:6; 19:27; 24:5; Rom 10:18; Rev 3:10; 16:14).

134. See Heb 1:6 (cf. 2:5; Acts 4:5; 17:31; Rev 12:9).

135. E.g., Isa 10:14, 23; 13:5, 9; 14:17, 26; 23:17; 24:1, 4; 27:6; 34:1; 37:16, 18; 62:4; Dan 2:38; 3:2, 45.

136. E.g., Pss 18:5; 23:1; 88:12; 89:2; 92:1; 95:10, 13; 97:9; Prov 8:31; Jer 10:12; 28:15; Isa 10:14; 13:11.

137. France, *Matthew*, 909.

138. Keener, *Matthew*, 572; Davies, *Matthew*, 167, notes that in both Jewish and

to argue, as France does, that to take the expression, τοῦτο τὸ εὐαγγέλιον τῆς βασιλείας ἐν ὅλῃ τῇ οἰκουμένῃ εἰς μαρτύριον πᾶσιν τοῖς ἔθνεσιν, in the universal sense of world evangelization is to take it out of context.[139]

Away from the Discourse itself, in Matt 26:13, Jesus alludes to the universal reach of the gospel using the term κόσμος. The instances of κόσμος used by Jesus in Matthew all refer universally to the entire world.[140] Moreover, the case for the anticipation of Matt 28:18–20 in 24:14 is strong. Balabanski demonstrates the connection between these two passages. She argues that Matt 28:18–20 cannot be taken in isolation of other missional passages in Matthew, noting that 24:1–31, in particular, "offer a vital intertextual horizon for the interpretation of the 'great commission.'"[141] Similarly, Luz affirms that the fact that "Matthew puts the mission command at the end of the first main section [of the Discourse, i.e., 24:14], much as he puts the mission command at the end of his entire Gospel, shows how important the universal mission to the nations is for him."[142] Indeed, Matthew's overall emphasis on mission is well-recognized.[143] But this mission emphasis becomes diluted if, written post-70, the implied reader is meant to take 24:14 as already accomplished in the Pauline sense (Rom 10:18 or Col 1:6) prior to the end of the temple.[144] That Matthew intends such is very unlikely.

Therefore, with respect to France's concern for contextual reading noted above, it is important to state that reading the Matthean οἰκουμένη with a Pauline lens is certainly not taking it in context. Those who appeal to the Pauline use of οἰκουμένη in order to deny a universal meaning in Matt 24:14 should also be prepared to apply the Pauline and other NT uses of τέλος in 1 Cor 1:8; 15:24; 1 Pet 4:7; Heb 3:14; 6:11; and Rev 2:26 to τέλος in Matt 24:14. In all these instances, τέλος refers to the *parousia* and or final/universal end of history. One must be cautious with the all-to-easy tendency to harmonize details across texts, especially before exhausting literary investigation in a particular author.

---

apocalyptic expectations, God's judgment will involve all the nations.

139. France, *Matthew*, 907.

140. Cf. 5:14; 13:35, 38; 16:26; 18:7; 25:24; of these, 5:14 and 13:38 imply universal mission.

141. Balabanski, "Mission in Mission," 162.

142. Luz, *Matthew*, 194; cf. Gundry, *Matthew*, 480; Davies and Allison, *Matthew*, 3:344; Hagner, *Matthew*, 695–96; Burnett, *Testament*, 293.

143. For a recent and holistic discussion on this, see Bitrus, *Hermeneutic of Mission in Matthew*.

144. I say this for the sake of argument, not because I assume a post-70 date for Matthew's Gospel.

Τὸ τέλος

Apart from πᾶσιν τοῖς ἔθνεσιν, another co-text of οἰκουμένη in 24:14 is τὸ τέλος ("the end"). The two terms are related not semantically but in terms of mutual interpretive information. That is, a universal οἰκουμένη would also imply a universal τέλος and *vice versa*. Preterists who take the mission saying in 24:14 as already fulfilled prior to the destruction of the temple would also naturally take τέλος as a reference to the destruction of the temple understood as the end of the old covenant. I will proceed to demonstrate the problem with this view in dialogue with France, its major advocate.

To begin, we should note that τέλος ("end") occurs three times within the section—24:6, 13, and 14, the latter two instances in close proximity.[145] Commenting on 24:6, France states: "the question which Jesus is here answering was about when the temple would be destroyed, and that is the 'end' most naturally understood here."[146] This first occurrence in v. 6, he argues, corresponds to that in v. 14 and both "clearly have a more specific reference" to the destruction of the temple. But what about τέλος in v. 13? It will be helpful to quote France fully here:

> This verse repeats the exhortation of 10:22b; . . . We noted that "the phrase *eis telos*, 'to the end,' can hardly have . . . a specific reference, but simply means persevering for as long as may be necessary" and that "the thought loosely echoes Dan 12:12-13, a beatitude on those who remain faithful and will receive their reward 'at the end of the days.'" Here, however, it comes between two references to "the end" in vv. 6 and 14 which clearly have a more specific reference. If, as the context here suggests, that "end" is the destruction of the temple which is the subject of the disciples' question (see on v. 6), it would be possible to read *eis telos* here in the same sense: whoever stands firm throughout the historical process which will culminate in the destruction of the temple will be saved. But it is not easy to see what sort of "salvation" fits that scenario, and it is more likely that the adverbial phrase *eis telos* (not *eis to telos*) functions independently of the articular noun *to telos*, and has the same sense here that it had in 10:22b; in that case the call is for faithfulness "for as long as it takes," and the promise is of the ultimate spiritual security . . . of those who have stood firm in their discipleship. It is that promise, rather than physical safety at the time of the fall of

---

145. The occurrence in 10:22 is relevant, that in 26:58 is not.
146. France, *Matthew*, 903.

Jerusalem, which best matches the dangers to faith spelled out in vv. 9-12.[147]

Basically, the anarthrous (non-articular) character of the prepositional τέλος in v. 13 has led France to consider it indefinite (that is, referring to an indefinite time) and therefore to be distinguished from the arthrous (articular) τέλος in vv. 6 and 14 understood as a reference to the destruction of the temple. This may be right, but we must consider the text more critically.

In fairness to France, it is indeed crucial to maintain, in light Matt 10:22b, that τέλος in v. 13 refers not to physical safety but to ultimate spiritual salvation. It is unlikely that τέλος in Matt 10:22b refers to the destruction of the temple.[148] Matthew 10 makes no association with the destruction of the temple. There is nothing in Matt 10:22 alerting the implied reader to take τέλος there as the destruction of the temple. Also, while the saying in Matt 10:22 occurs in the context of a limited mission to Israel, its language and tenor are more closely aligned with the motif of final reward which can only be in the ultimate end.[149] This motif of final reward also occurs in the Eschatological Discourse only in the part that deals with final judgment (24:45—25:46).[150]

Moreover, the notion of "being saved" as a result of "enduring till the end" in both 10:22 and 24:13 appears to stand in contradistinction to "being saved" as a result of flight from danger in the event of the destruction of the temple (24:16-22).[151] In other words, while "salvation as final reward" at the end of time is suggested in the 10:22 and 24:13,[152] only physical safety is implied in connection with the destruction of the temple in 24:15-25. This is the import of the latter part of France's statement cited above.

However, the distinction France makes between τέλος in Matt 24:13 and τέλος in vv. 6 and 14 is unconvincing. Certain considerations will suffice to demonstrate the unlikelihood of this distinction.

---

147. France, *Matthew*, 907. Evans, *Matthew*, 404, says enduring to the end in Matt 24:13 does not refer to the "eschatological end of history as humans know it, but to enduring and not quitting or abandoning the faith." For Hill, *Matthew*, 321, the "end" means "finally, without breaking down—not to the End."

148. Contra Wright, *Jesus and the Victory*, 347n109.

149. See 10:41-42. Notice the comparably gnomic nature of the saying in both v. 22 and vv. 41-42.

150. Cf. Dan 12:12-13 (the motif of reward is associated with the resurrection [ἀνάστασις] at the end of time).

151. Cf. 4 Ezra 6:25.

152. Even if one is killed before that end of time, as v. 9 suggests, it is still one's endurance to the end; cf. Wilkins, *Matthew*, 776; Blomberg, *Matthew*, 356; Hendriksen, *Matthew*, 854.

The first consideration challenging the distinction between τέλος in 24:13 and τέλος in vv. 6 and 14 is thematic. The "end" to which τέλος in vv. 6, 13 and 14 refers corresponds to the "end" to which συντελεία ("consummation") in the disciples' question in v. 3 refers. According to Levinsohn, "when a semantic item is introduced, other items that the culture associates with the item are also 'accessed.'"[153] Applied here, this means that the implied reader is more likely to associate the "end" (τέλος) in vv. 6, 13, and 14 with the part of the disciples' question that deals with "end" (συντελεία) than with the part that deals with the destruction of the temple.[154] Συντελεία and τέλος are semantically coordinate in the mental processing of the Discourse; therefore they are interchangeable.[155]

The second consideration is the pragmatic use of the article. The lack of the article in association with τέλος in v. 13 does not render its referent indefinite or unspecific and thus distinct from the articular τέλος in vv. 6 and 14.[156] At least three factors may account for why τέλος in v. 13 is anarthrous: (1) Although not necessary, it may be due to the intervention of the preposition εἰς. There is a preponderance of "εἰς + article + object" constructions in Matthew. However, grammarians recognize the general tendency for objects of prepositions to be anarthrous.[157] (2) Since the substantive, τέλος, is already active, having been mentioned in v. 6, its lack of the article in v. 13 is purposive, serving to highlight the saying for prominence or significance.[158] And (3) Matt 24:3–14 reflects a significant discourse pragmatic in terms of the articulation of the two synonymous substantives (συντελεία and τέλος): in 24:3, συντελεία is anarthrous because it is the first introduction of the "end" theme in the Discourse; the second reference to the theme, τέλος (v. 6), is articular because it identifies the just-activated (anarthrous) theme, συντελεία. Thus, after τέλος is rendered anarthrous or reactivated for prominence in v. 13, it is reidentified as already known in v. 14, hence the reappearance of the article.[159]

---

153. Levinsohn, *Discourse Features*, 148.

154. Paul could combine τέλος and αἰῶνος in 1 Cor 10:11 (τὰ τέλη τῶν αἰώνων), although apparently neither referring to the temple's destruction nor to the ultimate end.

155. So also Keener, *Matthew*, 563n90; contra France, *Matthew*, 903n31, and Fuller, who tries in vain to set the two terms apart from each other ("Olivet Discourse," 159–60).

156. I have already noted that, as in the case of ἔθνος, the presence or otherwise of the article before a substantive may alter its referent; see n122 in chapter 1.

157. See Hill, "Exceptions," 4, 6.

158. See Levinsohn, *Discourse Features*, 148–67; Long, *Koine Greek Grammar*, 416–22.

159. See Long, *Koine Greek Grammar*, 73–76.

The Third consideration is proximity. While the discussion on the destruction of the temple begins in 24:15, just after the use of τὸ τέλος in v. 14, this cannot necessarily imply that the "end" to which this τέλος refers is the destruction of the temple. A closer proximity exists between vv. 13 and 14 since they together represent a complex sentence joined together by a connective καὶ. Thus, it is unlikely that the anarthrous τέλος in v. 13 refers to an "end" different than that of the articular τέλος in v. 14 (or v. 6 for that matter). France's distinction between the articular τέλος (v. 14) and the anarthrous εἰς τέλος (v. 13) requires the implied reader to make an unlikely abrupt mental adjustment from taking τέλος in v. 13 as an unspecific reference to that in v. 14 as a specific reference to the destruction of the temple.[160]

Based on these considerations, I conclude that τέλος (vv. 6, 13, and 14) and συντελεία (v. 3) refer to the same "end"—the ultimate end of history when the faithful will be granted eternal salvation—not "end" understood as the destruction of Jerusalem. Having dealt with some of the critical issues within the first section, I will now turn to the elements of particularization within the Discourse.

Particularization

If Matt 24:4–14 represents a generalization, then the rest of the Discourse consists of particularization in terms of the two "particulars" that make up the disciples' questions in 24:3—the destruction of the temple on the one hand and the *parousia* and consummation of the age on the other. The main thrust of this study is that these two "particulars" are addressed in an alternating pattern. First, events related the destruction of the temple are the subject of 24:15–25. Second, the *parousia* is introduced in vv. 26–28 and further developed in vv. 29–31. Third, reference to the destruction of the temple is taken up again in the form of an analogy in vv. 32–35. And fourth, the *parousia* is expanded with analogies in 24:36—25:46. In chapters 2 and 4, I presented the discourse-grammatical basis for this structural schema. What remains is to flesh out the corresponding interpretation to demonstrate the validity of the proposed structure.

---

160. Note that both articular and anarthrous τέλος are used in reference to the final end of history. Again, see 1 Cor 1:8; 15:24; 1 Pet 4:7; Heb 3:14; 6:11; and Rev 2:26.

a(T¹): vv. 15–25

This segment consists of two parts: the imperative or command to flee once the βδέλυγμα τῆς ἐρημώσεως is sited or discerned (vv. 15–20), and the substantiation or argument for the flight (vv. 21–25), i.e., θλῖψις μεγάλη introduced using γὰρ in v. 21. In v. 24, a second γὰρ is used to further qualify the nature of "those days" (ἐκείναις ταῖς ἡμέραις) in which the flight must happen. Thus, the two key interpretive elements in this segment are βδέλυγμα τῆς ἐρημώσεως and θλῖψις μεγάλη.

Τὸ βδέλυγμα τῆς ἐρημώσεως

In Matt 24:15, Jesus' response to the first part of the disciples' question references the βδέλυγμα τῆς ἐρημώσεως (lit. "abomination of desolation") spoken of by Daniel "the prophet."[161] The abomination of desolation will signal to them that the catastrophe predicted in 24:2 is about to happen. Therefore, they should flee for safety (vv. 16–20). But the referent of this abomination of desolation is one of the most difficult questions of the Eschatological Discourse.

The term, βδέλυγμα, is used in the earlier OT prophetic oracles to refer to Israel's idolatry, while ἐρημώσις represents divine judgment in the form of destruction.[162] The two terms are brought into close causal connection in Jer 51:22 and Ezek 33:28–29. However, apart from Matthew (and Mark), the genitival phrase, βδέλυγμα τῆς ἐρημώσεως, occurs only three times in Daniel.[163] While there is a universal recognition that here it alludes to the event of BC 167 when Antiochus IV Epiphanes erected an altar to Zeus in the temple and sacrificed to it,[164] in Matt 24 the referent is anything but clear. In what follows, I consider the grammar as well as the literary context

---

161. Grundmann, *Matthäus*, 505, notes that the fact that Daniel is called "prophet" here indicates that Matthew's community was reading the Septuagint, which regards Daniel as a prophet.

162. In the LXX, βδέλυγμα is the translation for two Heb. terms, תּוֹעֵבָה and שִׁקּוּץ, both meaning "abomination" or "detestable thing," with particular reference to idols (Isa 2:8, 20; 17:8; 44:19; 66:3, 17; Jer 2:7; 4:1; 7:10, 30; 11:15; 13:27; 16:18; 39:35; Ezek 5:9, 11; 6:9, 11; 7:5–8, 20; 8:10; 11:18, 21; 20:7–8, 30; 36:31); similarly, ἐρημώσις translates two Heb. terms, חָרְבָּה and שְׁמָמָה/שָׁמֵם meaning "waste," "devastation," "desolation"/"desolate" or "destruction" (Jer 4:7; 7:34; 22:5; 32:18; 51:6, 22).

163. Dan 9:26–27; 11:31; 12:11. It is widely held that שִׁקּוּצִים מְשֹׁמֵם is a Jewish wordplay derived from בַּעַל שָׁמַיִם (Lord of heaven = Zeus); see, e.g., Beasley-Murray, *Jesus and the Last Days*, 409.

164. See 1 Macc 1:54; 59; 6:7; 2 Macc 6:1–6; Josephus, *Ant.* 12.253; 320–22.

and co-texts of the phrase in Matthew. Following this, I will review extant interpretations and then submit a proposal.

The Grammar of τὸ βδέλυγμα τῆς ἐρημώσεως

The expression, τὸ βδέλυγμα τῆς ἐρημώσεως, is a genitive construct, and, just like all similar constructs, lends itself to ambiguity. Thus, it is important to consider its grammar before looking at the referent in relation to the destruction of the temple. Davies and Allison construe ἐρημώσεως as an epexegetical genitive.[165] An epexegetical genitive is appositional in the sense that it defines or redefines the head noun. In the present case, βδέλυγμα would, by definition, be equated or interchangeable with ἐρημώσεως and the expression may be rendered as "abomination *which is* desolation." Davies and Allison also add that the phrase "can mean either [abomination that] 'makes desolate' or 'causes horror' or [preferably] both at the same time"[166] Such a causal reading of βδέλυγμα τῆς ἐρημώσεως ("abomination *that causes* desolation") is grammatically possible.[167]

More likely, however, βδέλυγμα τῆς ἐρημώσεως is an attributive genitival construct. Wallace describes the attributive genitive as the scenario where "the genitive substantive specifies an attribute or innate quality of the head substantive"[168] In other words, while the head noun and the genitival noun are not semantically the same, they are simultaneous or inseparable. Applied here, the sense of the genitive, ἐρημώσεως, would be that of characterization rather than equation or causation. Consequently, the expression βδέλυγμα τῆς ἐρημώσεως is fittingly rendered "devastating pollution,"[169] or "desolating sacrilege."[170] The distinction is not absolute, but it becomes necessary to avoid the tendency to separate the two terms or to take ἐρημώσεως as a reference to the destruction of Jerusalem and the temple, exactly what Michael Theophilos has done in his recent study. Taking the genitive construct causally, Theophilos argues that Israel is the βδέλυγμα ("abomination" = their rejection of Jesus as Messiah) and the Roman army the inflictor of the ἐρήμωσις ("desolation" = the destruction of Jerusalem).[171] I will respond

---

165. Davies and Allison, *Matthew*, 3:346.

166. Davies and Allison, *Matthew*, 3:346.

167. So NIV, NIB; although notice how awkward it is to read these senses into the phrase, βάπτισμα μετανοίας ("baptism of repentance") in Mark 1:4.

168. Wallace, *Grammar*, 86–88.

169. France, *Matthew*, 896.

170. Hill, *Matthew*, 321; Hendriksen, *Matthew*, 857; so also RSV.

171. Theophilos, *Abomination*, 120–26, 198.

to this shortly. In the meantime, I note that K. D. Dyer rejects any such attempt to separate βδέλυγμα τῆς ἐρημώσεως into a two-part event, although he, as Theophilos, maintains the causal view.¹⁷²

Literary Context and Co-texts of βδέλυγμα τῆς ἐρημώσεως

Contrary to the causal view argued by Theophilos, a distinction between βδέλυγμα τῆς ἐρημώσεως and the destruction of the temple should be maintained. The attributive view helps make this clear, and such a distinction is contextually grounded. First, the term "desolation" (ἐρημώσεως) in the phrase βδέλυγμα τῆς ἐρημώσεως echoes the saying in 23:38, "your house is left to you desolate (ἔρημος)." By saying this, Jesus does not mean that the temple is already destroyed; 23:38 may only proleptically refer to a future destruction. Second, βδέλυγμα τῆς ἐρημώσεως in 24:15 is only a sign of the beginning of a great tribulation that will culminate in the destruction of the temple. Nor is it the case that βδέλυγμα τῆς ἐρημώσεως is the cause of the destruction of the temple. In Matthew's context, the rejection of Jesus, rather than the abomination of desolation, is the cause of the temple's destruction. Third, the βδέλυγμα τῆς ἐρημώσεως is something that will be "standing," or better, seen to "have stood" (ἑστὸς) in the "holy place" (τόπος ἅγιον). This can only imply that the temple itself remains standing.

Moreover, this distinction is also the case in Daniel where the "abomination of desolation" is strictly the "desecration" rather than necessarily the "destruction" of the temple.¹⁷³ That this is the case is clear from the use of καθαρίζω ("to cleanse") in Dan 8:13–14 to describe the eventual remedy.¹⁷⁴

We should further consider two significant co-texts of the βδέλυγμα τῆς ἐρημώσεως in Matthew. The first is the phrase ἐν τόπος ἅγιον which defines the location of the abomination of desolation. Unfortunately, the referent of τόπος ἅγιον also lends itself to ambiguity. Some take it to refer to Jerusalem in particular or Judea in general. The book of 2 Macc 2:18

---

172. See Dyer, *Prophecy*, 223–24.

173. So also Beasley-Murray, *Mark Thirteen*, 55; contra Ford, *Abomination*, 168; Dyer, *Prophecy*, 223, as well as Beasley-Murray's later interpretation of the βδέλυγμα in Mark 13:14 to include "both profanation and destruction" (*Jesus and the Last Days*, 357, cf. 410–11, 416). Keener suggests that in Dan 9:26, the language of "abomination of desolation" is applied to "the cutting off of an anointed ruler, close to the time of Jesus" (*Matthew*, 575–76).

174. Extra-biblical accounts of the event also do not indicate the destruction of the temple, only its cleansing and *re*consecration; see 1 Macc 1:54; 4:41–58; Josephus, *Ant.* 12.253, 316–25.

may seem to support the equation of "holy place" with "holy land."[175] But the context of this Maccabean passage (vv. 1-19) indicates that the referent is specifically the temple, to which the author desires that God may gather all Jews for a festive commemoration of its purification, not "holy land" in general.[176] Pierre Bonnard argues that "holy place" is a veiled reference to the church, hence the address to the reader to understand.[177] Such identification would be hardly conceivable to the implied reader. In fact, Matt 16:18 may already suggest that the church "cannot suffer abominable desolation." Gentry argues for both Jerusalem and the temple because he assumes that the βδέλυγμα τῆς ἐρημώσεως is the surrounding of Jerusalem by the Roman soldiers.[178]

I argue that the implied reader of Matthew would more readily understand ἐν τόπος ἅγιον as a direct definite reference to the temple.[179] The lack of article before τόπος ἅγιον does not render it indefinite and therefore a reference to anywhere in the land.[180] One might argue that the juxtaposition of "holy place" (v. 15) with flight from "Judea" (v. 16), in addition to the fact that flight from Jerusalem is not mentioned, suggests that the "holy place" represents Jerusalem as a whole.[181] This is not impossible, but the point assumes that "those in Judea" excludes "those in Jerusalem." Judea here must be taken as all-inclusive. Moreover, the equation of "holy place" and the temple is supported by the fact Matthew uses the term "holy city" when he intends to refer to Jerusalem as a whole (cf. 4:5; 27:53).

Redaction-critical interpreters take "holy place" as a clarification of Mark's more ambiguous ὅπου οὐ δεῖ ("where it ought not to be"). However, as Agbanou argues, Matthew's "holy place," as in the text of Daniel, is "more

---

175. See Ford, *Abomination*, 170; Plummer, *Matthew*, 332.

176. Cf. Grundmann, *Matthäus*, 506n18.

177. Bonnard, *Matthieu*, 351; Smith, *Matthew*, 285, suggests it refers to the new Matthean community; cf. Patte, *Matthew*, 338.

178. In Ice and Gentry, *Great Tribulation*, 46-47.

179. E.g., Dan 8:13; 11:31 (cf. 1 En. 25:5; 2 Macc 8:17-19; Acts 6:13-14; 21:28; Heb 9:25; 11:31); see Hagner, *Matthew*, 698, 700; Gundry, *Matthew*, 482; Luz, *Matthew*, 196; Gibbs, *Jerusalem and Parousia*, 183; France, *Matthew*, 912; Konradt, *Matthew*, 359; Nolland, *Matthew*, 970.

180. While Matthew can make an articular reference to the temple (e.g., ἐν τῷ ἱερῷ in 26:55), the phrase, ἐν τόπος ἅγιον, is stylistically anarthrous (perhaps for emphasis or prominence; cf. discussion on τέλος above) but not necessarily indefinite (cf. ἐν πνεύματι ἁγίῳ [3:11]; ἐν ὁρίοις Ζαβουλὼν καὶ Νεφθαλίμ [4:13]; ἐν ἡμέρᾳ κρίσεως [10:15]; ἐν μέσῳ λύκων [10:16]; ἐν πνεύματι θεοῦ [12:28]; ἐν μέσῳ αὐτῶν [18:2]; ἐν ὀνόματι κυρίου [23:39]).

181. Dyer questions why the flight is not addressed to those in Jerusalem as a basis for suggesting that a Vespasian coin sited in the north or south of Judea could be what is required in Mark 13:14 (*Prophecy*, 224, 227).

primitive" than Mark's "where it ought not to be."[182] If Matthew was writing post-70 and using Mark, how likely is it that he would make this change, more explicitly referencing the temple as if it still stood in its place?[183] Nothing in Matthew suggests that he could be thinking of a rebuilt future temple.[184]

The second significant co-text is the remark, ὁ ἀναγινώσκων νοείτω ("let the reader understand"). Most exegetes take it as a parenthetical aside addressed by Matthew (or Mark) to the reader of Daniel.[185] Some take it as Matthew's (also Mark's) address to the readers of his Gospel.[186] Jeannine K. Brown and Kyle Roberts suggest it somehow points both backward and forward.[187] However, these views seem inaccurate; there is no reason the saying cannot be attributed to Jesus. The fact that in all the other six instances in Matthew, the verb ἀναγινώσκω is found only in the mouth of Jesus in reference to an OT passage,[188] resists the view that the expression is a parenthetical aside by the implied author.[189] By "let the reader understand," Jesus apparently calls for the re-appropriation of the Danielic βδέλυγμα τῆς ἐρημώσεως. The imperative suggests a potential ambiguity, implying the need for a correct interpretation of temple events rather than a literal transfer of the Danielic tradition.[190]

---

182. Agbanou, *Discours*, 87–88; cf. Wenham, *Rediscovery*, 193, 196, 365, 369–70.

183. Since it is difficult to see why Mark is reticent to mention "holy place" or "temple"—a term he uses nine times (11:11, 15, 16, 27; 12:35; 13:1, 3; 14:49), the phrase, "where it ought not to be," fits a scenario where the temple is no longer standing but the fear remains that some might try to erect an abomination on the sacred temple ruins.

184. Several passages (Matt 5:23–24; 17:24–27; 23:16–22) suggest that the temple is still standing when Matthew wrote. For more on this, see France, *Matthew*, 19.

185. See Hagner, *Matthew*, 700; Gundry, *Matthew*, 481; Luz, *Matthew*, 195; Beasley-Murray, *Jesus and the Last Days*, 411.

186. Geddert, "Apocalyptic Teaching" in *DJG*, 23.

187. Brown and Roberts, *Matthew*, 217. Note that, taken as an interjection by Matthew, as most scholars do, the expression would seem unnecessary if the temple was already in ruins; its combination with the explicit reference to the temple on the one hand and the lack of clarity regarding the referent of the βδέλυγμα τῆς ἐρημώσεως on the other, weigh against the claim that Matthew wrote *vaticinum-ex-eventu*. It would be right then to question, as France does, what Matthew "had to gain by writing so cryptically, and by failing to achieve a satisfying tie-up with what would then [post-70] have been quite recent history" (*Matthew*, 913); cf. Keener, *Matthew*, 562.

188. Matt 12:3, 5; 19:4; 21:16, 42; 22:31; adding 24:15, this sevenfoldness compares to other sevenfold expressions such as the woes uttered by Jesus in Matt 23.

189. See Pitre, *Jesus*, 309–13.

190. The notions of ambiguity and "understanding" of the events of the βδέλυγμα τῆς ἐρημώσεως is an issue in Daniel (Dan 8:15–17; 9:22–23; 11:33; 12:9–10), so also is "understanding" of Jesus' revelatory teachings in Matthew (e.g., Matt 5:17; 16:9, 11; cf. 13:11).

Furthermore, in the Discourse context, βδέλυγμα τῆς ἐρημώσεως partly resonates with Jesus' words in 23:38, "your house is left to you desolate (ἔρημος)," which in turn might suggest that an unworthy Jewish activity (cf. 21:13) has profaned the temple in a sense, hence Jesus' departure from it (24:1).[191] A murder such as Jesus references in 23:35 may also constitute an example of polluting abomination.[192] In any case, Matt 24:15 is certainly not intended to deny that the Antiochian event was already fulfilled in the past. Nor does it suggest the second coming of Antiochus IV. In fact, βδέλυγμα τῆς ἐρημώσεως can be invoked with potentially varying interpretive emphasis.[193] Hagner asserts that the Antiochian event was "so horrific . . . that it became a convenient and elastic symbol for the great evils that were to engulf the people in the future."[194] Similarly, commenting on the referent of βδέλυγμα τῆς ἐρημώσεως, Beasley-Murray states that "The common extension of meaning given to OT passages in the NT forbids an insistence that our Lord's use of the expression must be identical with that in the Danielic passages," adding, "in any case by this time it may well have become proverbial."[195] Thus, the referent of βδέλυγμα τῆς ἐρημώσεως, although to be processed in light of the Danielic tradition, can admit a new application.

Various Interpretations of βδέλυγμα τῆς ἐρημώσεως

The many interpretations of βδέλυγμα τῆς ἐρημώσεως that have been proposed may be divided into three broad categories:[196] (1) the futuristic-antichrist view, which represents the most popular interpretation;[197] (2) the pagan-abomination views: a Roman statue (of Caligula, Titus, or Hadrian)

---

191. Cf. Konradt, *Matthew*, 359.

192. See 1 Macc 1:37; Josephus, *Ant.* 9.152; Josephus, *J.W.* 4.201.

193. E.g., in reference to it, the author of 1 Macc (1:54) emphasizes the pagan altar; the author of 2 Macc (6:4) says that "the temple was filled with riots and reveling by gentiles, who dallied with harlots within the circuit of the holy places and brought in things that were not lawful"; and it certainly gave rise to the Pauline "man of lawlessness" (2 Thess 2).

194. Hagner, *Matthew*, 700.

195. Beasley-Murray, *Commentary*, 55.

196. For a history of scholarship on the subject, see Ford, *Abomination*, 158–69; Beasley-Murray, *Commentary*, 59–72; Beasley-Murray, *Jesus and the Last Days*, 413–15; Theophilos, *Abomination*, 11–21.

197. Hill, *Matthew*, 321; Hare, *Matthew*, 278; Gundry, *Matthew*, 482; Beare, *Matthew*, 468; cf. Davies and Allison, *Matthew*, 3:356. Ford, *Abomination*, 161–63, argues that it likely refers "first to the armies of Rome, but including later manifestations of Antichrist."

or some idol,[198] Roman army,[199] standard,[200] or coin;[201] and (3) the Jewish-abomination views: the activity of zealots' in the temple,[202] or, more broadly, Israel's covenantal infidelity and consequent punishment.[203]

First, the antichrist view assumes (1) an *ex-eventu* date for Matthew's Gospel, (2) a parallel between the Matthean βδέλυγμα and the Pauline ἄνθρωπος τῆς ἀνομίας (2 Thess 2:3),[204] and therefore, (3) an individual (analogous to Antiochus IV) as the referent of βδέλυγμα τῆς ἐρημώσεως. The first assumption is uncertain,[205] the second unlikely,[206] and the third flatly erroneous.[207] The third assumption is refuted by the fact that the βδέλυγμα τῆς ἐρημώσεως in the LXX Daniel on which Matthew most likely depends, is a neuter object which "shall be" (ἔσται [9:27]), "they shall give" (δώσουσι [1:31]), or "is prepared to be given" (ἑτοιμασθῇ δοθῆναι [12:11]) in the temple, not a person.[208] The gender agreement between βδέλυγμα and ἑστός

---

198. Jerome, *Comm. Matt.* 272, claims it may refer to a literal Antichrist or to the image of Caesar placed by Pilate in the temple pagan [see Josephus, *Ant.* 18.3.55-59], or to the equestrian statue of Hadrian [Eusebius, *Hist. eccl.* 4.6.3], or "an idol which will be placed in the desolated and destroyed temple." Chrysostom, *Hom. Matt.* 75.2, takes the abomination of desolation to be the image of Titus; Baur, *Lectures*, 303, claims the image of Hadrian as the referent. Pfleiderer, "Komposition der eschatologischen," 135, originated the view that it refers to Emperor Gaius Caligula's attempt to set up his image in the temple (see Josephus, *Ant.* 18.257-309), a view followed by many recent interpreters; see Theophilos, *Abomination*, 15nn23 and 24.

199. Bengel, *Word Studies*, 1:270; Lightfoot, *Commentary*, 2:313; Ford, *Abomination*, 163; Tasker, *Matthew*, 229-30; Gentry, in Ice and Gentry, *Great Tribulation*, 48.

200. Wright, *Matthew*, 118-19; Talbert, *Matthew*, 268; Lampe, "AD 70 in Christian Reflection," 162; see also Josephus, *J.W.* 6.316; Eusebius, *Hist. eccl.* 3.5.3-4; 1QpHab. 6.3-5.

201. Dyer, *Prophecy*, 226-29; he hypothesizes that a Vespasian image-bearing coin minted in 69 CE, soon after he became emperor-elect, could have reached Judea ahead of Titus and his armies and would have signaled to Jewish Christians of imminent doom. As news of Nero's death came, Vespasian headed back to Rome, leaving the onslaught against Jerusalem to Titus (see Josephus, *J.W.* 4.486-91).

202. Recent advocates of this view include Sowers, "Circumstances and Recollection"; but more extensively, Balabanski, *Eschatology*, 122-34.

203. Theophilos, *Abomination*, 121, 178-98.

204. Cf. the Didachean κοσμοπλανὴς ("world-deceiver" [Did. 16:4]).

205. See nn. 101 and 102 in chapter 1.

206. Dodd calls the identification "hazardous," adding, "it is not clear that the βδέλυγμα τῆς ἐρημώσεως is properly an antichrist at all" ("Fall of Jerusalem," 53n10).

207. See Such, *Abomination*, 81-87; although he argues that an individual, Titus, is the abomination of desolation in Mark 13:14 (101-2).

208. In the Heb. Daniel the "abomination" is masculine singular (שִׁקּוּץ) in Dan 11:31 and 12:11, but masculine plural (שִׁקּוּצִים) in 9:27. Note that a wrong English translation of Dan 9:27b (e.g., RSV) creates the false impression that an individual is referenced,

(both accusative neuter singular) suggests that Matthew deliberately intends something impersonal.[209] Thus, the sign-performing ἄνθρωπος τῆς ἀνομίας of 2 Thess. 2:3 hardly fits the βδέλυγμα τῆς ἐρημώσεως of Matt 24. Moreover, in the latter, the role of signs and wonders is assigned to ψευδόχριστοι and ψευδοπροφῆται (vv. 23-26) not to the βδέλυγμα τῆς ἐρημώσεως, which is clearly a different category.[210] Nor was the notorious Antiochus a suprahuman performer of signs.

Second, regarding the pagan abomination views, the connection of the βδέλυγμα τῆς ἐρημώσεως with Gaius Caligula should be excluded. It is unlikely that Matthew would refer to Caligula's attempt to place his image in the temple in 40 CE, an event that did not materialize due to Caligula's sudden death in 41 CE. Similarly, any connection with emperor Hadrian's erection of a temple to Jupiter on the temple ruins in the second century (132–36 CE) is extraneous for its sheer lateness. On the view that Titus is the βδέλυγμα τῆς ἐρημώσεως, Davies and Allison note that there is no real evidence of the image of Titus or of Titus himself in the temple during the 70 CE war.[211]

Those who claim that the mere appearance of the Roman army in Judea with their standard, which bears the image of the emperor, fulfills the βδέλυγμα τῆς ἐρημώσεως, do so on the basis of Luke 21:20. Tasker, for example, argues that Luke's version, "when you see Jerusalem surrounded by armies," and the omission of the words, *standing in the holy place* in the Sinaitic MS of the Old Syriac version of Matthew, are the clues to what βδέλυγμα τῆς ἐρημώσεως means. He reasons that the Roman soldiers' approach to Judea with their ensign would have been readily accepted by the idol-hating Jews as the sign to commence flight.[212]

The challenge with this view is that Matt 24:15–16 does not say, "when you see the 'abominable sign' (a rendition Tasker seems to prefer) approaching Judea . . . then flee." While Luke's version of the Discourse may shed some light on Matthew's, at this point it is better to make sense of Matthew's text than to cheaply play it off against Luke's. We should observe that by the *unaffected* (i.e., self-standing) ἐρήμωσις in Luke 21:20, Luke means

---

but there is no such possibility either here or in 11:31, contra Such, *Abomination*, 87. "There is nothing in the Daniel passages or in 1 Maccabees to suggest giving a personal meaning to the βδέλυγμα τῆς ἐρημώσεως" (France, *Gospel of Mark*, 523).

209. Cf. Mark's use of masculine ἑστηκότα (13:14) which suggests an individual.

210. Cf. Beasley-Murray, *Jesus and the Last Days*, 414.

211. Davies and Allison, *Matthew*, 3:345n116; although *Genesis Rabbah* 10.7 claims, "when the wicked Titus entered the Holy of Holies, he dragged down the veil, blasphemed and reviled God."

212. Tasker, *Matthew*, 229–30.

the "destruction" of the city as a whole, whereas the *affected* meaning of ἐρημώσεως (i.e., in phrasal collocation with βδέλυγμα, as in τὸ βδέλυγμα τῆς ἐρημώσεως [Matt 24:15]) is specifically the "desecration" of the temple (cf. Daniel).[213] Thus, Tasker's view fails to account for this notion of cultic desecration. Moreover, a flight while the Roman army built a siege around Jerusalem, would have been unlikely, practically impossible. Gentry's argument that some providential opportunity of escape could have opened during that siege is unconvincing.[214] The reason is that the urgency of the command in Matt 24:16–19 assumes that the flight would be safe and thus requires it to be immediate rather than dependent on a providential opening when Roman soldiers momentarily withdraw from the siege.[215]

Furthermore, the Roman standard erected in the temple may be closely analogous to the Antiochus-led desecration of the temple with an idol. According to Josephus (*War* 6.316), when Roman soldiers invaded and set the temple and its surrounding buildings on fire in 70 CE, they erected their standards, sacrificed to them, and acclaimed Titus as imperator. However, this identification of the Matthean βδέλυγμα τῆς ἐρημώσεως is even more problematic. At this tail end of the war, flight would have been too late and the command to flee itself meaningless, especially from the perspective of one who had already lived through or is simply reporting the ordeal.[216] Thus, no solution for the quagmire can be found in the Roman-army view, whether at the point they surrounded Jerusalem or at the point they invaded and destroyed the temple.

K. D. Dyer's proposal that a Vespasian image-bearing coin fulfills the saying runs into similar problems. Dyer's work is based on Mark's version, and he seems to take "where *he* ought not to be" (Mark 13:14) to be anywhere in Judea, with the "he" referring to Vespasian's standing image engraved on the coin. He argues (a) that the coin "fits the traditional interpretation of the abomination as both a foreign ruler and a pagan image who threaten the temple," and (b) that Judeans will be able to see the coin and flee in time.[217] However, it is not at all clear how this view makes sense of the flight if, at the time the coin appears in Judea, Jerusalem was already

---

213. The words, *affected* and *unaffected*, are borrowed from Wallace, *Grammar*, 507; he defines them in terms of phenomenological and ontological meanings respectively.

214. See Gentry, in Ice and Gentry, *Great Tribulation*, 48–50.

215. Josephus, *J.W.* 4.486–90 and 4.585–88, all passages cited by Gentry (Ice and Gentry, *Great Tribulation*, 50) do not support the claim of providential opening for escape but rather contradict it.

216. That is, assuming the post-70 date of writing is correct.

217. Dyer, *Prophecy*, 228.

surrounded by a Vespasian siege.[218] More importantly, how could a coin somewhere in Judea have been taken as the abomination of desolation when a coin with Caesar's image had for long existed in Jerusalem (Matt 22:18–21/ Mark 12:16–17)? Obviously, a coin, even if bearing a standing image, is not the kind of thing that could have stirred Jewish Christians to flight. This singular point renders the hypothesis improbable—an improbability which Dyer himself suspects.[219]

Third, the view taking the referent of βδέλυγμα τῆς ἐρημώσεως as something Jews themselves did in the temple is not a new one,[220] but it has been more vigorously advanced in recent years. Two paths may be followed to arrive at the hypothesis. The first path is the account of Josephus. Clearly aware of the event of Antiochus alluded to in Daniel,[221] Josephus writes that "Zealots brought upon their country the fulfillment of the prophecies directed against it. For there was an ancient saying of inspired men that the city would be taken and the sanctuary burnt to the ground by right of war, whensoever it should be visited by sedition and native hands should be the first to defile God's sacred precinct."[222] By this, Josephus references the zealots' violent invasion of the temple in 67 CE when they deposed the high priest, Ananus, replacing him with a man named Phanni(as) who they selected by lot.[223]

Following this account, Balabanski provides a most comprehensive explication of the view that the Markan βδέλυγμα τῆς ἐρημώσεως is to be understood in relation to the activity of zealots in the temple. She claims that the notion that Jews themselves, rather than gentiles, will commit the desecration of the temple is supported by the Danielic tradition because "Dan. 8:11ff; 9:27 and 11:32 either link or at least permit the linking of the cultic transgression to Jews who violate the covenant."[224] Balabanski goes further to specifically argue that the Zealots' installation of the puppet priest is the referent of the Mark 13:14 oracle. In other words, Phannias is "the abomination standing where *he* ought not."[225] This interpretation depends

---

218. See Josephus, *J.W.* 4.486–91.

219. Dyer, *Prophecy*, 228.

220. For many nineteenth-century German scholars who held this view, see Ford, *Abomination*, 159.

221. Josephus, *Ant.* 12.253, 320–22; *J.W.* 5.394–95.

222. Josephus, *J.W.* 4.387–88 (cf. 4.147–63).

223. Josephus, *J.W.* 4.151–61.

224. Balabanski, *Eschatology*, 124.

225. Balabanski, *Eschatology*, 129; cf. Sowers, "Circumstances," 317–39.

on the "prevailing critical view,"[226] i.e., that the Jewish oracle behind Mark 13 was given at the time of this event (i.e., 67/68 CE), borrowing from the tradition in Daniel and 1 Maccabees.

The candidacy of Phannias as the abomination of desolation is appealing. Witherington considers Phannias a plausible referent in Mark while taking Titus as the referent in Matthew.[227] Theophilos considers Balabanski's view as "closest to the original intent of the saying in that it was a Jewish group who were the abomination of desolation."[228] Indeed, the view is to be commended for eliminating the chronological incongruity associated with the view that identifies βδέλυγμα τῆς ἐρημώσεως with the Roman standard erected in the temple while the temple burned in 70 CE. As already noted, the command to flee for safety in Matt 24:16//Mark 13:14b would be meaningless by the time the Romans overrun the temple.

However, while offensive in itself, since Phannias, according to Josephus, was ἀνὴρ οὐ μόνον οὐκ ἐξ ἀρχιερέων, ἀλλ' οὐδ' ἐπιστάμενος σαφῶς τί ποτ' ἦν ἀρχιερωσύνη ("a man not only not of the high priests, but neither understanding well what the priesthood was"), the mere illegal installation of an unworthy high priest could hardly have signaled to Jewish Christians that it was time to flee. Much corrupt politicking was already entrenched in the appointment of high priests, and Rome or Rome's client-kings often intervened.[229] In fact, Ananus, though of the line of priests, was himself a product of such corrupt appointments.[230] Theophilos points out that several Jews and Christians would not have been negative about the Zealots' appointment of Phannias owing to the high priest's bitter reproach of the people for sloth (see Josephus, J.W. 4.160).[231] Moreover, if we grant that Mark was writing during 67–68 CE and supposed that Phannias was the abomination of desolation, hence his use of the masculine perfect participle, ἑστηκότα, we are compelled to look for a different referent in Matthew since a personal referent cannot fit the Matthean use of the neuter form, ἑστός, which suggests an impersonal object or phenomenon.[232]

---

226. Dodd, "Fall of Jerusalem," 47.

227. Witherington, *Matthew*, 447.

228. Theophilos, *Abomination*, 20; cf. Morris, *Matthew*, 603.

229. See Smallwood, "High Priests and Politics," 14–34.

230. Josephus, *Ant.* 20.196–99.

231. Theophilos, *Abomination*, 20; although Sowers argues that the priesthood remained sacred for many Christians ("Circumstances," 318).

232. Balabanski does not think that βδέλυγμα τῆς ἐρημώσεως in Daniel refers to a person, only that Mark was thinking about the installation of Phannias (*Eschatology*, 122n38).

The second path to the Jewish-abomination hypothesis is the OT prophetic literature. Theophilos advances this approach in his study dedicated specifically to Matt 24:15. Despite his largely positive appraisal of Balabanski's view, his proposal is "a revised model" that follows a "contextual exegetical approach" and "gives due weight to Old Testament intertextual prophetic echoes." Theophilos's unique contribution, inspired by the denunciatory tone of Matt 23, is that "the phrase [βδέλυγμα τῆς ἐρημώσεως] was employed as a prophetic oracle of doom against Israel for her apostacy."[233] This thesis is further grounded in three foundations: (1) "that the language of βδέλυγμα (שִׁקּוּצִים) and ἐρημώσις (מְשַׁמֵּם) is attested in the prophetic literature and used in the description (i.e., abomination) and consequence (i.e. desolation) of Israel's covenantal infidelity"; (2) that Daniel's use of βδέλυγμα τῆς ἐρημώσεως was influenced by this earlier prophetic literature;[234] and (3) that these two trajectories influenced Matthew's use of the Danielic saying to describe the destruction of Jerusalem.[235] Theophilos concludes that, by a twist of irony, in Matt 24, as opposed to the Danielic tradition where Antiochus IV is both the abomination and desolator, Israel is the abomination while the Roman soldiers inflict the desolation (i.e., the destruction of Jerusalem) as a consequence.[236]

This interpretation by Theophilos strikes one as much less persuasive than Balabanski's. First, Theophilos's case appears to be methodologically unsound. It amounts to fragmenting the phrasal unit τὸ βδέλυγμα τῆς ἐρημώσεως in order to equate it with the semantic sum of its parts, wherever those parts occur. As such, it imposes too general an interpretation, especially on the term βδέλυγμα. Second, in relation to this first point, and as I argued above, the genitive construct, βδέλυγμα τῆς ἐρημώσεως, does not commend the segregation of βδέλυγμα and ἐρημώσεως as two separate events each performed by a different agent in a causal connection.[237] Third, the term, ἐρημώσεως, does not necessarily mean the destruction of Jerusalem

---

233. Theophilos, *Abomination*, 20. A similar case is made by Dodd from the perspective of Luke's version of the βδέλυγμα τῆς ἐρημώσεως (Luke 21:20); he contends that Luke's version neither derives from his editing of Mark nor from reflections on the capture of Jerusalem by Titus in 70 CE, but from the OT, especially the capture of Jerusalem by Nebuchadnezzar in 586 BC ("Fall of Jerusalem," 49–52).

234. Isaiah (1:7–17); but especially Jeremiah (4:1–7; 7:1—8:3; 13:24–27; 51:22) and Ezekiel (5:9–14; 6:8–14; 33:21–29); on the prophetic influence on Daniel, Theophilos notes the following: Is. 53:11 and Dan 12:3; Jer 25:11–12 and 29:10 in Dan 9:24–27; Ezekiel 1 and Dan 7; Ezek 20:6 and Dan 8:9; Ezek 1:28 and Dan 8:17; Dan 8:2 and Ezek 1:1.

235. Theophilos, *Abomination*, 178.

236. Theophilos, *Abomination*, 198

237. Again, see Dyer, *Prophecy*, 223–34.

either in the Danielic or Matthean use.²³⁸ Fourth, following Theophilos' interpretation, Matt 24:15 would mean, "when you see Israel's covenantal infidelity and the consequent destruction of Jerusalem and the temple, then flee." Nothing could be more inconsistent with Matt 24:15–16 and Matthew in general. The depiction of Israel's unfaithfulness has been ongoing in Matthew,²³⁹ but the "abomination of desolation" is a specific thing (event or phenomenon) to look out for in the temple.

We should note that in the Danielic tradition, the agent of the βδέλυγμα τῆς ἐρημώσεως is distinct from the βδέλυγμα τῆς ἐρημώσεως itself. Again, while closely associated, it is important to maintain this distinction as the following passages show:

1. Dan 9:27— ... καὶ ἐπὶ τὸ ἱερὸν βδέλυγμα τῶν ἐρημώσεων ἔσται ἕως συντελείας καὶ συντέλεια δοθήσεται ἐπὶ τὴν ἐρήμωσιν (... and in the temple, an abomination of desolations shall be until the end, and [then] an end shall be given on the desolation).

2. Dan 11:31—καὶ βραχίονες παρ' αὐτοῦ στήσονται καὶ μιανοῦσι τὸ ἅγιον τοῦ φόβου καὶ ἀποστήσουσι τὴν θυσίαν καὶ δώσουσι βδέλυγμα ἐρημώσεως (Forces from him shall stand and defile the holy place of fear and *they* shall give *the abomination of desolation*).

3. Dan 12:11—ἀφ' οὗ ἂν ἀποσταθῇ ἡ θυσία διὰ παντὸς καὶ ἑτοιμασθῇ δοθῆναι τὸ βδέλυγμα τῆς ἐρημώσεως ἡμέρας χιλίας διακοσίας ἐνενήκοντα (From what time the 'every-day' sacrifice is taken away and abomination of desolation is prepared to be given [shall be] a thousand two hundred and ninety days).²⁴⁰

In these three passages, the agent is a person(s), but the βδέλυγμα τῆς ἐρημώσεως is a thing "given" (set up) in the holy place. That the abomination of desolation is not a person is verified by the fact the βδέλυγμα τῆς ἐρημώσεως is earlier described in terms of ἡ ἁμαρτία ἐρημώσεως ("the sin of desolation" [Dan 8:13]).²⁴¹ As noted above, Balabanski's review of these passages leads her to the conclusion that, "it is not correct to say that the βδέλυγμα τῆς ἐρημώσεως refers to the entrance of Antiochus IV Epiphanes into the Temple."²⁴² I have already noted that the specific character of the βδέλυγμα τῆς ἐρημώσεως as something given in the holy place, rather than

---

238. So also Burnett, *Testament*, 337.
239. Esp. 3:7–10; 23:13–38.
240. Translations mine
241. Balabanski, *Eschatology*, 122n38, notes that this earlier "reference is clearly linked thematically to the later ones (9:27, 11:31, 12:11)."
242. Balabanski, *Eschatology*, 122.

a person, is also reflected in the Matthean definite and neuter phrase, τὸ βδέλυγμα τῆς ἐρημώσεως ... ἑστὸς ἐν τόπῳ ἁγίῳ (24:15). In other words, the saying in Matthew is concerned with what is placed or done in the holy place rather than with the agent by whom it is placed or done.

Proposed Interpretation of βδέλυγμα τῆς ἐρημώσεως

What then would have been most likely seen as the abomination of desolation by the disciples or Matthew's readers? Bearing in mind the issues raised regarding Balabanski's view above, I suggest that the most plausible candidate for the abomination of desolation in Matthew remains within the Zealot saga.[243] However, rather than Phannias, *it refers to the heap of dead bodies resulting from the Idumean massacre of Jews in the temple.*

After Phannias became substantive high priest, an uprising broke out against the zealots at the instance of the ousted priest, Ananus, leading to a standoff in the temple. Josephus reports that the zealots, frightened by the masses' upper hand against them, escaped into the inner court of the temple, defiling the sacred place with their blood-stained feet.[244] While stuck in there, and having been fed with a lie that Ananus had betrayed the city to the Romans, they invited the Idumeans to come to their aid.[245] The Idumeans, being by nature disposed to murder (φύσει τε ὠμότατοι φονεύειν) responded to this invitation, broke into the temple, and massacred many Jews stationed there. According to Josephus, the outer temple (τὸ ἔξωθεν ἱερὸν) was flooded with much blood as eight thousand five hundred dead bodies lay there that day. Once done with the massacre in the temple, the Idumeans descended on the city, plundering houses, and extending their killing spree. They also sought out and murdered Ananus, the high priest. Josephus considers this event, especially the murder of Ananus, to be the beginning of the destruction of Jerusalem.[246]

Of course, the challenge with this account lies in the potential unreliability of Josephus. Since he was once allied with the Jewish revolutionary

---

243. Cf. Keener, *Matthew*, 576–77 and Morris, *Matthew*, 603, although they stop short of identifying a specific thing.

244. Josephus, *J.W.* 4.201, 242.

245. Josephus, *J.W.* 4.202–352.

246. Josephus, *J.W.* 4.310–18 (cf. 5.3); this event precedes a later development in the civil war when, because of fighting among three splinters of the zealots, many worshippers and priests were killed while sacrificing in the temple (*J.W.* 5.15–20). Josephus sees this later event as equally abominable, but he does not regard it as the beginning of the destruction of the city as Keener, *Matthew*, 576, appears to suggest. Nolland, *Matthew*, 970–71, fails to properly delineate the former event.

movement, his anti-zealot rhetoric is likely extravagant and politically motivated. Davies and Allison even deny the historicity of the Zealots' occupation of the temple,[247] although they point to no evidence contradicting the account. How much weight should be given to the account of Josephus? Perhaps not a hefty weight, but not a zero weight either.[248]

It is true that a heap(s) of corpses in the temple, as reported by Josephus, is not exactly analogous to the idolatrous alter set up by Antiochus (none of the views is); but one must wonder with Beasley-Murray whether it is "methodologically justifiable to look for an exact correspondence ... between prophecy and a particular feature of history."[249] A heap of dead bodies may evoke the divine punishment for idolatry in which dead bodies are piled up on idols as if to equate them (see Lev 26:30). Such a gory "image" in the temple may also ironically represent a "human sacrifice" that evokes and rivals Antiochus' idolatrous sacrifice to Zeus in its abominable nature.

It is also true that murder in the temple is not unheard of,[250] but the "sacrifice" resulting in bloodied human corpses in the very place that sacrifice is offered to God would not only have been seen as a most outrageous and ominous desecration of the holy place but also is more likely to have been interpreted as the βδέλυγμα τῆς ἐρημώσεως than the installation of Phannias as high priest. It would have heightened the fear of impending doom in view of the fact that the Roman army had at the time already subdued Galilee in the north, providing ample justification for a Jewish-Christian flight based on the warning of Matt 24:16. Such a flight (in 67/68 CE), while indeterminable from the text,[251] would certainly have been

247. Davies and Allison, *Matthew*, 1:346n116.
248. See Balabanski, *Eschatology*, 125–26, 132.
249. Beasley-Murray, *Jesus and the Last Days*, 415–16.

250. Cf. Matt 23:35. Josephus knows of some he calls λησταὶ ("robbers") who used to target and murder perceived enemies during festive periods not only in some parts of the city but sometimes even in the temple (*Ant.* 20.164–66).

251. The tradition of Jewish-Christian flight at the time to the Transjordan town of Pella seems to remain plausible and may be the fulfillment of Matt 24:16. It is apparently, independently attested in the fourth century CE by Eusebius (*Hist. eccl.* 3.5.3–4) and Epiphanius (*Pan.* 29.7.7–8; 30.2.7; *Treat.* 15.15). According to Eusebius, the Romans set up the βδέλυγμα τῆς ἐρημώσεως in the temple "at the end" (ἐπὶ τέλει) of the war. However, he also records that, motivated by an oracle "before the war" (πρὸ τοῦ πολέμου), Christians had migrated from Jerusalem to Pella. Most scholars defend the historicity of this tradition, e.g., Sowers "Circumstances," 319; Koester, "Origin"; Balabanski, *Eschatology*, 101–34. Those who object to it include Brandon, *Fall of Jerusalem*, 168–78; Lüdemann, "Successors," 161–73; Gundry, *Matthew*, 482. Objections to the tradition because Pella is situated in the Transjordan valley rather than the Judean desert mountains as Matt 24:16 requires, is weak, since the text is silent on where Christians in Jerusalem should flee, and the Pella tradition concerns only a flight from Jerusalem. If

much safer at this time than at any other time, including during the later war among zealot splinters,[252] as Roman onslaught against Jerusalem would have become too close and inevitable.

Besides, there is some semblance in pattern between the murderous act of the zealot-Idumean coalition and the onslaught carried out by the forces of Antiochus. In both cases, (1) there is internal-external collusion: Jewish zealots with the Idumeans on the one hand, and certain Jews with the forces of Antiochus on the other,[253] and (2) the abomination of desolation in both cases first takes place in the temple, then followed by an advance into the city and attack against houses and people.[254]

Θλῖψις and Θλῖψις Μεγάλη

The second key theme in Matt 24:15-25 is θλῖψις ("tribulation"). Several studies have highlighted this subject as a central element in Jesus' eschatological consciousness, especially within the framework of Second Temple Jewish eschatology.[255] These studies show much evidence (unstandardized and variegated as it may be) of the belief that some eschatological Great Tribulation or messianic woes will precede the arrival of the messianic age.[256] Based on Matt 10:34-36 and 11:12 (and parr.),[257] Allison argues that, like his Jewish counterparts, Jesus not only believed in an eschatological Great Tribulation, he also understood it to have begun to manifest in his time, including the death of John the Baptist, his own death, and eventually that of his disciples.[258]

---

there was a flight at all, Pella would probably have been the reasonable destination for Christians in Jerusalem. It is not unlikely that Christians further south of Judea would have chosen to go in the southern and more mountainous direction.

252. Josephus reports that this later splinter war among zealots made any hope of flight (φυγῆς) impossible (J.W. 5.27-30). How much more difficult would it have been with the eventual Roman invasion!

253. This is not intended as a strict comparison between pagan Antiochian forces and the Idumeans. Nor were Idumeans completely external since they shared kinship as well as the temple itself with the Jews (see Josephus, J.W. 4.278, 311), but they nonetheless remain an *ethnos* distinct from Jews.

254. Cf. 1 Macc 1:52-58 and Josephus, J.W. 4.313-17.

255. Allison, *End of the Ages*, 5-25, 115-41; Allison, *Jesus of Nazareth*, 145-47; Wright, *Jesus and the Victory*, 576-92; Pitre, *Jesus*, 41-30; Pate and Kennard, *Deliverance*, 29-57.

256. Pitre, *Jesus*, 128-29, provides a helpful summary of elements of this belief.

257. Also, Luke 12:49-50; Mark 8:31; 9:31; 10:33-34.

258. Allison, *End of the Ages*, 117-41.

Indeed, many prominent scholars including Schweitzer, Dodd, Cullmann, Sowers, Jeremias, Meyer, Wright, McKnight, and Dunn have advocated the same or similar view.[259] Pate and Kennard argue that in Matthew, Jesus' death is presented not as a vicarious but as a mimetic atonement. Accordingly, "Jesus' afflictions were equated with the Great Tribulation" as the beginning of what his followers will experience. However, "while Jesus has been delivered from the Great Tribulation through the resurrection, his followers have not."[260] Similarly, from the Markan perspective, Pitre argues that Jesus embraced the messianic woes in order to atone for the sin of Israel, restore all the twelve tribes (not just Jews), and hence to bring about the final end of exile.[261] Pitre furthers this view by finding in the Eschatological Discourse (Mark 13) what he describes as "the *two-stage* pattern of eschatological tribulation" in Jesus' understanding. The first stage of this eschatological schema is a period of "preliminary eschatological 'birth pangs,'" and the second stage which he calls the Great Tribulation is "the final stage of unparalleled distress."[262] According to Pitre, "In short, Jesus taught that the tribulation had already begun in the death of John the Baptist and that it was Jesus' own mission to set in motion the 'Great Tribulation that would precede the coming of the Messiah and the restoration of Israel.'"[263] Furthermore, "just as he had interpreted the death of John the Baptist as a signal of the onset of the tribulation . . ., so too Jesus expected that he himself, and perhaps his disciples, would meet their end in the Great Tribulation still to come."[264]

While Jesus may have viewed his own sufferings as part of the eschatological woes, Allison's use of the term, Great Tribulation, to describe such sufferings creates a terminological confusion in relation to the Eschatological Discourse[265]—a confusion which Pate and Kennard, and Pitre have only perpetuated. Pitre's delineation of a consecutive two-stage eschatological schema in which a preliminary tribulation is followed by a final Great

---

259. See Pitre, *Jesus*, 383.

260. Pate and Kennard, *Deliverance*, 401–22 (esp. 404, 422).

261. Pitre, *Jesus*, 4, 381–507; this view stems from Wright, although he rejects Wright's redefinition of exile in political, metaphorical, and Jew-centered terms rather than in geographical and all-tribes-of-Israel terms; see his critique of Wright on pp. 31–40.

262. Pitre, *Jesus*, 318–19, 378.

263. Pitre, *Jesus*, 4; this view is fleshed out in light of OT scriptures connecting tribulation and restoration, such as Ezek 5:8–12, 14; Jer 30:3–9; Dan 12:1–2 (see 320–21, 334–36).

264. Pitre, *Jesus*, 505.

265. Allison, *End of the Ages*, 117–41, fails to consider the only instance in Jesus' teaching in which the expression Great Tribulation is used, the Eschatological Discourse.

Tribulation appears inconsistent with the view that Jesus initiated the Great Tribulation. As far as the Eschatological Discourse is concerned, Jesus' own suffering and death are distinct from the Great Tribulation. This term should be strictly reserved for the events leading to and surrounding the catastrophic fall of the temple.

I argue that in Matt 24, Jesus' response indicates a certain distinction between θλῖψις (generic tribulation) in 24:9 and θλῖψις μεγάλη (Great Tribulation) in 24:21.[266] These two expressions of tribulation have common accompanying features, such as the rise of false prophets or false Christs (or both [cf. vv. 11 and 24]), but they are nonetheless different. The distinction is strengthened by (1) the fact that both θλῖψις (v. 9) and θλῖψις μεγάλη (v. 21) are activated "anarthrously" (i.e., first mention without the article) but perhaps, most importantly, by (2) the fact that the disciples' expected response varies in each case.

On the one hand, the "generic tribulation" in 24:9 represents a "generalization" of period, the routine experience of all eschatological history extending up to the consummation. Throughout this period, followers of Jesus will from time to time and in different places be handed over to tribulation: they will be killed, hated by all nations; there will be earthquakes, famine, wars, and betrayals. Regarding this, the disciples' response is, ὁρᾶτε μὴ θροεῖσθε ("see that you are not frightened/troubled/alarmed" [24:6]), the implication of which is that "you must endure all this till the end to be saved" (24:13). On the other hand [the] Great Tribulation in 24:21 is a "particularization" in time, a unique and specific tribulation of an eschatological moment. In regard to it, the disciples' response is quite different. They are not to stay calm and *endure* till the end; rather they are to *escape* for their lives and be safe.

This distinction of [the] Great Tribulation from the generic tribulation has further bases in context. First, [the] Great Tribulation is unique and distinct from [the] generic tribulation because a tribulation like it never was from the beginning of the world, nor will one like it ever be. Comparable to the prediction in 24:2,[267] this saying in 24:21 is properly taken as apocalyptic hyperbole.[268] Yet it provides an important clue for understanding Jesus' view

---

266. Cf. Carson, *Matthew, Chapters 13 through 28*, 504–5; although his separation of v. 22 from v. 21 is unacceptable.

267. Keener suggests that the no-stone-upon another saying is hyperbolic (*Matthew*, 562).

268. Cf. Ezek 5:9; Joel 2:2; Dan 9:12; 12:1; Exod 9:18; 11:6; 10:14; 1 Macc 9:27; T. Mos. 8:1 and 1QM 1.11–12; Josephus, *J.W.* 1.12; 5.442; see Gibbs, *Jerusalem and Parousia*, 185; France, *Matthew*, 915; Gentry, in Ice and Gentry, *Great Tribulation*, 50–53; Beasley-Murray cites Plato (*Republic* 6.492E) as well to show that such a saying is a

of eschatological tribulation and for resolving one of the controversial questions regarding where [the] Great Tribulation falls—in the past, present, or future.[269] I will quote 24:21 fully here and then provide a diagrammatical representation of its hermeneutic import:

> ἔσται γὰρ τότε θλῖψις μεγάλη οἵα οὐ γέγονεν ἀπ' ἀρχῆς κόσμου ἕως τοῦ νῦν οὐδ' οὐ μὴ γένηται. ("for then there will be Great Tribulation such as never was from the beginning of the world until now, nor will ever be").

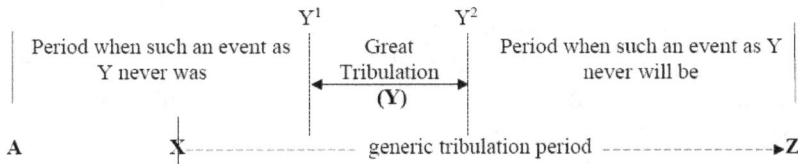

A Diagrammatic Representation of Matt 24:21.

In this representation of 24:21, "A" (the beginning of the world) implies "Z" (the end of the world).[270] In other words, the world will continue with various expressions of tribulation until the end, but a tribulation of the magnitude referred to will never occur again from the moment it happens forward until the end. The period, "XZ," is what I have designated eschatological history. It consists of "generic tribulation" (24:9) extending to the end of history "Z" as part of an ongoing period from Jesus' time "X". The broken line from X to Z is deliberate to indicate that tribulation in this period is not a continuous one. The Great Tribulation (Y) takes place at a moment within the larger period of generic tribulation,[271] with the unbroken line between

---

"traditional expression to denote severe tribulation" (*Jesus and the Last Days*, 418–19).

269. Allison's study on ancient Jewish literature concludes that where the subject is addressed, there is no standard view on the timing of the end-time tribulation; sometimes it is present, sometimes future, and other times past (*End of the Ages*, 8–25). On the scholarly debate, see Ice and Gentry, *Great Tribulation*, esp. 50–53, 95–101.

270. Cf. pp. 141–55.

271. Dan 12:1–2 may seem to connect a Great Tribulation to the time of resurrection at the end of history; however, since the reference is to the tribulation caused by Antiochus IV, this is an instance in which two events are closely aligned in the panoramic perspective of prophetic vision, even though they are, in reality, widely apart. Keener seems to suggest that an end-time Great Tribulation is meant in this Danielic passage (*Matthew*, 581).

Y¹ (24:15) and Y² indicating that the Great Tribulation is a single, continuous, but limited experience.[272]

Second, the Great Tribulation is distinct and unique by virtue of its temporal delimitation as expressed in vv. 15–20. Not only are the disciples the ones to see (ἴδητε [v. 15]), pray (προσεύχεσθε [v. 20]), and flee (φευγάτισαν [v. 16]), the locale of the event is specifically the "holy place" (temple [v. 15]) and generally Judea (v. 16). In v. 20, "sabbath" (conspicuous by its absence in Mark 13:18) points only to the land of Israel where sabbath limitations would make the enjoined flight difficult, and the use of γὰρ in v. 21 indicates that θλῖψις μεγάλη is Jesus' argument for why the disciples must flee when they see or discern the abomination of desolation. Moreover, the Great Tribulation "Y" is confined by the phrase, ἐν ἐκείναις ταῖς ἡμέραις ("in those days"). The close collocation of θλῖψις μεγάλη with ἐν ἐκείναις ταῖς ἡμέραις (used 3 times) in vv. 19–22, indicates a temporal limit which applies specifically to the θλῖψις μεγάλη.

Furthermore, insofar as the Great Tribulation specifically relates to Israel and the destruction of the temple, it follows that "the elect" because of whom the time of the Great Tribulation is shortened, are the true Israelites, that is, those Israelites "elected to salvation,"[273] not merely "the Jewish followers of Jesus,"[274] or "all true believers."[275] It also implies that πᾶσα σάρξ ("all flesh") is to be understood as a reference to Jews to whom the Great Tribulation specifically applies,[276] or, at the most, all those around Judea,[277] rather than as a universal reference to all humanity.[278] Since, in Matt 24:15–25, Jesus takes up the disciples' first question concerning when the temple

272. Carson, "Matthew," 557, is right in describing it as "one particularly violent display of judgment in the fall of Jerusalem"; cf. Keener, *Matthew*, 581; Russell, *Parousia*, 74.

273. Beasley-Murray, *Jesus and the Last Days*, 420.

274. Witherington, *Matthew*, 448.

275. Carson, "Matthew," 564.

276. Cf. LXX Ezek 21:6–9; Jer 12:12; 51:34–35; note also that the MT Jer 45:4–5 concerns כָּל־הָאָרֶץ הִיא ("all this land" = land of Israel; cf. KJV, NAB, NAS, RSV, NIB, ASV, NJB) in v. 4, contra NIV, NET; therefore כָּל־בָּשָׂר ("all flesh") in v. 5 should refer to all lives in the land of Israel rather than "all humanity," contra NET. Πᾶσα σάρξ may refer to all who dwell in the land of Israel in Ezek 21:4, 10, 12; Isa 66:23; it certainly points beyond Israel in connection with words like ἔθνεσιν (nations) or other contextual clues (e.g., LXX Zech 2:15–17; Jer 32:31); other uses are either universal or ambiguous (e.g., Isa 40:5–6; 49:26; 66:16, 24; Jer 32:27; Joel 3:1).

277. Cf. Beasley-Murray, *Jesus and the Last Days*, 418. Chrysostom applies the saying to Jews beyond Judea: "(by no flesh, He meaneth no Jewish flesh), both those abroad, and those at home. For not only against those in Judea did they war, but also those that were dispersed everywhere they outlawed and banished" (*Hom. Matt.* 76).

278. Contra Carson, "Matthew," 564; Evans, *Matthew*, 406–7.

will be destroyed (vv. 2–3a), the Great Tribulation must refer to events leading up to the destruction of the temple,[279] not to a future tribulation from that time on.[280] Without imposing the Lukan Discourse onto Matthew's, we should, at least, note that Luke corroborates this when he renders the Great Tribulation as "Great Distress (ἀνάγκη μεγάλη) . . . upon the land and wrath to this people" (Luke 21:20–24). Both preterists and futurists agree that this Lukan passage refers to the 70 CE event.[281] Accordingly, it is unlikely that Matt 24:15–20 refers to a future generation rather than that of Jesus and his disciples. Such a futuristic view is negated by Matt 24:34 which clearly declares "this generation," the first-century generation, as the time when the Great Tribulation will happen.

b(P¹): vv. 26–31

One of the contentions of this study is that Matt 24:26 begins a new particularization, introducing the theme of παρουσία and its nature. There are two signals for this transition. First, the statement, "behold I have forewarned you" in v. 25 is conclusive with respect to Jesus' warning against the rise and deceptive operations of false Christs and false prophets in the days of the Great Tribulation (vv. 23–24). Second, in v. 26, as in v. 15, the conjunction οὖν alerts the implied reader that a new turn or some new element is to be introduced in the progression of the Discourse. There is a repetition of the phrase, "if anyone/they say to you" in vv. 23 and 26, and the subject implied in the to-be verb, ἐστίν (v. 26), is only processed in relation to v. 23 (i.e., the Christ), but these should not detract from the two transition signals. Contrary to the view taking vv. 27–28 as a mere parenthetical aside,[282] v. 27 is strictly connected to and substantiates v. 26 using γὰρ,[283] while v. 28 is a pronouncement saying preliminarily concluding the introduction of

---

279. For the horror and famine occasioned by the events, see Josephus, *J.W.* 5.424–38, 510–19, 567–72; 6.193–213, 414–34.

280. So also Gibbs, *Jerusalem and Parousia*, 185; France, *Matthew*, 915–19. Keener holds to a combination of interpretive options advocated by different interpreters (i.e., that the great tribulation leads to Jesus' second coming, or that from temple destruction to the second coming is an extended period of tribulation, and or that the great tribulation is prophetically blended with the final one; however, he rejects the exclusively futurist view as "not tenable" (*Matthew*, 577–78).

281. See Ice and Gentry, *Great Tribulation*, 94, 98.

282. Again, see Wilson, *When Will These Things Happen?*, 154.

283. See Levinsohn, *Discourse Features*, 91; Runge, *Discourse Grammar*, 52; Wallace, *Grammar*, 673, regards γὰρ as an explanatory conjunction.

παρουσία via an asyndetic conjunction. The asyndetic connection between vv. 27 and 28 indicates strict cohesion and continuity (cf. v. 35).

The conjunction δὲ in v. 29 signals discontinuity but also resumption, focusing on the development or description of the παρουσία proper.[284] I will now proceed to analyze this particularization, focusing on the themes, παρουσία, the gathering of the ἀετοί, and the description of παρουσία in that order.

Introducing the Παρουσία (vv. 26–27)

Of the three synoptic Eschatological Discourses (Matt 24–25, Mark 13, and Luke 21), the term παρουσία (*parousia*) occurs only in the Matthean version.[285] This raises three pertinent questions: (1) What is the meaning of *parousia*? (2) How does the implied author of Matthew intend it to be understood by the implied reader? (3) Why is the term *parousia* used in this instance (v. 27) and in the Eschatological Discourse as a whole?

The first question borders on definition. The term *parousia* occurs in both canonical and extra-canonical writings. In the latter, it is used in connection with an individual or dignitary,[286] a group of individuals,[287] or a divinity.[288] In the NT, the term is used for Paul's visit or presence,[289] Paul's companions' coming to visit,[290] the coming of the antichrist,[291] but more frequently for Jesus' coming.[292] Thus, BDAG defines *parousia* first as the "state of being present at a place" and second as "the arrival as the first stage in

---

284. So also Evans, *Matthew*, 409.

285. Matt 24:3, 27, 37, 39.

286. E.g., Jdt 10:18.

287. E.g., 2 Macc 8:12; 13:21; 3 Macc 3:17.

288. Josephus describes God's manifestation in the OT tabernacle using the word *parousia* (*Ant.* 3.203); cf. *T. Jud.* 22:2; and the coming of God's eschatological agent is also referenced using the term (*T. Levi* 8:15). For Hellenistic *parousia* of divinities, see Oepke, "Παρουσία," in *TDNT*, 5:860–61.

289. 2 Cor 10:10; Phil 1:26; 2:12.

290. 1 Cor 16:17; 2 Cor 7:6; 7:7.

291. 2 Thess 2:9.

292. Matt 24:3, 27, 37, 39; 1 Cor 15:23; 1 Thess 2:19; 3:13; 4:15; 5:23; 2 Thess 2:1, 8; Jas 5:7–8; 2 Pet 1:16; 3:4, 12; 1 John 2:28. Some consider this a technical use of the term, e.g., Vena, *Parousia*, 209; cf. Rowland, "Parousia," in *ABD*, 5:166; Oepke, "Παρουσία," in *TDNT*, 5:865–66; others think the term is non-technical since it is used for individuals other than Jesus; e.g., Holleman, *Resurrection and Parousia*, 98–99. For Plevnik, *Paul and the Parousia*, 4, 43, "παρουσία is not a technical term," but "a technical use is truer ... in the later writings (Matt 24:3, 27, 37, 39; Jas 5:7–8; 2 Pet 1:16; 3:4, 12; 1 Jn 2:28) than in Paul's."

presence." Under this second definition, BDAG further identifies two developments in the use of the term: (a) a "usual sense" involving the coming of an individual, and (b) a more technical sense involving (i) "the coming of a hidden divinity" whose presence is disclosed in acts of power or recognized in cultic celebration, and (ii) the official visit of a dignitary to a province.[293] In short, the term *parousia* has three related nuances: "presence," "arrival," and "coming/advent."

The second question regards how the implied author of Matthew might intend *parousia* to be understood by the implied reader. Traditionally, discussions on the *parousia* of Jesus draw on a rich historical and cultural background—the OT motif of the "coming" of God and the Jewish tradition of the coming of the God's heavenly eschatological agent form a primary background,[294] so also the Hellenistic background for *parousia* in relation to the coming or visit of dignitaries or divinities.[295] In all, the *parousia* of Jesus is understood to refer to his second coming, his visible descent from heaven to earth.[296]

However, some interpreters have challenged this traditional understanding. For example, although Wright retains the belief in the second coming as a yet-future event,[297] he considers the use of the term *parousia* for it as "misleading ... since it merely means 'presence.'"[298] Commenting on Matt 24, in particular, Wright judges that Matthew's use of *parousia* "in terms of historical reconstruction looks initially the least plausible of the three [synoptics]," and he further rejects the notion that the Discourse is about the end of the world or second coming.[299] In Wright's view, this *par-*

293. BDAG, "παρουσία," 780–81.

294. Such Jewish traditions may be late; see Verheyden, "Describing the Parousia," 534–40; Plevnik, *Paul and the Parousia*, 11–44; Holleman, *Resurrection and Parousia*, 103–14; Vena, *Parousia*, 59–74.

295. See Oepke, "Παρουσία, πάρειμι" in *TDNT* 5:858–71; Deissmann, *Light from the East*, 368–73; Moore, *Parousia*, 7–34; Vena, *Parousia*, 33–52. Holleman, *Resurrection and Parousia*, 95–122, also has a helpful background discussion, although he thinks it "highly unlikely that the historical Jesus predicted his coming in the future" (115); cf. n78 in chapter 1.

296. Some church fathers even used the word *parousia* to refer to Jesus' first visible coming/presence in the incarnation; see Ign. *Phld.* 9.2; Clement of Alexandria, *Strom.* 6.15.128.

297. Wright, *Surprised by Hope*, 127, states: "The 'son of man' texts aren't 'second coming' texts at all, despite their frequent misreading that way ... the second coming has not yet occurred." Contra Russell, for example, who takes the *parousia*, second coming, the resurrection of the dead, final judgment, and the last day as all contemporaneous with the destruction of Jerusalem (*Parousia*, 32–33, 121–22, 126).

298. Wright, *New Testament and the People*, 462–63.

299. Wright, *Jesus and the Victory*, 341–42, 345–46. Nor does Wright think that the

ousia, as applied to Jesus, most naturally means "something like 'arrival on the scene,' in the sense of enthronement."[300] This enthronement, Wright argues, is what the disciples were asking. Thus, Jesus' unsurprising response is "with a reworking of scriptural passages about great cities being destroyed, and about the vindication of the true people of Israel's god." In other words, Jesus' response is that the temple will be destroyed and this would constitute "his own vindication," that is, "his own 'coming'—not floating around on a cloud, of course, but his 'coming' to Jerusalem *as the vindicated, rightful king*."[301] This is indeed a fascinating interpretation, one that several interpreters have shared in one form or the other, as noted in chapter 1.[302] However, there are several issues with such understanding of the Matthean Discourse.

First, Wright's interpretation does not consider the fact that the implied author does also rework scriptural passages, including Jesus' sayings (as Jesus himself is supposed to have done scriptures) in light of his own context and intended communication goal. A cursory synoptic comparison makes clear how the evangelists have re-appropriated the traditions.[303] In fact, several fulfillment passages in Matthew are simply scriptures reworked or reapplied in light of or in relation to Jesus.[304]

Second, Wright's interpretation cannot explain why the Matthean Discourse (Matt 24–25) includes not only the destruction of the temple but also the gathering before and judgment of "all the nations" (πάντα τὰ ἔθνη) by the Son of Man in 25:31–46,[305] a judgment which would entail the final separation of the wicked from the righteous, *eternal punishment* (κόλασιν αἰώνιον) for the former and *eternal life* (ζωὴν αἰώνιον) for the latter. If all this was fulfilled in the destruction of the temple, then any post-70 evangelistic endeavor would have been meaningless. As I argued in chapter 1, Russell's

---

second coming of Jesus itself will mean descent from heaven to earth (cf. *Surprised by Hope*, 124–36; *Paul*, 1082–83). Such a descent from heaven, in his view, "is the real novelty" of which Judaism knows nothing about, although the concept is "not an arbitrary innovation" (*New Testament and the People*, 462). In *Jesus and the Victory*, 635, he calls it a "post-Easter innovation."

300. Wright, *Jesus and the Victory*, 341n95; 346.

301. Wright, *Jesus and the Victory*, 342.

302. See n78 of chapter 1; cf. Jeremias, *Parables*, 51, 53; and the more extreme view of Russell, *Parousia*, 32–33, 121–22, 126.

303. E.g., the βδέλυγμα τῆς ἐρημώσεως appears to mean different things in the three Synoptics: Mark 13:14 appears to refer to a man in the temple; Luke 21:20, the surrounding of Jerusalem; and Matt 24:15, a thing in the temple; cf. the Pauline ἄνθρωπος τῆς ἀνομίας (2 Thess 2:3).

304. E.g., Matt 2:15–18.

305. As I argued earlier, πάντα τὰ ἔθνη in 25:32 picks up from 24:14 and anticipates 28:19.

thoroughgoing preterist view, i.e., that the judgment in Matt 25:31–46 involves only "the tribes of Palestine" understood as the referent of πάντα τὰ ἔθνη in 25:32, is as unacceptable as the view of Wright and others that the judgment represents a process that happens throughout history. Against the former view is not only that we already have the term οἰκουμένη (Matt 24:14) describing more than just the tribes in Palestine, but also that Matt 25:31–46 alludes to 13:37–43 where Jesus envisions a global judgment involving the κόσμος ("world"). The later view is essentially a concession that the Discourse is not simply about the destruction of the temple.

Third, Wright considers the idea of Jesus literally coming down from heaven "so strange and unJewish an idea" that it would have been very difficult for the disciples to grasp.[306] I contend that grasping or not grasping something has nothing to do with whether or not the thing is real. But how really inconceivable would such an idea have been for those who saw Jesus walk on water (Matt 14:25–26), who already understood that the Son of Man *remains* to come in the glory of his Father with his angels for final judgment and reward (Matt 13:41–51; 16:27[307]), and who saw him transfigured on the mount and Moses and Elijah literally appearing and later covered with him in a "bright cloud" (νεφέλη φωτεινὴ [17:1–6])? If we ignore all these scenarios and take Wright's interpretation, we should demand his answers to several questions: how Jewish is the idea that the destruction of the temple would be "the end of Israel's period of mourning and exile and beginning of her freedom and vindication"?[308] How more plausible is it that the disciples would have grasped this, as Wright assumes? Apparently, Wright seems unduly selective about what idea the disciples could or could not have grasped.

Examining the text closely, the sense of the simile in 24:27 relative to v. 26 is that the *parousia* will be as the lightning (ἡ ἀστραπή),[309] which implies that it will occur with "unmistakable clarity and suddenness."[310] It will be resplendent,[311] universal, and so visible that no one will need to be told.[312]

---

306. Wright, *Jesus and the Victory*, 345.

307. As discussed in chapter 3, Adams, *Stars Will Fall*, 147–48, challenges Wright's view based on the Markan parallel to this passage (Mark 8:38).

308. Wright, *Jesus and the Victory*, 346.

309. Cf. 2 Bar. 53:8–10.

310. Hagner, *Matthew*, 706; while public, the destruction of the temple was anything but sudden.

311. Cf. Vena, *Parousia*, 52n73.

312. According to Luz, *Matthew*, 199n142, "the use of lightning as an image for something that is visible everywhere is widespread." Meier says that what is stressed is not suddenness but the *parousia*'s "open and public character" (*Matthew*, 286).

As such, the disciples are not to be misled into believing that the Christ has come and is in the "wilderness" or in some "inner room."[313] The tight link between vv. 26 and 27 via a γὰρ-substantiation supports the notion of *parousia* as visible "coming." Not only is such "coming" implied in 16:27 as already noted,[314] it is clearly stated in Matt 24:30, and severally implied in the parables within the Discourse particularly the parables of the ten virgins (25:1-13), the talents (25:14-30), as well as the final assize (25:31-46), all of which requires that the disciples think of the *parousia* in terms of Jesus' visible return to earth.

As it appears, the prohibition, μὴ ἐξέλθητε ("do not go out," that is, to *meet* a supposed Christ who has come [24:26]) has its genuine opposite in 25:6 where the command is, ἐξέρχεσθε εἰς ἀπάντησιν [αὐτοῦ] ("go out to *meet* [him]").[315] One can argue that this command is in a parable and, therefore, "go[ing] out to meet [him]" should not necessarily be expected to transpire literally. Yet the parables require some concrete analogical semblance to the *parousia* to be meaningful. Whether or not a literal descent of Jesus from heaven would have made sense to the disciples (*per* Wright's argument) is immaterial; what is important is that Matthew's Gospel indicates or, at least, suggests that *parousia* entails such literal visible return of Jesus to earth.

Of course, based on the notion of *parousia* as the non-literal descent of divinities,[316] one may argue that *parousia* as applied to the second coming of Jesus (now a 'hidden divinity') entails not his visible descent to earth but the intense or powerful manifestation of his presence on earth while he remains in heaven.[317] However, the Matthean literary context should take priority. And by extension, since all the instances in the NT text involves literal visible presence, it is more than likely that *parousia*, as used in Matt 24, is intended to be understood as the visible return of Jesus from heaven to earth.[318]

---

313. Luz further states: "Matthew pictured the parousia as an external and cosmic event. For him, the possibility does not exist of limiting it to a local event, as do the contemporary false prophets, or of internalizing it, as do earlier spiritual or modern psychological interpretations" (*Matthew*, 199).

314. This verse implies a universal judgment/reward; we do not have a sense that the reward of everyone according to works transpires contemporaneously with the temple's destruction as Russell, *Parousia*, 36-38 avows.

315. Cf. ἐξῆλθον εἰς ὑπάντησιν τοῦ νυμφίου ("they went to *meet* the bridegroom [25:1]"). The word ἀπάντησιν/ ὑπάντησιν is used only two other times in the NT—in 1 Thess 4:17 where it relates to the second coming of Jesus, and in Acts 28:15.

316. See BDAG's first technical sense above; cf. Josephus, *Ant.* 3.203.

317. So suggests Wright, *Surprised by Hope*, 134-35; Wright, *Paul*, 1082-83.

318. NT support (esp. 1 Thess 4:16; Acts 1:11) for Jesus' *parousia* as his visible return from heaven to earth appears unassailable despite existential, realized eschatological, or

The third pertinent question concerns why the implied author feels the need to introduce the term *parousia* in this Discourse at all. In both vv. 3 and 27, it would have been possible, given the lack in all of Matthew till this point, to construct the disciples' question without the term *parousia*. A likely construction in 24:3 might simply have been, τί τὸ σημεῖον ὅταν ἐλεύσετε;[319] In v. 27b, it would have been quite possible to say, οὕτως ἔσται ὅταν ἔλθῃ ὁ υἱὸς τοῦ ἀνθρώπου.[320] It is my considered view that Matthew is aware of the already prevailing application of *parousia* to Jesus' second coming. Therefore, it is most likely that the introduction of the term is meant to set the stage for how he wants the *coming* (ἐρχόμενον) of the Son of Man in v. 30 to be understood.

Moreover, since vv. 29–31 most likely relates to the disciples' second question (v. 3b) and develops vv. 26–28, as indicated by the conjunction δὲ (v. 29) and other thematic correspondences, and insofar as the phrase "coming of the Son of Man" using ἔρχομαι is capable of referring to different things, the term *parousia* has been used to ensure that the implied reader takes v. 30 to describe the visible descent or second coming of Jesus the Son of Man.

Gathering of the ἀετοί (v. 28)

The saying, ὅπου ἐὰν ᾖ τὸ πτῶμα, ἐκεῖ συναχθήσονται οἱ ἀετοί ("wherever the corpse may be, there the eagles/vultures shall be gathered together"), has remained a puzzle for interpreters. C. H. Dodd once despaired that we could know what phenomena the saying depicts.[321] It is considered a "parable,"[322] "bizarre metaphor,"[323] "sapiential riddle,"[324] "synthetic proverb,"[325] or allegory with some hidden or spiritual meaning. Most interpreters would agree that it "has a proverbial ring to it";[326] and similar sayings occur in both bibli-

---

hyper-preterist reinterpretations; see Moore, *Parousia*, 35–79; cf. Luz's submission in n313 above). For definitions of the *parousia* of Jesus as a descent from heaven in the NT expectation, see Robinson, *Jesus and His Coming*, 18; Marshall, "Parousia," 194.

319. Cf. Mark 13:4; Acts 1:11.
320. Cf. Matt 25:31.
321. Dodd, *Parables*, 88.
322. Morrison, *Matthew*, 520.
323. Nolland, *Matthew*, 981.
324. Witherington, *Matthew*, 449:
325. Davies and Allison, *Matthew*, 3:355.
326. Evans, *Matthew*, 408.

cal and extra-biblical writings.³²⁷ Of the several interpretations that have been proposed,³²⁸ I consider three categories here:

First, a host of interpreters through the ages have taken the saying in a positive sense. According to Chrysostom, the eagles are angels, Martyrs, and all the saints.³²⁹ Many patristic and some Reformation interpretations applied it to the eschatological or present salvific gathering (uniting) of saints to Jesus.³³⁰ Most recent interpreters, however, connect the saying specifically to the *parousia* as a proverbial reinforcement of the immediately preceding verse (27) intended to counter the notion of secrecy in vv. 23-26. In this sense, "the consensus of recent commentators" as Davies and Allison states, is that "the coming of the Son of Man will be as public and obvious as eagles or vultures circling over carrion."³³¹ In other words, the saying merely repeats the notion of unmistakability or universal visibility of the *parousia*.³³² Some commentators emphasize both the visibility of the *parousia* and the gathering of the saints to Jesus. Thus, Nolland states, "Nobody will need to

---

327. Job 9:26; 15:23; 39:27-30; Hab 1:8; Ezek 39:17-20; Rev 19:17-18, 21 (cf. Deut 28:26; 1 Sam 17:44; Ps 79:2; Ezek 32:4); see Seneca, *Ep.* 95.43; Lucian, *Nav.* 1; Aelian, *Nat. an.* 2.39, 46.

328. Allison and Davis, *Matthew*, 3:355-56, identify eight possible meanings arranged from the most likely to the least likely. Bridge, *"Where the Eagles Are Gathered,"* 3-21, isolates, categorizes, and critiques "20 exegetical options" based on Luke's version.

329. Chrysostom, *Hom. Matt.* 76. 3.

330. Irenaeus may imply present or eschatological participation in Jesus' glory (*Ad. Haer.* 4.14.1). Some take πτῶμα as the death/body of Jesus, e.g., Jerome, *Comm. Matt.* 4.24.28; Apollinaris (*Frag.* 126), Hippolytus (*Matt. 24*, 205); Origen (*Frag.* 478). Luther affirms this sense when, concerning "the body," he says, "From this carcass we have eternal life" (*Luther's Werke* 40:607). However, Calvin, *Harmony*, 3:91-92, 102-3, rejects the view that the "body" represents the death of Christ, arguing instead that the expression means both the unity of the saints in Christ and their gathering to Christ for protection not only in the last day but also during dangers faced by his followers. For further patristic views, see Bridge, *"Where the Eagles Are Gathered,"* 16, 151-55. Bridge's own interpretation based on the Lukan parallel is that "Luke uses the ἀετοί saying to portray the glorious deliverance of the saints," in which case τὸ σῶμα signifies the crucified Lord as a living entity, i.e., the resurrected Christ (4, 59-68). On Matthew's version, Hill, *Matthew*, 322, comments, "It is unlikely that πτῶμα (body) includes a reference to the crucified body of Christ."

331. Davies and Allison, *Matthew*, 3:355-56.

332. See Luz, *Matthew*, 199-200; Hagner, *Matthew*, 707; France, *Matthew*, 918-19; Wilson, *When Will These Things Happen?*, 153; Senior, *Matthew*, 270; Meier, *Matthew*, 286; Beare, *Matthew*, 470; Gardner, *Matthew*, 346; Evans, *Matthew*, 409; Guenther, "When 'Eagles' Draw Together," 142-43, 145. For Gibbs, *Jerusalem and Parousia*, 187, it refers to the "self-revelatory character of the parousia"; for Konradt, *Matthew*, 261, the "general perceptibility" of the *parousia*. M'Neile, *Matthew*, 351, thinks the saying "expresses inevitableness" in light of Amos 3:3-8. For Maier, *Matthäus-Evangelium*, 2:288, vv. 27 and 28 are linked together, highlighting the *certainty of the parousia*.

direct Christian disciples to the Son of Man: as unerringly as the vultures gather to the corpse, so they will find themselves gathered without prompting to the Son of Man."³³³

Second, several interpreters take 24:28 in connection with v. 24, in which case, the ἀετοί, understood as vultures are the false prophets and false Christs who destroy or lead Israel astray. Toussaint, for example, interprets πτῶμα more allegorically as lifeless and putrefying Israel upon which false prophets will feast.³³⁴ There is, indeed, contextual connection between v. 28 and the preceding verse(s). However, a direct hermeneutical connection between vv. 28 and 24 is remote. There is also no evidence that I have seen of false prophets or false Christs represented as flesh-eating birds. The *Animal Apocalypse* has a parable in which birds attack God's sheep to destroy them (see 1 En. 90:1–5). If this passage is of any relevance (a doubtful proposition), it is clear that "false prophets" (and or false Christs) would fall into the category of shepherds and therefore are distinguished from the eagle-led birds of heaven that attack God's people (the sheep).

Third, many interpreters take Matt 24:28 as a reference to judgment, although there is no consensus on what judgment is meant or against whom it is directed. To some, the saying refers to the eschatological judgment immediately before or in connection with the return of Christ.³³⁵ More interpreters think it rather refers to the judgment of Israel in the destruction of Jerusalem by the Romans, in which case, the ἀετοί, understood as eagles, is a reference to the Roman army whose standards have the image of eagles.³³⁶ Those who take this view see an allusion to the warning of Judgment on the temple in Jer 7 (esp. v. 33),³³⁷ or to several literary uses of eagle as an allusion to the Romans.³³⁸ For example, Wright asserts, "the eagles—the Roman eagles, presumably—would gather round the carcass ['the great city"

---

333. Nolland, *Matthew*, 981; see Bridge, "Where the Eagles Are Gathered," 16–19.

334. Toussaint, *Behold the King*, 276; cf. Plummer, *Matthew*, 334; Lenski, *Interpretation*, 2:946; Smith, *Matthew*, 288.

335. Hendriksen, *Matthew*, 861; Keener, *Matthew*, 582–83; Morris, *Matthew*, 608; Glasscock, *Matthew*, 473, takes the saying to refer to "the carnage of the Tribulation"; Turner, *Matthew*, 579: it may reference the "final eschatological battle." Some interpreters of the Lukan parallel think of it in terms of universal judgment; see Bridge, "Where the Eagles Are Gathered," 11–13.

336. See Pliny, *Nat.* 10.5.16; Josephus, *J.W.* 3.123 describes the eagle as "the king and bravest of all the birds," Rome's "symbol of empire" and "omen of victory" against adversaries.

337. So Robinson, *Jesus and His Coming*, 75–76; Glasson, *Second Advent*, 84–85.

338. Ezra 11–12; 14:18; 1QpHab 111.11 (Romans = Kittim); *T. Mos.* 10:8 (see Charlesworth, *Old Testament Pseudepigrapha*, 1:932, note *e*).

of Jerusalem] to pick it clean."³³⁹ However, although the saying might evoke the idea of corpses being eaten by birds,³⁴⁰ such an interpretation is too literalistic for a proverb.³⁴¹ Moreover, "the saying itself" as Guenther notes, "does not speak explicitly of judgment."³⁴²

Warren Carter maintains the judgment view but argues that the judgment is against imperial Rome (eagles) instead of Jerusalem. He alleges six erroneous assumptions of the "commentators' consensus" that the saying refers to the public and obvious nature of the coming of the Son of Man as eagles or vultures circling over carrion. First, Carter argues that this consensus view misidentifies ἀετοί as vultures, arguing that ancient writers distinguished between ἀετοί (eagles) and γύψ (vultures).³⁴³ Second, Carter rightly emphasizes the fact that eagles are not characteristically carrion eaters.³⁴⁴ Third, he observes that a connection is always made between γύψ (vulture) and πτῶμα (dead body) but never between ἀετοί and πτῶμα as in Matt 24:28. Fourth, the saying itself does not involve a verb of eating or circling. Fifth, the consensus view falsely "assumes that eating is the obvious activity of ἀετοί and the most natural link between them and the corpse."³⁴⁵ And sixth, the biblical material rarely presents πτῶμα as food. Based on these six points of objection,³⁴⁶ Carter concludes that Matt 24:28 does not illustrate the nature of Jesus' coming but the consequence of his coming

---

339. Wright, *Jesus and the Victory*, 360; cf. Gaston, *No Stone*, 353; Tasker, *Matthew*, 230; Carter, "Are There Imperial Texts?," 467–87. Based on the Lukan parallel, Lang, "Where the Body Is," 324–26, takes eagles as Rome, arguing that σῶμα (the body) corresponds to Jesus himself while eagles are the hostile forces who come to arrest him. The logion, thus, foreshadows the arrest of Jesus in Luke 22 and the division of the disciples.

340. See Keener, Matthew, 582–83.

341. As France, *Matthew*, 919 argues, "to allegorize it [the saying] as depicting the 'corpse' of Jerusalem surrounded by the 'eagles' (military standards) of the Roman army is to look for too literal a reference in proverbial language."

342. Guenther, "When 'Eagles' Draw Together," 148–49; so also Luz, *Matthew*, 199–200: "in Matthew, the saying about eagles hardly speaks of judgment"; Hagner, *Matthew*, 707: while judgment may be "the most natural application of the imagery, . . . there is no reference to judgment in the immediate context." Even Gundry who regards the saying as a "warning of judgment" concedes that by being linked to the lightning metaphor, the vulture metaphor "loses its judgmental meaning," and instead, "signifies the unmistakable visibility of the Son of Man's coming" (*Matthew*, 486–87).

343. Carter, "Are There Imperial Texts?," 469–71.

344. Aelian, *Nat. an.* 2.36, 46 says that the eagle, as opposed to the vulture, will eat nothing it did not kill. In 1 En. 90:2–4, eagles lead the birds of the heavens to attack and eat living not dead "bodies."

345. Carter, "Are There Imperial Texts?," 471.

346. Some of the criticisms also stand against the view represented by Wright and others above.

in relation to Rome: it "depicts the Roman army symbolized by the eagles, destroyed in the final eschatological battle when Jesus, Son of Man, returns to judge Roman imperial order and to establish God's reign."[347]

In agreement with Carter's first objection, it is clear that ancient writers made technical distinctions between eagles and vultures.[348] However, it is equally true that both birds were often confused in other or ordinary settings.[349] The combination of πτῶμα ("dead body") and ἀετοί (eagles) in Matt 24:28 suggests that vultures or, at least, vulture-like eagles are meant.[350] But even if we maintain ἀετοί in this verse as eagles,[351] it would still not make Carter's interpretation legitimate for several reasons: (1) An allusion to Romans using "eagle" cannot be taken for granted.[352] That "eagle" is generously applied to a wide range of entities makes a strict application to the Romans unnecessary.[353] (2) When Carter says that the idea of a "circling" carrion is absent in the saying, he misses the point expressed by the word συναχθήσονται. In Carter's view, "the verb 'gathered together' (συναχθήσονται) supports the claim that eschatological judgment on Rome is the focus of Matt 24:28," implying that "what happens to the corpse happens to the eagle."[354] This line of reasoning seems improbable, even extraneous. The verb συνάγω in and of itself does not suggest destruction or judgment.[355] (3) Carter's case

---

347. Carter, "Are There Imperial Texts?," 468; he claims that Matt 22:7 is an indication that Matthew views Rome as an agent of God in destroying Jerusalem (477).

348. See Lev 11:13; Deut 14:12; Aristotle, *Hist. an.* 6.5–6.

349. Aristotle, *Hist. an.* 9.32, describes a specie of eagle (percnopterus) which is like the vulture in appearance and preys on dead animals; cf. Pliny, *Nat.* 10.3; see Topel, "What Kind of a Sign?," 404–5; Harb, "Meaning of Q," 283. Luz, *Matthew*, 199, citing Wolfgang Speyer, states: "in antiquity, people knew little about vultures and often confused them with eagles."

350. Cf. Nolland, *Matthew*, 981n93; Dodd, *Parables*, 88n1.

351. Carter, "Are There Imperial Texts?," 460–70.

352. According to Hagner, *Matthew*, 707: "a reference to the Romans does not make sense here"; Broadus, *Matthew*, 489 considers a reference to Romans "hardly possible" and even fanciful; Plummer, *Matthew*, 335, says, "a direct reference to the eagles on the Roman standard is less likely"; Evans, *Matthew*, 408; thinks that reference to Romans is probably not the original intention of the saying although post-70 readers may make the association. Cf. Hill, *Matthew*, 322; M'Neile, *Matthew*, 351.

353. God is compared to an eagle in his deliverance (Exod 19:4) and protection (Deut 32:11); those who wait on the Lord will mount up with wings like eagles (Isa 40:31); in Hos 8:1, eagle alludes to Assyria; in Deut 28:49, Babylon is anticipated and compared to the eagle (cf. Hab 1:8); Ezek 17 gives a parable of two great eagles, Babylon and Egypt); 1 En. 90:2 most likely alludes to Greece using eagle; see Reynolds, *Between Symbolism and Realism*, 208–15, 262.

354. Carter, "Are There Imperial Texts?," 478.

355. Cf. Matt 13:30, 47; 18:20; 22:10, 34, 41; 25:24, 26; 26:3, 57; 27:17, 27, 62; 28:12.

is further weakened by his identification of πτῶμα with Rome as well. "The identification of the corpses as Rome condemned by God at Jesus' coming," he claims, "also explains the use of the collective singular noun πτῶμα."[356] How Rome can be both ἀετοί and πτῶμα in the same saying is, to say the least, difficult to see. (4) The notion that Matt 24:28 is a veiled anti-imperial rhetoric seems less supported by the tenor of Matthew's Gospel as a whole. Witherington is right to note that "unlike Revelation, we do not seem to find much anti-imperial rhetoric elsewhere in the Gospel."[357]

Like many interpreters in the second category of views above, I argue that the saying in Matt 24:28 is an extension of v. 27. The asyndetic link suggests it is meant to reinforce the *parousia* saying in vv. 26–27[358] with the added element not merely of the visibility or certainty of the *parousia*, but of the universal gathering before the Son of Man—an inevitable gathering not only of the disciples (*per* Nolland), but also of *all peoples*. Blomberg simply takes this view but does not provide any support for it.[359] I contend that, in relation to the word συναχθήσονται (*they shall be gathered together*), 24:28 anticipates or alludes to the final assize (25:31–32) where it is said that when the Son of Man comes and sits on his glorious throne, "all the nations (πάντα τὰ ἔθνη) *will be gathered together* (συναχθήσονται) before him." Its primary and explicit emphasis is "gathering together" rather than judgment; the notion of judgment is not necessary to the saying itself.

One might plausibly argue that the "gathering together" in 24:28 corresponds to the "gathering together" of the elect in v. 31. Bridge thinks that the association of these two gatherings "appears coincidental."[360] I argue that although vv. 29–31 develops vv. 26–28, the gathering in v. 28 is not the same as that in v. 31. The difference lies in the change in gathering terminology—συναχθήσονται in v. 28 and ἐπισυνάξουσιν in v. 31. While semantically correspondent, the formal variation of the verb indicates a referential difference within the Discourse in its broader context.[361] On the one hand, the "gathering" in v. 31 using ἐπισυνάγω specifically involves only the elect. It alludes to 23:37 where the same variant is used for Jesus' desire to gather

---

356. Carter, "Are There Imperial Texts?," 479.

357. Witherington, *Matthew*, 449n10.

358. Cf. vv. 34–35 where an asyndetic link similarly represents a complementary connection.

359. Blomberg, *Matthew*, 361: "Verse 28 then concludes the paragraph by describing metaphorically how *all people* will be drawn to see Christ upon his return, just as certainly as vultures gather to devour a corpse or animal carcass" (italics mine).

360. Bridge, "*Where the Eagles Are Gathered*," 19.

361. I will argue that the variant ἐπισυνάγω in v. 31 refers to the same thing it does in Matt 23:37.

(ἐπισυναγαγεῖν) Jerusalem's children. Thus, it represents the initial gathering of the saints to the Son of Man at his return. On the other hand, the "gathering" in v. 28 using συνάγω has nothing to suggest that the gathering will involve only the elect.[362] But the generic nature of v. 28 corresponds to the generic nature of 25:31–32. Only in this connection do we know that the gathering in v. 28 will involve judgment, the final judgment of all nations.

I will shortly focus more directly on 24:31. In the meantime, one major objection to this generic *parousia*-gathering interpretation is that the saying in 24:28 is somewhat unsavory since it implies that Jesus represents himself as a cadaver (dead body) around which people as vultures gather. For example, Guenther describes it as an "ugly and offensive saying."[363] Michael J. Wilkins claims that "the metaphor doesn't really make a parallel with Jesus' coming," wondering, "does the Parousia correspond to a carcass?"[364] Bridge also raises a similar objection by claiming that "neither the material prior to Mt. 24:28, nor that which intervenes (vv. 29–30), indicates that Matthew intends to correlate the ἀετοί logion with the reference to the collection of believers." "As for Luke" [like Matthew], he goes on to argue,

> the proverb—taken as a simile—makes an awkward comparison. It seems incredible that the evangelist (or Jesus) would have employed an image as grotesque as vultures over cadaver to denote a spectacle as exalted as the heavenly assembly. Moreover, there are no particles of comparison (e.g., ὡς, ὡσεί) to indicate this intent.[365]

These objections are invalid. Firstly, the interpretation offered above makes it unnecessary to determine whether ἀετοί means eagles or vultures or to focus on the unsavory nature of cadaver (*per* Wilkins); the saying simply makes certain that all peoples will be inevitably gathered to the Son of Man. Secondly, as also argued above, the saying does not claim to be a "heavenly assembly" supposedly of believers with Jesus (*per* Bridge). Thirdly, the assumption that either Jesus or the evangelist could not use such grotesque imagery for a gathering to himself has little or no merit. The very assumption presumes a literal and unnecessary correspondence

---

362. Cf. Luke 17:37. In connection with the emphasized motif of "being gathered together" (ἐπισυναχθήσονται), Luke's use of σῶμα ("body") instead of Matthew's πτῶμα ("carcass") makes it even clearer that the saying is not intended to mean judgment, although Luke, lacking the final assize tradition, has applied it to those taken (= ἀετοί); they are taken to be "gathered together" to the Son of Man (= σῶμα) while those left await judgment.

363. Guenther, "When 'Eagles' Draw Together," 140.

364. Wilkins, *Matthew*, 782n30.

365. Bridge, "*Where the Eagles Are Gathered*," 18–19.

between metaphor and reality. Adolf Schlatter rightly asserts that finding it objectionable to apply the "carrion" metaphor to Jesus indicates that one has used the wrong method of interpretation.[366] Indeed, it should be observed that the Discourse uses other seemingly inappropriate or shocking imageries for the person of Jesus. In 24:43, Jesus could compare himself to a thief who breaks in at night. He could also take the role of a hard (vicious) man "reaping where you did not sow and gathering where you did not winnow" (25:24, RSV).[367] Therefore, it is unlikely that Jesus would be as concerned as Wilkins or Bridge about the implication of cadaver to his person or his *parousia* in a generic proverbial statement.

Fourthly, contrary to Bridge's view, and whether it is Matthew or Luke, the absence of particles of comparison is hardly a strong basis for rejecting the association between the gathering of vultures/eagles to a carcass and the gathering of people to the Son of Man when he comes.[368] In Matt 21:33-43, Jesus gives an extended parable that compares God to a householder and Jewish leaders to tenants without any particle of comparison. Matthew 24:28 is to be taken as a reduced or implicit metaphor,[369] not repeating the sense in v. 27 (i.e., publicity and suddenness), but supplying what it lacks (i.e., inevitable gathering). In so far as it seamlessly completes the thought of v. 27 by adjoining to the suddenness and publicity of the *parousia* the inevitability of gathering, it draws from the ὥσπερ ... οὕτως comparative construct of v. 27 to make an implicit comparison between the gathering of vultures/eagles to carrion and the inescapable gathering of all peoples to the Son of Man.

Describing the Παρουσία (vv. 29–31)

This passage is no doubt the most controversial within the Discourse. The problem that it poses breaks down into several points of inquiry: Are the cosmic signs in v. 29 to be taken literally or metaphorically? What is the sign of the Son of Man and the meaning of the coming of the Son of Man in v. 30? What does the sending of the angels to gather the elect in v. 31 mean? I introduced current discussions on these questions in chapter 3 of

---

366. Schlatter, *Matthäus*, 709.

367. Like Bridge, Joachim Jeremias, is in error when he thinks it "hardly conceivable" that Jesus would so compare himself (*Parables*, 59).

368. As I noted above (n358), even Luke 17:37 appears to eliminate any grotesqueness in the saying.

369. It does not explicitly equate the *parousia* gathering with the vultures gathering over carrion.

this study, especially noting the contributions of Caird, Wright, Allison, Adams, and others. To recall, while Allison and Adams advocate the traditional understanding of these verses as referring to some cosmic catastrophe associated with the end-of-the-world *parousia* or second coming of Jesus and the gathering of the saints to him, Caird, Wright, and many others including France; Gibbs, and Wilson,[370] have argued for a figurative understanding in light of similar apocalyptic imageries in the OT prophetic and apocalyptic traditions.[371] According to Wright,

> The whole passage [Mark 13] seems to me (a) to refer clearly to the forthcoming destruction of Jerusalem, and (b) to invest that event with its theological significance. This is not to 'demythologize' the apocalyptic language concerned. Nor is it to reduce it to 'mere metaphor'. It is to insist on reading it as it would have been heard in the first century, that is, *both* its very this-worldly, indeed revolutionary, socio-political reference *and* with its fully symbolical, theological, and even 'mythological overtones'.[372]

Of course, Wright thinks that Matthew's version is not different. In this sense, the *coming* of the Son of Man is interpreted as his vindication and exaltation to the throne based on the earth-to-heaven-direction reading of Dan 7:13–14;[373] and "the gathering of the elect by angels" is taken to symbolize the messengers or disciples spreading the gospel throughout the whole world and gathering people into Jesus' kingdom.[374]

Earlier in this chapter, I highlighted Pitre's important work, *Jesus, the Tribulation, and the End of the Exile*. Pitre agrees with the interpretation of Mark 13:24–27 (Matt 24:29–31) as a reference to the destruction of

---

370. See Beasley-Murray, *Jesus and the Last Days*, 423–27; Hatina, "Focus of Mark"; Bauer, *Gospel*, 212.

371. Esp. Isa 13:6–13; 34:3–4; Ezek 32:5–8; Joel 2:10–11 (cf. Amos 8:9; Zeph 1:15; T. Mos. 10:1–10).

372. Wright, *Jesus and the Victory*, 342.

373. Wright, *Jesus and the Victory*, 361. One might wonder how "very this-worldly" Wright's reading is if Mark 13:26//Matt 24:30 refers to upward movement/enthronement in haven. Gibbs does not appeal specifically to such a reading of the Danielic passage; instead, he maintains the vindication-in-heaven interpretation via a rather curious (hardly justifiable) grammatical decision that takes ἐν οὐρανῷ in Matt 24:30a adjectivally rather than adverbially, such that the verse means that a sign "will appear, that which shows this man, who is in heaven" (*Jerusalem and Parousia*, 198–99).

374. Wright, *Jesus and the Victory*, 362–63; cf. France, *Matthew*, 919–27; Gibbs, *Jerusalem and Parousia*, 187–204; Wilson, *When Will These Things Happen?*, 156–58. Bauer maintains this interpretation, but he hesitates to equate "angels" in 24:31 with Christian messengers, stating that "the exalted Christ [will] harness the power of his angels to assist the church in the evangelization of the nations" (*Gospel*, 213).

Jerusalem. However, he claims to differ from Wright by positing that the cosmic "imagery is much more than 'metaphoric language' meant to invest a 'historical' event with 'theological significance;' rather, "it is, in fact, *literal* language meant to describe the *cosmic* effects of an event that is *both* historical and eschatological: the destruction of Jerusalem."[375] Following Allison,[376] Pitre insists that first-century Jews such as Josephus interpreted cosmic signs "very literally."[377]

Pitre further appeals to *4 Ezra* 13:29-49 to posit that the saying in Mark 13:24-27 (Matt 24:29-31) points to the messianic restoration of Israel.[378] Thus, the *coming* of the Son of Man on the clouds of heaven is "his arrival" as Messiah,[379] which "will bring about a cosmic tumult that will signal the destruction of the city of Jerusalem already inaugurated by the abomination of desolation." Following this, the angels are sent "to gather the elect, the scattered remnant of Israel from among the nations." While Pitre allows that the "elect" will "perhaps" include "those among the nations who will turn to the God of Israel and to the Son of Man," he concludes that "this gathering will represent the true, the final, the eschatological End of the Exile and the beginning of the long-awaited restoration of Israel."[380]

I commend Pitre's interpretation. But he essentially exploits Allison's traditional stance in order to affirm Wright's preterist reading of the passage. It should also be observed that the signs mentioned by Josephus are neither quite the same as those in Matt 24:29, nor did they occur during or "'immediately *after* (μετὰ)' the tribulation of Jerusalem described in Matt 24. Rather, as Josephus says, they took place long before as "*prior*-signs portending the desolation to come" (προσημ ἔρχομαι αἴνουσι τὴν μέλλουσαν ἐρημίαν τέρασιν).[381] Although I lean toward Pitre's more literal interpreta-

---

375. Pitre, *Jesus*, 336–37 (emphasis original).

376. Allison, "Jesus and the Victory," 126–41; Allison, *End of the Ages*, 83–100; Allison, *Jesus of Nazareth*, 152–69.

377. Pitre, *Jesus*, 336–37.

378. Pitre, *Jesus*, 346–47.

379. Unlike Wright and others, the association Pitre makes between Matt 24:30 and Dan 7:13–14 is not that of a vindication or enthronement in heaven but rather of "coming" as messiah (*Jesus*, 340–41).

380. Pitre, *Jesus*, 348. While this conclusion echoes Wright, France, Gibbs, and Wilson take 24:31 as the general missions to the whole world rather than a reference to the end of Israel's exile.

381. E.g., (1) a sword-like star standing over the city for a year before the desolation, (2) a light as bright as day breaks into the alter in the ninth hour of the night during the feast of unleavened bread, (3) a heifer gives birth to a lamb in the temple as it was being led to the priest for sacrifice, (4) the bolted iron gate of the inner court swings open on its own accord, (5) chariots of soldiers seen running around in the sky and

tion, his interpretation raises questions regarding how Matt 24:29–31 would have been "very literal" in 70 CE when Jerusalem fell, or in what sense these verses represent literal "cosmic effects" of the fall itself.

The major challenge with Pitre's interpretation, as well as with Wright's and others, however, is that the Discourse does not equate the destruction of Jerusalem and the temple with the coming of the Son of Man. Nor does it present the coming of the Son of Man as a cosmic *signal* for the destruction of Jerusalem. Also, Matthew (or Mark and Luke for that matter) gives no indication anywhere that he is thinking in the ancient exile category; the implication that God already dwells in the temple (Matt 23:21; cf. 21:13) negates the exile hypothesis. It is possible to borrow the restoration language of the OT without implying that what is currently addressed is restoration from that exile. Moreover, gathering "the elect" of both Israel and the nations appears quite different from ending Israel's historical or even ideological exile.[382]

Before I offer the view taken in this study, I would highlight Ryan Juza's interpretation in his recently published work. First, "Matt 24:29," Juza believes, "is primarily an allusion to two prophetic ["Day of YHWH"] texts from the OT: Isa 13:10 and 34:4," with additional influence from Joel 2:10 and 3:15 [4:15 LXX]."[383] Thus, apparently in agreement with Wright, Juza concludes that "Matthew uses the language of 24:29 similar to an OT prophet in order to communicate theological content concerning a historical event." Second, although Juza allows that Luke's version favors the view that v. 29 refers to the destruction of the temple, he argues that the Matthean context demonstrates that, in employing this language, Matthew has shifted from describing "'a day' of YHWH" as in the OT prophetic tradition, to describing "the Day itself, the parousia." In this way, Juza maintains the traditional interpretation of Matt 24:29–31 as a reference to the *parousia* rather than the destruction of Jerusalem, adducing 8 supporting bases. I will paraphrase (or quote for clarity) each adduced reason:

1. Matthew alone, of all the Synoptics, uses the word *parousia* which should be prepared for.

---

surrounding the city, (6) on a Pentecost, priests feel a quake in the temple and heard a sound of multitude saying, "let us remove hence." Josephus interprets these literally as clear omens of the desolation (Josephus, *J.W.* 6.288–300).

382. Luke even supposes the beginning of another exile for unbelieving Jews (21:24) rather than the end or what Pitre considers "the beginning of a long-awaited restoration of Israel."

383. Juza, *New Testament*, 39.

2. The Discourse divides into four main units (24:1–3, 4–14; 15–31, and 24:32—25:46) with each part ending with a reference to the *parousia* and/or the end of the age.

3. The disciples ask about the "sign" of the *parousia* (24:3), therefore it makes sense that "the sign of the Son of Man" in 24:30a refers to the *parousia*.

4. "Those days' in 24:19, 22, 29, 38 most likely refers to a period of suffering and witness which is broader in scope than the period surrounding Jerusalem's destruction. This implies that the event which follows 'immediately after the suffering of those days is the parousia."

5. "The language of 24:29–31 has many similarities to 25:31–46 (esp. v. 31), which is a description of the final judgment."

6. "While some texts in Matthew do refer to a "coming" of the Son of Man other than the parousia (cf. 10:23; 16:28; 26:64),[384] other texts more than likely describe the parousia (cf. 16:27; 19:28; 25:31). Furthermore, the majority of occurrences of "come" (ἔρχομαι) in the discourse refer to the parousia (24:5, 30, 39, 42, 43, 44, 46; 25:10, 11, 19, 27, 31, 36, 39)."

7. "The language of 24:30–31 is interpreted with more exegetical ease as a description of the parousia than as a description of the temple's destruction."

8. "In the rest of the NT, this sort of language is normally applied to the parousia (e.g., 1 Thess 4:13–18)."[385]

I believe that Juza has provided a most helpful contextual defense for the traditional *parousia* understanding of Matt 24:29–31. However, as noted in chapter 1 and demonstrated in the preceding section, Juza's structure of the Discourse fails to correctly assign 24:26–28; some of Juza's interpretation in vv. 29–31 may appear inaccurate. Nor does he treat the latter part of the Discourse adequately enough. In what follows, I take on vv. 29–31 to further demonstrate why its traditional understanding as the description of the *parousia* should be maintained. I will consider the passage under the following headings: (i) the phrase, εὐθύς δὲ μετὰ τὴν θλῖψιν τῶν ἡμερῶν (ii) cosmic catastrophe (ii) the sign and appearing of the Son of Man, and (iv) the angelic gathering of the elect.

---

384. Juza's view is that Matt 10:23 and 16:28 refer to the destruction of Jerusalem. I noted in chapter 3 that they refer to the resurrection instead.

385. Juza, *New Testament*, 44–46.

Εὐθύς δὲ μετὰ τὴν θλῖψιν τῶν ἡμερῶν ἐκείνων ("immediately after the tribulation of those days" [v. 29a])

Every element of this phrase has interpretive significance in relation to the preceding sections and what follows in vv. 29b-31. I have already argued that δὲ both signals discontinuity as well as resumes the development of the *parousia* theme introduced in vv. 26-28. The arthrous θλῖψιν (tribulation) indicates previous anarthrous activations of the term in both vv. 9 and 21. Consonant with all the uses in Matthew as a whole, the adverb, εὐθύς, is used here not merely stylistically but deliberately to connect contiguous events.[386] Perhaps the phrase, τῶν ἡμερῶν ἐκείνων ("those days") is of the most importance. The "tribulation of 'those days'" may be taken to refer to the events associated with the destruction of the temple, in which case, "those days" merely picks up from "those days" in vv. 19-22 and nothing more. If this is the case, then what follows v. 29a (i.e., vv. 29b-31) must be strictly connected to that Great Tribulation, that is the destruction of the temple. Then the traditional view of 29b-31 as a future *parousia* would immediately collapse.

Indeed, it would seem that "those days" in v. 29a constitutes a conundrum for the traditional interpretation of vv. 29b-31. However, this is far from being the case. At least, three reasons for distancing vv. 29b-31 from the destruction of the temple may be adduced.

First, if the distinction I have argued between "generic tribulation" (24:9) and "[the] Great Tribulation" (vv. 15-25) is valid, it has implications for the scope of "those days" in v. 29a. The term θλῖψις is activated anarthrous ([-] = without the article) in both vv. 9 and 21. This leaves the possibility that the arthrous instance in v. 29a is meant to embrace these two previous activations. That the qualification using μεγάλη ("great") is dropped in v. 29a seems to support this. Moreover, while "those days" appears to relate specifically to the shortened days of vv. 19-22, the phrase is semantically equivalent to τότε ("then"/"at that time") in v. 9. In other words, "those days" in v. 29a may be summative in the sense that it embraces both the Great Tribulation/temple destruction (v. 19-22) and the more extensive generic tribulation of all time (v. 9) as shown in the diagram below:

---

386. Cf. εὐθέως (Matt 4:20, 22; 8:3; 13:5; 14:22, 31; 20:34; 21:2; 25:15; 26:49, 74; 27:48); εὐθύς (Matt 3:16; 13:20-21; 14:27; 21:3); see Wilson, *When Will These Things Happen?*, 154.

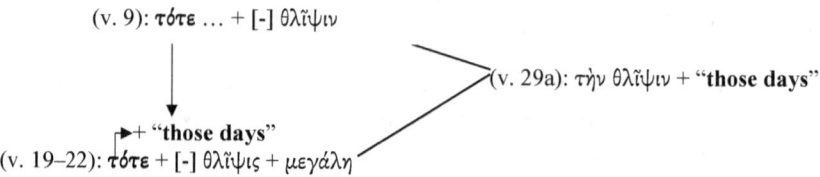

"Those Days" in Context.

Second, the tenor of v. 29a indicates that the destruction of the temple is itself the Great Tribulation or the climax of what has already started with the abomination of desolation (v. 15). In light of Mark's "in those days after that tribulation" (13:24), Pitre argues rather that the Coming of the Son of Man is the climax of "those days" of the Great Tribulation/temple destruction.[387] But this is hardly the intention of the Markan text, nor could the Matthean text admit such an interpretation. *To say that the Son of Man will come "immediately after" a Tribulation which includes the destruction of the temple is already to deny that that Tribulation/destruction of the temple is the same as the Coming of the Son of Man.* There is thus the inevitable implication that the destruction of the temple itself is not described in Matt 24.[388]

Third, in the immediate context, the phrase "those days" is used to describe the days before the flood as analogous to the days before the *parousia*. At the end of Matthew, the entire post-resurrection period is described in 28:20 as πάσας τὰς ἡμέρας ἕως τῆς συντελείας τοῦ αἰῶνος ("all the days until the end of the age"). Given these observations and the certain distinction between the tribulation/destruction of the temple on the one hand and the Coming of the Son of Man in vv. 29b–31, understood as the *parousia* on the other, "those days" in v. 29a, admits of an expansive meaning to include all the days of generic tribulation leading up to the consummation.[389]

Accordingly, the flood analogy (24:36–38), referring to the day of the Coming of the Son of Man just described in vv. 29–31, presents a different scenario than is feasible in the days immediately after the Great Tribulation/destruction of the temple. Precisely, this analogy implies that the *parousia*, as with the flood, will occur unsuspectedly following a generally "peaceful" time—a time of "eating and drinking, of marrying and giving in marriage."

---

387. Pitre, *Jesus*, 331–32.

388. This is not at all surprising. As Hare, *Theme of Jewish Persecution*, 178, points out, it is not out of character for Matthew, who can give a long mission discourse (chapter 10) without mentioning the mission itself.

389. Cf. Juza, *New Testament*, 46 (point #4).

This notion of peaceful and celebratory abandon contrasts sharply with what one would expect during or "immediately after" Jerusalem's Great Tribulation/destruction of the temple.[390] Therefore it is legitimate to conclude that v. 29b and what follows up to v. 31 refer to events that will usher in the consummation immediately following the end of the days of generic tribulation. The identification, "generic tribulation", is just that; it implies random tribulation throughout the course of history until the end but in a generally "peaceful," at least, unsuspecting world. Based on this interpretation, there is no need to argue, as Fuller has done, that "immediately after" simply implies "next" after the fall of Jerusalem but "many other events may intervene."[391]

Cosmic Catastrophe (v. 29b)

Much has already been said about v. 29b. I agree with the majority of interpreters that the apocalyptic language here and, by extension, vv. 30–31, is similar to OT theophany passages depicting YHWH's manifestation for judgment or salvation.[392] The most important of these passages are:

1. Isa 13:9–10 (LXX): "See, the day of the LORD is coming, [a day] of wrath and fierce anger, to make the whole earth a desolation and to destroy its sinners from it. *For the stars of the heaven and the orions and all the constellation of the heaven will give no light, and the sun will be darkened while rising and the moon will not give its light.*"

2. Isa 34:2–5 (LXX): "Because the Lord is enraged against all the nations and angry against all their host, to destroy them and to hand them over to slaughter. Those of them slain shall be cast out and the dead and their stench shall go up; the mountains shall rain with their blood. *The heaven shall roll up as scroll and all the stars shall fall as leaves from the vine and as leaves fall from the fig tree.* My sword is made drunk in heaven; see, it shall descend upon Edom and upon the people for destruction with judgment."

3. Joel 2:10 (LXX): "*The earth shall be confounded before him and the heaven shall be shaken. The sun and the moon shall darken, and the stars shall withdraw their brightness*" (cf. 3:4; 4:14–16 LXX).

---

390. The notion of careless and celebratory abandon is also implied in 24:48–49.

391. Fuller, "Olivet Discourse," 161; he takes "the tribulation of those days" to be the destruction of Jerusalem and vv. 30–31 as the *parousia* with an indefinite period intervening.

392. See Vena, *Parousia*, 59–74.

4. Ezek 32:7-8 (LXX): "And [in the day] I put you out, I will veil the heaven and darken its stars; I will cover the sun with cloud and the moon shall not give its light. All the shining light of heaven will go dark over you and I will put darkness upon your land says the Lord."

All these prophetic utterances refer to now past manifestations of the Day of the Lord in judgments against nations and or in relation to Israel. No one thinks that such cosmic unraveling in which the sun and moon lose their light, the stars fall, and the heavens and earth are shaken did indeed pan out literally in the historical events referred to.

So, when such language is used in the Matthean Eschatological Discourse, in what sense is it used? While it is my considered opinion that apocalyptic language in general is largely symbolic,[393] the principle I adopt here is to take the language figuratively or symbolically if a literal meaning is extravagantly bizarre, "patently false . . . [and] or contextually incongruent";[394] that is, to interpret it more literally than metaphorically only as compelled by contextual or literary phenomena.[395] Allowing for some degree of hyperbole,[396] Matthew's use of this language seems more literal than metaphoric.

As a foundation, certain preliminary observations should be noted: (1) None of the OT passages above is cited directly in Matt 24:29b-31. In other words, Jesus or Matthew is free to blend and use this language in ways that are different. (2) Unlike these theophany passages in which cosmic catastrophic language describes judgment/tribulation itself, the language in Matt 24:29b is distinguished from the tribulation/destruction of the temple using the adverbial phrase εὐθέως δὲ μετὰ, which indicates that a different event is in view, the coming of the Son of Man (vv. 30-31). And (3) The language in Matt 24:29b appears measured; the mountains do not rain with blood, and the heavens do not dissolve or roll up as scroll, implying utter destruction.[397] Of course, none of these changes the apocalyptic nature of the language, but together, they point to the need to process the language in light of the present literary context.

---

393. Out of five categories of views on v. 29 found by Juza, four describe it using the word "metaphorical." The four include Adams and Allison, who nonetheless maintain the *parousia*/end of the world referent of the passage (see Juza, *New Testament*, 19-21).

394. Black, "More about Metaphor," 34.

395. See also Bauer and Traina, *Inductive Bible Study*, 149.

396. Cf. Matt 24:2.

397. Cf. Isa 34:4; 2 Pet 3:10. Transformation or renewal rather than destruction of the cosmos is the point that Juza has helpfully made in his *Future of the Cosmos*, esp. 64, 305-6; he correctly notes that Matt 24:30-31 indicates that the earth remains intact, although he could still talk of "the destruction of heavenly bodies" (50).

As the implied reader will conceivably understand it, the language of Matt 24:29b leans toward literal than metaphorical. That this is plausibly the case is supported by three scenarios in Matthew. First is the *transfiguration* scenario in 17:1–8. There, Jesus is transfigured into a visible blinding glory; Elijah and Moses appear literally on the Mount, a "bright cloud" (νεφέλη φωτεινή) later envelopes them, and the divine voice speaks audibly from the cloud.[398] If this scene is proleptic of the *parousia* glory of Jesus, as seems to be the case,[399] it would prepare the implied reader to, at least, expect visible *parousia* events. Second is the *passion* scenario. The implied author knows and the implied reader either knows or will soon learn that darkness literally covered the land as a prelude to Jesus' death. When Jesus finally dies, a literal earthquake takes place and rocks are split. These things occur literally since it is because of them that Jesus is acknowledged as indeed the Son of God by those watching (27:45, 51–54).[400] Third is the *resurrection* scenario. In Matt 28:2, the resurrection of Jesus is accompanied by "a great earthquake" and the descent of an angel who rolls away the stone and the sight of whom strikes the guards with deadening terror.

These three scenarios are, in one degree or another, analogous to the *parousia*, suggesting that literal cosmic disruption at the coming of the Son of Man is and will more likely than not be the interpretive mental framework for the implied author and readers in 24:29b–31 respectively. This literal framework would also embrace a phenomenon of falling stars, perhaps a reference to meteorites falling as a result of cosmic tremor.[401] It is in this light that the shaking of the "powers of heavens" should be understood, although there remains the question about the referent of this "powers of heavens."

Based on the commonly accepted tradition of ancient people associating heavenly bodies with angelic beings who control the destiny of humans,[402] some have viewed this "powers of heavens" as a reference to astral divinities or angelic beings. However, on closer examination, none of the texts (Ezek 32:7–8; Joel 2:10, 31; 4(3):15; Hag 2:6, 21; Rev 6:12–13; 1 En. 80:4; 2 Esd 5:4; As. Mos. 10:5) cited by Gundry supports this view.[403] Juza's claim that

---

398. 2 Pet 1:17–18 attests to the authenticity of the tradition.

399. So also Keener, *Matthew*, 437.

400. Cf. Allison, "Jesus and the Victory," 131.

401. According to Gundry, *Matthew*, 487, "the falling of stars refers to a shower of meteorites." It "is no mere shower of meteors" insists Beare, *Matthew*, 471.

402. So Beare, *Matthew*, 471; Gundry, *Matthew*, 487; Meier, *Matthew*, 287; Nolland, *Matthew*, 983; Morris, *Matthew*, 609–10; Juza, *New Testament*, 48n113 only notes Deut 32:8 (LXX).

403. Gundry, *Matthew*, 487.

"in Isa 34:4 LXX, 'the powers of heaven' are not merely heavenly bodies, but also represent angelic rulers whom God conquers as he descends on the Day of the Lord"[404] is clearly untrue. Concerned only with the judgment of Edom, the Isaianic text neither uses the words "powers of heaven" nor gives any hint of the conquering of angelic rulers.[405] In Deut 4:19 and 17:3, the expression, τὸν κόσμον τοῦ οὐρανοῦ ("constellation/host of heaven"), is mentioned as a summation of all the heavenly bodies (sun, moon, and stars, cf. Isa 13:10). This is also the sense of πᾶσαν τὴν στρατιὰν τοῦ οὐρανοῦ ("all the army of heaven") in Jer 8:2 (LXX)" as well as of the expression, πάσῃ τῇ δυνάμει τοῦ οὐρανοῦ ("to all the *power of heaven*"), in 2 Kings 23:5.[406]

In fact, apart from the Pauline concepts of πνευματικὰ τῆς πονηρίας ἐν τοῖς ἐπουρανίοις ("spiritual forces of wickedness in the heavenly places" [Eph 6:12]) and στοιχείων τοῦ κόσμου (often translated "elemental spirits of the world" [Gal 4:3, 9; Col 2:8, 20]),[407] I found no text clearly warranting the equation of "power(s) of heaven(s)" with angelic beings. These particularly Pauline concepts should not be uncritically imported into Matthew.

Although Juza could only note Deut 32:8 as evidence that ancient people "routinely associated heavenly bodies with angelic beings," he claims that "Matthew appears to hold this common belief when he talks about the magi being led by the Messiah's 'star,' which properly refers to an angel (2:2, 7, 9, 10)."[408] But this interpretation of the star as an angel is unlikely. The implication of αὐτοῦ τὸν ἀστέρα in Matt 2:2 and the tenor of 2:9–11 is that the star is Jesus himself (cf. Rev 22:16) not an angel.[409] Despite Juza's effort to force "enemy" in Matt 13:24–30, 36–43 and 22:44 to mean "powers of heavens,"[410] Matthew appears to show no interest in the judgment of "heavenly powers" understood as angelic beings. Moreover, it is unlikely that the judgment of angelic beings will be represented in Matt 24:29b by such angelic beings merely being shaken (σαλευθήσονται).

Consequently, it is better to take the last καὶ in Matt 24:29b as an ascensive καὶ ("even") and therefore αἱ δυνάμεις τῶν οὐρανῶν ("the powers of

---

404. Juza, *New Testament*, 48.

405. Not only do Rev 6:12–13 and Apoc. Pet. 5:4 Eth. not support the view as Juza acknowledges; but also, against Juza's claim, in T. Levi 4:1, the phrase "invisible spirits" clearly represents a different category than the celestial bodies.

406. So also, Filson, *Matthew*, 256.

407. Cf. Jer 8:2 which lists sun and moon.

408. Juza, *New Testament*, 48.

409. Note the intercalation (i.e., A-B-A order):"τὸ παιδίον" (v. 9) . . . "Ἰδόντες δὲ τὸν ἀστέρα ἐχάρησαν χαρὰν μεγάλην σφόδρα" (v. 10) . . . "τὸ παιδίον" (v. 11).

410. Juza, *New Testament*, 48n115.

heavens") as a summative reference and amplification of all celestial bodies.[411] These heavenly powers rule the day (sun) and night (moon and stars);[412] but they will be shaken, causing them to lose their lights.[413] The resulting cosmic disruption and darkness will serve to compel the attention and bewilderment of the nations and reveal the One coming in the clouds. Turner may be right that "the cosmic chaos portrayed here hints at the need for cosmic renewal."[414]

That none of the ideas of the literal darkening, shaking, and dislocation of heavenly bodies appears inconceivable in Matthew leads to the conclusion that the language of Matt 24:29b, though apocalyptic in character and deriving from OT metaphorical theophany passages, lends itself to be understood in more literal a way than metaphorical. By this, I mean that room should be given for hyperboles, even clear symbols, as is the case with σάλπιγγος μεγάλης ("great trumpet") in v. 31. One may not understand in this verse a literal trumpet any more than one may take Rev 19:15 to mean that Jesus will come with a literal sword in his mouth.

The Sign and Appearing of the Son of Man (v. 30)

As argued in chapter 4, τὸ σημεῖον in v. 30 resonates with τὸ σημεῖον in the disciples' question in v. 3b, making it most likely that a reference is being made here to the *parousia* about which they asked.[415] However, owing to the way v. 30a is constructed, the knottier issue concerns the referent of the "sign" itself. On this, the proposed views are (1) the cross,[416] (2) an ensign or

---

411. See Toussaint, *Behold the King*, 276; Mounce, *Matthew*, 226; Filson, *Matthew*, 256.

412. Gen 1:16.

413. Trilling's rendering of δυνάμεις τῶν οὐρανῶν as "pillars of heaven" (*Matthew*, 2:201) is farfetched, but it may be accommodated based on the notion of cosmic shaking.

414. Turner, *Matthew*, 582, although his cross-reference to Matt 19:28–29 implies that he takes παλιγγενεσίᾳ to mean cosmic renewal, an unlikely view in my opinion.

415. So also Lunde, "Salvation-Historical Implication," 177–79; Juza, *New Testament*, 45.

416. Chrysostom, *Hom. Matt.* 76.3. According to Schweitzer, *Matthew*, 455, "the Church very early thought of sign as a cross appearing in the sky," citing Did. 16:6, Apoc. Pet. (chapter 1), Apoc. El. 32, Ep. Apos. (16), and the Gos. Pet. (39).

standard,[417] (3) the Son of Man himself,[418] (4) the destruction of the temple,[419] (5) cosmic signs of v. 29,[420] (6) a combination of (1) and (2): cross as an ensign,[421] (7) a combination of (2) and (3): Jesus himself with an ensign,[422] and (8) a great light (especially based on Matt 24:27).[423] According to Wilson, "most contemporary commentators are reluctant to make any decisive judgment between the various views."[424] Witherington's suggestion of the sign referring back to the signs in v. 29 (view 5) is nullified by the composite conjunction, καὶ τότε, which signals a distinction between the cosmic upheaval of v. 29 and the sign of v. 30. Glasson's interpretation (view 2) and the combination views are unnecessary belaborings of τὸ σημεῖον.[425]

I consider Gibbs' argument for temple destruction as the sign (view 4) as unacceptable, yet as worth further engagement. Gibbs makes two exegetical moves in v. 30: First, he translates τὸ σημεῖον τοῦ υἱοῦ τοῦ ἀνθρώπου as "the sign of this man," taking it as an objective genitive, i.e., "that which shows this man." Second, Gibbs takes the prepositional phrase ἐν οὐρανῷ ("in heaven") adjectivally (modifying τοῦ υἱοῦ τοῦ ἀνθρώπου ["this man"]) instead of adverbially (modifying φανήσεται ["will appear"]). Thus, v. 30 reads, "that which shows this man who is in heaven will appear,"[426] that

---

417. Glasson, "Ensign," 299–300, argues that "the σημεῖον of xxiv. 30 and the trumpet of xxiv. 31 . . . should be taken together and σημεῖον should be translated 'standard,'" citing Isa 6:12; 49:22; 27:13; 28:3; Jer 4:21; 6:1; 51:27 (cf. 1QM 3:13–15; Isa 5:26; 11:10; 18:3; 62:10). See Hill, *Matthew*, 323. Hagner, *Matthew*, 713, is uncertain but thinks this is possible.

418. Smith, *Matthew*, 288; Luz, *Matthew*, 3:201–2; Gundry, *Matthew*, 488; Juza, *New Testament*, 51.

419. Gibbs, *Jerusalem and Parousia*, 198–99; France, *Matthew*, 926; Bauer, *Gospel*, 212. Garland, *Reading Matthew*, 238–39, claims: "the sign . . . is perhaps some heavenly sign that appeared over Jerusalem as a portent of its destruction," citing Josephus account of a sword-shaped star seen over the city for a year before its ruin (*J.W.* 6.5.3).

420. Witherington, *Matthew*, 452.

421. Davies and Allison, *Matthew*, 3:360.

422. Talbert, *Matthew*, 269, considers the two views as "perhaps two sides of one coin." Similarly, Evans, *Matthew*, 410–11, thinks that "the sign of the Son of Man will be his appearance in heaven, coming . . . with his battle ensign ready to execute judgment."

423. Waetjen, *Origin*, 229 (cf. *Matthew's Theology*, 248).

424. Wilson, *When Will These Things Happen?*, 157, citing France, *Gospel according to Matthew*, 344–45; Hagner, *Matthew*, 713–14; and Higgins, "Sign," 380–82.

425. According to Agbanou, *Discours*, 112, to translate σημεῖον as ensign "has the disadvantage of giving the word a meaning it never has in the NT and a second meaning in the same context [with respect to] v. 3."

426. Or as Bauer, *Gospel*, 212, renders it, "then will appear the sign of the heavenly Son of Man." See also France, *Matthew*, 926n102.

which shows him in heaven being "the complex events around the destruction of Jerusalem and the temple."[427]

Gibbs' exegesis seems flawed. As I will show shortly, the structure of v. 30 and many other factors refute his interpretation. In the meantime, it is important to note the following: First, Gibbs' interpretation is based on a scantily attested variant, τοῦ ἐν οὐρανῷ ("who is in heaven").[428] Second, it seems unlikely that "complex events" that transpired over the course of 2–3 years would be described with φαίνω (to appear, to shine, to flash]). This same verb (φαίνω in v. 30) has just been used in v. 27 to describe the *parousia* in terms of lightning, suggesting suddenness, something which occurs in a moment. Third, in Matthew, the phrase used to indicate that the Son of Man is in heaven is "*sitting* at the right hand of power." It is true that this expression is in 26:64 strictly inseparable from the phrase, "*coming* on the clouds of heaven."[429] However, it should be taken into consideration that "the sign of the Son of Man in heaven" and his "coming in the clouds of heaven" are in a context dealing not merely with the temple's destruction but also with the *parousia*, a "coming" that will involve final judgment (24:3c, 27; 25:31). And fourth, Gibbs' rendition, "the sign that this man is in heaven will appear," is as Juza has argued "grammatically improbable."[430] Gibbs himself describes his exegesis as "not the natural grammatical understanding" and, therefore, "not the easier rendering."[431]

Herman C. Waetjen's view (8) that the sign is a great light is not lightly dismissed. He compares it both to the nativity star as well as to the new creation light (cf. Rev 21:23–25; Isa 60:1–5).[432] The challenge is that the lightning in v. 27 is only an analogy of the *parousia* not a sign of the Son of Man—ὥσπερ γὰρ ἡ ἀστραπή... οὕτως ἔσται ἡ παρουσία τοῦ υἱοῦ τοῦ ἀνθρώπου ("for as the lightning ... so shall the *parousia* of the Son of man be").

If Isa 60:1–5 and Rev 21:23 are of any relevance to the sign in Matt 24:30, then, the light would be the Son of Man himself whose great glory will lit up the cosmic darkness.[433] This goes to support view number 3 for which I will now present further evidence. First, the third view is

427. Gibbs, *Jerusalem and Parousia*, 198–99.

428. This reading is found only in the fifth- to sixth-century codex Bezae (D); Gibbs, *Jerusalem and Parousia*, 198n200, puts too much weight on it.

429. Gibbs, *Jerusalem and Parousia*, 201, may be right to take the two expressions as parallel in Matt 26:64.

430. Juza, *New Testament*, 50n121.

431. Gibbs, *Jerusalem and Parousia*, 198.

432. Waetjen, *Matthew's Theology*, 248n124.

433. Cf. Juza, *New Testament*, 51.

grammatically consistent. Contrary to Gibbs' translation, v. 30a should retain its most grammatical reading: "then will appear in heaven the sign of the Son of Man." The expression, τὸ σημεῖον τοῦ υἱοῦ τοῦ ἀνθρώπου, is properly taken as a genitive of apposition and read as "the sign *who is the Son of Man*." In other words, the genitive ("of the Son of Man") elucidates what sign is meant, corresponding to what Wallace describes as "ambiguity–clarification."[434]

Second, this most natural and grammatical translation is supported by the rhetorical structure of v. 30. What we have is, in a sense, a thematic intercalation (A-B-A):

A καὶ τότε <u>φανήσεται</u> τὸ σημεῖον τοῦ υἱοῦ τοῦ ἀνθρώπου ἐν οὐρανῷ,
  B καὶ τότε <u>κόψονται</u> πᾶσαι αἱ φυλαὶ τῆς γῆς
A¹ καὶ <u>ὄψονται</u> τὸν υἱὸν τοῦ ἀνθρώπου ἐρχόμενον ἐπὶ τῶν νεφελῶν τοῦ οὐρανοῦ
                          μετὰ δυνάμεως καὶ δόξης πολλῆς

In this arrangement, although B and A¹ constitute a two-sentence complex with the same subject, held together by a single τότε, and separated only by a simple καί, A and A¹ are somewhat parallel.[435] The verb φανήσεται ("will appear") is closely synonymous to ὄψονται ("they shall see"), since the one implies the other. A and A¹ also correspond in terms of the prepositional phrases: ἐν οὐρανῷ = ἐπὶ τῶν νεφελῶν τοῦ οὐρανοῦ. It is noteworthy that ἐπὶ τῶν νεφελῶν τοῦ οὐρανοῦ modifies not the Son of Man directly, but the verbal adjective, ἐρχόμενον. Importantly, in the absence of a repeat of τότε in A¹, and if for a moment we eliminate B, there is a clear suggestion then that A¹ represents a restatement and expansion of A. As such τὸ σημεῖον τοῦ υἱοῦ τοῦ ἀνθρώπου(A) = τὸν υἱὸν τοῦ ἀνθρώπου(A¹). The verse taken together indicates that the Son of Man himself (not something different or a perception of an event on earth) has appeared in the "sky" and is moving on the clouds towards the tribes of the "earth" with power and great glory[436]—a *parousia* movement that climaxes in the event of 25:31–32. The equating of the "sign" and the "Son of Man" agrees with the lightning analogy in v. 27. Aside from preparatory atmospheric events (cf. v. 29), lightning is so sudden it is its own sign.

Third, the view that the Son of Man is himself the sign in v. 30a is supported by Matt 12:39-40 (16:4) where τὸ σημεῖον Ἰωνᾶ τοῦ προφήτου ("the sign of Jonah the prophet") is Jonah himself.[437] The implied reader

434. Wallace, *Grammar*, 95.

435. So also Gibbs, *Jerusalem and Parousia*, 201.

436. As v. 27 suggests, οὐρανός here implies "sky" rather than "heaven" the abode of God; cf. similar use in Matt 16:1-4 (NIRV, NAS, NIB, and NAU).

437. Notice Luke's rendition, "for just as Jonah *became* (ἐγένετο) a *sign* to the

having already encountered this saying will readily take τὸ σημεῖον τοῦ υἱοῦ τοῦ ἀνθρώπου as referencing the Son of Man himself. With this clear parallel not too far from the Discourse, it is unnecessary to try to support an already awkward translation by comparing prepositional phrases in completely dissimilar sayings as Gibbs does.[438]

Fourth, outside of Matthew, the Messiah of Israel is described both in the OT and NT as himself a sign: (1) Isa 11:10 (MT) reads, "And there shall be in that day the root of Jesse standing (עֹמֵד) as a sign (נֵס) for the peoples, him the nations shall seek and his resting place shall be glorious."[439] (2) In Luke 2:12, the angel says, "And this [will be] the sign (τὸ σημεῖον) for you: you will find a baby wrapped in swaddling clothes and lying in a manger" by which is clearly meant that the sign is the baby himself. Moreover, the lack of σημεῖον in Mark 13:26 and Luke 21:27 also supports this interpretation.

Furthermore, that the Son of Man is the sign himself coming visibly downward explains why the tribes of the earth would mourn in v. 30b, since it is unlikely that people would mourn because of some unknown celestial sign or phenomenon. In relation to this, the statement, καὶ τότε κόψονται πᾶσαι αἱ φυλαὶ τῆς γῆς should be translated universally ("and all the tribes of *the earth* shall mourn)[440] rather than locally ("and all the tribes of *the land* shall mourn").[441] It is true that the only other occurrence of φυλή in Matthew's Gospel (19:28) refers to the "tribes" of Israel. It is also true that instead of φυλή, Matthew uses ἔθνος in a generic or plural sense to refer to all people of the earth (24:7; 25:32). In fact, even the OT texts—LXX Zech 12:10–14 and Amos 8:9–10—alluded to by v. 30b, both refer specifically to Israel:[442] in Zech 12:10–14, the mourners are specifically τὸν οἶκον Δαυιδ καὶ τοὺς κατοικοῦντας Ιερουσαλημ ("the house of David and those living in Jerusalem"), and in Amos 8:9–10, the term γῆ means not the *earth* but the

---

Ninevites, so also shall the Son of Man to this generation" (11:29–30); cf. "sign of circumcision" (= circumcision itself) in Rom 4:11.

438. See Gibbs, *Jerusalem and Parousia*, 198n191–97.

439. Contrary to the assumption in view (2), Isa 11:12 (וְנָשָׂא נֵס לַגּוֹיִם וְאָסַף נִדְחֵי יִשְׂרָאֵל ["he shall raise a sign for the nations and gather the outcasts of Israel"]) does not intend to distinguish the root of Jesse in v. 10 from the sign; rather as v. 11 indicates, it is YHWH (יהוה = אָדוֹן [cf. 10:23, 33; 5:25–25]) who does the raising, while the root of Jesse is the sign.

440. Hagner, *Matthew*, 714; Luz, *Matthew*, 201; Witherington, *Matthew*, 453; Juza, *New Testament*, 53–55.

441. Gibbs, *Jerusalem and Parousia*, 199–201; France, *Matthew*, 923–26; Wilson, *When Will These Things Happen?*, 157–58; Bauer, *Gospel*, 212; Garland, *Reading Matthew*, 238.

442. See Juza, *New Testament*, 53–54.

land.[443] Why then should the saying be universal in Matt 24:30b instead of a reference only to Israel?

The answer to this question lies in the principle of re-appropriation, combined with Matthew's particular emphasis on universality: Zech 12:10–14 especially (synthesized with Dan 7:13) is re-appropriated universally in Matt 24:30b in relation to the *parousia*.[444] This re-appropriation is suggested by at least four facts: (1) While the particularistic Israel-specific mourning in Zech 12:10–14 is penitential, no such penitence is suggested in Matt 24:30b; there will be no room for repentance, only deliverance for the elect of the whole earth, followed thereafter by the judgment of all the nations. (2) Not only Zech 12:10–14, but also Isa 11:12 (cf. Deut 30:4; LXX Zech 2:10), which only concerns the regathering of Israel, is alluded to but re-appropriated universally in Matt 24:31 as reference instead to the elect of all nations. Even Gibbs and France are of the view that those gathered in 24:31 are not only Jewish elect but the elect from all over the world, and *they do not attempt to argue that the OT Israel-specific gathering is brought over here*.[445] If 24:30 refers to Israel-specific mourning because it alludes to some OT passage, 24:31 must also refer to Israel-specific gathering by the same token of OT allusion. Thus, if the latter is a universal gathering of the elect rather than a particularistic gathering of Israel, then the former must refer to a universal rather than an Israel-specific mourning. Anything contrary would appear exegetically inconsistent. (3) The scope of the gathering in v. 31b ("from the four winds, from one end of heaven to the other") strengthens the universal character of 24:30b. (4) The implied reader will most likely relate 24:30 to 8:11–12 and understand it universally. Moreover, the universal scope of Rev 1:7 is an indication of how first-century writers, including Matthew, were re-appropriating Zech 12:10–14 (LXX) and Dan 7:13 in relation to the *parousia*.[446]

Finally, on the direction of the "coming of the Son of Man in the clouds of heaven," a more plausible indication is "movement" from heaven to earth rather than "ascent" to a heavenly throne. First, in Matt 24:30, the distinction between γῆ ("land" which is on earth) and heaven is maintained. Thus,

---

443. In general, γῆ may be translated "earth" 21 times (Matt 5:5, 13, 18, 35; 6:10, 19; 9:6; 10:34; 11:25; 12:40, 42; 16:19[x2]; 17:25; 18:18[x2], 19; 23:9, 35; 24:35; 28:18), "land" 13 times (2:6, 20, 21; 4:15[x2]; 9:26, 31; 10:15; 11:24; 14:24, 34; 27:45, 51), and "ground"/"soil" 8 times (10:29; 13:5[x2], 8, 23; 15:35; 25:18, 25).

444. Cf. Ham, "Reading Zechariah," 85–97; contra Gundry, *Use of the Old Testament*, 234.

445. See Gibbs, *Jerusalem and Parousia*, 202; France, *Matthew*, 927.

446. So also Juza, *New Testament*, 53; cf. Lunde, "Salvation-Historical Implication," 177n69 on the relevance of Zech 14:6–7.

those who "see" the Son of Man are on earth and not in some heavenly space as apocalyptic "seers" often are. Second, unlike in 26:64 where the term "see" is best taken metaphorically as mental perception,[447] there is nothing grammatically or contextually constraining "see" in 24:30 to be construed metaphorically.[448] In other words, "they will see" (ὄψονται) in this context is more likely to suggest to the implied reader the visible descent of Jesus. Third, and concerning this second point, while the priest and Jerusalem specifically are those who will "see" in 26:64, in the present context, it is πᾶσαι αἱ φυλαὶ τῆς γῆς ("all the tribes of the earth") that will see. What this means is that, while "coming in the clouds of heaven" in 26:64 relates to the judgment of the temple, this latter verse should not be uncritically blended into 24:30.[449] Fourth, and most importantly, the Son of Man's coming *with* (μετὰ) power and great glory here both alludes back to 16:27 (not to 16:28)[450] and points forward to 25:31.[451] The connection of these three passages (16:27; 24:30; and 25:31) verifies that the Son of Man's "coming in the clouds of heaven" referred to in 24:30 is that *coming to earth* in which the power and glory of his Father are already his possessions not that which he *goes up* to be vested with in *heaven*.[452]

The Angelic Gathering of the Elect (v. 31)

I have already commented in brief on this verse with respect to its allusion to Isa 11:12 (and the like) as well as its universality. What is left is to consider the use of ἄγγελος here and the meaning of their gathering activity. First, how is τοὺς ἀγγέλους to be understood—as a reference to human messengers or to angels? As already clear from earlier discussions, the case for the missiological interpretation of Matt 24:31 has been persuasively made

447. Most likely, Matt 26:64 refers to Jesus' vindication in the destruction of Jerusalem. The verb "see" controls 64a and 64b separated by a simple καί. Thus, insofar as "'see' the Son of Man seated at the right hand of power" (64a) does not mean that they will see him thus seated, the seeing of him "coming in the cloud of heaven" (64b) is, accordingly, not to be construed literally as a visible descent. Therefore, "see," in this context, is a metaphor for perception or realization; cf. Gundry, who also takes it as "mental seeing" (*Matthew*, 545).

448. Cf. "see" in 24:15, 33.

449. As Gibbs, *Jerusalem and Parousia*, 198–99, has done.

450. Contra France who while linking 16:28 to either the resurrection or possibly the transfiguration curiously continues to tie it also to 24:30 (*Matthew*, 640–41).

451. Both France, *Matthew*, 639–40 and Gibbs, *Jerusalem and Parousia*, 107–8 connect 16:27 to the final judgment of 25:31–46.

452. Contra Wright, *Jesus and the Victory*, 361–63; France, *Matthew*, 923–24; Gibbs, *Jerusalem and Parousia*, 200–201.

by Wright, France, Gibbs, and others.⁴⁵³ These scholars all see τοὺς ἀγγέλους as human messengers sent to spread the gospel throughout the world. I find this interpretation unsustainable, perhaps even allegorical.⁴⁵⁴ While it is true that ἄγγελος also means "human messengers," it is used so only once in Matthew.⁴⁵⁵ In the remaining 19 instances,⁴⁵⁶ it means "angels" as it does in almost all the 175 instances in the NT. The implied reader is already too conversant with the angelic role as the eschatological reapers (Matt 13:39, 41, 49; 16:27) to understand ἄγγελος here as human messengers. Taking the whole Discourse as a unit, 24:31 is to be interpreted in connection with 25:31. As such, there is no reason why τοὺς ἀγγέλους in the former cannot also refer to πάντες οἱ ἄγγελοι μετ' αὐτοῦ ("all the angels with him") in the latter. In light of 16:27, we must assume that the angels who come *with him* (μετ' αὐτοῦ) in 25:31 are also the angels coming *with* the Son of Man in 24:31, not messengers on earth. It would take an unlikely revolutionary imagination for the implied reader to understand τοὺς ἀγγέλους going to gather the elect in 24:31 as the disciples (messengers), especially since the disciples are themselves part of the elect as 24:20–26 suggests.⁴⁵⁷

---

453. Note a 1979 article in which Schuyler Brown, assuming Matthew's redaction of Mark and taking Mark 13:24–27 as a fulfilled prophecy, claims, "A missiological interpretation of [Matt 24] v. 31 is confirmed by the special Matthean material which separates the sign of the Son of man from the reference to his coming [in v. 30]: 'and then all the tribes of the earth will mourn'" ("Matthean Apocalypse," 13). This claim is unwarranted since, as I noted above, v. 30 B and A¹, while thematically different, constitute a two-sentence complex with the same subject; and they are held together by a single τότε and separated only by a simple καί. Even supposing Matthew's redaction of Mark 13:24–27, Matt 24:30b would be an unlikely way to suggest a missiological understanding of v. 31.

454. The same sort of interpretation that France, *Matthew*, 919, rejects when he says that to allegorize "corpse" as Jerusalem and "eagles" as the Roman army in 24:28 "is to look for too literal a reference in proverbial language"; except that what we have here is not a proverbial language.

455. Matt 11:10.

456. Matt 1:20, 24; 2:13, 19; 4:6, 11; 13:39, 41, 49; 16:27; 18:10; 22:30; 24:31, 36; 25:31, 41; 26:53; 28:2, 5.

457. Gibbs, *Jerusalem and Parousia*, 186n134, opines that "'the elect' [in 24:22, 24] refers to 'the elect in Judea,'" but he has no way to prove they exclude the disciples—the supposed messengers. Since the disciples are addressed as capable of being led astray in 24:4, they must also be part of the elect capable of being led astray in 24:24. According to Hagner, *Matthew*, 632, "'elect' . . . in 24:22, 24, 31 [is a] shorthand for the disciples of Christ." "'Elect' is "perhaps a fixed technical term for the messianic community of salvation" in 22:14 (Davies and Allison, *Matthew*, 3:207); cf. Witherington, *Matthew*, 448; Bauer, *Gospel*, 211; France, *Matthew*, 827–28, 915–16.

Second, if this plain understanding is taken, the gathering in v. 31, therefore, cannot be understood in terms of human missiological gathering.[458] Instead, taking the verse in its plain sense, what we have is the first part of a twofold *parousia* gathering, the second part of which will then follow for the final judgment. The same angels are involved,[459] but this first part of the gathering is distinguished from the second using the term ἐπισυνάγω as opposed to the regular συνάγω. While cognates, these terms refer to two distinct gatherings associated with the *parousia*.

In the Discourse, the first instance of the gathering motif occurs in the generic saying of 24:28 using συνάγω, proleptically referring to the general gathering in 25:31–32 which also uses συνάγω. In contrast, 24:31 uses ἐπισυνάγω for a priority gathering involving only the elect at the coming of Jesus and alludes back to the only other two instances in 23:37 where Jesus expresses his desire "to *gather* (ἐπισυναγαγεῖν) your children as a hen *gathers* (ἐπισυνάγει) her chicks under her wings." The gathering schema is as follows:

---

458. Missiological gathering is always depicted as an extended period of gathering that includes both the good and the bad, culminating in the final eschatological moment of judgment/separation; see Matt 13:47–48; 22:10. Gibbs, *Jerusalem and Parousia*, 203, uncritically assumes a parallel between these passages and 24:31, arguing for a missiological gathering in the latter. However, the parable of the Dragnet depicts missiological *gathering* (συνάγω) activity as different from angelic *separation* (ἀφορίζω) activity in 13:47–49. Precisely, the casting of net in 13:47 represents missionary activity, but in light of v. 49, the separation in v. 48 is by angels ἐν τῇ συντελείᾳ τοῦ αἰῶνος. Gibbs also fails to notice important differences between the parable of the Wedding Feast (22:1–14) and the Discourse: (1) while the "burning of city" in 22:7 temptingly appears to reference the destruction of the temple predicted in chapter 24, the two are not the same, and any connection remains uncertain, (2) the gatherers in the Wedding Feast are *servants* (δοῦλοι) as opposed to *angels* (ἀγγέλοι) in 24:31, (3) the gathering terminology is also different, συνάγω in 22:10 but ἐπισυνάγω in 24:31, (4) while both the good and the bad are gathered in 22:10, only the elect are gathered in 24:31, and (5) on the one hand, the gathering in 22:10 is defined missiologically in 22:14 (the saying, "many are *called* but few are *chosen*," implies a protracted missionary activity of an all-inclusive invitation [καλέω]); on the other hand, the gathering in 24:31 is a punctiliar precision angelic gathering of the elect.

459. Cf. Matt 3:12; 13:30; 24:28; 25:32; see Witherington, *Matthew*, 453.

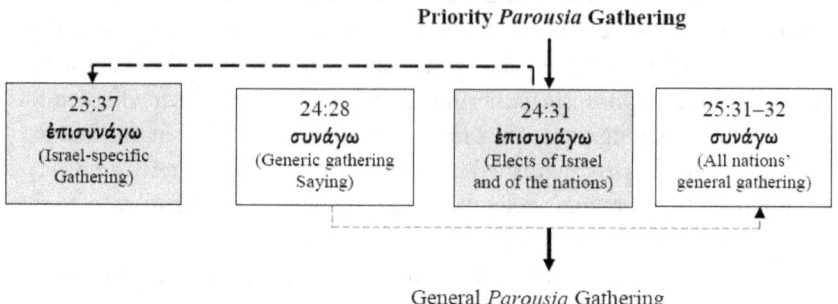

Gathering Terminology in Context.

Gibbs takes the connection between the gathering of 23:37 and 24:31 in terms of contrast, which he believes "fits well into Matthew's schema of the turning of the mission to the Gentiles." "Jerusalem's children," he says, "were not willing to be gathered either by Jesus or by the missionaries he will send (23:34). His missionaries accordingly will turn to gather the elect from among all the nations."[460]

This is an inaccurate interpretation; it suggests the closure of mission to Israelites, or that Israelites are *per se* rejected. Against such a notion is that Matt 23 suggests that by "Jerusalem" (23:37) Jesus means the religious establishment. In light of the parable in 21:33–45, Israelites are not rejected any more than the vineyard is rejected. Rather, it is the tenants (Israelite leadership) that are replaced (esp. v. 45).[461] Thus, it is not "Jerusalem's children" who were unwilling to be gathered, but Jerusalem's religious leaders who would not let "your children" be gathered. Moreover, Gibbs ignores 24:16–18 which addresses Jerusalem's children and "the elect" on whose account the time of the Great Tribulation will be shortened (vv. 22, 24). This notion of "elect" clearly indicates the enduring place of Israelites ordained unto salvation.

Thus, properly understood, 24:31 implies that although Jerusalem rejected Jesus' attempt, this universal gathering using ἐπισυνάγω speaks of the faithfulness of Jesus to Israelite elects as an integral part of the elects of all the nations. As such, contrary to the missiological reading of this verse, the point is hardly that evangelized individuals from all the nations are now the elect, and Israelites are not.[462] While the Israelite nation as a whole will face the desolating judgment coming on the temple, what we have in the

---

460. Gibbs, *Jerusalem and Parousia*, 202; cf. Brown, "Matthean Apocalypse," 14.
461. Cf. 1 En. 90:6–39.
462. See Bauer, *Gospel*, 213 (cf. 209).

aftermath, as I have earlier argued, is the *ethno*sization rather than the end of mission to or rejection of Jews. Consequently, I conclude that Matt 24:31 is better taken as a reference to the angelic gathering of all the elect (of Israel and of the nations) to Jesus as the first part of the *parousia* gathering rather than to the missiological gathering activity of human messengers.

a(T²): vv. 32–35

In this subsection, Jesus shifts to his temple-specific response in relation to the disciples' first question. To be sure, there is thematic resonance between εὐθέως ("immediately") in v. 29 and ἐγγύς ἐστιν ἐπὶ θύραις ('it is near, at the doors") in v. 33 of the subunit, suggesting that all of vv. 29–35 should be held together as one subunit.[463] However, the opening δέ conjunction, in combination with the parabolic character of vv. 32–34, indicates discontinuity from the preceding material while developing and finalizing the temple response analogically. Moreover, the fig tree is a symbolic representation of the temple establishment.[464] By using the fig tree analogy, Jesus alludes back to Matt 21:12–20. There, in connection with the "fruitless" temple, Jesus curses a fig tree which, though full of leaves, has no fruit. Similarly, in 24:32, the reference is to a fig tree that has merely "put forth leaves," signaling the imminence of summer. The theme of nearness in 21:20 using the adverb παραχρῆμα ("immediately") to describe how quickly the fig tree withers also occurs in 24:33 using the expression, ἐγγύς ἐστιν ἐπὶ θύραις ("it is near, at the doors"), to describe the imminent destruction of the temple following the signs that the disciples will see.

While the actual destruction of the temple is not described, this connection makes clear what the analogy is about, helping to clarify the referent of ἐστιν in 24:33. Although this third-person εἰμί verb also means "he" (cf. 24:26), and therefore may refer to the Son of Man,[465] it is more properly translated "it" as a reference specifically to the destruction of the temple (cf. 24:3).[466] That this is the case is supported by the fact that the phrase, ὅταν

---

463. So Evans, *Matthew*, 409.

464. So also Keener, *Matthew*, 589; and Witherington, *Matthew*, 453, who, on the basis of this, resolves the Discourse into an A-B-A-B schema that appears to correspond to the structure argued in this study.

465. So Hagner, *Matthew*, 715. Davies and Allison, *Matthew*, 3:366, also suggest this based on the image of a door (cf. Jas 5:9; Rev 3:20); so also Evans, *Matthew*, 412, who references Gen 19:11; Prov 9:14; and Wis 9:17.

466. I agree with Gibbs here, except that he overloads the εἰμί verb with both temple destruction (understood as what vv. 29–31 describes) and the fullness of the gentile mission (*Jerusalem and Parousia*, 204).

ἴδητε ("when you see"), is used in v. 33, as is also in v. 15 where it specifically relates to the temple's fate.

The most important debated element in the subunit, however, has to do with the referent of "all these things" (πάντα ταῦτα) in vv. 33 and 34. Some have argued that it refers to all the events previously noted in vv. 4-31.[467] According to Carson, it refers to "the distress of vv. 4-28" understood as "the tribulation that comes on believers throughout the period between Jesus' ascension and the Parousia."[468] Turner takes it to refer only to the "preliminary signs that anticipate Jesus' coming" (i.e., vv. 29).[469]

These views are inaccurate. There is a slight distinction between "all these things" in v. 33 and that in v. 34.[470] The former refers to the things that will signal to the disciples the imminent destruction of the temple. Specifically, it includes the abomination of desolation (v. 15), the miserable conditions occasioned by it (v. 21), and the appearance of false Christs and prophets who would try to deceive many through signs and wonders (vv. 23-24). Just as the fig tree putting forth leaves alerts of summer, when the disciples see "all these things," they will know that the temple is about to be destroyed. The latter "all these things" comprehends both the things that the disciples will see and the temple destruction itself.

Together, except for v. 8 which relates to eschatological signs in general, "all these things" (vv. 33 and 34) is used strictly in connection with the fate of the temple just before and throughout the Discourse. First, in 23:36, it specifically refers to the things that will come upon Jerusalem in relation to the temple's desolation/destruction alluded to in 23:38. Second, the solemn declaration of certainty in 24:35 repeats the emphatic prophetic word in 24:2 where "all these things" refers only to the temple with no association with the Son of Man's coming. And third, the reduced form—"these things" (ταῦτα)—in the disciples' first question (v. 3) pertains to the temple's destruction as distinct from the *parousia* question.

All of this leads to the conclusion that "all these things" refers to the temple's destruction and related signs. In other words, it seems unlikely that the events of vv. 29-31 are included in the "all these things" of vv. 33 and

---

467. Evans, *Matthew*, 412; so also Gibbs, *Jerusalem and Parousia*, 205; Agbanou, *Discours*, 107; Beasley-Murray, *Jesus and the Kingdom*, 334; Hagner, *Matthew*, 715, limits the scope to vv. 4-28.

468. Carson, "Matthew," 569.

469. Turner, *Matthew*, 586; of course, since Turner takes "all these things" in vv. 33 and 34 as the same, he can rightly argue that including the Coming of the Son of Man itself will amount to tautology.

470. Contra Fuller, "Olivet Discourse," 162; Talbert, *Matthew*, 270; Turner, *Matthew*, 586.

34.[471] If at all the Discourse has anything to do with the *parousia* of Jesus as distinct from the destruction of the temple, as most commentators agree, the implied reader, compelled by the correspondence of τὸ σημεῖον in vv. 3 and 30, is more likely to understand vv. 29–31 plainly as a reference to that *parousia* about which the disciples ask than figuratively as a reference to the destruction of the temple. As I shall further demonstrate, it is incorrect to argue that reference to the *parousia* only begins in v. 36.

Furthermore, Jesus solemnly declares that "this generation" (ἡ γενεὰ αὕτη) will by no means pass away until all the things the disciples will see and the destruction of the temple take place. As I earlier argued, this directly relates to and satisfies the disciples' first question regarding when the temple will be destroyed in 24:3 (i.e., this generation). Contrary to the notion of "qualitative generation"—that is, a generation of the same quality but which is located in the distant future, as argued by Gundry,[472] what we have here is chronological generation. Since Matthew only uses the term "generation" in the plain rather than idealistic sense,[473] it is clear that by "this generation," Jesus certainly means the first-century generation. In association with 23:38, the prior and similar solemn declaration, ἥξει ταῦτα πάντα ἐπὶ τὴν γενεὰν ταύτην ("all these things shall come upon this generation") in 23:36 supports both the contemporary and temple-specific reference of 24:34. Finally, as already argued, 24:35 is a pronouncement saying asyndetically connected to and concluding the subunit (cf. v. 28).

b(P²): vv. 36—25:46

Having completed the temple-related response to the disciples' first question, in this long section, Jesus begins a series of analogies of the *parousia*. It may be wondered whether or not Jesus said all of these analogies in the one sitting of the Discourse starting in 24:3. But this is beside the point. The important thing is that in the present literary context, 24:36—25:26 is

---

471. Keener, *Matthew*, 589, notes that "these things" in Matthew 24 apply to the desolation of the temple to occur within that generation." Hagner, *Matthew*, 715, also argues "it cannot include the coming of the Son of Man"; so also Carson, "Matthew," 569; cf. Blomberg, *Matthew*, 364. Even in Luke's version where the Discourse depends on a singular question (21:7), the way the response pans out in vv. 22–33 suggests a distinction between the destruction of Jerusalem/temple (vv. 22–24) and the Coming of the Son of Man (vv. 25–27); and "these things" in vv. 28, 31, and 32 all appear to refer back to vv. 22–24, so that the redemption/kingdom that draws near (vv. 28 and 31) is the event of vv. 25–27. The alternative is to equate vv. 22–24 with vv. 25–27, which creates the problem of leaving the redemption that is drawing near hanging in the air.

472. Gundry, *Matthew*, 490–91; Chrysostom, *Hom. Matt.* 77.1.

473. Matt 1:17; 11:16; 12:39, 41–42, 45; 16:4; 17:17; 23:36.

united in further developing and explicating the subject of *parousia*. Accordingly, this section takes up three themes we have already encountered in the introduction and description of the *parousia* and develops them using illustrations. First, the notion of *suddenness/unknownness* in v. 27 is taken up and developed in vv. 36-44. Second, and in close relation to this, the initial *priority gathering* of the elect in v. 31 is illustrated in vv. 40-44. And third, the theme of *general gathering* in v. 28 is taken up and developed in 25:31-46. All this is done while highlighting the need for the followers of Jesus to be constantly watchful and ready (24:42—25:30). This watchfulness and readiness manifest in wisdom and faithfulness.

Thus, contrary to many treatments limited to ch. 24,[474] it is imperative to take ch. 25 along to interpret the Discourse fully and correctly. We should also avoid the tendency to treat this section as merely stacked subunits.[475] In what follows, I demonstrate that 24:3—25:46 taken as a unit not only coheres structurally but also further strengthens the analyses offered so far.

Structural Transition and Implication of the flood-thief Analogy (vv. 36-44)

The Structural Significance of v. 36

In 24:36, δὲ is used again to mark both discontinuity with the immediately preceding material and further development of the *parousia* theme. The phrase, περὶ δὲ, strengthens this discontinuity and development. Although most commentators ignore the structural significance of this phrase, several have highlighted its structural function as a new topic marker, especially based on its epistolary use.[476] However, in the Gospels and Luke-Acts, περὶ δὲ, glossed as "but concerning," is a development marker used to re-enter a topic already in the process of description within the immediately preceding context. For example, in 22:31 (the only other occurrence glossed the same way in Matthew apart from 24:36), περὶ δὲ, while marking a shift in frame, reintroduces and develops the already established description of resurrection (v. 30) which is in question.[477] Similarly, περὶ δὲ in Matt 24:36 nei-

---

474. See n2 in chapter 2.

475. See e.g., Gibbs, *Jerusalem and Parousia*, 207-13.

476. E.g., 1 Cor 7:1, 25; 8:1; 12:1; 16:1, 12. In each of these cases, the gloss should be "now concerning." See Hart, "Chronology," 228; Gibbs, *Jerusalem and Parousia*, 172; France, *Matthew*, 963; Wilson, *When Will These Things Happen?*, 224.

477. Cf. Mark 12:26; 13:32; John 16:11; Acts 21:25. In Matt 6:28, καὶ περὶ is used in a similar way. The two other Matthean uses of περὶ δὲ do not have the same gloss, "but concerning," but as references to time (i.e., 20:6; 27:46).

ther introduces a new subject nor signals a major (bipartite) hinge,[478] only a limited structural discontinuity in order to re-enter and develop an aspect of an already described theme.

Gibbs argues that περὶ δὲ in 24:36 "reaches back to the beginning of the Discourse and brings into focus the disciples' second question concerning the *parousia* and consummation of the age.[479] This is partly true, but it represents a "fly-over treatment" of the text. That is, it overlooks *parousia*-related comments already made between vv. 36 and 3, or simply regards any mention of such in vv. 3–35 as an aside. The disciples' question is clearly about "the sign" (v. 3) not about "that day and hour" (v. 36). Thus, the phrase, περὶ δὲ τῆς ἡμέρας ἐκείνης καὶ ὥρας ("but concerning *that* day and hour"), assumes that the matter of sign (of the parousia) has already been dealt with.

Since the disciples' question is about the sign of the *parousia*, the mere reference to the unknownness of "that day and hour" in v. 36 says nothing about the *parousia* itself as some event other than the destruction of the temple. In other words, the expression, "that day and hour" here could well refer to the moment when the temple's destruction (understood as the *parousia*) happens. Thus, the implied reader could only know that an event other than the temple's destruction is in view starting in v. 36 only if that event itself has been previously described in relation to its associated sign(s). That description is not satisfied by the mere introduction of the parousia in vv. 26–28, but especially in relation to the sign(s) and events of vv. 29–31. Both passages refer to the *parousia* (*parousia* (v. 27) = *coming* of the Son of Man (v. 30)). This is verified thematically and structurally by the fact that (1) the term "coming" (ἐρχόμενον) used in v. 30 recurs eight times in 24:36—25:46 only in reference to the *parousia*,[480] (2) the *parousia*-ἐρχόμενον sequence in vv. 27 and 30 is also the sequence from v. 36 on, with the event concerned first re-entered using the term *parousia* in vv. 37–39 and from there on, an ἔρχομαι verb is used throughout,[481] and (3) 25:31 resonates with and thematically complements 24:30–31; it is unlikely that the implied reader will understand these two passages in two different ways as assumed by the bipartite structure advocated by Gibbs and France.

---

478. Contra France, *Matthew*, 936; Gibbs, *Jerusalem and Parousia*, 172, 207.
479. Gibbs, *Jerusalem and Parousia*, 172–74.
480. 24:42, 43, 44, 46; 25:10, 19, 27, 31; cf. Juza, *New Testament*, 46.
481. 24:42, 44, 46; 25:27, 31 (cf. 24:43; 25:10, 19).

The Flood- and Thief-Parousia Analogies (vv. 36–44)

The emphasis in this section is eschatological unknownness, what Davies and Allison call "eschatological ignorance."[482] But it also includes eschatological suddenness in relation to the Coming of the Son of Man. No one except the Father knows the day or hour of the *parousia* (v. 36). This unknownness and suddenness of the *parousia* timing is substantiated using the flood analogy from v. 37. Thus, just as "they did not know until the flood came and swept them away, so shall the *parousia* of the Son of Man be" (v. 39). However, this unknownness and suddenness hardly imply the exclusion of all signs. In Noah's time, the flood water seems not to have been suddenly dumped all at once; it would have been preceded by visible signs of storm, followed by persistent rain, resulting in an overwhelming flood, even though such signs would have been too late to be of any use. Similarly, as I have argued earlier, to say that the *time* of the parousia is unknown is different from denying that a sign(s) will precede the occurrence. The sign(s) in vv. 29–30a relate to the *parousia* even without the benefit of forewarning. In fact, the disciples' second question does not necessarily require that the sign represent a forewarning. Thus, rather than deny that Jesus responds to the disciples' question concerning signs, vv. 29–30a seems to indicate that while the *parousia* will indeed be heralded by sign(s), the sign(s) will be too sudden or too late to be of any use. Hence, the best one can do is to be constantly watchful (v. 42) and ready (v. 44).

The most controversial point in this unit, however, is the meaning of the saying, μία παραλαμβάνεται καὶ μία ἀφίεται ("one will be taken and the other will be left") in vv. 40–41. Some consider the matter neither clear nor significant;[483] Gibbs completely avoids it;[484] but the Discourse cannot be done adequate justice without the determination of the referent of the one "taken" and the one "left." Among both postribulationists[485] and certain pretribulationists,[486] the logion is used to support the view of rapture in which those taken are raptured to heaven. While these two opposing schools disagree on the timing of the rapture, they interestingly agree in taking the word παραλαμβάνεται as positively referring to the ones "taken" or received in favor, while the ones "left" are judged or left for judgment. This positive interpretation of παραλαμβάνεται enjoys the support of most

---

482. Davies and Allison, *Matthew*, 3:374.

483. E.g., Carson, *Matthew, Chapters 13 through 28*, 509.

484. Gibbs, *Jerusalem and Parousia*, 208.

485. Ladd, *Blessed Hope*, 144–45; Reese, *Approaching Advent*, 29, 208, 214–15; Gundry, *Church and the Tribulation*, 135–39, 158.

486. Esp. of the *Left Behind* series view.

interpreters.[487] However, the view has increasingly been opposed by many commentators,[488] including hyperdispensational pretribulationists.[489] These commentators are of the view that those "taken" are taken into judgment while those "left" are the saved ones. They argue that the context of the saying in vv. 40–41 is judgment and that ἦρεν ("taken/swept away") in v. 39 parallels παραλαμβάνεται ("taken") in vv. 40–41. Witherington adds that "the saying about the angels gathering the elect [v. 31] is remote from this saying [vv. 40–41] compared to the immediately preceding Noah story." Thus, he concludes that "those 'left behind' are the fortunate ones, while those taken are taken away in or by judgment, as the Noah analogy makes clear."[490]

Although this latter interpretation is now gaining wide acceptance, it represents, in my view, an overreaction against the popular rapture theology, and the exegetical bases for it are anything but solid.[491] The context of Matt 24:37–41 is both of salvation and judgment, and the claim of parallelism between ἦρεν and παραλαμβάνεται misapprehends the flood analogy as will soon be clear. But also, the notion of remoteness between v. 31 and vv. 40–41, as Witherington argues, ignores the fact that vv. 37–41 in whole aims to explicate vv. 30–31, a passage which describes the *parousia* as Witherington also appears to maintain.[492]

The key to interpreting the saying in vv. 40–41 is of course to relate it back to the flood analogy, but it must also be related to the following thief-in-the-night analogy. First, properly understood, the flood analogy depicts Noah as the *parousia-Christ*, as the one who takes the one and leaves the other. This is clear from Gen 7:1–2 (MT). Noah is commanded, "*go you* (בֹּא־אַתָּה)[493] *and all your household into the ark,*" and to "*take to yourself*

---

487. E.g., Broadus, *Matthew*, 495; Hare, *Matthew*, 282; Meier, *Matthew*, 291; Marvin, *Luke*, 332; Glasscock, *Matthew*, 477; Hagner, *Matthew*, 720; Hendriksen, *Matthew*, 870; Bock, *Luke 9:51—24:53*, 1437; Bruner, *Matthew*, 2:526; Wilkins, *Matthew*, 801; Nolland, *Matthew*, 994; Marshall, *Luke*, 668; cf. Wilson, *When Will These Things Happen?*, 228n220. France, *Gospel according to Matthew*, 348 and Gundry, *Church and the Tribulations*,135–39, 158 once held this positive view.

488. See France, *Matthew*, 941; Gundry, *Matthew*, 494; Blomberg, *Matthew*, 36; Wright, *Jesus and the Victory*, 366; Mounce, *Matthew*, 229; Witherington, *Matthew*, 454; Osborne, *Matthew*, 905; Evans, *Matthew*, 414.

489. E.g., Walvoord, "Is Posttribulation Rapture Revealed?," 257–66; Pettegrew, "Interpretive Flaws," 187–88.

490. Witherington, *Women*, 45–46; Witherington, *Matthew*, 454.

491. To be clear, I do not share this escapist flight-to-heaven rapture theology made popular by LaHaye and Jenkins; see, e.g., their *Left Behind*.

492. Witherington, *Matthew*, 452–54.

493. Or LXX, εἴσελθε σὺ ("you go/enter").

(תִּקַּֽח־לְךָ֒)⁴⁹⁴ *select* faunae from all the beasts of the field. In fulfilling this, Noah separates his household and the select faunae from the rest (see Gen 7:15-16 MT). This act of selection and separation by Noah is what is assumed and summed up in the phrase, ἄχρι ἧς ἡμέρας εἰσῆλθεν Νῶε εἰς τὴν κιβωτόν ("until the day Noah entered into the ark" [Matt 24:38b]), corresponding to the theme of Jesus bringing *with him* his angels (Matt 24:31; 25:31), and gathering his *elect* to himself by separating them from the rest of people (24:31; 25:10).⁴⁹⁵ The flood story pervades the Discourse from here, especially helping to explicate 24:40-41. Thus, in as much as "the rest" in the Noah story are left to be swept away by the flood, "the rest" in the Discourse (i.e., the ones not taken or gathered to Jesus) are the ones left for judgment.

Second, the thief-in-the-night saying that follows in vv. 43-44 is intended to further reiterate what has just been said in vv. 37-42 in terms of the suddenness of the *parousia* and the need for constant readiness.⁴⁹⁶ Although distinct, and separated from the flood analogy by the use of a discontinuous δὲ in v. 43, the thief-in-the-night analogy implies as well as clarifies the meaning of being "taken" and being "left." When a thief breaks into a house, he does not remove the bad properties and leave the good ones behind. On the contrary, he takes the good and the house is left broken and robbed. In the same way, vv. 43-44 implies that the coming of the Son of Man will be as a thief suddenly breaking upon the world and taking (gathering to himself) the good (saints) and leaving behind those to be judged. This comports well with the analogy of Noah gathering to himself his household and some select animals while leaving others. It also comports with the theme of angelic precision gathering in 24:31 which will be followed by the general assize in 25:31. Nothing in these texts, however, warrants the notion of saints being whisked away to heaven.

Given this two-directional connection, the interpretation of the saying could not be clearer: the ones taken are the saints, while the ones left are the wicked. This interpretation is also grounded in the relationship and significance of the terms αἴρω, παραλαμβάνω, and ἀφίημι on the one hand, and the *discourse priority of saints* within the Discourse on the other.

---

494. Or LXX, εἰσάγαγε πρὸς σε ("lead to you" = take with you).

495. Note the corresponding phrase in Matt 25:10, εἰσῆλθον μετ' αὐτοῦ εἰς τοὺς γάμους καὶ ἐκλείσθη ἡ θύρα ("they entered with him into the wedding *and the door was shut*"); cf. Gen 7:16b, καὶ ἔκλεισεν κύριος ὁ θεὸς ἔξωθεν αὐτοῦ τὴν κιβωτόν ("*and God shut from outside the ark*").

496. I earlier argued that the shocking character of the thief-in-the-night analogy in relation to the person of Jesus compares to the bizarre or grotesque character of the cadaver saying also in relation to Jesus in 24:28.

First, the relationship between the two terms αἴρω (v. 39) and παραλαμβάνω (vv. 40–41) is antithetical, not synonymous parallelism. While αἴρω in this context certainly means to "sweep away," παραλαμβάνω means to "take with/along" in a positive sense.[497] It is used exclusively in this sense in the LXX,[498] and overwhelmingly so in Matthew[499] and the rest of the NT.[500] The only exceptions are the instances in Matt 27:27 and John 19:16–17. In relation to the first instance, Matthew shows awareness of the use of παραλαμβάνω in a non-cordial way. However, his preferred use of the term is positive, referring to being taken alongside in an approving manner. In other words, this exception cannot be taken as the rule. This is in no way to imply that frequency necessarily fixes meaning. Rather it is to affirm that an author's established pattern and literary context should have greater hermeneutical weight anytime doubt arises.

Second, the term ἀφίημι can be glossed in a number of different ways.[501] Several times in Matthew, it is used to refer to something or someone forsaken or abandoned.[502] In particular, it has the negative meaning of abandonment, judgment, and or destruction within the Discourse context itself: (1) Jesus employs ἀφίημι in 23:38 to allude to the destruction of the temple—"see, your house is left (ἀφίεται) to you desolate." And (2) concerning the coming destruction of the temple, Jesus further states, "No stone will be left (ἀφεθῇ) here upon a stone which shall not be destroyed" (24:2),

---

497. According to BDAG, "παραλαμβάνω," 767–77, it means (1) *to take into close association take (to oneself), take with/along* (e.g., Matt 24:40–41); (2) *take over, receive*; and (3) *accept* with emphasis sometimes on agreement or approval.

498. Gen 22:3; 31:23; 45:18; 47:2; Num 22:41; 23:14, 20, 27–28; Josh 4:2; 2 Chr 25:11; Esth 5:1; Sol 8:2; Jer 30:17–18; 39:7; Lam 3:2; Dan 4:31; 6:1, 20, 29; 7:18. Challenged by this exclusive meaning of παραλαμβάνω, Merkle, "Who Will Be Left behind?," 170–72, resorts to the OT remnant theology by using passages like Isa 3:1–3; 4:2–4; Zach 13:8; Zeph 3:11–13; and Jer 6:11 to support the view that those left behind are always the blessed ones while those taken are those that go into captivity. Similarly, Keener, *Matthew*, 941, notes passages like Pss. Sol. 13:11 and Sir 44:16–17 which might support the view. However, there is no contextual or verbal correspondence between these passages and παραλαμβάνω in Matt 24:40–41. Ps. Sol. 13:11 uses αἴρω in connection with the judgment of sinners and thus has a sense similar to Matt 24:39 but not vv. 40–41; Sir 44:16–17 simply makes the point that the earth was repopulated through Noah.

499. Matt 1:20, 24; 2:13–14, 20–21; 4:5, 8; 12:45; 17:1; 18:16; 20:17; 24:40–41; 26:37; 27:27.

500. Mark 4:36; 5:40; 7:4; 9:2; 10:32; 14:33; Luke 9:10, 28; 11:26; 17:34–35; 18:31; John 1:11; 14:3; 19:16; Acts 15:39; 16:33; 21:24, 26, 32; 23:18; 1 Cor 11:23; 15:1, 3; Gal 1:9, 12; Phil 4:9; Col 2:6; 4:17; 1 Thess 2:13; 4:1; 2 Thess 3:6; Heb 12:28.

501. In Matthew, it may mean "let," "let go," "leave," "permit," "forgive," or "abandon"; see BDAG, "ἀφίημι," 156–57.

502. E.g., 4:20, 22; 19:27, 29; 26:56.

by which he means that every stone will be left in ruins. This clearly sets the stage for the implied reader's understanding of the term's sense in 24:40–41.

Third, Matt 24–25 reflects *the discourse priority of the saints*. By this, I mean a pattern throughout the Discourse giving the saints (their deliverance or blessing) referential priority or priority of reference. Letting alone 24:40–41 for a moment, this pattern is evident in several instances: (1) As Jesus warns in 24:15–20, the disciples are to take their flight *first* before destruction comes on the city. (2) Based on the motif of gathering, the elect are *first* gathered in 24:31 and afterwards all the nations are gathered in 25:32. (3) In 24:38–39, Noah's entrance into the ark (implying the "being taken to safety" of all those with him) has discourse priority of reference, followed by (a reference to) the destruction of the wicked.[503] (4) In 25:10–12, the *entrance* of the five wise virgins to the wedding takes place and is mentioned *first*, followed by a reference to the remaining five who are left out rejected. (5) The faithful servants of the parable of the talents in 25:14–30 are referenced and admitted *first* into the joy of the Father before the fate of the wicked servant is announced and executed. And (6) the judgment scene in 25:31–46 unfolds in a two-step process: (a) The Son of Man will separate the sheep from the goat, the sheep *first* to the right, and *then* the goat to the left (vv. 32–33), and (b) the King mentions and admits the faithful servants on the right into the kingdom *first*, followed by the pronouncement of the fate of the wicked (25:33–46). Undoubtedly, this observation applies to and indeed makes clear the one-taken-and-one-left saying in 24:40–41. It is very unlikely, in light of these observations, that the saying will be understood differently than that the ones referenced *first* ("taken") are the righteous and the ones referenced second ("left") are the wicked.

But before I conclude, it is necessary to consider one likely objection to this observation and interpretation. That is that, in the parable of the Tares (Matt 13:24–30, 36–43), the Tares (that is, the wicked) are said to be removed first, leaving the righteous (the wheat) to inherit the kingdom. Although a valid objection, there is a problem with this parable that prevents it from being used to determine who is taken or left in Matt 24:40–41. It represents an odd and unlikely harvest practice, which, if taken on face value as the standard, would contradict the already established procedure in Matt 3:12 and in Matt 13 (vv. 47–48) itself.

---

503. Notice Luke's connection of the saying with both Noah's and Lot's stories (17:26–37). The two analogies are linked with ὁμοίως (likewise) in v. 28, indicating the same sense: as Lot was first taken out by the angel before the city is judged (cf. Gen 19:15–17), so those with Noah were first taken out before the flood, and so the saints will be "taken"—first gathered to the Lord before the general judgment; see also Nolland, *Luke*, 862; Fitzmyer, *Luke*, 1172.

The apparent contradiction is resolved once the order in the parable of the Tares is understood in terms of *rhetorical topicality effect*. By this I mean the observation that when a discourse unit is binary, the element which is emphasized either by it being topical or by it taking more of the material, takes referential precedence.[504] Thus, because the parable is primarily about the Tares rather than the Wheats (*per* 13:36),[505] their removal is accorded rhetorical precedence without suggesting actual harvest procedure. In fact, the danger of such a harvest procedure is clearly stated in 13:29, and this, without any note of amelioration in v. 30. Since such a harvest procedure is unlikely, therefore, the parable of the Tares does not explicate the one-will-be-taken-and-one-will-be-left saying or negate the interpretation above.[506] Moreover, Matt 24–25 represents Jesus' fuller eschatological vision. Based on these constraints, it must be concluded that the ones "taken" are the saved, and the ones "left" are the damned.

Eschatological Vigilance: Analogies of Faithfulness and Wisdom (24:45—25:30)

In Matt 24:45—25:30, Jesus gives further analogies of the *parousia* from the perspective of the disciples' preparedness, further accentuating the motifs of *unknownness* of the time and *suddenness* of the *parousia* (24:36; cf. vv. 42, 44, 50 and 25:13) with the added notion of eschatological *delay* (24:48; 25:5, 19).[507] These motifs altogether compel eschatological vigilance: Jesus'

---

504. Cf. the bad and the good (Matt 22:8–13); the foolish and the wise (25:1–13); the wicked and the righteous (25:41–46).

505. The common identification of the parable as the "Parable of Wheat and Tares" is erroneous.

506. Contra Merkle, "Who Will Be Left Behind?," 172–73, 176.

507. The notion of delay is often taken to imply crisis within the early Christian circle. Schweitzer, who of course denies the authenticity of the synoptic Apocalypse, claims that "the real inner history of it [Christianity], is based on the delay of the Parousia" (*Quest*, 358, 387n1). The parables in Matt 24–25 are said to be originally crisis-parables aimed at the Jewish leaders or Jesus' contemporaries regarding an imminent catastrophe, but which the church has reapplied to itself as *parousia*-parables in view of a different crisis—the delay of *parousia*; so Dodd, *Parables*, 154–74; Jeremias, *Parables*, 48–63. However, Davies and Allison, *Matthew*, 3:389, maintain that "there is no good reason to speak of a 'crisis' in connexion with this theme in Matthew," adding, "Matthew is concerned with unpreparedness because of the delay in Jesus' coming, not with the delay itself." The assumption of crisis based on a mirror-reading of the text ignores the hypothetical nature of the parables as opposed to the flood analogy. And in fact, to maintain that the time of the *parousia* is unknown is, in a sense, to offset the notion of delay; cf. Wright, *New Testament and the People*, 462; Witherington, *Jesus, Paul, and End*, 15–48; Sim, *Apocalyptic Eschatology*, 150–74. For a recent treatment of the subject of the delay of the *parousia*, see Hays et al., *When the Son of Man Didn't Come*.

followers must be ready at all times for his *parousia* by being faithful and wise. This is the main point of the three analogies within this section.

First, on the one hand, *the* faithful and wise servant who is occupied with his master's business will be blessed when his master returns. On the other hand, *that* evil servant who ignores his office and indulges in drunkenness and bullying of fellow servants will have his master suddenly arrive on a day he does not expect; the consequence will be judgment, the same fate as the hypocrites or wicked in general (24:45-51). The phrase, "*that* evil servant" (ὁ κακὸς δοῦλος ἐκεῖνος) in 24:48 appears to make reference back to *the* hypothetical "faithful and wise servant." Some interpret it in this manner.[508] But this would appear awkward and unnecessary. It is better to take *that* evil servant as a different hypothetical servant,[509] likely introduced in anticipation of the wicked and slothful servant in the parable of the Tenants later in 25:14-30.

Second, the parable of the Ten Maidens highlights the eschatological virtue of wisdom (25:1-13): five wise Maidens are prepared for the arrival of the bridegroom in contrast to the five foolish ones who fail to prepare. Eschatological vigilance is not a matter of night vigil but of making the wise decision of extra provision. Thus, at the arrival of the bridegroom, "in the middle of the night" (25:6),[510] the wise Maidens "summon their reserve" (implied) and enter (εἰσῆλθον) with him into the wedding while the foolish ones are shut out and sternly rejected, left for judgment (vv. 10-12). There is an allusion here to 24:38 and Gen 7:13-16 where Noah's household and the select animals enter with him into the ark and God shuts the door.

Third, the parable of the Talents highlights the eschatological virtue of faithfulness (25:14-30): two business-minded and faithful servants are blessed at their master's return in contrast to the wicked and slothful one who faces judgment.

As is common with apocalyptic materials (cf. ch. 3), these analogies represent threefold mutually clarifying iterations of the same eschatological necessities. Although discrete, they cohere thematically. Thus, the two attributes of eschatological vigilance—faithfulness and wisdom—are first generalized in the hypothetical faithful and wise servant (24:45-47), and then particularized and developed alternatingly in the parables of the Maidens and the Talents. The opposite attributes of *that* evil servant, generalized in 24:48-51, are placed in juxtaposition and similarly particularized and developed in the two parables as well. This may be graphically represented as follows:

508. E.g., Luz, *Matthew*, 224.
509. So Hagner, *Matthew*, 724.
510. Cf. Thief in the night (24:43).

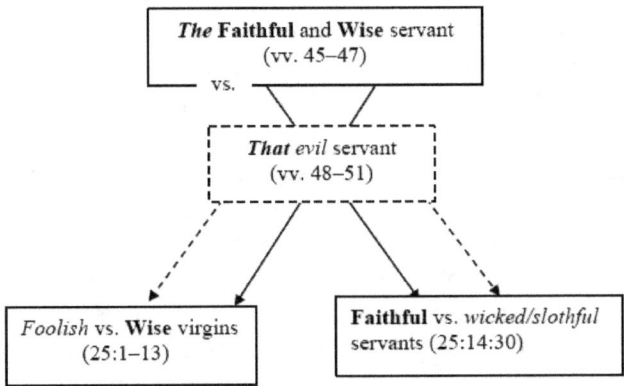

Connecting the Analogies of Matt 24:45—25:30.

In other words, the two parables in 25:1–30 are co-opted to make the same points by elaborating on the motifs of faithfulness and wisdom in the servant of 24:45–47 as well as the opposite motifs of unfaithfulness and sloth of the servant in 24:48–51.[511] Thus, as the *wisdom and faithfulness* of the servant in 24:45–47 relates to the wisdom of the five wise virgins (25:1–13) and the faithfulness of five- and two-talent servants (25:14–23) respectively, so also the wickedness of the servant in 24:48 relates to the foolishness of the five foolish virgins in 25:1–13 and the unfaithfulness of the one-talent servant in 25:24–30.[512] The reward of the wise and faithful servant is the same in 24:47 as that of the faithful servants in 25:21, 23 (i.e., "being set over much"). Similarly, the fate of *that* evil servant in 24:48–51 is the same as that of the wicked and slothful servant in 25:24–30 (i.e., "weeping and gnashing of teeth").

This interconnectedness is structurally and theologically significant. First, it verifies the unity and coherence of Matt 24 and 25 which is also further strengthened by the alternation:

A (faithful and wise servant exhorted to vigilance [24:44; cf. v. 42])
   B (punishment of *that* wicked/weeping and gnashing of teeth [24:51])
A (faithful and wise servant exhorted to vigilance [25:13])
   B (punishment of the wicked servant/weeping and gnashing of teeth [25:30]).

---

511. Note Matt 13:31–33, 44–45; see chapter 3, n484.

512. Slothfulness (ὀκνηρός) of the wicked servant in 25:26 implies his foolishness (cf. Prov 6:6). France, "On Being Ready," 180, describes 24:45–51 as "the parable of the 'wise' and 'foolish' slaves."

Second, it obviates the curious soteriological implication of damnation based just on one's failure to multiply one's talent. In other words, the fate of the one-talent servant in 25:30 is caused not merely by the failure to increase his talent but also by the unfaithfulness and foolishness characterized in 24:49 and 25:3, 24–27.

So far, I have discussed the analogies in 24:36—25:30 in terms of three motifs, the *unknownness* of time, *suddenness*, and *delay* of the *parousia*. The other motif running through the entire section is *separation*. The *parousia* will entail the separation of the righteous from the wicked. Although 24:45—25:30 is particularly ecclesiastical in that it addresses those who are already servants of the gospel, the analogies both reflect the initial angelic separation of the elect in 24:31 and point to the eventual outcome of the general gathering in 25:31–46.

The final Assize (25:31–46)

Much hermeneutical energy has been invested in this last part of the Eschatological Discourse.[513] Part of the reason for the great interest as Gray puts it, is the passage's "tremendous influence on Christian teaching, preaching, praxis, literature, and art." According to Gray, the "two problem areas" in Matt 25:31–46 are the referents of πάντα τὰ ἔθνη (v. 32) and ἑνὶ τούτων τῶν ἀδελφῶν μου τῶν ἐλαχίστων (vv. 40, 45).[514] I take this to be correct. However, two other issues are also critical: the genre and the soteriology of the passage.

The Genre of Matt 25:31–46

To begin with, Matt 25:31–46 is traditionally approached from the standpoint of tradition history—form, *Sitz im Leben*, and redaction—often with the presupposition or result that it lacks originality to Jesus and/or unity with the preceding material.[515] As the present study has demonstrated, it is impossible to make sense of the *parousia* subject without these last verses.

---

513. Although Gray's *Least of My Brothers* remains the most extensive survey of the history of interpretation of Matt 25:31–46. Apart from many articles, other recent extensive studies include Pond, "Interpretive Issues"; Leverett, "Looking for the Least."

514. Gray, *Least of My Brothers*, 8–9.

515. See Bultmann, *History*, 123–24, 125; Catchpole, "Poor on Earth," 365–78. Cope, "Matthew," 42, claims, "the passage is not highly original, . . . it does not reflect a situation in the life of Jesus," adding, "The arguments against its being a saying of Jesus are collectively compelling." See also Robinson, "Parable," 232–37.

The thematic and structural unity of the entire Discourse up to 25:46 is evident even to some who have cause to doubt its root in the teaching of Jesus.[516] Importantly, the implied reader will understand the Son of Man's coming "in his glory" and "sitting on his glorious throne" (Matt 25:31) as the culmination of the *parousia* journey began in 24:30–31, where also we have the motif of "coming... with power and great glory" (v. 30). Thus, the gathering in 25:32 is the second half of an event of which 24:31 is the first half. The one text that represents that event in whole is the generic *parousia* saying of Matt 24:28.

Regarding the question of genre, Matt 25:31–46 has been regarded as a parable,[517] a Hebrew poem,[518] an allegory,[519] a *mashal* (=parable) in the form of "apocalyptic revelation" like 1 En. 37–71,[520] or more strictly, an "apocalyptic vision."[521] Most commentators implicitly follow or cite the authority of Jeremias, taking the passage as a parable,[522] but they seem to miss his actual understanding of its more apocalyptic character. I will argue that "apocalyptic" is the most accurate designation of Matt 25:31–46. Precisely, the passage is to be taken as an *illustrative apocalyptic, perspectivally describing the Last Judgment as a reality*.[523] It takes the form of actual realization of

---

516. E.g., Cope, "Matthew," 44, maintains that "the passage is wedded to its [literary] context," concluding, "The isolation of xxv 31–46 as an independent saying is the most glaring mistake of the traditional exegesis of this passage."

517. A view that goes back to Paschaius Radbertus (ca. 785–860); see Davies and Allison, *Matthew*, 3:418. Those maintaining the passage as a parable include Manson, *Sayings*, 242–52; Wenham, *Parables*, 88–89; Lambrecht, *Once More Astonished*, 212–13; Keener, *Matthew*, 602.

518. Burney, "Matthew."

519. Gaechter, *Literarische* Kunst, 38.

520. Jeremias, *Parables*, 16n22, 60; 206n77 (he entitles the pericope, *description of the Sentence pronounced at the Last Judgment*). Cope, "Matthew," 36, thinks that Matt 25:31–46 may have originally been a Hebrew Poem (*per* Burney), but like Jeremias, he maintains: "The passage is no ordinary Synoptic parable, its closest literary parallels are found in the Similitudes of Enoch, although Jeremias thinks it an error to call 1 En. 37–71 a 'Similitude.'"

521. Beare, *Matthew*, 492; and Gardner, *Matthew*, 357. Witherington, *Matthew*, 468, calls it an "apocalyptic prophecy"; Hultgren, *Parables*, 310, "an apocalyptic discourse with a parabolic element"; Waetjen, *Matthew's Theology*, 258, "an apocalyptic parable," and Friedrich, "apocalyptic revelation-discourse" (cited in Catchpole, "Poor on Earth," 356).

522. See France, "On Being Ready," 189–90.

523. By "perspectivally," I mean that 25:31–46 is one way of describing the reality of the final judgment; there are other ways of describing the event (cf. 12:36–37, 41–42). Leverett, "Looking for the Least," 165–90, analyzes identifications of the passage as parabolic, apocalyptic, and predictive. He seems to take the view that although using apocalyptic parlance, the passage is intended as "a factual and detailed reporting of an

a parable rather than the parable itself, in the same sense that Matt 13:37–43 (the meaning of the parable of the Tares) is no longer a parable (13:24–30) but its actual and apocalyptic realization.[524]

After the series of parables on eschatological vigilance (24:43—25:30), Matt 25:31–46, proceeding in the same apocalyptic mood of 24:27–31, 36–42, is the actual realization of the separation entailed or represented pictorially in these preceding parables.[525] The mere use of shepherd-sheep-goat metaphor in 25:32 does not make the passage a parable any more than the reintroduction of Tare simile in 13:40 means that Jesus is still talking in parables in 13:37–43. Instructively, the comparative conjunction ὥσπερ ("just as") used in 25:32 is also used to liken the *parousia* to the lightning (24:27) and Noah's flood (24:37), and no one thinks that the lightning and flood analogies are parables.[526] Thus, we ought not to talk of the "parabolic nature of Matt 25:31–46"[527] or of its allegorical nature (*per* Gaechter), but of its apocalyptic nature. The reality of the passage strengthens the fact that apocalyptic can refer to concrete phenomenon without fading into either mere symbolism or wooden literalism.

Referent of πάντα τὰ ἔθνη

Centuries of interpretation have differed sharply on the referent of πάντα τὰ ἔθνη in 25:32.[528] Grays' historical survey shows the majority view to be that πάντα τὰ ἔθνη refers to all humanity.[529] However, some consider it a

---

eschatological judgment" (184). In excluding the "parabolic" view, Cope, "Matthew," 34, states: "No imagination, recognition, or insight is necessary on the reader's part," adding, "the statements are unambiguous and forthright"; see also Gibbs, *Jerusalem and Parousia*, 214; Filson, *Matthew*, 266.

524. To use the words of Linnemann, *Parables*, 24, Matt 13:24–30 constitutes the "picture part" of a parable while 13:37–43 is the "reality part." Matthew 25:31–46 compares to 13:37–43 as an expression of the reality rather than the picture.

525. Plummer, *Matthew*, 349, thinks that Matt 25:31–46 is the revealed and plain meaning of the several parables of judgment (18:23–34; 20:1–16; 21:33–41; 22:1–14; 24:45–51; and 25:1–12).

526. The conjunction ὥσπερ can introduce or be used within non-parables/realities (12:40; 13:40; 20:28) as well as parables (25:14–30); but the latter is clearly a picture rather than a reality.

527. So Gray, *Least of My Brothers*, 351. Gray thinks that not considering the parabolic nature of the passage is one of the pitfalls of centuries of interpretation.

528. Gray, *Least of My Brothers*, 331–51.

529. Those holding this view today include Gundry, *Matthew*, 511–12; Blomberg, *Interpreting the Parables*, 398; Davies and Allison, *Matthew*, 3:422; Beare, *Matthew*, 493; Luz, *Matthew*, 275; Gibbs, *Jerusalem and Parousia*, 214, 216–17; France, *Matthew*, 961; Nolland, *Matthew*, 1024–25; Snodgrass, *Stories*, 554–55.

reference to only Christians,[530] while two views—all non-Christians,[531] and all non-Jews[532]—only emerged in the modern era, although not widely attested.[533] The last view is mostly held by dispensationalists for whom πάντα τὰ ἔθνη refers only to gentile nations (i.e., excluding Israel and the church) who survive the Tribulation; they will be judged based on how they treated Israel.[534]

The phrase πάντα τὰ ἔθνη ("all the nations") here is already anticipated by two other occurrences in the Discourse (24:9,14), and is itself the ground for the instance in 28:19 (cf. Luke 24:47). According to its common or predominant use, πάντα τὰ ἔθνη primarily *refers* to all gentile nations. However, other than what Carson describes as the fallacy of "false assumptions about technical meaning,"[535] there is no cogent reason in Matthew to limit πάντα τὰ ἔθνη to gentile nations in 25:32. In fact, there is substantial reasons to the contrary.

First, I argued earlier that within the Eschatological Discourse, there is, at least, the implicit assumption that Israel has been *ethnos*ized and, therefore, subject to both the Great Commission and the Last Judgment in the same way that gentile nations are. To recall, this *ethnos*ization is informed by 24:9 in light of 23:34–35 and strengthened by 18:15–17. Second, in 24:30, we are told that "all the tribes of the earth will mourn" at the sight of the sign of the Son of Man in his *parousia*. The tribes of the earth not only include Israel but also, their reaction reflects the anticipation of judgment that has yet to be accounted for in the Discourse. All we encounter in connection with the *parousia* from 24:30 on is analogies and parables until we get to the judgment scene in 25:31–46. Third, outside the Discourse, the Israel-inclusive nature of πάντα τὰ ἔθνη in 25:32 is further verified by several other passages in Matthew. Thus, in Matt 10:15, Jesus declares that it will be

---

530. Michaels, "Apostolic Hardships," 29–30, represents this interpretation based on 24:45–51 and Gal 6:6: "all nations" are those who had the gospel preached to them (or Christians), not those who had not.

531. Cf. Ladd, "Parable," 199.

532. E.g., Runesson, *Divine Wrath*, 25–26; 414–25.

533. Gray, *Least of My Brothers*, 349.

534. See Pond, "Interpretive Issues," 81–82; Pond, "Who Are the Sheep?," 288–301; although Ware, a dispensationalist, thinks that the Discourse is only about Israel, not the Church ("Is the Church in View?," 171). Cope, "Matthew," 37, argues that "the judgment of Israel and of the Church have been dealt with earlier in the gospel," although he later says it "perhaps includes Israel" (43); Lambrecht, *Once More Astonished*, 222–23, 227, thinks that Israel does not belong to "all the nations" in 25:32 since they have already been condemned as indicated by the parable of the Wicked Tenant; cf. Hare, *Matthew*, 288–89.

535. Carson, *Exegetical Fallacies*, 45–47.

more tolerable on *the day of judgment* for Sodom and Gomorrah than for gospel-rejecting Jewish towns. In Matt 11:21–24, he reiterates that Tyre and Sidon will fare better on *the day of judgment* than Israelite cities—Chorazin, Bethsaida, and Capernaum. Again, in Matt 12:41–42, the people of Nineveh and the queen of the South will arise (ἀναστήσονται/ἐγερθήσεται) at the judgment *with* (μετὰ) "this generation" (i.e., Jesus' Jewish contemporaries) and condemn it.

The matter could not be clearer, but I must make three observations in relation to Matt 25:32: (1) The *day of Judgment* in these pronouncements must refer to the eschatological "D-Day," by which I mean the decisive and final Day of Judgment when humans in general (οἱ ἄνθρωποι) will give account (Matt 12:36).[536] (2) The third pronouncement (Matt 12:41–42) implies that the judgment referred to is associated with the resurrection of the dead. The One Judgment in which (a) the dead will rise, and (b) all the nations are gathered before the Divine Judge, is the Last Judgment (i.e., 25:31–46).[537] And (3) against the dispensational interpretation, Matt 25:46 indicates finality, with the judgment leading either to eternal life or eternal punishment with fire (v. 41),[538] not to some temporary millennial existence.[539] Therefore, it must be concluded that for all these pronouncements to be true, the judgment in question (a) must refer to the One Last judgment and (b) must include Israel.[540]

Waetjen maintains that neither the Jews nor the disciples are in the judgment of Matt 25:31–46. Yet he argues, "if it may be presupposed that they are present," they are, according to 19:28 "seated on twelve thrones judging the twelve tribes of Israel, while Jesus ... is seated on his own throne of glory."[541] Gibbs also argues that "Jesus directs the attention of both the righteous and the wicked to 'these' brothers of his who are *standing* with him at the judgment," adding that it corresponds with the promise in 19:28

---

536. Cf. Cullmann, *Christ and Time*, xix, for whom the D-Day is the coming of the kingdom in its already-form and the consummation the V-Day.

537. Gray, *Least of My Brothers*, 349: "The understanding of the first sixteen centuries is that Matt 25:32 presupposes a resurrection of the dead."

538. Cf. Matt 25:46 and Dan 12:2; see also Waetjen, *Matthew's Theology*, 259.

539. Contra Walvoord, *Kingdom Come*, 200; Pond, "Interpretive Issues," 82 (cf.105–15, 149–52); Toussaint, *Behold the King*, 288–89. Nothing in the text could commend the dispensational Tribulation-millennial interpretation which presupposes a distinction between judgment here and the white-throne judgment to the implied reader; cf. Ladd, "Parable," 196; Snodgrass, *Stories*, 552.

540. Commenting on "all the nations" in 25:32, Snodgrass, *Stories*, 554, affirms that Jesus' "picture of judgment subverts the usual picture by placing Israel with the other nations."

541. Waetjen, *Matthew's Theology*, 258–59.

that "they would, at the regeneration, *sit* on twelve thrones and judge the twelve tribes of Israel."[542] Martin Down takes a similar view when he claims that the brothers of Christ "are more likely with him on the throne" based on John 5:25, John 3:18, and Rom 8:1.[543]

Of course, there is verbal correspondence between Matt 19:29 and 25:31. But there are serious issues with interpreting the latter in light of the former. First, it is clear that in the Gospels, the same expression can communicate different aspects of reality in the same way that "the coming of the Son of Man" (cf. "kingdom of God") does.[544] Second, the near demonstrative (τούτων) in Matt 25:40/45 suggests that those referred to as ἑνὶ τούτων τῶν ἀδελφῶν μου τῶν ἐλαχίστων are "pre[sent] and visible" at the judgment,[545] not as judges, but as participants, indeed, as candidates themselves of the final reward of eternal life. Contrary to Gibbs' view, they cannot be *standing* at the judgment and at the same time be *sitting* on thrones, which is what 19:28 requires. Third, the *hapax legomenon*, παλιγγενεσίᾳ (rebirth, renewal or regeneration) in 19:28 admits of a different meaning.

Against most scholars who take παλιγγενεσίᾳ to refer to the cosmic re-creation of the final eschaton,[546] this saying, I argue, is another way of referencing the coming of the Son of Man in his kingdom in relation to his resurrection and ascension to the throne. Like 10:23b, 19:28 also alludes to Dan 7:9–14 which in turn echoes Ps 122:3–5 (cf. Ps 110:1).[547] Both 10:23b and 19:28 lack the notion of coming in the clouds, there is no angelic entourage, and when the final judgment plays out in 25:31–46, there is neither a hint of the twelve sitting on twelve thrones judging Israel as a separate group nor any notion of an intermediate kingdom, since the judgment leads immediately to either eternal life or eternal punishment.

Thus, the correct understanding of 19:28 (cf. Luke 22:28–30) is that with Jesus' resurrection and ascent to the throne, the disciples will also "sit on thrones judging the twelve tribes of Israel," by which is meant their assumption of apostolic and spiritual authority over the new Israel of God, and in which sense, they, being once "the last," will become "the first" (19:30).[548] In other words, the resurrection of Jesus (not to be separated

542. Gibbs, *Jerusalem and Parousia*, 219n329 (italics mine).

543. Down, "Exegetical Note," 588.

544. See chapter 3, pp. 82–83, 85.

545. So Quarles, *Matthew*, 306.

546. Evans (*Matthew*, 347–48) follows Burnett, "Παλιγγενεσία"; and Sim, "Meaning of παλιγγενεσία." Cf. France, *Matthew*, 742–43; Witherington, *Matthew*, 372; Keener, *Matthew*, 479–80.

547. See Evans, *Matthew*, 347–48.

548. "Twelve tribes of Israel" in this saying is symbolic of the new people of God;

from his session on the throne) is his "coming" in his kingdom, his entry into his glory (cf. Luke 24:26), and with this, the reconstitution of the kingdom and people of God around himself and his apostles in the power of the Spirit—the *palingenesia*.[549] This will be the fulfillment of what Jesus says to Israel's leaders in Matt 21:43: "I tell you, the kingdom of God will be taken away from you and given to a nation producing the fruits of it" (cf. 16:19; Luke 12:32; Dan 7:22).[550]

Moreover, the Johannine and Pauline texts appealed to by Down, reflect an *already*-soteriology quite different from Matthew's *not-yet* eschatological salvation. As such, they cannot provide an explanation for Matt 25:31–46. In short, Matt 25:31–46 gives no warrant for the idea that any other persons are sitting on the throne, or that there are two sets of judgment going on at the scene.

Referent of ἑνὶ τούτων τῶν ἀδελφῶν μου τῶν ἐλαχίστων

The expression, ἑνὶ τούτων τῶν ἀδελφῶν μου τῶν ἐλαχίστων, is commonly translated as "one of the least of these my brothers."[551] It is traditionally taken

---

they take up the tribal shape of Israel—twelve tribes; cf. Rev 21 where the new Jerusalem is described in terms of Israel's tribal shape.

549. This term evokes the Stoic idea of cosmic conflagration and regeneration (see discussion in Diog. Laert. *Vit. philos.* 7.140–43). It also occurs in Philo who refutes the Stoic idea, maintaining that the world is indestructible (*Aet.* 85–88). Matthew's use of *palingenesia* is more likely closer to Josephus' for whom it means the restoration of Israel from exile and thus their reconstitution (*Ant.* 11.66). Josephus also uses the phrase γενέσθαι τε πάλιν in association with the resurrection (*Ag. Ap.* 2.218). It is instructive that "resurrection" was originally a metaphor for Israel's restoration and reconstitution (Hos 6:2; Isa 26:19; Ezek 37). In the NT, the reconstitution of Israel (God's new people) takes place with the resurrection of Jesus. The only other occurrence of *palingenesia* is in Titus 3:5 where it refers to the "regeneration" of the Holy Spirit (given following the resurrection and exaltation of Jesus to the throne). Derrett, "Palingenesia," 51–58, argues that the true meaning of *palingenesia* is resurrection, by which he means the general eschatological resurrection. However, as implied in 1 Cor 15:20–24, Jesus' own resurrection is the beginning of the eschatological resurrection. Therefore, it properly represents the beginning of the *palingenesia*.

550. See discussion in chapter 1, pp. 21–23, and n122 there. Notice also that the word "judging" in 19:28 suggests continuing activity as opposed to the momentary judgment in Matt 25:31–46. Nor could the "judging" pertain to the final earthly kingdom of Christ, for then it would not only imply the segregation of the people of God (Israel on the one hand and the rest on the other with some other judges) but also that conditions requiring judgment will remain in that perfect kingdom; Matthew knows nothing of the so-called "millennial reign."

551. So RSV, NET, NIV, KJV, NKJV, NLT. NAS's and NAU's ascensive translation is not better.

as a reference to the poor and needy in general,[552] a view lending 25:31–46 to modern liberation theology and social justice or welfare advocacies.[553] Dispensationalists consider it a reference to Jewish remnant/evangelists of the Tribulation.[554] Others interpret it as a reference specifically to the disciples of Jesus,[555] needy Christian missionaries,[556] or Christians in general."[557]

One of the reasons the issue has remained unresolved has to do with translation. While "one of the least of these my brothers" is a plausible translation,[558] it is not a necessarily correct one. The problem with this translation is its "partitiveness," implying some form of distinction between "the least" on the one hand, and "these my brothers" on the other, thereby, in a sense, prioritizing or privileging "the *least* of my brothers"[559] over against "the *rest* of these my brothers." Following this understanding, it should be asked why a favor done to only the least of Jesus' brothers would be more eschatologically determinative in the Last Judgment than that done to the *rest* of his brothers? Such a distinction cannot be the saying's intent and therefore is to be rejected.

Against the traditional translation, the word order of the saying should be preserved and the phrase translated as written. Accordingly, 25:40 should read, "in as much as you did [it] to *one of these my brothers [who are] the least ones.*"[560] The difference is exegetically significant. In the traditional

---

552. Wenham, *Parables*, 91; Beare, *Matthew*, 495; Hare, *Matthew*, 290; Snodgrass, *Stories*, 557; Hultgren, *Parables*, 320–24; Via, "Ethical Responsibility."

553. E.g., Schottroff, *Parable*, 224; Wilson, *For I Was Hungry*; cf. Luz, *Matthew*, 267–70. Waetjen, *Matthew's Theology*, 259, limits the scope to "all human beings among the Gentiles." But Cope, "Matthew," 44, refutes this interpretation: "Matthew xxv 31–46," he bluntly states, "*cannot* provide a legitimate basis for Christian concern for the poor and needy of the world," insisting, "Such an interpretation violates the text by eisegesis," and concluding, "'The least of these my brethren' are the disciples"; cf. Donahue, "Parable."

554. Pond, "Interpretive Issues," 80, cites many examples.

555. Ladd, "Parable," 197–99; Gibbs, *Jerusalem and Parousia*, 217–20; cf. Lambrecht, *Once More Astonished*, 223–27; Gardner, *Matthew*, 359; Michaels, "Apostolic Hardships," 28; Hagner, *Matthew*, 745; Witherington, *Matthew*, 466; Cope, "Matthew xxv 31–46," 44. Brown, "Faith, the Poor and the Gentiles," 173–74, thinks of them as missionary disciples or the Matthean community.

556. E.g., Court, "Right and Left."

557. This view is nuanced differently by different commentators, e.g., Blomberg, *Interpreting Parables*, 400; Gundry, *Matthew*, 514; Hill, *Matthew*, 330; France, *Matthew*, 964–65; Gray, *Least of My Brothers*, 358. For more, see Keener, *Matthew*, 605–6n236.

558. Waetjen, *Matthew's Theology*, 259, thinks that although "my brothers" is missing in some Mss including Codex Vaticanus, "it probably is originally Matthean."

559. Or the "humblest" as Bornkamm, "End-Expectation," 24, calls them.

560. Cf. NAB's "one of these least brothers of mine." See Brown, "Faith, the Poor and the Gentiles," 173.

rendition, *the least* are a subgroup of *these my brothers*; in the translation argued here, *the least* are *these my brothers*. In other words, ἐλαχίστων ("least") is not a superlative of subdivision or partition, but a superlative of modification. Put differently, ἐλαχίστων is epexegetical or appositional to τῶν ἀδελφῶν, not some subunit of it. This understanding is not only grammatically sound, it is also the one supported by the Discourse context.

First, consider a similar saying, μίαν τῶν ἐντολῶν τούτων τῶν ἐλαχίστων, in Matt 5:19. By this expression (v. 19a), Jesus hardly means in v. 19b that what matters is simply the observance of the *least* or insignificant parts of the commandments as opposed to the *rest*. On the contrary, the preceding verse (v. 18) makes it clear that he is concerned about the law in general. He means that the whole OT law is God's least commandment, the least expected of men. This is verified by the fact that he would then go further to enjoin higher dimensions of God's law in vv. 21–48. Thus, the phrase should not be translated, "one of the least of these commandments" but rather, "one of these least commandments," similar to the translation of 25:40 I have argued above.

Second, consider Matt 10:42 and 18:2–6. In 10:42, Jesus, addressing the disciples, declares, "And whoever gives to *one of these little ones* only a cup of cold [water], in the name of a disciple, truly, I say to you, he will certainly not lose his reward." The parallel with 25:31–46 is clear, but the more important point to note is that the demonstrative, "these" (τούτων), points not to a third party, but to the same twelve disciples addressed (10:1). The use here is what I would call the "demonstrative of undifferentiated reference to the second person."[561]

In 18:2–6, Jesus compares his disciples to a child. "Whoever humbles himself like "one such child" (ἓν παιδίον τοιοῦτο; vv. 4–5) is the greatest in the kingdom of heaven. In v. 6, the expression, "one of these little ones *who* believe in me" (ἕνα τῶν μικρῶν τούτων τῶν πιστευόντων εἰς ἐμέ) implies that faith in Jesus is the attribute of the one like a child.[562] In v. 10, no "one of these little ones" (ἑνὸς τῶν μικρῶν τούτων) should be despised. Furthermore, in vv. 12–13, the followers of Jesus are compared to a flock of hundred sheep. Should one be missing, the shepherd would leave the ninety-nine and go after it. The meaning of this is given in v. 14; that is, it is not God's will that "one of these little ones" (ἓν τῶν μικρῶν τούτων) should perish. Then the missing-sheep metaphor is applied to a brother who strays by sinning against a fellow brother, with the injunction for the offended brother

---

561. In the mission discourse, first person (speaker) = Jesus, second person (addressee) = the twelve, third person = null.

562. Notice that the inclusion of *who* in the translation here is as legitimate as it is in the translation proposed for 25:40 above.

to restore the offending one. All of this implies (1) that ἓν τῶν μικρῶν τούτων ("one of these little ones") is Jesus' designation for the disciples as a whole, not a subgroup of them (cf. 10:42)[563] and (2) that the disciples, like the sheep, are fellow brothers of equal status, not thought of according to neediness or status in life, or any other criteria.

Third, and most importantly, the saying in Matt 25:40 recurs in v. 45 in the abbreviated form: ἐφ' ὅσον οὐκ ἐποιήσατε ἑνὶ τούτων τῶν ἐλαχίστων. Here then, with the removal of τῶν ἀδελφῶν, we have the actual import of the longer version in v. 40. Translated, it reads, "in as much as you did not do [it] to *one of these least ones*"). The referent of the plural near demonstrative (τούτων) is the same in both v. 40 and v. 45. Therefore, τῶν ἀδελφῶν is the same as τῶν ἐλαχίστων. In v. 40, τούτων represents an undifferentiated second party referent—Jesus refers to those on the right, the same party he addresses as *these* my least brothers (cf. 10:42), and in v. 45 it represents a differentiated third-party referent—Jesus addresses those on the left and points to all those on the right as these my least brothers.[564]

Accordingly, the question the saying in 25:40/45 raises is not, who are *the least of these my brothers*? Rather, it is simply, who are *these my brothers*? Once the question is phrased correctly in this way, the answer becomes clear, and we can find it in connection with two passages—Matt 12:49–50 and 24:29–31.

In Matt 12:49–50, Jesus points to the disciples and says, "Behold my mother and my brothers."[565] He then substantiates this pronouncement in the following verse using γὰρ: "For whoever does the will of my Father who is in heaven is my brother, and sister, and mother" (v. 50). The implications of these verses are that (1) the disciples do or have done the will of the Father, (2) every other person who has done or does the will of the Father, just as the disciples, is Jesus' brother, and (3) in saying "brother, sister, and mother," Jesus implies that his brothers are not simply the twelve but all who, like the twelve do the will of the Father.

More importantly, these brothers of Jesus in 25:40/45 must be the same as the elect already gathered to the Son of Man in his coming in 24:31. It is fascinating that although many commentators think that both 24:29–31

---

563. Cf. Talbert, *Matthew*, 136–37. Commenting on Matt 10:42 in connection to 18:6–14, France, *Matthew*, 415, states that this designation is "a metaphor for all members of the disciple community, old as well as young, in their insignificance and vulnerability" (cf. 964).

564. Cf. Gray, *Least of My Brothers*, 358: the purpose of the demonstrative τούτων "is to set 'the least' apart from πάντα τὰ ἔθνη rather than to distinguish τῶν ἐλαχίστων from τῶν ἀδελφῶν."

565. Cf. Matt 28:10.

and 25:31–46 are both *parousia* passages, they hardly make any connection between the *least brothers of Jesus* or the sheep in the latter and *the elect* in the former.[566] If the two passages refer to the *parousia*, as they indeed do, then "all the nations" who are gathered in 25:32 must also be the tribes of the earth that mourn in 24:30. They must thus be juxtaposed with the elect already gathered from all over the earth in 24:31. I argued earlier that these two gatherings are related as two sides of the same event. Thus, as Jesus comes in his glory, the elect—his brothers—are first gathered to meet and welcome him. The direction of movement is not back up to heaven but to the final assize in 25:31–46.[567] At this destination, "all [the rest of] the nations"(the mourners in 24:30) are gathered (25:32), and together with the elect who are already gathered to Jesus (24:31), that is, all his least brothers (25:40), reconstitute a general assembly of all humanity for the purpose of final judgment, reward, and/or separation.[568]

The discourse unity of Matt 24–25 necessitates this interpretation.[569] Consequently, I conclude that the *least brothers* of Jesus in 25:40/45 are not the Jews, or gentiles, or the poor, needy and underprivileged in general.[570] They are also not any and every human being, or a subgroup of Christian missionaries or missionaries in general. On the contrary, *these my brothers, the least ones*, are all the elect, consisting of the disciples and all who like them have done the will of the Father, all the righteous from all over the nations. Having been temporarily *gathered* (24:31) or *taken* (24:40–41), they arrive with Jesus at the great assize for the final judgment leading to the eternal age of life or punishment; the text indicates no intervening millennial kingdom. The eschatological schema is as follows:

---

566. Tasker, *Matthew*, 238, does identify the sheep with the elect gathered from the corners of the earth.

567. In agreement with Gray, *Least of My Brothers*, 358, 25:31–46 portrays the classic judgment associated with the parousia."

568. Cf. Bornkamm, "End-Expectation," 23.

569. Cf. Heil, "Double Meaning," 5.

570. Bauer, *Gospel*, 214, rightly insists that we should "rule out the notion that the 'least of these my brethren' pertains to the poor in the world in general."

AN INTERPRETATION OF MATT 24:3—25:46

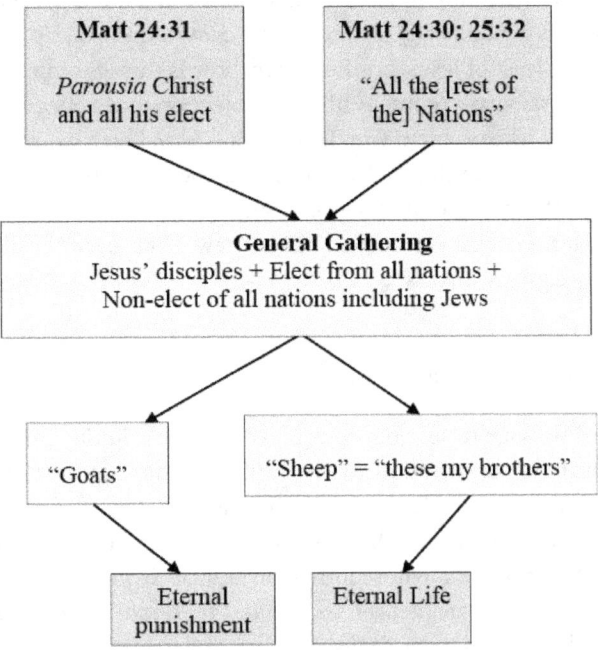

Showing Matt 24:31 and 25:32 as Two Parts of the Same Event.

There are two likely objections to this interpretation. First, it may be asked why the elect/brothers should be taken/gathered first only to recombine them with "all the nations." The reason for this is clear: According to 12:36, the Last Judgment and/or reward requires all humans (οἱ ἄνθρωποι) without exception to be present. But the initial gathering in 24:31 does not reflect a notion of Judgment and/or reward. Thus, the final assize in 25:31–46 must be that all-inclusive scene of judgment. Also, the schema may allude to ancient Hellenistic *parousia* imagery apparently first articulated by Theodoret of Cyria (ca. 458): "When a king enters some city, people in office and of highest station meet him at some distance, while those accused of crimes await the arrival of the judge inside."[571] As I shall show in the final chapter, this interpretation helps fill the gap in Paul's description of the *parousia* in 1 Thess 4:16–17: the saints will meet the Lord in the air and the whole entourage will from then head to the one last and general judgment leading to the eternal age to come (25:31–46).

---

571. Theodoret of Cyrus, *Comm. Paul*, 118; see also Wright, *Surprised by Hope*, 132–33; Witherington, *Jesus, Paul and the End*, 157–58.

A second objection might be based on the fact that even the sheep are ignorant of having done any favor to Jesus (25:37). If the disciples are part of the sheep, the least of Jesus' brothers here, how is this ignorance or element of surprise possible for them? While this objection may appear legitimate, it is unnecessary. The problem with it is that it is based on a wooden literalism that absolutizes the exchange by ignoring the apocalyptic and perspectival character of the passage. In a sense, Jesus was never naked or sick and in prison, at least not that is recorded in Matthew. Thus, even the disciples can legitimately express surprise.

The Soteriology of Matt 25:31–46

Finally, this passage raises questions regarding the criteria of the Last Judgment or the basis for salvation. Will salvation in the judgment day be based simply on how individuals treated the brothers of Jesus?[572] Such a criterion would contradict already established soteriological givens in Matthew, such as the fact that salvation will require deliverance "from sins" (1:21) and repentance (3:2; 4:17; 12:41; cf. 11:20, 21) and therefore not merely an award for charitable gestures towards Jesus and his followers.

As pointed out above, Matt 10:42 parallels the judgment criterion in 25:31–46. Snodgrass' claim that the context of 10:40–42 (mission) is different from that of Matt 25:31–46,[573] is invalid since the latter both stands in relation to mission in the Discourse itself (24:14) and has mission as its very basis (28:19–20). However, Snodgrass rightly wonders whether there is "evidence elsewhere that Matthew or Jesus thought entrance to the kingdom could be obtained merely by being nice to missionaries, regardless of theology and conduct." He is of the view that, "The support from 10:40–42 for this view is superficial." This is a legitimate point, but Snodgrass makes it because he wants to insist that "these least brothers of mine must be understood generally of those in need."[574]

Exactly what reward is meant in 10:42 is unclear,[575] but even if it is eternal life or inheritance of the kingdom as in 25:31–46,[576] the latter passage

---

572. For more on this, see Leverett, "Looking for the Least," 76–90; Snodgrass, *Stories*, 158–59.

573. Snodgrass, *Stories*, 557.

574. Snodgrass, *Stories*, 557.

575. The reward is likely related to what is said in 10:6–8, 11–13, that is, rewards in terms of blessings received through the ministry of prophets or preachers. In Matthew, rewards can be earthly (6:3–4, 6, 17–18), heavenly (5:12), or both (19:29; cf. Luke 18:29–30).

576. So France, *Matthew*, 414.

is, as I have argued above, a perspectival description of the judgment. That is, while concerned with reality, it only describes it from a particular point of view for the sake of contrast between the righteous and the wicked. Again, other perspectives of the same judgment also occur in Matthew. For example, in 12:36–37, the final judgment is said to be based on careless words, and in 12:41–42, repentance is entered as a factor.[577] These facts make it necessary to conclude that Matt 25:31–46 does not teach work-based salvation as opposed, for example, to repentance- or faith-based salvation. Such soteriological concern is better left to Pauline and other relevant doctrinal statements and not imposed on an apocalyptic description of reality.[578]

If we must belabor the apocalyptic passage with the question on what constitutes the last judgment's criteria for inheriting the kingdom and or eternal life, the answer again depends on the proper identification of the sheep who have done the act and to whom they did it. I have argued that those who do the favor are the same as the least brothers of Jesus. They are all disciples (not only the twelve) who believe and follow Jesus and do the will of the Father (Matt 12:49–50). The motif of "doing the will of the Father" is associated with what it means to be Jesus' least brothers; it is said to be the criterion for entering the kingdom, and it relates to the hearing of the words of Jesus and the doing of them (Matt 7:21–24).[579] In 21:29, 31, the motif involves repentance and obedience.[580] The sheep are those who follow Jesus (Jew and gentile)—his least brothers, the elect (24:31), the righteous (25:37), the doers of the Father's will, and the ones who inherit the kingdom and eternal life (25:34, 46b). The goats are the exact opposite, consisting of Jews and gentiles alike.

Conclusion

This chapter has attempted to show, above all things, that Matt 24–25 must be held together to be adequately interpreted. I have argued that 24:3

---

577. For other criteria of the last judgment in Matthew, see Leverett, "Looking for the Least," 127–29.

578. As is obvious, I do not share Wright's interpretation of the Discourse, but I agree with his statement: "All Christian language about the future is a set of signposts pointing into a mist. Signposts don't normally provide you with advance photograph of what you will find at the end of the road, but that doesn't mean they aren't pointing in the right direction. They are telling you the truth [the reality], the particular sort of truth that can be told about the future" (*Surprised by Hope*, 132).

579. Cf. Matt 25:41 and 7:21–23; see also Snodgrass, *Stories*, 557 who notices this connection but still misses the referent of "these my brothers."

580. Jesus himself epitomizes the doing of the will of the Father (Matt 26:42).

consists of two legitimate questions which refer to the fate of the temple and the *parousia* or second coming of Jesus as two distinct events. The interpretation offered affirms the alternating structure argued and vice versa. In sum, the Discourse reflects an indefinite period of tribulation until the *parousia*, with a unique near intervening moment of Great Tribulation associated with the destruction of the temple in 70 CE. The *parousia* itself will unfold as a sudden yet complex event with cosmic upheavals, an initial gathering of the elect of all nations to meet and welcome Jesus the arriving King, leading to the great assize where all nations—Jew and gentile—will stand before the King for final judgment and the ushering in of the eternal state. I provide a more extensive summary in chapter 7 of this study.

6

The Function of the Eschatological Discourse in Matthew

Introduction

HAVING TAKEN PAINS TO interpret the Eschatological Discourse, the goal of this chapter is to determine how it functions within the overall structure and aim of Matthew. In chapter 4, I highlighted a few narrative structures of Matthew, specifically as advocated by Kingsbury, Matera, and Carter. While leaning towards Kingsbury's view on Matthew's overall aim, that is, Jesus—his person, proclamation, and passion, I contended that one critical weakness of his tripartite division of the Gospel is that it leaves the Eschatological Discourse with no proclamative or structural significance.[1]

To be precise, to take 4:17—16:20 as "the Proclamation of Jesus Messiah" and to subsume Matt 24-25 within 16:21—28:20 as "the Suffering, Death, and Resurrection of Jesus Messiah," as Kingsbury does, is to give the erroneous impression that the Eschatological Discourse, let alone chs. 17-23, is not itself a proclamation.[2] The Discourse clearly has nothing to contribute to the passion of Jesus,[3] and while it depicts Jesus as victor, there

---

1. So also the kernel-block structures proposed by Matera and Carter; see chapter 4, pp. 95-98.

2. The hints in Matt 17:9, 22-23; 21:37-39 regarding the suffering, death, and resurrection are not enough to allow this title to embrace the whole of chs. 17-25.

3. One could argue a sense in which the motif of Jewish rejection of Jesus in Jerusalem (Matt 21-23) might foreshadow the passion but we cannot technically speak of such rejection as the passion itself, otherwise we would have to include practically most

is no resurrection motif there. Moreover, although we should say "Amen" to Kingsbury's view that Jesus as Son of God is the one central object in Matthew, when the structure of Matthew is taken as I have argued, the Discourse will be shown to fill not a dispensable or marginal role but a central objective in Matthew's Gospel as a whole. As Wright says concerning Mark 13,[4] Matt 24–25 is not merely one of several discourses or some stand-alone apocalyptic that may be neatly ripped off and read in isolation without damaging the whole structure and meaning of the First Gospel.

Function vs. Interpretation

Before proceeding, it needs to be clarified whether there is a distinction between the interpretation of a passage and how it functions. In a sense, it may seem that a text cannot function in isolation from what it means in relation to the broader text. There is room for ambiguity here since interpretation and function may be interwoven and mutually informing in some cases. However, this interrelationship does not negate the essential distinction between the two terms. Interpretation deals with the question of meaning. But by function, it is meant how a passage is structurally situated and the contribution it makes to the central or overall goal of a literary work (here, Matthew's Gospel as a whole). The argument presented in this chapter will bolster this distinction

The fact that the Eschatological Discourse is the last of Jesus' teachings or discourses suggests a strategic structural and hermeneutical implication. As Ellis notes,

> The strategic value of the final position in narrative or discourse has long been known. It is the place for a climax, a summary of conclusions, the solution to problems, the interconnection of hitherto disconnected themes. It is the logical place for a farewell address or for memorable words and ideas. In a chapter or section of a literary work, it can serve the above functions in addition to serving as the normal place for a transition from one part of a work to another. Matthew's brilliant exploitation of the strategic value of the final position in his narratives and discourses and in the ending of his gospel as a whole, supplies the reader with another key to his methodology and to the message his methodology serves.[5]

---

if not all of Matthew (see 2:12–15; 4:1–11; 12:14).

4. See Wright, *New Testament and the People*, 393.

5. Ellis, *Matthew*, 17.

Ellis is specifically concerned with "ending pericopes."[6] However, this comment applies no less to whole sections. The final position of the Eschatological Discourse, its length relative to the whole (cf. the other Synoptics), and its unique elements indicate a whole-book significance. Thus, we can legitimately ask what its function is in relation to the overarching goal of Matthew.

Jonathan Lunde argues that the "climactic position" of the Eschatological Discourse "as the final of Matthew's five discourse implies that it assumes, at least in part, what has transpired previous to it in the gospel" as well as "the events of the passion and resurrection which follow it."[7] Similarly, David P. Scaer, observes that "Because the Fifth Discourse [Matt 24–25] is placed immediately before the narrative of the suffering and resurrection of Jesus, it occupies a special place in Matthew's Gospel." Scaer goes on to say that "this final discourse provides an interpretation of the Gospel's conclusion, which is anticipated in the other four discourses." Each discourse, "beginning with the Second Discourse . . . takes into itself all that has preceded it." Therefore, in its final position, the Eschatological Discourse "assumes the previous discourses and takes all of them into itself."[8]

Both Lunde and Scaer appear to be correct. However, it remains to be shown in what specific terms the Discourse is of central importance relative to the larger whole. The clue, as I shall argue later, is to be found in relation to the revelatory character of its apocalyptic.

Views on the Function of Matt 24–25

Sorting through the literature, one finds four views representing how exegetes have understood Matt 24–25 to function within Matthew, its major emphasis, or whole-book significance. The most common tendency is to take the Discourse merely as Matthew's or Jesus' piece on eschatology; some emphasize its ecclesiological function; some, its salvation-historical implication; and others its Christological goal. Matthew appears to weave all these together, so that none can exist in isolation. The four views are highlighted below. In the end, I will follow up with an explication of the view advocated in this study.

---

6. Ellis, *Matthew*, 17–19.
7. Lunde, "Salvation-Historical Implication," 2–3.
8. Scaer, *Discourses*, 354.

Eschatology for the Sake of Eschatology

Majority of exegetes understand Matt 24–25 to concern not only the fate of Jerusalem but also the future and consummation or end of the world. The Discourse represents Jesus' prophetic view of the future at large. Thus, in many of the commentaries and specialized studies, it is treated merely as a treatise on eschatology.[9] And most of the few monographs fall short of investigating its broader theo-structural significance.[10]

This problem is not unconnected with the earlier emphasis on Mark 13 as or in relation to some self-existing Little Apocalypse, which not only explains why Matt 24–25 was for so long ignored, but also informs how it has mostly been treated—as a mere derivate and expansion of Mark 13. Thus, Burnett complains that the predominant treatment of the Discourse as simply "Jesus' eschatological teaching" led to the result that "Matthean theology in the Eschatological Discourse has suffered exegetical malnutrition; it has been studied largely with an interest only in recovering an earlier apocalypse behind Mark 13, or in seeking to ascertain Jesus' view of the future."[11]

While the little apocalypse theory is largely abandoned,[12] much of the discussions on Matt 24–25 has remained purely eschatological for eschatology sake. In other words, eschatology is both what it means and how it functions within Matthew. I will highlight Bauer's view shortly, but he rightly maintains that "the function of the eschatological discourse is not to satisfy inquisitiveness regarding the future."[13]

Eschatology for the Sake of Ecclesiology

With greater emphasis shifting to the compositional or redactional context, Matthew 24–25 came to be viewed as a window into the situation in life of the Matthean Church in relation to the outsiders. Exegetes sought to discover how the Discourse functioned within the Matthean community. Primarily, it is said to function as a paraenetic, that is, concerned with the

---

9. See Rand, "Survey"; Walvoord, "Christ's Olivet Discourse," 113–14.

10. E.g., neither Agbanou's *Discours* nor Gibbs' *Jerusalem and Parousia* goes beyond interpretation; Burnett's *Testament* and Wilson's *When Will These Things Happen?* attempt to close this gap by exploring how the Discourse relates to the person of Jesus in Matthew's Gospel.

11. Burnett, *Testament*, 12–13.

12. See n47 in chapter 1.

13. Bauer, *Gospel*, 215.

ethics (discipling) of the church. But also, its function embraces missiological and consolatory concerns.

As discussed in chapter 1, Bornkamm's seminal article, "End-Expectation," opened a new vista for the study of the judgment motif in Matthew. To recall, Bornkamm makes the case that the theme of judgment, especially in Matt 25, functions in relation to the church. It is meant by Matthew to encourage a new standard of righteousness by showing that the church itself and not only the gentiles will be judged according to how they treated the humblest.[14] Daniel Marguerat affirms Bornkamm's view,[15] taking judgment as "a theme of first importance for Matthew the evangelist"[16] and Matt 24–25, in particular, as Matthew's thematization of the church's relationship to the coming of judgment.[17]

Bauer also shares this concern of judgment for those within the church as a significant emphasis of Matt 24–25. Accordingly, the Discourse functions "to provide paraenesis to the readers of the Gospel of Matthew as they meet with persecutions and tribulations in the future." Its central purpose within the broader context is to encourage faithfulness and watchfulness as conditions for eschatological deliverance and eternal life. In this way, the disciples are, on the one hand, to be like Jesus, who, through faithfulness and watchfulness obtained victory over death, and universal authority (Matt 26–28). On the other hand, they are to be unlike disobedient and faithless Israel (21–23).[18]

Schuyler Brown notes that "chapters 24–25 of Matthew's Gospel occupy a key position in the structure of the work,"[19] suggesting that it has a particularly missiological function, concerned with mission to gentiles. Based on the assumption that the apocalypse (esp. 24:4–31, 34) is an already fulfilled prophecy in the Jewish war from the perspective of Matthew, he goes on to argue that "because of the hatred suffered from the *ethne* during the Jewish war and the *anomia* which this has brought forth among the disciples, the Matthean community has forgotten its vocation."[20] As Brown thinks, despite being a fulfilled prophecy, Matthew still finds a way to make

14. Bornkamm, "End-Expectation," 23–24.

15. Marguerat, *Jugement*, 563.

16. My translation. In French, "un thème théologique de première importance pour l'évangéliste Matthieu" (Marguerat, *Jugement*, 3).

17. Marguerat, *Jugement*, 566; So also Charette, *Theme of Recompense*, 159–68.

18. Bauer, *Gospel*, 215–16.

19. Brown, "Matthean Apocalypse," 2.

20. Brown, "Matthean Apocalypse," 9. In another article, Brown hypothesizes that controversy over gentile mission is central to understanding the contradiction between Matt 10:6 and 28:19 (see "Matthean Community").

the apocalypse speak to his community's current situation. According to him, "the flight motive has a secondary metaphorical significance." It is to be understood allegorically to mean that they should "abandon Judaism" and focus on mission to the gentiles.[21] This missiological function comes to a head in 25:31–46 believed by Brown to be a "*captatio benevolentiae.*" It "prepares the community for the responsibility of the universal mission (28:19). Its purpose is to heighten the community's sense of its own importance: The Messiah king will understand as done to himself whatever is done to them."[22]

Others who interpret the Eschatological Discourse ecclesiologically emphasize its more consolatory function. For Hare, "Matthew's purpose in this last discourse (chs. 24–25) is not to show how Jesus' predictions have been fulfilled in the event of AD 70 but to prepare Christians for enduring faithfulness during the indefinite period that remains" before the glorious coming of the Son of Man.[23] Stanton argues that apocalyptic in Matthew, as evidenced in 24:10–12, indicates "the community's sense of alienation from the outside world and the evangelist's concern to reinforce group solidarity"; 25:31–46, in particular, serves the purpose of "consolation and encouragement to a community acutely aware of the hostility of the Jewish and Gentile world." In whole, "the apocalyptic themes [of Matt 24–25] are the response to the trauma of parting of ways from Judaism to the perceived hostility . . . and to serious internal dissension within the community."[24]

Similarly, Sim's reconstruction of the setting of the Matthean community takes its cue from the historical and sociological functions of apocalyptic. Although Sim addresses apocalyptic eschatology in Matthew's Gospel as a whole, it is clear that Matt 24–25 plays a prominent role in elucidating the worldview.[25] Thus, as in other apocalypses, Matthew employs apocalyptic to identify and legitimate the sectarian nature of Matthew's community, explain their current circumstances, elicit future hope, depict the fate of opponents, and encourage group solidarity and social order.[26] According to Sim, 25:31–46 "functions primarily to satisfy the missionaries' desire for vengeance on their particular opponents." Further, it "performs a consolatory function which is necessary for the successful completion of the task.

---

21. Brown, "Matthean Apocalypse," 10, 14.

22. Brown, "Matthean Apocalypse," 18 (cf. "Faith, the Poor and the Gentiles," 172–73).

23. Hare, *Theme of Jewish Persecution*, 178–79 and *Matthew*, 273.

24. Stanton, *New People*, 163–65.

25. Sim, *Apocalyptic Eschatology*, 150–69.

26. Sim, *Apocalyptic Eschatology*, 222–49.

They can undertake their mission firm in the knowledge that those who oppose them are earmarked for the eternal fires of Gehenna."[27]

The views advanced by Sim going back up to Bornkamm was addressed in chapter 3. The sum of the critique offered there is that while promising much interpretive insight, the conclusions of the redactional and especially the socio-ecclesiological approaches remain questionable. Bornkamm indeed influenced subsequent studies in Matthew. However, as Wilson has observed, the problem with his treatment lies in its narrow focus on redacted elements in Matthew instead of the narrative whole. Wilson also questions the connection Bornkamm makes between eschatology and ecclesiology which "gives the impression that eschatological teaching is intended to have purely paraenetic function."[28] On the more sociological approach which Sim epitomizes, the problem lies in what it assumes, namely, that a text necessarily provides a transparent window into the conditions in which it originates, or in this case, that a hypothesis on the Matthean community's *sitz im leben* must be taken as the rule.[29] There is just no way to say with absolute certainty what specific situation Matthew is addressing or, with respect to Balabanski's claim discussed in chapter 5,[30] what parts of the Eschatological Discourse reflect the past or current experience of the Matthean community.

Eschatology for the Sake of Soteriological History

The concept of "salvation history" (*Heilsgeschichte*) understood as the unfolding of events within God's overall plan of salvation, is somewhat controversial. Critics consider the concept unscientific, pointing to the biblical story's lack of continuity and the inexplicability of some of its events using historical criteria. Some reject the terminology for its association with the Hegelian philosophy. However, Oscar Cullmann not only justifies the concept, but also the use of the term "salvation history," even if as a heuristic hermeneutical tool, that is, "in the absence of a better expression."[31] Against Schweitzer, Bultmann, and their followers who reject the idea as a later development,[32] Cullmann insists that Jesus' eschatological expectation was

27. Sim, *Apocalyptic Eschatology*, 234.
28. Wilson, *When Will These Things Happen?*, 38.
29. See chapter 3, pp. 61–62, and chapter 5, p. 144 on the view advanced by Balabanski.
30. See p. 144.
31. Cullmann, *Salvation in History*, 74–78.
32. E.g., developing Bultmann's existential eschatology, Conzelmann argues that

rooted in a redemptive-historical conviction and in a tension of "already and not yet."[33]

Several scholars such as W. Trilling, G. Strecker, R. Walker, and others have viewed *Heilsgeschichte* as the dominant structural and theological framework of Matthew's Gospel. These scholars all see Matthew as concerned with elucidating three epochs of salvation history—the time of Israel, the time of Jesus, and the time of the church. For Trilling, Matthew is so concerned because he considers the church now as the "true Israel"; and for Strecker, he is motivated by the delay of the *parousia*. As Kingsbury argues, in the thinking of these scholars, the church (ecclesiology) is the central or controlling object of Matthew's Gospel.[34] On his part, Kingsbury contends that Matthew's salvation history consists of two epochs—the time of Israel (OT/prophecy) and the time of Jesus (earthly-exalted/fulfillment), with the latter subsuming the so-called time of the church, spanning from Jesus' birth to his *parousia*.[35] This helps Kingsbury substantiate his threefold Christological structure of Matthew's Gospel. But Kingsbury himself fails to see how the Eschatological Discourse is central to Matthew's superstructure and Christology, viewing it not only as unconnected with the destruction of the temple but especially as merely ecclesiologically focused, in agreement with Hare.[36]

However, in his 1996 dissertation, Jonathan Lunde seeks to draw out Matthew's salvation-historical view specifically from Matt 24–25. According to Lunde, Matthew achieves his salvation-historical perspective in the Eschatological Discourse by weaving together two major strands—the eschatological and the Christological.[37]

First, eschatologically, Matthew not only understands the Jewish war as a punishment for Israel's rejection of Jesus and his messengers but also as the final eschatological tribulation preceding the *parousia*. Lunde argues that based on this interpretation of the Jewish war, and in keeping with evidence from apocalyptic literature (especially Daniel), "Matthew expects the universally-visible parousia to occur soon after 70 CE." The parabolic thief and bridegroom imageries do not imply that Matthew expects the *parousia*

Luke devised the concept of salvation history (understood as a perversion of Jesus' view of eschatological imminence) to resolve the problem of delay of the *parousia*; see his *Theology of Luke*, 95–234.

33. Cullmann, *Christ and Time*, xvii–xxx.

34. See Kingsbury, *Matthew*, 25–26; and discussion in Lunde, "Salvation-Historical Implication," 1–18.

35. See Kingsbury, *Matthew*, 31–37.

36. See Kingsbury, *Matthew*, 29.

37. Lunde, "Salvation-Historical Implication," 296.

will be delayed. Instead, "they serve to portray the interim between the resurrection and the parousia and to emphasize the unknowability of the latter's timing" and thus the need for vigilance.[38]

Second, Christologically, and influenced by the apocalyptic tradition in Daniel, Matthew presents Jesus as the 'true Israel,' the Son of Man and ultimate fulfillment of the obedient, suffering people of God, one who eclipses Israel's greatest heroes, including David and Moses.[39] Israel's rejection of him leads to his departure from the temple (24:1). Their persecution of him, which is completed in his crucifixion, results in the judgment and destruction of the temple (Matt 24) while Jesus himself is vindicated in his resurrection and rewarded with the Kingdom authority as confirmed by Matthew's use of Danielic enthronement themes in 28.18–20.[40]

Importantly, Lunde claims that "Matthew's use of the title Son of Man for Jesus is very suggestive of his salvation-historical perspective."[41] Those from every nation who share in Jesus' suffering in the interim will also share in his vindication at his *parousia*. However, because of Israel's rejection of Jesus as the Son of Man, argues Lunde, it has been removed from its privileged position and has been numbered among the nations.

Lunde's perception of Matthew's salvation-historical view in the Eschatological Discourse is commendable. As I earlier argued, the clearest indication of the *ethnos*ization of Israel as a nation comes when we read Matt 24:9 in connection with 23:34–35 and in light of 18:17 (cf. 21:43; 22:1–14). It is also Matthew's understanding that the title, Son of Man, applies to Jesus messianically in light of Dan 7:13–14. Moreover, the language of Matt 28:18–20 also clearly echoes the Danielic apocalyptic tradition. In all of this, and indeed in many important interpretive details within the Discourse, the present study agrees with Lunde's interpretation and its implication.

However, there are at least three issues with Lunde's interpretation. First, we should observe that the Eschatological Discourse itself does not present Jesus as the suffering Son of Man. Second, although the title, Son of Man, outnumbers all others in Matthew,[42] it is not central to Matthew's Christology or salvation history, being more of Jesus' own self-identification than it is a Matthean argument. And third, while the salvation-historical implication in Matthew that Lunde has argued is generally correct, this

---

38. Lunde, "Salvation-Historical Implication," 298–300.
39. Lunde, "Salvation-Historical Implication," 204.
40. Lunde, "Salvation-Historical Implication," 206.
41. Lunde, "Salvation-Historical Implication," 205.
42. 8:20; 9:6; 10:23; 11:19; 12:8, 32, 40; 13:37, 41; 16:13, 27, 28; 17:9, 12, 22; 19:28; 20:18, 28; 24:27, 30(x2) 37, 39, 44; 25:31; 26:2, 24(x2), 45, 64.

implication, as I shall demonstrate soon, is subsidiary to Matthew's central aim in the Discourse.

Eschatology for the Sake of Christology

In general, Christology is recognized as a major, albeit, debated theme in Matthew's Gospel.[43] As earlier noted, Kingsbury, and most recently, Bauer, offer thorough expositions of Matthew's view of Jesus' identity.[44] While failing to account for the place of the Eschatological Discourse, they persuasively make the case that the title "Son of God" has primacy over all other titles and, therefore, shapes both the Christology and structure of Matthew.[45] Although Hagner focuses on more sociological functions of apocalyptic in Matthew,[46] he suggests a correlation between apocalyptic language and heightened Christology in the Gospel. "Christology, so important in this Gospel," he says, "will always entail apocalyptic-like language."[47]

It may be questioned, however, whether Matt 24–25, the most apocalyptic portion of the Gospel, has anything to do with Christology. For example, in responding to Burnett's work, *Testament of Jesus-Sophia*, Hare, who is more ecclesiocentric in his view of how the Discourse functions, claims that the "attempt to extract Matthew's Christology from this segment [i.e., Matt

---

43. For the divergent views, see Kingsbury, "Figure of Jesus," n1. Cf. Hill, "Figure of Jesus." The two scholars especially differ over whose point of view is normative in Matthew for the story and identity of Jesus—Kingsbury (God), Hill (Jesus). For some balance, see Choi, *Messianic Kingship*, 129–31.

44. Kingsbury, *Matthew*, 40–127; Bauer, *Gospel*, 237–75.

45. While many would take Son of God as dominant in Matthew, not all agree with Kingsbury's view. Hill begs to differ. Based on Matt 12:18–21 (which cites Isa 42:1–4), Hill argues that "Servant" expresses Matthew's conception of the role of Jesus ("Son and Servant," 12). Hill is right, but Matthew can use an imagery to express Jesus' vocation without intending it to be central to Jesus' person and destiny. This remains the case even with Allen Mawhinney's argument in light of 2 Kgs 16:7 that the titles "Son" and "Servant" significantly overlap ("Baptism," 39). In fact, Hill would conclude his essay with the admission: "Matthew's dominant Christological title may indeed be 'son of God': I think it is: but the sonship is expounded, given content, possibly even validated by Matthew . . . in terms of Jesus' servanthood in general and by his exemplification of the Servant, *Ebed Yahweh*" ("Son and Servant," 15). Contra Hill, it is unlikely that the single OT reference to "servant" in Matt 12:18–21 has controlling significance over what Matthew thinks of Jesus. In short, "Servant," though important, is not how Matthew wants to depict the person and destiny of Jesus. So also Choi, *Messianic Kingship*, 149. Thus, although I concur with Kingsbury and Bauer that Son of God is at the center of Matthew's Christology, I will demonstrate later that that center is thicker and more intertwined than they assume; that is, the Son of God title is not alone in that center.

46. Hagner, "Apocalyptic Motifs," 73–77.

47. Hagner, "Apocalyptic Motifs," 69; cf. Käsemann, "Beginnings," 40.

24] is misplaced, because the passage itself is not Christologically focused."[48] This claim is incorrect and needs to be addressed before we can proceed.

First, such a claim is rooted in the erroneous prioritization of sociological and or, as in this case, ecclesiological concerns,[49] over against the controlling vision of apocalyptic writers—the triumph of God. That is to say, the primary function of apocalyptic is to legitimize an apocalyptic figure, to affirm the figure, his eschatological victory or vindication, to make clear that God, after all, is Sovereign.[50] Thus, it is because of the ultimate victory and vindication of the divine apocalyptic figure and therefore how this apocalyptic figure acts or will act in history that apocalyptic has ecclesio-hortatory or paraenetic power. For this reason, Scaer may be right in characterizing the eschatological discourse "as concluding theological interpretation" relative to the whole of Matthew.[51]

Second, while we must affirm its hortatory and paraenetic significance, the Eschatological Discourse in its form as apocalyptic (revelatory) is also, at its core, a vindication of Jesus-Messiah.[52] In relation to this, (1) the disciples' question is, in essence, about Jesus—the judgment *he* thrusts into motion, and *his* coming; (2) the Discourse significantly represents the juxtaposition of the "coming of false Christs" (24:5, 23–24) with the "coming of Jesus, the real Christ" (24:27, 30, 37, 39, 40, 42, 44; 25:31), so that we can firmly say, "Jesus is the Christ, others are not"; (3) the high point of the Discourse is the majestic and terror-provoking descent of Jesus depicted in 24:31 and 25:31; and (4) Jesus is both the speaker and chief actor in the Discourse. All of this goes to support the Discourse's Christological focus, both affirming and deepening the identity of Jesus.

Given these observations, it is, therefore, no wonder that several interpreters have highlighted the Christological function of Matt 24–25. However, these interpreters, in my view, fail to grasp the correct or exact Christological function of the Discourse. The first view to be noted is that of Ellis in his *Matthew: His Mind and Message*. Ellis argues that each Discourse in Matthew functions to accentuate the central themes of Jesus' teaching in each preceding narrative section.[53] Therefore, since we have the judgment motif all through chs. 19–22, he concludes that the last Discourse (taken as chs. 23–25) functions to provide two answers to the unanswered question in

48. Hare, "Testament," 66.
49. Cf. chapter 3
50. Cf. Murphy, *Apocalypticism*, 9; Murphy, *Early Judaism*, 132–33.
51. Scaer, *Discourses*, 354–93.
52. Cf. Wright, *Jesus and the Victory*, 343, 510–19.
53. Ellis, *Matthew*, 14–15.

22:41–46. Of these answers, the first, provided in Matt 23, is that Jesus is the eschatological prophet of Deut 18:18, while the second, given in chs 24–25, presents and emphasizes "Jesus as the Son of Man who will come at the end of time to judge all nations."[54]

Ellis himself notes the difficulty in proving that "Matthew wishes to present Jesus as the eschatological prophet predicted by Moses in Dt 18:18."[55] But there are other issues with Ellis's view. First, as I argued in chapter 4, Ellis chiastic structure for Matthew in which ch. 13 represents the Gospel's center (a center which, by the way, Kingsbury affirms) is flawed. Second, "judgment motif"/ "Jesus as Judge" goes beyond the narrative section preceding the Eschatological Discourse. We see the theme(s) way back in 3:11–12, in 7:21–23, and others. So then, the web of Matt 24–25 goes beyond accentuating merely what is taught in the preceding narrative section alone to exert significance for the whole book. Third, it does not seem that Jesus' question in 22:41–46 is completely unanswered since the passage implies that Jesus is, at least, not merely the Son of David, but certainly, one greater than David. Third, Ellis, I believe, not only fails to bring this observation to bear on the overall structure of Matthew[56] but also assumes emphasis on the wrong title, Son of Man. As I have already argued in response to Lunde above, since Jesus identifies himself with the title phrase, "Son of Man," it is unlikely that Matthew intends to emphasize it. I will comment further on this later. In the meantime, I will consider two others who have argued a Christological function for Matt 24–25.

Burnett, in his *Testament of Jesus-Sophia*, views Matt 24 as functioning Christologically. According to him, "The function of the discourse [24:3–31] in terms of the whole gospel is that of a farewell speech of Jesus as Wisdom and as the soon to be exalted Son of Man."[57] Although Burnett also recognizes the apocalyptic form of Matt 24,[58] he questions the strict apocalyptic Christological approach that simply says: "Jesus is the apocalyptic Son of Man who will come at the End of the Age as Judge"—a view compelled by Matt 25.[59] For him, "Matt 24 should not be read too quickly in light of the apocalyptic judgment and Christology of chapter 25." Rather, when the context of Matt 24 is properly discerned in relation to chs. 23–25

---

54. Ellis, *Matthew*, 88–89.

55. Ellis, *Matthew*, 89n158.

56. See Ellis, *Matthew*, 12–13.

57. Burnett, *Testament*, 29. For more on the Discourse as a farewell speech, see chapter 3, n92.

58. Burnett, *Testament*, 190.

59. Burnett, *Testament*, 15, 17.

and Matthew as a whole, a different Christological thrust emerges, showing that Matt 24 functions as a testament of Jesus as Sophia.⁶⁰ Burnett argues this because he believes that "Matthew's apocalypticism is informed [less by the prophetic tradition but] by that stream of Jewish wisdom tradition which constrained the notions of Sophia's rejection, withdrawal to heaven, and appearance again from there as (or somehow associated with) the figure of the Son of Man."⁶¹

Importantly, Burnett contends that "the primary way the evangelist achieves the identification of Jesus with Wisdom is by his redaction of the Q material in 23:34." "Matthew," he says, "redacts what ... is the Q reading of ἡ σοφία τοῦ θεοῦ εἶπεν (Luke 11:49) to read ἰδοὺ ἐγὼ ἀποστέλλω (23:34), a change [which] not only attributes a saying of Wisdom to Jesus but [also] identifies him with Wisdom."⁶²

As I have argued above, contrary to Hare's criticism,⁶³ the issue with Burnett's claim is not that Matt 24 (and we should now add ch. 25) has nothing at all to do with Christology. Rather, the issue, apart from emphasizing the Son of Man title about which I have already hinted and will later make clear the position taken here, is whether indeed the passage supports a Wisdom Christology. Although much has been made about Matthew's view of Jesus as Wisdom,⁶⁴ several factors make a Sophia-Christology in Matt 24–25 based on 23:34 a weak proposition: (1) It seems unlikely that Matthew would want to identify Jesus with Wisdom in 23:34 by eliminating the attribution ἡ σοφία τοῦ θεοῦ in Q (Luke 11:49). (2) Even if Matthew intended such identification by substituting ἐγὼ for this attribution, the implied reader would have to have known the hypothetical Q saying or Luke to make the Christological judgment that Burnett argues. This too seems unlikely. (3) Σοφός, a cognate of σοφία is used in the same saying (Matt 23:34) to refer to the *sent* rather than the *sender*, suggesting the subordination of wisdom *to* rather than identification *with* Jesus.⁶⁵ (4) In relation to this third point, it is true that Jesus employs language found in the wisdom

60. Burnett, *Testament*, 17–28.
61. Burnett, *Testament*, 26; see 1 En. 42; Sir 24:8–12.
62. Burnett, *Testament*, 31.
63. Contra Hare, "Testament," 66.
64. Burnett follows Suggs, *Wisdom*. Other advocates include Deutsch, *Lady Wisdom*, 68–73; Gench, *Wisdom*; Witherington, *Matthew*, 16–21; Witherington, *Jesus the Sage*; Brown and Roberts, *Matthew*, 388–91. For critiques of the view, see Johnson, "Reflections," 55; France, *Evangelist and Teacher*, 302–6; Bauer, *Gospel*, 264–66.
65. The simple καὶ-linking of the substantives (προφήτας καὶ σοφοὺς καὶ γραμματεῖς) suggests that the same persons are the prophets, wise, and scribes (i.e., the disciples; cf. 24:9; 28:16–20).

tradition.⁶⁶ It is also true that he displays extraordinary wisdom (e.g., 13:54). However, Matthew prefers that Jesus be seen as greater than Wisdom: "a greater than Solomon is here" (12:42). (5) Matthew 11:19c is generic and does not identify wisdom directly and/or solely with Jesus.⁶⁷ And (6) There is no explicit Sophia motif in the Eschatological Discourse to bear a Christological or structural burden in relation to Matthew's Gospel as a whole.⁶⁸ These facts make it improbable that what Matthew expects the implied reader to take away from the Discourse is that Jesus is Sophia.

Moreover, Burnett's four reasons for limiting the Discourse to 24:31 (=Mark 13:27) are anything but cogent.⁶⁹ The structure and interpretation I have argued in chapters 4 and 5 make clear that Matt 24 cannot be correctly interpreted without ch. 25. In sum, Burnett's Wisdom-Christological reading of Matt 23:34 and ch. 24 is unconvincing. It is not in the least clear how Matt 24 is more reflective of a Wisdom Christology than an apocalyptic Son of Man Christology or something else.

Another Christological view regarding the function of the Eschatological Discourse is by Wilson. In general, Wilson's work is a reaction against Marcus Borg and others who have advocated a non-eschatological Jesus.⁷⁰ But in relation to how Matt 24–25 functions, his view is closely synonymous to that of Burnett, differing only in the fact that he takes into account both the prophetic and the wisdom traditions in relation to Jesus. Wilson argues that the Discourse, taken along with chs. 21–23, presents Jesus as the Eschatological Judge: The Judge-Prophet and Judge-Sage.⁷¹

Wilson succeeds in demonstrating not only that Jesus' self-understanding was eschatological but especially that he is depicted as the Judge in

---

66. E.g., Matt 11:25–30 echoes much of Job 28:12–28; Sir 6:23–31; 51:23–27.

67. If we take ἔργον in 11:19c as alluding back to ἔργον in v. 2, then the saying would appear to apply wisdom to Jesus only (cf. Keener, *Matthew*, 343). However, the switch to an inclusive tone beginning in v. 16 and focusing on the response of "this generation" to both John and Jesus hardly permits the identification of wisdom solely with Jesus to the exclusion of John; see Bauer, *Gospel*, 182; Turner, *Matthew*, 296–97. Moreover, to base Matthew's identification of Jesus with wisdom on Matt 11:28–30 is to ignore the immediate context in which Jesus is rather Son of God and revealer of the Father (vv. 25–27); cf. Kynes, *Christology*, 93–100.

68. The closest term φρόνιμος does not refer to Jesus (24:45; 25:2, 4, 8–9; cf. 7:24; 10:16).

69. (1) That the *parousia* question is answered definitively in 24:30–31, (2) 24:29–31 is a transition pericope to seven *parousia* parables, (3) the "seeing" of the sign of the Son of Man in 24:31 balances off the prediction in 23:39, and (4) 24:3–31 contains the necessary elements of a testament (Burnett, *Testament*, 194–97).

70. See Borg, *Conflict*; Crossan, *Historical Jesus*.

71. Wilson, *When Will These Things Happen?*, 181–247.

the Discourse. However, in using this as a basis to pivot to Jesus as Judge-Prophet and Judge-Sage as the Christological aim of Matt 24–25 in the context of chs. 21–25, Wilson misses an important opportunity. Therefore, he comes under the same sorts of critique offered above in relation to Burnett's view. Although Jesus operates in Prophetic manners and in ways consistent with Wisdom in Matthew in general and chs 24–25 in particular, "Prophet" and "Sage" neither drive the Christological logic of Matthew nor define the function of the Eschatological Discourse.

In fact, Witherington knows well the prophetic character of Jesus and his teachings, but he could assert that in Matthew, "there is hardly a mention of Jesus as a prophet," adding, "'Prophet' does not seem to have been seen by this evangelist as either a Christological or an eschatological term."[72] As Witherington thinks, the "Prophet" saying in Matt 13:57 is more of "a general maxim" rather than a direct self-identification.[73] This assessment is even more so with the "Wisdom" saying in 11:19c. That is to say, in neither 13:57 nor 11:19c does Jesus directly call himself "Prophet" or "Wisdom" respectively.[74]

Matthew's Gospel is certainly a Christological mosaic, whose contours include "all of the above"—Son of Man, Servant, Shepherd, Wisdom, Teacher, Law Giver, Prophet, etc.—but we must still ask of his main outline. With this, I turn to the position taken in this study regarding how the Eschatological Discourse functions in Matthew.

Matt 24–25 in Relation to Matthew as a Whole

The Eschatological Discourse undoubtedly performs several immediate and internal roles. There is no question regarding the Discourse's consolatory and missiological bents. There is also no doubt about its paraenetic or hortatory inclination. I note, in particular, Bauer's view above, underscoring the contrast between the expected faithfulness and watchfulness of the disciples and the faithlessness and disobedience of Israel in Matt 21–23 on the one hand, and the similarity between this expected faithfulness and watchfulness and the experience of Jesus in chs. 26–28 on the other. While this view

---

72. Witherington, *Jesus the Seer*, 339. Note that in Matt 21:11, the multitude identifies Jesus as "the prophet from Nazareth," although 16:14–17 implies that seeing Jesus merely as a prophet indicates blindness to his real identity.

73. Witherington, *Jesus the Seer*, 339; cf. Witherington, *Matthew* 15–16.

74. Jesus also operates in ways reminiscent or typical of Moses, but this does not make him another Moses. For discussions on this, see Allison, *New Moses*; Baxter, "Mosaic Imageries"; cf. Bauer, *Gospel*, 263–64.

is persuasive, it is surprising, however, that Matthew does not make this contrast and comparison clear to the implied reader by explicitly applying the terms "faithfulness" and "watchfulness" to Israel and Jesus. In any case, the contrast and comparison are within the immediate context and controls less than half of Matthew's Gospel.

In relation to the overarching goal of Matthew, that is, taking all the material (chs 1-28) into account, and in line with the fourth view above, I will argue that the Eschatological Discourse exists in Matthew for the sake of Christology. With this, I remain in agreement with Kingsbury and Bauer on the centrality of Jesus as the Son of God in Matthew, although I believe that the structural framework they have advocated to arrive at or in support of this conclusion is faulty in diminishing the significant Christological and structural role of the Eschatological Discourse.

My specific claim, in accordance with the structure argued in chapter 4, is that Matt 24-25 functions to reveal the identity of Jesus as the Universal Judge-King.[75] Accordingly, the title, "King" in 25:31-46, rather than function in an "auxiliary capacity" within its limited pericope, as Kingsbury suggests,[76] is at par with "Son of God," both intertwining and equally elucidating the central Christological thrust of Matthew. Put differently, Jesus as "Son of God"[77] and "Universal Judge-King"[78] are two halves of Matthew's contention regarding Jesus' identity; the one is ontological, the other functional. On close examination, the second half is the contribution of the Eschatological Discourse to the Christological superstructure of Matthew.

Based on the concept of recurrence structure,[79] the following diagram shows the two aspects of Jesus' identity untwined and fitted into the structure of Matthew I argued in chapter 4:

---

75. Cf. Wilson's "Judge-Prophet" and "Judge-Sage" (discussed above).

76. Kingsbury, *Matthew*, 99. Ellis, *Matthew*, 19 thinks that the scene [25:31-46] sums up the eschatological implications of the whole discourse and makes Jesus' final teaching before the passion a revelation on the finality of a loving "yes" or a selfish "no" to his whole messianic work." What is argued in this study is that, in terms of overall function, the scene is most importantly a revelation of Jesus as the Universal Judge-King.

77. Jesus thinks of God rather than David as his father (Matt 7:21; 10:32, 33; 11:25, 26, 27[3x]; 12:50; 15:13; 16:17, 27; 18:10, 14, 19, 35; 20:23 [cf. 24:36]; 25:34; 26:29, 39, 42, 53; 28:19).

78. The motifs of kingdom and Judgment abound: kingdom (3:2; 4:8, 17, 23; 5:3, 10, 19-20; 6:10, 33; 7:21; 8:11-12; 9:35; 10:7; 11:11-12; 12:25-26, 28; 13:11, 19, 24, 31, 33, 38, 41, 43-45, 47, 52; 16:19, 28; 18:1, 3-4, 23; 19:12, 14, 23-24; 20:1, 21; 21:31, 43; 22:2; 23:13; 24:7, 14; 25:1, 34; 26:29); judgment (3:10-12; 5:21-22; 7:19; 10:15; 11:22, 24; 12:18, 20, 36, 41-42; 13:40, 42, 50; 18:8-9; 23:33; chs. 24-25).

79. See discussion in chapter 2.

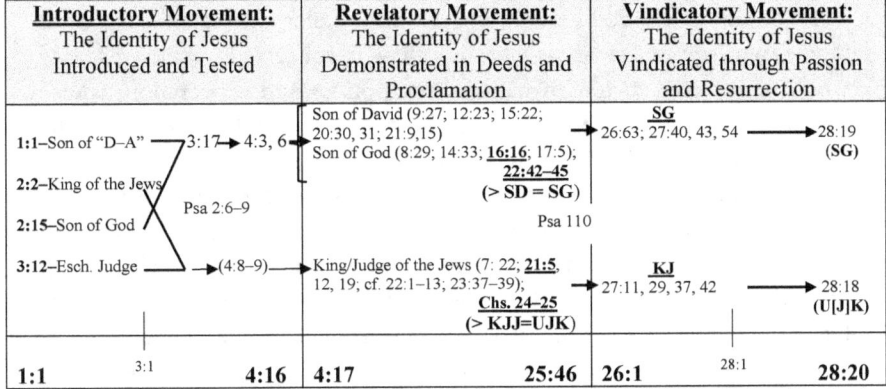

Table 6: Showing Relation between Christological Titles and Matthew's Structure

Within this tripartite structure, two complimentary identity trajectories relate to the two main questions or challenges faced by Jesus.[80]

On the one hand, Jesus is introduced as the Son of David (Matt 1:1), but is he better or, more importantly, the Son of God? Although Son of David evokes Son of God in Jewish messianic expectation (2 Sam 7:12–16), just being Son of David is not enough qualification for being Messiah; Joseph is called son of David in Matt 1:20. It should be asked why Matthew would use "Son of David" in this non-messianic way if he is intent on demonstrating Jesus to be the Son of David. Why is it that the kinds of people who call Jesus "Son of David" are the blind (9:27; 20:30, 31), a foreign woman (15:22), the multitudes who were not only unsure (12:23) but also vacillated between him as Son of David and "the prophet from Nazareth" (21:9, 11), and children (21:15). In fact, the title seems so public that almost no one would want to waste time trying to prove Jesus' Davidic Sonship, even if it also invites ponder (12:23). The genealogy indicates that Matthew takes it for granted. No revelation is needed at all throughout Matthew to discern that Jesus is Son of David; he is publicly known to have been born to Joseph, Son of David and carpenter (1:20; cf. 13:54–56).

But more importantly, why does Matthew extend Jesus' genealogy beyond Son of David to Son of Abraham (1:1)? Because it is taken for granted that Matthew is presenting Jesus as the Son of David, there appears to be

---

80. Kingsbury, *Matthew*, 97, does say that Matthew is concerned throughout "to qualify Jesus-Messiah in two directions in terms of 'King of the Jews (Israel)' on the one hand and 'Son of God' on the other."

only a scanty reference to such a concern in current discussions.⁸¹ But might it not be the case that, as is said in relation to Solomon (12:42), "a greater than David/son of David" is what Matthew is concerned with here,⁸² one who is unfettered to Jewish nationalistic politics and expectation, whose power and authority is boundless, embracing πάντα τὰ ἔθνη τῆς γῆς as the Abrahamic promise states in Gen 22:18?⁸³

Indeed, it is not long before the supreme superiority of Jesus is introduced in the announcement of his Spirit-mediated conception (1:18) and encapsulation of Israel (2:15).⁸⁴ In light of the Abrahamic connection above, one would have expected that Matthew would have made much about Jesus being the Seed of Abraham. But Matthew, fearing no omission or contradiction, aims, in my view, at the very acme of Christology. It is Matthew's goal to demonstrate, as his central burden, that far greater than Son of David, Jesus is the Son of God. Thus, the further divine introduction, οὗτός ἐστιν ὁ υἱός μου ὁ ἀγαπητός (3:17), which alludes to Ps 2:6–9,⁸⁵ is the subject of contention in the tempter's double challenge, εἰ υἱὸς εἶ τοῦ θεοῦ (4:3, 6). Thus begins to unravel, in the "Introductory Movement," the first strand or aspect of Jesus' identity within Matthew's central Christological goal.

Within the "Revelatory Movement,"⁸⁶ a tension develops in the recurrence of Jesus as "Son of David" and as "Son of God" motifs. Without necessarily rejecting the former, the tension is resolved in favor of the latter.⁸⁷

---

81. See Huizenga, "Son of Abraham." He contends that "Son of Abraham" in Matt 1:1 introduces a sacrificial motif which suggests that, along with "Son of David," Matthew is presenting Jesus as a new Isaac. However, while Jesus' submission to death might echo Isaac's, we do not see any specific hint relating Jesus to Isaac in Matthew. The importance of "Son of Abraham" in 1:1 is hardly to necessarily imply that Jesus is a new Isaac, although "ransom" motif occurs in 20:28. Moreover, it was not Isaac who died, a lamb did in his place.

82. Cf. Witherington, *Matthew*, 15–16.

83. Cf. Matt 24:9, 14; 25:32; 28:19.

84. Cf. Hos 11:1; Nolan, *Royal Son of God*, 209, following the scribe of Codex Sinaiticus, argues that 2:15 rather echoes Num 23:22; 24:8, both read in light of the star of David in Num 24:17. His overall claim is that the royal Davidic theology integrates all of Matthew's Christology (see 13). For others, see Kingsbury, *Matthew*, 99.

85. According to Keener, *Matthew*, 135, "scholars generally agree that one text here [in 3:17] is Psalm 2:7." Although the expression, "in whom I am well pleased" is taken from Isa 42:1, the Isaianic "My Servant" is not part of the enthronement context of Ps 2 which is the text upon which Matthew seems most fixed.

86. An apt title in keeping with the use of the term ἀποκαλύπτω in 10:26; 11:25, 27; 16:17 (cf. 24:30). Chs. 24–25 is most apocalyptic, thus, as Bauer and Traina say, it would serve to "make real what is hidden" (*Inductive Bible Study*, 149).

87. Kingsbury, *Matthew*, 100, prefers to say that Son of David is subjected to "a double restriction," that is, related only to healings, and to particular individuals rather

Thus (1) Jesus is revealed by the Father to be the Son of God in 16:16–17 and 17:5, and (2) as already mentioned above, there is almost a critique of the assumption of Jesus' Davidic sonship by Jesus himself in 22:42–45.[88] While this passage indicates that Pharisees, at least, expected a Davidic Messiah-King (v. 42), it certainly implies Jesus' divine superiority and Lordship over David.[89] To my mind, Bauer seems a bit too sympathetic to Jesus' Davidic Sonship when, on this passage (22:41–46), he comments that "the Matthean Jesus sees it [Son of David] as deficient unless supplemented by the transcendent category of Son of God."[90] Properly taken, however, what Jesus seems to imply is the supplanting of Davidic Sonship by his divine Lordship over David, not the supplementation of the former by the latter

This might explain why it is the case that from this point, the title, Son of David, never occurs again in Matthew, trumped by the Son of God motif.[91] Thus, within the "Vindicatory Movement," the priest himself asks whether Jesus was "the Christ, the Son of God" (26:63); and following this, Jesus is mocked for his claim of being the Son of God (27:40, 43; cf. 26:64). Furthermore, in 27:54, the divine introductory affirmation "*this* is my beloved Son" (3:17) meets its human counterpart affirming Jesus' divine Sonship: "Truly, the Son of God *this* was" (ἀληθῶς θεοῦ υἱὸς ἦν οὗτος). This affirmation is quite interesting in that it comes from the lips of a gentile centurion for whom a connection between Son of David and Son of God would have been unlikely. Finally, in 28:19, Jesus sets himself within the eternal Godhead as the Divine Son, completing the first half of Jesus' identity upon which Matthew is centrally fixed—his ontological identity.

On the other hand, within the "Introductory Movement," Jesus is introduced as the king of the Jews (2:2) as well as their Judge (3:12).[92] Then he

---

than to the masses.

88. Note Selvanayagam, "Interpreting a Riddle," 262–68. Challenging what he calls "the uncritical glorification of David in Christian tradition," he argues that the title, Son of David, in the Gospels should not lead to the conclusion that Jesus is a type of David who comes to reunite and rule over the kingdom of Israel. On the contrary, Selvanayagam suggests that Jesus' geographical, ministerial, and administrative identifications would indicate that he has come to challenge and correct the Davidic regal tradition.

89. Cf. Wright, *Jesus and the Victory*, 507–9. Choi, who after analyzing the use of Son of David in Matthew, concludes, "It is evident that Matthew intends to develop his Christology beyond a mere Davidic kingship into something that closely resembles Yahweh by attributing to Jesus such authority as was exclusively ascribed to Israel's deity" (*Messianic Kingship*, 204).

90. Bauer, *Matthew*, 247.

91. So also Kingsbury, *Matthew*, 102.

92. Although non-Jewish Magi come to worship him, they do so only as homage to him in his capacity as king of the Jews.

is tempted with universal kingship (4:8), again alluding to Ps 2:6–9 where this equation holds: My Son = My King (Judge).[93] Although the "Judge" title is muted moving forward, several passages within the "Revelatory Movement," especially 7:22 and chs. 21–25, depict Jesus as Judge either implicitly or explicitly.[94] In 21:5, Jesus' ride into Jerusalem unveils him as the King of the Jews, and his activities portray him as their Judge (esp. 21:12, 19; 22:1–13; 23:37–39). The significance of chs. 24–25 is not merely that there will be judgment, but that Jesus will be the Judge.[95] However, and most importantly, this Final Discourse reveals Jesus as more than the King and Judge of the Jews, but as the "Universal Judge-King."[96] His judgment is pronounced upon Jerusalem, to be realized in the fall of the temple (a major theme in Matt 24). And ultimately, he will sit on his glorious throne and judge all nations in his capacity as the divine Universal King (25:31–46). The sudden switch from "Son of Man" to "King" in 25:31–34 represents an unveiling of the universal regal dimension of Jesus' identity. With this, the "Revelatory Movement" reaches its culmination; Matthew's two-stranded portrait of Jesus is completed.

Furthermore, there exists a critical link between the two trajectories or intertwining strands of Matthew's central Christological burden. The link is the enthronement tradition of Ps 110 cited by Jesus in the exchange in 22:42–45. By citing this Psalm and posing the question he does, Jesus claims divine superiority over David, which manifests itself in his being both Universal Judge and King, hence the judgment motif in Matt 24,[97] and especially his sitting on his throne in Matt 25:31–32.[98] Thus, while there is hardly a connection between Jesus' Kingship in this universal scene and his being David's Son,[99] there is indeed a connection between his Kingship here and his being David's Lord, the Son of God. In other words, to recall what

---

93. Note the motif of universality and judgment in Ps 2.

94. See Wilson, *When Will These Things Happen?*, 72–73, 78–79.

95. Scaer, *Discourses*, 354.

96. Contra Willitts, who paints a picture of Jesus simply as a nationalistic King (*Matthew's Messianic Shepherd-King*).

97. Note also the judgment motif in Ps 110.

98. Cf. Wright, *Jesus and the Victory*, 343, 507–9. I do believe that if we read Matt 22:42–45 with the full context of this Psalm in mind, we might as well add the title "Universal Priest" in view of the divine oath, "You are a priest forever in the order of Melchizedek." In that case, Wright will be right in arguing that Jesus is also depicted as the Priest who replaces the temple upon which his judgment will fall. However, while priesthood is true for Jesus in general, it is only a legitimate inference rather than an explicit Matthean argument. Similarly, I also think that the vindication of Jesus as a prophet as Wright argues is beneath the ultimate goal of Matthew.

99. See Bauer, *Gospel*, 246–47.

has been said above, "King" in 25:34, 40 does not function in "an auxiliary capacity" limited to its pericope. Rather, this universal Kingship of Jesus, in relation to his divine Sonship, is all along what Matthew aims to prove.

Accordingly, what this shows is that, rather than being merely one of several Discourses, and without denying its paraenetic effects in relation to the disciples to whom it is addressed, Matt 24–25 functions at the broader Christological and structural levels to fill the second half of Matthew's two-tiered construction of Jesus' identity—his functional identity. Within the "Vindicatory Movement," the recurrence of this functional identity of Jesus takes place again in the form of questions and mockery of him as the King of the Jews (27:11, 29, 37, 42), but it is ultimately resolved in Jesus' claim of universal rather than nationalistic authority in 28:18.

Overall, then, Matthew is properly the Gospel of the Son of God, the Universal Judge-King—"the Divine Royal."[100] This study claims that these two aspects of Jesus' identity together constitute the central object of the First Gospel. Matthew has glued these two aspects together using a mix of materials from LXX Gen 22:18, Ps 2, and Ps 110.

But why set apart "Son of God" and "Judge-King" in this way as the most important of Jesus' identity? I have shown that the recurrence structure of Matthew from the beginning to the end supports the view. What about the Son of Man phrase title? On this, it is to be observed that it is not Matthew's intention to demonstrate that Jesus is the Son of Man. This may sound surprising at first, given the preponderance of the phrase/title in the Gospel.[101] Yet several factors buttress the point.

First, Matthew's Gospel neither opens with an introduction of Jesus as Son of Man (see the section "Introductory Movement" in proposed structure) nor does it close with any reference to him as such.[102] Second, although also quite messianic in its evocation, Jesus alone uses the phrase/title as his common personal designation. Third, and most importantly, the fact that no one in Matthew wonders at such self-identification or asks about what it means, suggests, as Kingsbury argues, that for Matthew it serves only as "'public title' that does not divulge the identity of Jesus."[103] In his response to Kingsbury, Hill also concedes that in contrast to Son of God, "it [Son of

---

100. With the addition of "Judge," Choi, *Messianic Kingship*, 131, is right in using this term to describe Matthew's Christology.

101. Matt 8:20; 9:6; 10:23; 11:19; 12:8, 32, 40; 13:37, 41; 16:13–16, 27, 28; 17:9, 12, 22; 19:28; 20:18, 28; 24:37, 39, 44; 25:31; 26:2, 24, 45, 64.

102. The introduction and conclusion are usually key to an author's purpose.

103. Kingsbury, "Figure of Jesus," 29.

Man] is simply the peculiar way of referring to himself attributed to Jesus by the tradition . . . and accepted without question by Matthew."[104]

Given all that I have argued above, one conclusion may be reached regarding the titles, Son of Man and Son of David: they are nominal placeholders for the two intertwining strands of Jesus' identity that form the central burden of Matthew's Gospel; the one is a nominal apocalyptic placeholder, the other a nominal nationalistic placeholder. Matthew's Jesus is "Divine Royal": Son of God and Universal Judge-King. Thus, the First Gospel comes full circle with a perceptible *inclusio* of universality, so that the universal promise to Abraham (Gen 22:18, hence "Son of Abraham" in Matt 1:1) is fulfilled in the revelation and vindication of Jesus' divine Sonship and Universal Kingship. In a sense, it should be wondered why Matthew would spend a tone of ink to prove that Jesus is Son of David when even the blind,[105] a foreigner,[106] commoners,[107] and children[108] know him to be so. But when God affirms the divine Sonship and Universal Kingship/Judgeship of Jesus;[109] when Satan presupposes it,[110] and demons know it,[111] but the authorities reject and influence subjects to ridicule it,[112] then it would be time to demonstrate and vindicate it through words and deeds. This strongly seems to be why Matthew has written. In the end, Jesus' sonship is only caught as or by means of revelation.[113]

Conclusion

This chapter aimed to show how the Eschatological Discourse functions within the overall structure and central purpose of Matthew. I began by asserting a distinction between interpretation and function. Next, I highlighted several views on how the Discourse functions. Essential to the whole discussion is the fact that eschatology, ecclesiology, salvation-history, and Christology are all interconnected in Matthew. However, I have argued

---

104. Hill, "Son and Servant," 3.
105. 9:27; 20:30, 31.
106. 15:22.
107. 12:23.
108. 21:15.
109. 3:17; 17:5.
110. 4:3, 6, 8–9.
111. 8:29.
112. 26:63; 27:40, 43. Cf. Satan's presupposition-drive challenge (4:3, 6, 8–9) and human rejection-driven challenge (27:40).
113. 16:16; 27:54.

that with reference to the overarching or controlling aim of Matthew, Matt 24–25 functions Christologically not to present Jesus as the Son of Man, or to display his prophetic genius, or demonstrate his identification with Wisdom. Rather, the Eschatological Discourse, in its strategic final position, completes Matthew's portrait of Jesus by unveiling him as Universal Judge-King. This identification along with the title Son of God constitute the core argument of the First Gospel.

7

Conclusions and Correlation within the NT

Introduction

THIS STUDY HAS BEEN concerned with a holistic investigation into the Eschatological Discourse of Matt 24–25. I have explored different aspects of the Discourse, its literary character, structure, interpretation, and function within the Gospel as a whole. The aim of this last chapter is twofold: (1) to draw together the major conclusions from the study, including a summary of the interpretation offered in chapter 5, and (2) to carry out a limited exercise in correlation, highlighting the eschatology expressed in the Discourse and how it intersects or otherwise with what is thought in the NT as a whole in relation to current debates.

Conclusions and Summary of Interpretation

The key findings of this study begin in chapter 3. There, I examined the literary nature of Matthew's Gospel, showing that while it is biographical in form, many scholars recognize it as apocalyptic in content or worldview. Importantly, I argued that because Matthew's Jesus is, in a unique sense, both a prophetic and an apocalyptic figure, Matt 24–25 is properly taken as a prophetic-apocalyptic in that it combines a prophetic reality specific to Israel and an apocalyptic expectation of cosmic consummation.

The literary character of prophetic-apocalyptic requires that one consider the language with care. Approaches to the apocalyptic language have remained divided between those who take it metaphorically and those who advocate a literal interpretation. The view taken in this study is that one must consider general matters such as the rhetorical, poetic, and dynamic nature of prophetic-apocalyptic, avoiding wooden literalism without resorting to absolute metaphorical or allegorical interpretation. Along with these general concerns, one must also consider specific matters of structure, intertextuality, and context. While it is the case that apocalyptic language is, in general, to be processed in symbolic manners, these specific considerations may warrant more literal than metaphorical interpretations or something in-between.

Chapter 4 dealt with the structure of Matthew in general and the Eschatological Discourse in particular. First, I argued a tripartite Christological structure of Matthew's Gospel, consisting of three movements: (I) Introductory Movement: Jesus identified and tested (1:1—4:16); (II) Revelatory Movement: the identity of Jesus demonstrated and/or unveiled in his deeds and proclamations (4:17—25:46); and (III) Vindicatory Movement: the identity of Jesus vindicated in his passion and resurrection (26:1—28:20). The Eschatological Discourse concludes the Revelatory Movement.

Second, combining inductive study categories and insights from the discourse grammatical approach (specifically in relation to the use of the conjunctions καί, δέ, τότε, οὖν, and asyndeton), I argued that the Discourse, delimited to 24:3—25:46, is structured in terms of "problem" (the disciple's question; 24:3) and "solution" (Jesus' response; 24:4—25:46), with the latter consisting of generalization (24:4—14) and particularization (24:15—25:46). In the generalization, Jesus surveys all the period from the time of his speaking to the *parousia*. In the particularization, Jesus delineates the two elements of the disciple's question (temple destruction and the *parousia*/end of the age) woven together alternatingly through the Discourse. In the structure that emerges, the temple's fate (a[T^1]) is the focus in 24:15-25, the *parousia* and end of the age (b[P^1]) in 24:26-31, the temple's fate (b[T^2]) in 24:32-35, and the *parousia* and end of the age (b[P^2]) in 24:36—25:46. The conjunctions οὖν and δέ provide the basis for this structural decision.

Chapter 5 constitutes the central body of this study. Based on the literary and structural foundations laid in chs. 3-4, I undertook to offer an interpretation of the Discourse, exploring its various issues, themes, and eschatological thrust. Because of the length of the chapter, I have broken down the interpretation into ten broad and summative conclusions:

1. Based on synoptic, contextual, and grammatical warrants, I argued that the disciple's question in Matt 24:3 must be taken as twofold—the destruction of the temple and the *parousia* as two separate events which are, in the character of apocalyptic visions, connected as though simultaneous. The disciples' question is neither singular nor threefold. Nor is it necessary to posit a fourfold question as has most recently been done by Juza, whose work I thoroughly appreciate. The twofold view is supported by the likely but not necessary evocation of the motif of "coming" in 23:39. But more importantly, this twofold view is supported by the fact that the disciples are aware that Jesus had previously spoken of the *parousia* and end of the age in a context where the destruction of the temple could not be implied (16:27). Ultimately, the term συντέλεια (24:3c) is consistently used in Matthew to refer to that "end" in which there will be final reward, the consignment of some to eternal fire and the admission of others to eternal life. The destruction of the temple does not satisfy this notion of ultimate finality.

2. In relation to this first point, while it is possible to psychoanalyze the disciples, there is nothing in the text that crystallizes confusion in their question. The disciples are told to beware of deceptions regarding the arrival of the end, but the warning is really about a deception that could come externally to them rather than one already resident in them. Accordingly, Jesus neither corrects the disciple's question nor ignores any part of it as some have claimed.

3. The Eschatological Discourse evinces two aspects of tribulation—the Great Tribulation, now a past event, and routine tribulations as a continuing experience until the end. In a panoramic manner, Jesus articulates the nature of all the eschatological period from the time of his disciples to the end of history (i.e., *parousia* and end of the age) in 24:14. All this period will be characterized by routine tribulations with a near and particularly explosive moment in the Great Tribulation, the events leading to and including the 70 CE destruction of the temple. After this event, routine tribulations will continue until the *parousia* and end of the age.[1] One important indication of this is the varied action of the disciples as directed by Jesus—*flee* and *endure* till the end. On the one hand, with respect to the Great Tribulation/destruction of the temple, the disciples must *flee* for safety. On the other hand, with respect to the routine tribulations of all time, they must endure

---

1. Not to exclude the possibility of other moments of Great-Tribulation-like events in history but in view of the expression οὐδ' οὐ μὴ γένηται ("nor ever will be"), no future tribulation will be like the destruction of the temple.

persecution, which will turn deadly at times, till the end. Put simply, *flee* and *endure* are two different directives; they cannot refer to the same tribulation experience.

4. In connection with the Great Tribulation/destruction of the temple, I proposed that the enigmatic expression, βδέλυγμα τῆς ἐρημώσεως, is better understood in relation to the sacrilegious activity of Jewish zealots, specifically the murderous act which their Idumean collaborators carried out in the temple as described by Josephus. While somewhat speculative and external to the text, none of the other alternative interpretations—the futuristic antichrist view, the pagan-abomination views, and the Jewish-abomination/infidelity views—better fits the text.

5. Informed by Matt 21:43, and the connection between 23:34–35 and 24:9, the disciples are the new-Israel in Jesus, while unbelieving Jews are merged with the nations of the world. The possible revulsion some might feel about the "strange" proposal of Israel's "*ethnos*ization" will likely be assuaged when it becomes clear that even some in the community of faith in Jesus could experience the same fate according to Matt 18:15–17.[2] The implication of "*ethnos*ization" is not that unbelieving Israel is rejected but that they are subject to the proclamation of "this gospel of the kingdom" (24:14), that is, *the gospel of Jesus' vindication as Son of God and Universal King*.

6. The *parousia* and end of the age will take place at an unknown time after the gospel has been proclaimed to the whole world. Contrary to the preterist view which limits the intended scope of the gospel in 24:14 to the then-known world or the Roman empire, the significance of the term οἰκουμένη is to be processed in association with the immediate co-texts (πᾶσιν τοῖς ἔθνεσιν) and more broadly in relation to the universal motif in the Discourse's judgment scene (25:31–46) and in the Great Commission (28:18–20).

7. Jesus introduces and describes the *parousia* in Matt 24:26–31. The proverbial gathering of eagles in 24:28 refers to the general gathering at the *parousia*; it is a parabolic allusion to the Great Assize in 25:31–46. The apparent emphasis of the saying is "gathering." Therefore, the unsavory character of the saying is immaterial. Closely related to this consideration, the expression, "immediately after the tribulation of those days" in 24:29 is best taken as a reference to the end of the routine tribulation that will continue till the end. And compelled by the

2. See chapter 5, n121.

resonance between τὸ σημεῖον in the disciple's question in 24:3c and τὸ σημεῖον in v. 30, the controversial "coming of the Son of Man" in vv. 30–31 should be understood as a reference to the *parousia*.

8. Because NT writers do re-appropriate OT and apocalyptic materials in a variety of ways, it is important to carefully consider the literary context and goal of each author. For example, Matt 24:31 alludes to Isa 11:12 (cf. Deut 30:4; Zech 2:10) which deals specifically with the gathering of Israel. Yet none of those who take a preterist view of 24:30–31 *attempt to argue that the OT Israel-specific gathering* is what is meant here. This attests to the NT authors' practice of re-appropriation of inherited tradition, which makes it plausible to interpret both the "coming of the Son of Man" and the "sending of angels to gather the elect" not only universally but also in a manner more literal than metaphorical.

9. Since the time of the *parousia* will be unknown, Jesus employs several analogies to illustrate to the disciples the need for eschatological vigilance. Such vigilance will be characterized by wisdom and faithfulness. At the end, when Jesus descends at the *parousia*, there will be a sudden separation. Some will be "taken", and others will be "left." Contrary to the now popular interpretation of the words "taken" and "left" as "being taken for judgment" and "being left for salvation" respectively, the plain meaning is to be preferred in light of the flood analogy. Just as Noah separated some animals "taking" them with himself and his household into the ark for preservation, and "leaving" the rest for the flood judgment, so it will be in the end. The saints will be "taken" to meet with Jesus at his *parousia* and the rest of humanity as a whole will be "left" for the judgment that Jesus brings.

10. Matthew 24 and 25 exist in inextricable unity; the one cannot be fully grasped without the other. Consequently, 24:30–31 and 25:31–46 must be interpreted as complementary halves of the *parousia* event. The gathering of the elect by the angels to the Son of Man when he steps into time (24:30–31) represents the being "taken" (24:40b, 41b) and the first half of the *parousia* journey. The second half of the *parousia* is represented by the great assize described in 25:31–46 where, on arrival, all the nations—those "left" (24:40c, 41c)—are gathered before Jesus for judgment. Although perspectival, this judgment represents the final judgment of all the nations, including Jews; it will lead immediately to two eternal destinies—eternal life for the righteous (i.e., Jesus' least brothers = the sheep = elect Jews and gentiles) and eternal punishment for the wicked (i.e., the goat, both Jew and gentile). In

other words, when Jesus arrives at his *parousia*, that will be the end of this *present age* of tribulations and the beginning of the eternal state *to come*.

Finally, in chapter 6, I considered how the Eschatological Discourse functions in relation to the overall goal of Matthew. It was argued that the Discourse is placed in a strategic position structurally. In such a position, it functions to complete Matthew's central Christological argument by revealing Jesus as Universal Judge-King.

Matt 24–25 in Correlation with other NT Data

Bauer and Traina define correlation as "the process of bringing together or synthesizing the interpretation (and appropriation) of individual passages so as to arrive at the meaning of larger units of biblical material."[3] At the heart of correlation is "the consideration of both *unity* and *diversity* in the theological teachings of the Bible."[4] In other words, correlation deals with developing a biblical theology in relation to the interpreted passage. However, as Bauer and Traina rightly point out, this is a difficult exercise. Critical to the problem is the question of whether there is such a thing as biblical theology, that is, whether the Bible as a whole (in this case, the NT) reflects a theological unity. Some have argued against such a theological harmonization, advocating instead the theological diversity of each Bible book.[5]

In relation to eschatology as an aspect of theology, it may indeed seem difficult to harmonize much of the details in each NT book. I acknowledge the advice from Bauer and Traina that correlation is vulnerable to subjectivity. Yet I agree with them that the exercise "is not finally a matter of subjective individual judgment because correlation focuses on the objective data of the text."[6] Thus, while allowing for tentativeness and openness to conversation in what follows, I hope to show that despite apparent diversity in many details, the NT data supports the eschatology reflected in Matt 24–25 as interpreted in chapter 5 of this study. The motifs of *parousia* and *tribulation*, as well as the concept of *temporal dualism*, will constitute the key foci of the exercise.

---

3. Bauer and Traina, *Inductive Bible Study*, 337.
4. Bauer and Traina, *Inductive Bible Study*, 339.
5. Bauer and Traina, *Inductive Bible Study*, 339–40.
6. Bauer and Traina, *Inductive Bible Study*, 341.

Diversity and Unity in the Synoptics

The Eschatological Discourse certainly reflects several elements of diversity within the Synoptics. For example, one can observe how the material is reused in different contexts.[7] Also, several details, such as the disciples' question and the identity of the abomination of desolation, may be interpreted differently. In relation to the disciples' question, the Synoptics seem to evince varying degrees of connection between the temple destruction and the coming of Jesus. While the distinction is more apparent in Matthew, it is less discernible in Mark and Luke since the disciple's question in the two latter instances appears to refer only to the destruction of the temple (cf. Mark 13:4; Luke 21:7). Moreover, Mark and Luke neither use the term *parousia* nor the expression συντέλεια [τοῦ] αἰῶνός.

What is the significance of these differences? One way to resolve the differences is to read Mark's or Luke's version of the question into Matthew's, as hyper-preterists do, and therefore assume that the destruction of the temple, the end, and the coming of the Son of Man are all one and the same. Or the differences may be exploited to support the claim that the disciples confused the temple destruction with the *parousia* in their question. I have shown that the Matthean Discourse resists either of these moves. The reason for the almost indiscernible distinction between the temple destruction and the coming of Jesus in Mark and Luke is to be found not in the disciples' confusion but more likely in the prophetic perspective of Jesus.[8]

First, Mark's Jesus responds to the disciple's temple-specific question in Mark 13 with 8:38 in view. Since Jesus can speak of two kinds of "comings" in close succession (Mark 8:38—9:1; cf. Matt 16:27-28), it is not unlikely that he would do the same in Mark 13, even if based on a temple-specific question. Like Matthew, Mark betrays a universal evangelistic reach. Thus, in 13:10 the gospel must be proclaimed to πάντα τὰ ἔθνη πρῶτον, with the word πρῶτον ("first") implying "before the 'end'" (τέλος). Those who endure to the end will be saved (v. 13; cf. Matt 24:14). Also, if the "tribulation such as has not been from the beginning of creation until now, nor will ever be" (Mark 13:19) includes the destruction of Jerusalem and the temple as is likely (and as I argued in Matt 24:21), then Mark's "in those days after that tribulation"

---

7. Note esp. Luke 12:35-48: the parable on watchfulness and the coming of the Master occurs in a different context than the Eschatological Discourse (cf. Matt 24:43-51). See Luke 17:30-31 (where the warning for those on the housetop not to come down and those in the field not to return home is in connection with the day the Son of Man is revealed) and Matt 24:15-21 (where the warning is in connection with siting of the abomination of desolation in the temple).

8. I discussed prophetic perspective in chapter 3.

(13:24a) plausibly distinguishes between the temple's destruction on the one hand, and the coming of the Son of Man (13:24b–27) understood as the *parousia* on the other. In other words, the words, "in those days" envisages an indefinite tribulation period that extends beyond the destruction of the temple. Juza not only subscribes to this interpretation[9] but also takes it as a given that "Mark appears to adopt the same structural scheme as Matthew," arguing that Mark's Eschatological Discourse "refers to both the destruction of the Jerusalem temple and to the second coming of Jesus."[10]

Second, Luke's overall eschatological outlook also accords with that of Matthew and Mark. Although Juza denies that Luke, just as Mark, has both the destruction of the temple and the second coming in view, he acknowledges that his position flies in the face of the consensus of "the vast majority of interpreters" on Luke 21.[11] On close examination, Luke 21:24–27 indicates a clear distinction and an indefinite gap between the "Great Distress" (ἀνάγκη μεγάλη) which includes the destruction of Jerusalem and the temple on the one hand, and the coming (ἐρχόμενον) of the Son of Man understood as the *parousia* on the other.[12] Thus, in both Mark 13 and Luke 21 (as in Matt 24–25), the coming of the Son of Man as an event at the end of an indefinite and extended period of tribulation, is discernibly set apart from the more proximal event of the destruction of the temple.

Furthermore, the broad unity between the Matthean Discourse's eschatology as interpreted, and those of Mark and Luke is affirmed by the shared motif of two-age dualism.[13] The Synoptics exhibit a clear sense of both tension and differentiation between "the present age" and "the age to come." This motif of temporal dualism is also expressed in terms of the "coming of the kingdom of God" which is in turn virtually equivalent to the "coming of the Son of Man."

It is to be observed that, in clear contradiction of Dodd's realized-only eschatology, the Synoptic Gospels represent the kingdom of God not only as a present or inaugurated reality (e.g., Matt 12:28; Mark 3:26–27 [cf. 1:15; 9:1]; Luke 11:20; 17:21) but also as a future reality (e.g., Matt 16:27–28; Mark 8:38; Luke 9:26–27; 18:8).[14] In relation to this, Matthew's Jesus distinguishes

9. Juza, *New Testament*, 74–75.

10. Juza, *New Testament*, 67; cf. Stein, *Jesus*, 50–135; Beasley-Murray, *Jesus and the Last Days*, 350–75.

11. Juza, *New Testament*, 93.

12. The latter would be consistent with Luke's view in Acts 1:11.

13. For the NT conception of time based on the term "age" (αἰών) see Cullmann, *Christ and Time*, 45–50.

14. For a comprehensive discussion, see Beasley-Murray, *Jesus and the Kingdom of God*.

between "this age" and "the age to come" (12:32). The term συντέλεια αἰῶνός (consummation of the age) also implies this two-age duality. With the kingdom of God having broken in, the present age is a mixture of good and evil, but at the consummation of the age, the Son of Man will return to usher in the age to come, that is, the kingdom of God with the absolute and final exclusion of evil (Matt 13:39–43, 49).[15] Within the Matthean Eschatological Discourse, the motif of "consummation" of this present age characterized by tribulations implies and anticipates the eternal age of life for the righteous and punishment for the wicked (25:46). But the kingdom of God is present with the disciples in Jesus "until the end of the age" (28:20).[16]

Similarly, Mark and Luke share in this overarching temporal dualistic frame. Thus, in 10:29–30, Mark implies the presence of kingdom blessings already within the present age (καιρῷ τούτῳ) in association with persecutions and in contradistinction to the age to come when eternal life will be inherited. Luke's Jesus also implies kingdom blessings in "this [present] time," but eternal life awaits "the age to come" (18:29–30). The latter will be associated with the resurrection of the dead (20:35). In all these instances, the age to come is not associated with the destruction of the temple.

Given these observations, it is clear that while differences in details occur, the Synoptic Gospels exhibit agreement in overall eschatology that corresponds with the interpretation of Matt 24–25 offered in chapter 5. The outline consists of an indefinite period of kingdom experience/witness and routine tribulation (with one explosive moment in the destruction of the temple) until the consummation of the age.[17]

Diversity and Unity between Matt 24–25 and Acts

Much of the discussion on eschatology in Acts involves the place or hope of Israel. This will require a different investigation, especially with respect to the notion of "restoring the kingdom to Israel" in Acts 1:6–7. This expression may seem to diverge and indeed contradict the argument made so far, since it suggests a future in which an Israel-specific kingdom will be restored. However, such an Israel-specific kingdom would not only constitute an overinterpretation of the text, but it is also hardly supported anywhere else in Acts. Just as in the Synoptics, there is no mention of kingdom to/

---

15. For my representation of the salvation history arising from this, see appendix 4; cf. Kingsbury, *Matthew*, 25–36; Lunde, "Salvation-Historical Implication," 1–18, 310.

16. For more on Matthew's dualism, see Sim, *Apocalyptic Eschatology*, 75–87.

17. See chapter 5, pp. 141–55.

of Israel anywhere in Acts,[18] and the expression, "restoration of all things" in 3:19–21, is hardly to be restricted to Israel.[19] It would require a different study to fully demonstrate this, but since this would go beyond the scope of this study, I grant, for the sake of argument, that a future restoration of Israel is in view here, as some have claimed,[20] representing a divergence from the broad eschatological outline argued above. However, in relation to the notion of *parousia* and the nature of the time before it, Acts is consistent with the Synoptic Gospels.

First, Luke's understanding of the second coming of Jesus is clear in Acts 1:11. Jesus *will come* (future of ἔρχομαι) from heaven in the same way the synoptic Eschatological Discourses apocalyptically describe the *coming* (participle of ἔρχομαι) of the Son of Man. Thus, whether or not Wright's view of such a coming being a "post-Easter innovation" is warranted,[21] this corresponds with or represents Luke's concrete interpretation of the eschatological hope.

Second, concerning the nature of the interim period, the kingdom of God is both a present reality in the power of the Spirit (Acts 1:6–7; 2:1–47)[22] and remains to be finally and fully brought about in the future (8:12; 19:8; 20:25; 28:23, 31). Importantly, the present period, as Luke has Paul say, is also a time of tribulation. Paul, in Acts 14:22, was encouraging believers to stand firm in the faith, reminding them that διὰ πολλῶν θλίψεων δεῖ ἡμᾶς εἰσελθεῖν εἰς τὴν βασιλείαν τοῦ θεοῦ ("through many tribulations we must enter into the kingdom of God"). Evidently, consistent with the interpretation of the Eschatological Discourse offered in chapter 5, neither Luke nor Paul in Acts thinks that the tribulation will come after Christians have escaped to heaven.

---

18. Always it is "kingdom of God" (1:3; 8:12; 14:22; 19:8; 20:25; 28:23, 31).

19. What we have in this 3:19–21 is a statement regarding Israel's need to repent and receive the benefits of the kingdom which is already present through the Spirit (vv. 19–20), and the "restoration of all things," a reference to cosmic renewal (v. 21); so also Juza, *New Testament*, 124–25. The issue in Acts is not a future Israel-specific kingdom but entrance into eternal life. Both Jews and gentiles will inherit eternal life based on their response to the gospel of the kingdom (see Acts 13:45–46, 48).

20. E.g., Buzzard, "Eclipse of Biblical Kingdom," 207; Keener, *Acts*, 2:1109–12. For extended discussions on this, see Kurz, "Test of the Role of Eschatology"; Lennartsson, *Refreshing & Restoration*.

21. Cf. n294 in chapter 5.

22. See Dunn, "Spirit and Kingdom," 36–40; Smalley, "Spirit, Kingdom, and Prayer."

Unity and Diversity between Matt 24–25 and Pauline Corpus

The Thessalonian letters are properly where to begin when considering Pauline eschatology. Much verbal correspondence between these letters and the Eschatological Discourse betrays some form of relationship.[23] Many scholars believe that Paul drew from Jesus' Eschatological Discourse either in written or oral form.[24] Inclined to a pre-70 date of Matthew, Carson goes as far as to declare that "the discourse itself is undoubtedly a source for the Thessalonian epistles."[25] I will demonstrate the correlation between Paul's and the synoptic eschatological views by highlighting the Pauline view on our three themes of interest—the *parousia*, tribulation, and the two-age motif.

First, for Paul, the term *parousia* means "presence," "arrival," or "coming." As I argued on the use of the term in the Matthean Eschatological Discourse,[26] in relation to Jesus, Paul believes that the *parousia* will involve a personal descent from heaven: "the Lord *himself* with a loud command ... will descend from heaven" (αὐτὸς ὁ κύριος ἐν κελεύσματι ... καταβήσεται; 1 Thess 4:16); he shall come "with all his holy ones" (i.e., "his angels"; 1 Thess 3:13), "revealed from heaven with the angels of his power" (2 Thess 1:7; cf. Matt 25:31; Mark 8:38). Paul also believes that the *parousia* will involve the resurrection of the saints with whom the living saints will be "snatched," "seized," or "caught" away (ἁρπάζω) into the clouds to meet (ἀπάντησιν) Jesus in the air (1 Thess 4:13–17).[27]

Given the broader cultural context regarding the visit of dignitaries,[28] and by its very nature, this statement implies a meeting *to welcome* rather than a meeting *to be whisked away*.[29] In relation to the Eschatological Discourse, the motif of ἁρπάζω in 1 Thess 4:17 most likely represents Paul's version or interpretation of παραλαμβάνω in Matt 24:40–41. Although lexically different, the two terms resonate semantically as the "taking" of saints

---

23. See Keener, *Bible Background*, 590.

24. See Orchard, "Thessalonians"; Waterman, "Source of Paul's Teaching"; Wenham, *Rediscovery*, 365, 369–70; Wenham, "Paul and the Synoptic Apocalypse," 2:345–75; Witherington, *Problem with Evangelical Theology*, 117.

25. Carson, "Matthew," 549.

26. See chapter 5, pp. 177–82.

27. The phrase, ἄξει σὺν αὐτῷ ("he shall bring with him"), in v. 14 is explicated in v. 16 as the raising of saints from the dead, not the bringing of them with Jesus from heaven; these saints are said to be asleep in death (vv. 13, 14, 15).

28. See nn. 295 and 571 in chapter 5.

29. As Brown and Keener succinctly put it, "Jesus does not meet us on our way up to heaven; rather, we meet him on his way down to rule the earth" (*Not Afraid of the Antichrist*, 149).

to meet with Jesus.³⁰ Once this is granted, it becomes clear, in light of the interpretation laid out in chapter 5, that 1 Thess 4:17a is an abbreviation of the earthward *parousia* journey of Jesus. In other words, the silence in the statement regarding where the saints are taken to after meeting Jesus in the air is supplied by the fullness of the eschatological schema of Matt 24–25: the saints are caught away/taken to meet the descending Son of Man in the air, and from there the journey continues downward to the great assize described in Matt 25:31–46.³¹ Against the popular rapture theory based on 1 Thess 4:16–17, if the saints were to be secretly removed from earth to heaven, it would make no sense for the Lord *himself* to descend from heaven in a personal and visible way, as Paul says, in order to do that. And it would be pointless to say that the Lord *himself will descend* if he will be invisible.

Second, although Paul may use the term tribulation (θλῖψις) more broadly at times, in many of the instances, and as already clear in Acts 14:22, the term denotes the routine tribulation that believers experience till the end of the age.³² Accordingly, while believers will not be subject to God's *wrath* (ὀργή), that is, the eternal condemnation of the wicked (1 Thess 5:9),³³ they are not exempt from *tribulation* (θλῖψις).³⁴ This is also clear from 2 Thess 1:4–7 where Paul says that the increasing faith and love of the Thessalonians in the midst of the tribulations and persecutions which they endure is "evidence" (ἔνδειγμα) of God's righteous judgment in order that they might be counted worthy of the kingdom of God.³⁵ Paul goes on to say that

30. Contra Witherington, *Matthew*, 455, and many others who view the latter term in terms of judgment; cf. Keener, *Matthew*, 591–92. Witherington had previously emphasized the parallel between 1 Thess 4:16—5:7 and Matt 24:30–49, especially giving Matt 24:31, 40–41//1 Thess 4:17 the title, "believers gathered to Christ" (*Problem with Evangelical Theology*, 117; cf. Witherington, *Jesus, Paul and End*, 159–60).

31. This is also verified by the fact that the *gathering* (ἐπισυναγωγή; cf. chapter 5, pp. 206–9) of saints to Jesus and his "destroying of the man of lawlessness who takes seat in the temple of God" takes place consecutively during the same *parousia* event (2 Thess 2:1, 8). If he will thus destroy him at his *parousia*, certainly there cannot be an Antichrist-driven post-rapture Great Tribulation.

32. Cf. Rom 8:35; 12:12; 2 Cor 1:4, 8; 4:17; 6:4–6; 7:4; 8:2; Eph 3:13; 1 Thess 1:6; 3:3, 7; 2 Thess 1:4.

33. This verse sets up a contrast between ὀργή (wrath) and σωτηρία (salvation), indicating that while the latter means eternal salvation, the former means eternal damnation; cf. Brown and Keener, *Not Afraid of the Antichrist*, 123–26.

34. The two terms, wrath and tribulation, must be distinguished. Fee, *First and Second Thessalonians*, 50n89, states that the failure "to distinguish between these two terms . . . was one of the great failings of historic Dispensationalism."

35. Cf. Phil 1:28–29. Opinions vary on what element in the passage the term ἔνδειγμα specifically refers to. One widely held view is that the believers' afflictions themselves are the evidence of God's righteous judgment understood in light of

they will be granted "rest" (ἄνεσιν) from these tribulations, *not escape*, "at the revelation of the Lord Jesus from heaven with his mighty angels" (ἐν τῇ ἀποκαλύψει τοῦ κυρίου Ἰησοῦ ἀπ' οὐρανοῦ μετ' ἀγγέλων δυνάμεως αὐτοῦ). In other words, Paul believes that the end-time tribulations were already in progress and will last until Jesus' *parousia*. Even "the mystery of lawlessness" (μυστήριον . . . τῆς ἀνομίας) is already at work (2 Thess 2:7) as a necessary prelude to the *parousia*.

Third, for Paul, the kingdom of God is both present[36] and future[37] within the overarching temporal dualism of "present age"[38] and the "age to come."[39] The "end of the ages" in 1 Cor 10:17 should be taken as reference to the "last of all past ages."[40] Paul can also speak of all ages without present-future differentiation (1 Tim 1:17). Overall, he shares the temporal dualism implied in the Eschatological Discourse and evident in the Synoptic Gospels as a whole. It needs to be pointed out that, like the synoptics, Paul lacks any notion of a distinct future millennium intervening between the present age and the age to come. On the contrary, in echoing the notion of Jesus' vindication that we see in Matthew's Eschatological Discourse (cf. Matt 28:18), he views Jesus as already reigning as Universal King, a reign that will continue until *the end* (τὸ τέλος) when all his enemies are defeated and the kingdom (the age to come) is once and for all turned over to the Father (1 Cor 15:24).[41]

One challenging difference between Paul and the Matthean Eschatological Discourse might relate to the meaning of 2 Thessalonians, especially the identity or referent of the "man of lawlessness" who shall take his seat in the temple of God (2 Thess 2:1–12). What "temple of God" does Paul have in mind in v. 4 (if a future rebuilt temple is unlikely)? And to whom does this "man of lawlessness" refer? Paul says that "the Lord will slay him with the breath of his mouth and destroy him by the appearing of his *parousia*" (v. 8). If the letter was written before the fall of the temple in 70 CE as is most likely,[42] does this not mean that the *parousia* either happened in the past in connection with that event, is that event (hence the hyper-preterist

---

contemporary Jewish suffering theology, e.g., Bassler, "Enigmatic Sign."

36. Cf. Rom 14:17; 1 Cor 4:20; Col 1:13; 1 Thess 2:12.

37. Cf. 1 Cor 6:9–10; 15:50; Gal 5:21; Eph 5:5; 2 Thess 1:5; 2 Tim 4:1, 18; Acts 14:22.

38. Cf. Rom 12:2; 1 Cor 1:20; 2:6, 8; 3:18; 2 Cor 4:4; Gal 1:4; Eph 1:21; 2:2; 1 Tim 6:17; 2 Tim 4:10, 18; Titus 2:12.

39. Cf. Eph 1:21; 2:7.

40. Cf. Eph 3:9; Col 1:26.

41. Cf. Matt 24:3c, 14.

42. 2:4 appears almost an impossible statement after the temple was no more. See Witherington, *1 and 2 Thessalonians*, 12–13.

view), or failed to happen at all, in which case, both Jesus and Paul would have been wrong?

As I have argued earlier, the hyper-preterist view here would still be unlikely since no incident, including Caligula (whose failed assault on the temple Paul would have known) and Titus, fulfills the role of the "man of lawlessness" in 2 Thess 2:4. In fact, although these are legitimate questions, for 2 Thess 2:1–12 to constitute a problem for or deviation from the overall unity in eschatological view argued here, it must be proven that the same scenario as the Eschatological Discourse is necessarily being described.

Given Paul's gentile audience, as well as his redefinition of the "temple of God" in terms of the church,[43] it cannot be taken for granted that by "temple of God" in 2 Thess 2:4, he intends them to understand the temple of Jerusalem.[44] Nor should Paul's "man of lawlessness" or antichrist be equated with the "abomination of desolation" in Daniel/the Eschatological Discourse,[45] although the latter has inspired the Pauline tradition. The identity of the "man of lawlessness" would require a different investigation. But in the final analysis, it is not likely that any harm will be done to the broad eschatological unity demonstrated above when all the details are known and factored in.[46]

Diversity and Unity between Matt 24–25 and the Petrine Corpus

Eschatology is a significant theme in both 1 and 2 Pet. In the former, Peter encourages believers facing or on the verge of a fiery trial.[47] Unlike the Eschatological Discourse, 1 Pet does not use the word θλῖψις (tribulation),[48] but the term ποικίλοις πειρασμοῖς ("various trials"; 1:6) has a similar sense in context. Peter believes that the present time (in his day) is already within the end of the age (1:20); "the end of all things," he declares, "has drawn near" (4:7). The present "suffering," a prominent theme in the letter,[49] is in a sense

---

43. 1 Cor 3:16, 17; 6:19; 2 Cor 6:16; Eph 2:21 (cf. John 2:19, 21; Rev 3:12).

44. See Beale, *1 and 2 Thessalonians*, 207–8. For an overview of the debates, see Johnson, "Paul's 'Anti-Christology,'" n23.

45. See 156–71, esp. 161–69.

46. Certain that by "temple of God" in 2:4, Paul means the Jerusalem temple, Witherington, *1 and 2 Thessalonians*, 12, 212, reflects on how Paul would have rationalized the event of the day in relation to the second coming.

47. 1 Pet 1:6, 4:1, 12; 17–19.

48. Nor does 2 Pet.

49. 1:6; 4:12 (πειρασμός); 1:11; 4:13; 5:1, 9 (πάθημα).

part of the eschatological woes or judgments heralding the end of the age; the time was already ripe for judgment to begin "from the house of God" (4:17).[50] However, the believers' fiery trials will result in praise, glory, and honor at the *revelation* (ἀποκάλυψις) of Jesus Christ, that is, the *parousia* (1:7; cf. 4:13; 5:1). This comports with the eschatological notion in Matt 24–25 that followers of Jesus will go through tribulation until the end.

In 2 Pet, eschatology is introduced as "part of the [author's] ongoing argument about ethical and immoral living."[51] Juza offers a helpful discussion on the subject, especially in relation to the destiny of the cosmos.[52] Second Pet appears to lean more toward a literal fiery dissolution of the cosmos than appears to be the case in the Eschatological Discourse (or elsewhere[53]). Whereas in the latter, the heavens are shaken, so that (as I think) the celestial bodies lose their light, and the stars fall,[54] the present heavens and earth, the author of 2 Peter says, are stored up for conflagration on the day of judgment. Even the very elements (στοιχεῖα) of the heavens will be dissolved by fire (2 Pet 3:7,10).[55] I believe our author here employs extreme hyperbolism.[56] But such a description makes rhetorical sense given 2 Peter's overarching aim to persuade radical ethic of faith-righteousness (1:1; 3:11, 14).

The important point to make, however, is that the eschatology portrayed in 2 Peter remains within the broad outline known from the Synoptics and Paul.[57] The power of Jesus is already in operation in the present age (1:3,16); and the fact that the prophetic word is already "as a lamp shinning in a dark place" (1:19), might suggest ongoing opposition to the gospel, even suffering for Christians (cf. 2:9). Yet the future coming of Jesus and the full realization of his kingdom remains certain despite insinuations by certain mockers to the contrary (1:16; 3:3–5).

Significantly, 2 Peter is neither aware of believers being flown into heaven to be with Jesus there,[58] nor of some transitional future earthly mil-

---

50. See Dubis, *Messianic Woes*.

51. Reese, *2 Peter and Jude*, 190.

52. Juza, *New Testament*, 205–47.

53. Although see similar motifs in Mark 9:49; Luke 12:49; Heb 10:27; 12:29.

54. Cf. Heb 12:26–27.

55. Some favor stoic philosophy as the source of this language, while others favor Jewish apocalyptic; see Juza, *New Testament*, 210–14.

56. Cf. Matt 24:2; Jesus predicts the destruction of every stone, but the actual event left some stones intact; see Keeener, *Matthew*, 562.

57. Juza, *New Testament*, 214, highlights the author's familiarity "with Paul (3:15–16), the Jesus tradition (e.g., 1:16–18; 2:20; 3:10a), the flood tradition (2:5; 3:6), and the tradition of the watchers (2:4)."

58. The idea of rescuing the godly out of trial in 2:9 is better understood in terms of

lennium. Rather, the hope of Christians is τὴν αἰώνιον βασιλείαν τοῦ κυρίου ἡμῶν ("the eternal kingdom of our Lord," 1:11) ushered in at his *parousia* when he will execute the final judgment (cf. Matt 25:31-46). In 2 Peter, the Day of the Lord is the day of Jesus' *parousia*. It will come like a thief (cf. Matt 24:43); and on that day the entire cosmos and the ungodly will be judged (3:7, 10), leading immediately to the age to come, the eternal state. The author of 2 Peter is clear and specific about the Christian expectation. "According to his promise," he declares, "we wait (not for some time in heaven or some intermediate kingdom on earth but) for new heavens and a new earth in which righteousness dwells" (3:13).

Diversity and Unity between Matt 24– 25 and the Johannine Corpus

Striking diversities, including structural, theological and/or stylistic diversities, exist both between John's Gospel and the Synoptics and within the "Johannine corpus" as a whole.[59] Strauss and Dodd promoted the notion that John's Gospel consists of a completely realized eschatology.[60] Consequently, most contemporary scholars consider the book of Revelation to be too futuristic to have been written by the same author as John's Gospel/ letters,[61] although some have argued that the Apocalypse concerns events all fulfilled in the first century, especially the fall of Jerusalem.[62] None of these claims seems to be consistent with the data.[63] Again, I will focus on

---

deliverance *through* trial than *escape* or avoidance of it.

59. I use "Johannine corpus" broadly to refer to NT writings attributed to or claimed to be written by "John," including the book of Revelation.

60. Strauss viewed the Fourth Gospel as a theological invention which is both inferior to and irreconcilable with the Synoptic Gospels, claiming that while not unacquainted with eschatology, John has deliberately spiritualized it; see Schweitzer, *Quest*, 84–87. According to Dodd, "In the Fourth Gospel, the crudely eschatological elements in the *kerygma* are quite refined away . . . [the] promise of a second coming is realized in the presence of the Paraclete, the Holy Spirit, in the life of the Church. . . . The evangelist, therefore, is deliberately subordinating the 'futurist' element in the eschatology of the early Church to the 'realized eschatology'" (*Apostolic Preaching*, 65–66).

61. See discussion in Carson and Moo, *Introduction*, 702–7.

62. Revelation, it is claimed, was written pre-70, before the destruction of the temple and during the reign of Nero, e.g., DeMar, *Last Days Madness*, 21, 388, 390. Revelation 11:1–3 might seem to support this, but John is capable of re-appropriating "temple" language/custom for a new reality. See Rev 3:12 where "the temple of my God" is linked with "the city of my God" defined as "the new Jerusalem" (cf. John 2:19, 21); see Beale, *Revelation*, 557–65.

63. Apart from the observation in n58 above, many other factors (external and

the eschatological themes of *parousia*, tribulation, and temporal dualism to show that a common eschatological view exists not only within the Johannine corpus but also with the rest of the NT as surveyed above.

First, Jesus teaches in John's Gospel that judgment has already taken place (3:18), and that those who believe in him have already obtained eternal life, having passed from death to life (John 5:24–25; 6:47, 54; 10:28; 17:3). As such, the kingdom of God has broken into the present and can be entered into through new birth (3:5). However, this does not imply a lack of or even the subordination of the unrealized or future eschatology in John. On the contrary, in relation to the subject of *parousia*, Jesus speaks also of the *coming hour* "in the last day" (τῇ ἐσχάτῃ ἡμέρᾳ) when the dead will be raised to inherit either eternal life or be condemned (5:28–29; 6:39–40, 54; 12:48).[64] Jesus' "realized" response to Mattha's "futurist" hope in 11:24–26 represents neither the rejection nor the subordination of future eschatology.[65] In 21:22–23, Jesus answers Peter's inquiry regarding the beloved disciples by implying a future second coming. This balances off any such notion of rejection or subordination of apocalyptic eschatology in John.

As in Mark and Luke, the term *parousia* does not occur in the Fourth Gospel. Nor does it occur in the book of Revelation for that matter. However, it is used to refer explicitly to the second coming in the First Johannine Letter (2:28), a letter in which eternal life is both a present reality (5:11, 13) and a future promise to be received in connection with the second coming (2:25, 28).

Turning to Revelation (1:4, 8; 4:8), Jesus is "the one who is to come" (ὁ ἐρχόμενος). This identification covers three aspects of Jesus' coming.[66] The first aspect is a *spiritual* always-imminent coming. Jesus is already at the door and will enter in with his people for eucharistic fellowship and blessing

---

internal) argue against the early date. E.g., it would seem unlikely that a pre-70 author of Revelation would have equated Rome with Babylon. Most likely, Rome is seen as a type of the ancient Babylon in relation to the destruction of the temple of Jerusalem. In other words, Rome's destruction of Jerusalem must have already happened to evoke such a cryptic namesake. Based on the more widely held late date (90s), it is my considered opinion that Revelation draws together events that are (1) already history or in progress (Rev 12), (2) envisaged in the near future (1:1), and (3) remain for the end of time (20:11—21:1–5). Like what we have in Matt 24–25 (Jerusalem and *parousia*), and in the character of "prophetic perspective," it foresees God's judgment on Rome (as the triumph of Jesus and the vindication of Christians who suffer under its tyranny) held in relation to the *parousia* and ultimate end of history.

64. See Cullmann, *Christ and Time*, 89; contra Bultmann, *History and Eschatology*, 47.

65. Contra Bultmann, *History and Eschatology*, 48; Dodd, *Apostolic Preaching*, 66.

66. Notice how DeMar fails to consider the nuances of the "coming quickly" theme in Revelation (*Last Days Madness*, 40–41, 72, 206, 217, 358–59).

(3:20; cf. John 14:23).⁶⁷ The second aspect is a *symbolic* coming in the form of judgment. Accordingly, he warns the churches, especially Ephesus and Pergamum (2:5,16; 3:11), that he will come to them "quickly" (ταχύς) for judgment if they fail to repent.⁶⁸ This coming "quickly" relates to the broader coming for the judgment of Babylon (=Rome),⁶⁹ but certain preliminary judgments are expected to "arrive" or "come quickly" (9:12; 11:14). In due time, Jesus' time to judge Babylon came (14:7-8); and in an hour Babylon's judgment came (18:10). The expressions, "things that must happen quickly/soon" (1:1; 22:6), "I am coming quickly/soon" (22:7, 12, 20), and "the appointed time is 'near'" (ἐγγύς; 22:10) must be interpreted in relation to these two aspects of "coming."

But following this coming "quickly" (which will ultimately culminate in the eventual judgment of Rome) and preceded by a "1000-year" reign (20:1-10), is the third aspect of Jesus' coming, the *second coming* or *parousia* (20:11-15). Initially described in 1:7 (cf. Matt 24:30), this "coming" corresponds to the time of final judgment and eternal reward (11:18b), and it is likely the event described as "coming like a thief" in 16:15 (cf. Matt. 24:43).⁷⁰

Before leaving this *parousia* motif in the Johannine corpus, it is important to step back and comment on John 14:2-3. Jesus' words, "In my Father's *house* are many *rooms*,⁷¹ I go to prepare a place for you," and the promise that he would come again to take his followers to himself, are uncritically taken to refer to Jesus' second coming or his going to heaven and coming back to rapture the church. But this is a severe misreading of the passage. It should be observed that the passage belongs to the broader context of Jesus' *Paterological 'Discourse'* (chs. 14-16).⁷² Consistent with this context, John

---

67. This may thus be called "eucharistic coming" (cf. Cullmann, *Christ and Time*, 74).

68. The term ταχύς means "quickly," "in a relatively short time," or "soon" with emphasis on speed; see BDAG, "ταχύς," 993. There appears to be lacking any need to distinguish between the notions of manner ("quickly") and time ("soon") in the term as Thomas Ice does in Ice and Gentry, *Great Tribulation*, 107-14.

69. Cf. 4 Ezra 3:28, 32; 2 Baruch 11:1.

70. Although this "thief" motif can also apply to the other aspects of "coming." Apocalyptic symbols or motifs are not monovalent, having the same referent always. For a similar but inconclusive take on the aspects of coming identified here, see Gregg, *Revelation*, 23-26.

71. So RSV, NIB, NIV, NIRV, NLT; contra KJV's "mansions." On the problem with translating μονή as "mansion," see Whitacre, *John*, 348-49, although he still misses the point of the passage as a whole—correctly rejecting the notion of a materialistic heaven but maintaining the second coming interpretation.

72. I use the term "paterological" (from πατήρ = father) to indicate what the discourse is about. Thirty percent of the word "father" as a reference to God by Jesus in John's Gospel occurs here, although the section is often called "farewell discourse," a

14:2-3 must be interpreted in light of Jesus' explanation in 16:25—Ταῦτα ἐν παροιμίαις λελάληκα ὑμῖν ("these things I have spoken to you in figurative language").

This is not to imply that everything Jesus says in chs. 14-16 is a parable or metaphor, only that much of the "going-to-the-Father" language is figurative. Jesus would further explain this in terms of a painful but brief absence that will result in joy (16:16-22) and in connection with "that day" (ἐκείνῃ τῇ ἡμέρᾳ) when the disciples will begin to pray to the Father in Jesus' name (16:23-26). While leaving the world and going to the Father is said to make plain sense to the disciples in 16:28-29, the expression "that day" here can only refer to Jesus' resurrection, not to be separated from his ascension to the Father.

Furthermore, the words, "in my Father's house" (14:2) echoes Jesus' earlier reference to the temple as "my Father's house" and to himself as its replacement (2:16, 19).[73] Read in these connections, 14:2-3 is a figurative reference to Jesus' imminent death and resurrection/ascension ("temple destroyed and rebuilt = prepared") by which he would purchase for his followers a place in himself in relation to the Father. This means that the motif of being where Jesus is in 14:3b is a relational rather than a topographical one.[74] In other words, Jesus himself (not some material "place") is the Father's house fully prepared through death and resurrection/ascension to accommodate the disciples in his intimacy with the Father. This is also why he would go ahead in 17:15 to say: "I do not pray that you take them out of the world, but that *you may keep them from* (τηρήσῃς αὐτοὺς ἐκ) the evil [one]."

This then leads us to consider the motif of tribulation. The interpretation offered in Matt 24-25 regarding the tribulation as the characteristic of all the period until Jesus' *parousia* is supported by Jesus' clear warning and consolation in John 16:33—"in this world you will have tribulation (θλῖψιν), but take courage, I have overcome the world" (cf. 16:2). John believes that the tribulation is already in progress, and the antichrist is already in the world (1 John 2:18, 22; 4:3; 2 John 1:7). When we come to the book of Revelation, we find that everyone in heaven got there through the "great tribulation" (7:14).[75] The promise, "*I will keep you from* (σε τηρήσω ἐκ) the hour of trial" in 3:10 is, in light of 3:12 (which encourages *overcoming*), a promise of *preservation through* rather than *escape from* tribulation (cf. John 17:15).

---

designation which says nothing about the passage.

73. See Keener, *John*, 2:936.

74. Cf. vv. 10, 11; 17:24.

75. Evoking the events associated with the fall of Jerusalem, by "great tribulation" is meant the ordeal of Christians under Rome ("mystery Babylon the great, ἡ μήτηρ τῶν πορνῶν καὶ τῶν βδελυγμάτων τῆς γῆς" [Rev 17:5]).

Moreover, Rev 3:10 is a promise specifically to the church in Philadelphia. Thus, there is no cogent basis in the Johannine corpus for the view that the church will be whisked away from the earth to avoid [the] tribulation. Nowhere does John's Apocalypse envision such a thing either explicitly or implicitly, either allegorically or chronologically.[76]

Finally, on the motif of temporal dualism, it would appear that rather than two ages—the present age, and the age to come—the book of Revelation teaches a three-age temporal schema—the present age, the millennial (1000-year) age (20:4–6), and the eternal state. This may appear to represent a divergence from what we have seen so far in the Synoptics, Pauline, and Petrine letters. However, such a three-age schema would be too curious an exception in the NT in particular; it would seem to be uncharacteristic of the apocalyptic thought in general. Such a view would also ignore the mostly symbolic nature of apocalyptic numerology.

Viewed correctly, in light of the comments above on the "coming" theme in Revelation, the millennium about which Rev 20:6 speaks is neither a period beginning at the birth or resurrection of Jesus until the *parousia*, nor one that will follow the *parousia*.[77] Rather, from John's point of view, it is the apocalyptically envisioned indefinite duration between the judgment of Rome and the *parousia*.[78] In other words, Revelation's "millennium" is the post-Rome continuation of "the present age," while "the age to come" is described as that new heaven and new earth that will commence with the *parousia* after Jesus has judged and rid the world of all evil as depicted in 20:11—21:1–5. This agrees with the fact that in Matt 25:31–46 when Jesus arrives in *parousia* and judges the nations, what follows is the eternal state—eternal life or eternal punishment—not an intervening temporary millennial kingdom.

General Conclusions and Implications

The result of the correlation exercise above shows that despite differences in details, the eschatology of Matt 24–25, as interpreted, is consistent with the view reflected in the NT as a whole. The NT passages surveyed in the

---

76. Contra LaHaye, *Revelation*, 100. He is aware that the "The Rapture of the Church is not explicitly taught in Revelation 4," yet claims, "but [it] definitely appears here chronologically at the end of the Church Age."

77. For discussions on these and other views, see Gregg, *Revelation*, 27–34; Bock, *Three Views*; Blomberg and Chung, *Case for Historic Premillennialism*; Riddlebarger, *Case for Amillennialism*, 13–45; Schwarz, *Eschatology*, 331–37.

78. This may be designated "revised amillennial view."

correlation will require specific and more extended investigations. But when such is carried out, giving due attention to the text over against the interpreters settled tradition, and properly accounting for the specific contexts and goals of the biblical authors, it seems unlikely that an eschatological schema quite contrary to the one reflected in Matt 24–25 will emerge.

In sum, apart from structurally functioning to complete the "Divine Royal" portrait of Jesus that Matthew is centrally aimed at, the Matthean Eschatological Discourse reflect three important keystones of NT eschatology. The first keystone is that all of history, from the time Jesus gave the Discourse until the end, will be a time of *tribulations*. Within this spectrum of time, and from the present point of view, the Great Tribulation, referring to the events surrounding the fall of Jerusalem in 70 CE, is past. But as Matt 24–25 envisions, the followers of Jesus will experience tribulations through the course of their proclamation of the gospel of Jesus the Son of God and Universal Judge-King. NT writers believed they were already living in the time of eschatological judgments or woes, and the church of Jesus Christ has always experienced times of tribulation, some sever and others mild. Jesus makes it clear that while no tribulation will ever be like the one associated with the destruction of the Jerusalem temple, tribulations will continue until the end. Even so, the present time is a time of tribulation. In relation to the indefinite time, Jesus further declares that it is those who endure (not those who escape) the tribulation till the end that will be saved.

The second element of the eschatology of Matt 24–25 is that the *parousia* can happen at any time, but that time will remain unknown. Much eschatological prognostications and permutations have continued in recent times. They have always failed and will continue to fail. There is no biblical key for decoding the time of the *parousia*. As Jesus says, only God the Father can determine when the proclamation of the gospel to the whole world according to Matt 24:14 is fulfilled, or indeed when the end of the tribulations has come. At the end of present time of tribulations, the *parousia* will take place, the saints will be gathered to meet and welcome Jesus to earth. Contrary to the common rapture theology, the *parousia* will be the Lord's home-coming not the saints' flight away from the earth. He will come to judge the nations, to finally rid the earth of evil, and to usher in the fullest manifestation of God's eternal kingdom, as both 2 Peter and Revelation describe it, the new heaven and the new earth.

The third element of the eschatology of Matt 24–25 is *temporal dualism*—the present age versus the eternal age to come. Insofar as the judgment of Matt 25:31–46 is universal and leads to either eternal life or eternal punishment, it implies that there is no such period as an intermediary earthly millennium during which, as some teach, an Israel-specific kingdom will be established and the promise of God to Israel is fulfilled. On the contrary, the findings in this study verify the view that Jesus has fulfilled Israel's hope; he already reigns as the Son of God and Universal King; he has already poured out the Spirit. As far as Matthew and Jesus are concerned, unbelieving Israel has been *ethnos*ized—merged with the nations. Consequently, they are subject to evangelism and discipleship in the present. In Matt 25:31–46, the sheep—those on the right hand—are also the elects of God, consisting of both Jews and gentiles. There is no warrant in the Eschatological Discourse for either a secret pre-tribulation rapture of the church or such Israel-church distinction that pervades popular eschatological thinking.

Appendix 1

My Diagrammatical Representation of Carson's Structure of Matt 24

(Numbers are verses of Matt 24)

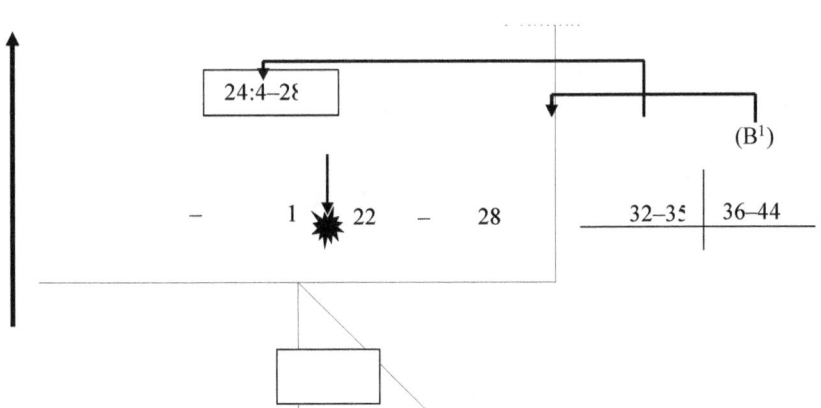

Appendix 2

Comparative Analysis of Matt 2:19—4:18[1]

	Matt 2—3:1	Matt 4:1–18	
2:19–21	- Herod dies ("leaves him") - Angel ministry	- Satan departs ("leaves him") - Angel ministry	4:11

2:22–23	(*Subject infered = some continuity*)
	- Ἀκούσας δὲ ὅτι…
	    → (+Disc. +Dev.)
	- Relocation to Galilee
	- Move to Nazareth
	- Fulfillment formula
		(*Subject infered = some continuity*)
		- Ἀκούσας δὲ ὅτι…
		    → (+Disc. +Dev.)
		- Relocation to Galilee
		- Move to Nazareth & to Capernaum
		- Fulfillment formula
			4:12–16

xxxxxx	xxxxxxxxxxxxxxxxxxxxxxxx	(*Explicit re-entry of subject*) Ø Ἀπὸ τότε ἤρξατο ὁ Ἰησοῦς κηρύσσειν	4:17
3:1	(*Entry of new subject*) Ἐν δὲ ταῖς ἡμέραις ἐκείναις……… Ἰωάννης ὁ βαπτιστὴς → (+Disc.> +Dev.)	(*Subject infered, proclamation theme dev.*) Περιπατῶν δὲ παρὰ τὴν θάλασσαν τῆς Γαλιλαίας εἶδεν………… κηρύσσων (Mat 4:23) → (+Disc. +Dev.)	4:18

1. Notes: (1) At the minimum, the similarity between 2:19—3:1 and 4:11–16

implies that they should be held together. (2) The use of δὲ in 3:1 signals a high-level discontinuity but not a whole-book division since such division would make John the Baptist more prominent for the entire book than the implied author intends. (3) The parallel between 2:22 and 4:12 involves discontinuity but also some significant degree of continuity since the subject must be inferred from what precedes. (4) In light of 3:1, a case can be made for the ministry of Jesus beginning in 4:18. However, 4:18 has two points of connection to 4:17—the explicit subject and the theme of proclamation (4:23). Therefore, 4:18 is better taken as a development of v. 17 moving forward. Thus, there is more continuity between v. 17 and v. 18 than there is between in 3:1 and what precedes. (5) The asyndetic conjunction in 4:17 appears to relate to what follows than to what precedes. (6) 4:17 has no parallel in chs. 2–3:1, making it unique and therefore a conspicuous and memorable point of departure; the clause stands almost like a topical heading for what follows, and the implied reader will most likely hear it so.

Appendix 3

Proposed Structure of Matthew[1]

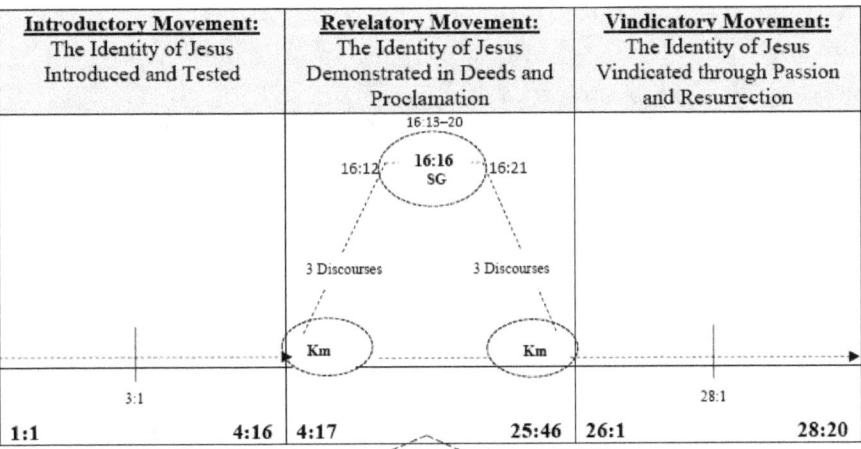

N^t (4:17–25); **D^1** (5:1–7:28); N (8:1–9:34); **D^2** (9:35–10:42); N (11:1–12:50); **D^2** (13:1–52); N (13:53–16:12); **H (16:13–20)**; N (16:21–17:27); **D^4** (18:1–35); N (19:1–22:48); **D^5** (23:1–39); N^t (24:1–2); **D^6** (24:3–25:46);

---

1. Nt = short transitional narrative; N = Narrative; D1–6 = Discourses; H = Hinge passage; SG = Son of God; Km = Kingdom motif opening (4:17) and closing (25:31–46).

Appendix 4

Salvation-Historical Outline Arising from the Interpretation of Matt 24–25

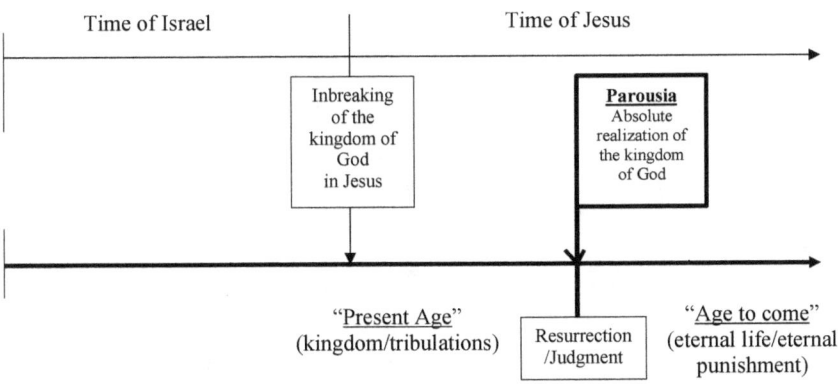

Bibliography

Adams, Edward. *The Stars Will Fall from Heaven: Cosmic Catastrophe in the New Testament and Its World*. London: T. & T. Clark, 2007.
Alford, Henry. *Alford's Greek Testament: An Exegetical and Critical Commentary*. Grand Rapids: Guardian, 1976.
Allen, Willoughby C., and L. W. Grensted. *Introduction to the Books of the New Testament*. 3rd ed. Edinburgh: T. & T. Clark, 1929.
Allison, Dale C., Jr. "Apocalyptic." In *DJG*, edited by Joel B. Green et al., 17–20. Downers Grove, IL: InterVarsity, 1992.
———. *The End of the Ages Has Come: An Early Interpretation of the Passion and Resurrection of Jesus*. Eugene, OR: Wipf & Stock, 1985.
———. "Jesus and the Victory of Apocalyptic." In *Jesus & the Restoration of Israel: A Critical Assessment of N.T. Wright's Jesus and the Victory of God*, edited by Carey C. Newman, 126–41. Downers Grove, IL: InterVarsity, 1999.
———. *Jesus of Nazareth: Millenarian Prophet*. Minneapolis, MN: Fortress, 1998.
———. "Matt. 23:39 = Luke 13:35b as a Conditional Prophecy." *JSNT* 18 (1983) 75–84.
———. *The New Moses: A Matthean Typology*. Minneapolis, MN: Fortress, 993.
———. "A Plea for Thoroughgoing Eschatology." *JBL* 113 (1994) 615–68.
———. "The Structure of the Sermon on the Mount." *JBL* 106 (1987) 423–45.
Agbanou, Victor Kossi. *Le Discours Eschatologique de Matthieu 24–25: Tradition et Rédaction*, EBib 2. Paris: Lecoffre, 1983.
Aquinas, Thomas. *Commentary on the Four Gospels: St. Matthew*. Oxford: James Parker and Co, 1874.
Arthur, Green, ed. *Jewish Spirituality for the Bible through the Middle Ages*. New York: Crossroad, 1986.
Aune, David E. "The Apocalypse of John and the Problem of Genre." *Semeia* 36 (1986) 13–96.
———. *Apocalypticism, Prophecy, and Magic in Early Christianity: Collected Essays*. Grand Rapids: Baker Academic, 2008.
———. "Greco-Roman Biography." In *Greco-Roman Literature and the New Testament: Selected Forms and Genres*, edited by D. E. Aune, 107–26. SBLSBS 21. Atlanta: Scholars, 1988.
———. *The New Testament in Its Literary Environment*. Philadelphia: Westminster, 1987.

———. *The Westminster Dictionary of New Testament and Early Christian Literature and Rhetoric.* Louisville: Westminster John Knox, 2010.
Bacon, Benjamin W. "The 'Five Books' of Moses against the Jews." *Exp* 15 (1918) 56–66.
———. *Studies in Matthew.* New York: Holt, 1930.
Balabanski, Vicky. *Eschatology in the Making: Mark, Matthew, and the Didache.* SNTSMS 97. Cambridge: Cambridge University Press, 2005.
———. "Mission in Mission." *NTS* 54 (2008) 161–75.
Barbieri, Louis A., Jr. "Matthew." In *The Bible Knowledge Commentary,* edited by John F. Walvoord and Roy B. Zuck, 76–81. NT Edition. Wheaton, IL: Victor, 1983.
Barclay, J. M. G. "Mirror-Reading a Polemical Letter: Galatians as a Test Case." *JSNT* 31 (1987) 73–93.
Barthes, Roland. *La mort de L'auteur.* https://www.ubu.com/aspen/aspen5and6/threeEssays.html#barthes.
Bauckham, Richard J., ed. *The Gospel for All Christians: Rethinking the Gospel Audiences.* Grand Rapids: Eerdmans, 1998.
———. *Jesus and the Eyewitnesses.* 2nd ed. Grand Rapids: Eerdmans, 2017.
———. "The Rise of Apocalyptic." *Themelios* 3 (1977) 10–23.
Bauer, David R. *The Gospel of the Son of God: An Introduction to Matthew.* Downers Grove, IL: InterVarsity, 2019.
———. *The Structure of Matthew's Gospel: A Study in Literary Design.* JSNTSup 31. Sheffield, UK: Almond, 1988.
Bauer, David R., and Robert A. Traina. *Inductive Bible Study: A Comprehensive Guide to the Practice of Hermeneutics.* Grand Rapids: Baker, 2011.
Baur, Ferdinand Christian. *Lectures on New Testament Theology.* Edited by Peter C. Hodgson. Translated by Robert F. Brown. Oxford: Oxford University Press, 2016.
Baxter, Wayne S. "Mosaic Imageries in the Gospel of Matthew." *TJ* 20 (1999) 69–83.
Beale, G. K. *1 and 2 Thessalonians.* Downers Grove, IL: InterVarsity, 2003.
———. *The Book of Revelation.* NIGTC. Grand Rapids: Eerdmans, 1999.
———. *Handbook on the New Testament Use of the Old Testament: Exegesis and Interpretation.* Grand Rapids: Baker, 2012.
Beardslee, William A. "New Testament Apocalyptic in Recent Interpretation." *Int* 25 (1971) 419–35.
Beare, Francis W. *The Gospel according to Matthew: Translation, Introduction, and Commentary.* Peabody, MD: Hendrickson, 1981.
———. "The Synoptic Apocalypse: Matthean Version." In *Understanding the Sacred Text: Essays in Honor of Morton S. Enslin on the Hebrew Bible and the Christian Beginnings,* edited by John Reumann, 115–33. Valley Forge, PA: Judson, 1972.
Beasley-Murray, G. R. *A Commentary on Mark Thirteen.* London: Macmillan, 1957.
———. *Jesus and the Kingdom of God.* Grand Rapids: Eerdmans, 1986.
———. *Jesus and the Last Days: The Interpretation of the Olivet Discourse.* Peabody, MD: Hendrickson, 1993.
Bassler, Jouette M. "The Enigmatic Sign: 2 Thessalonians 1:5." *CBQ* 46 (1984) 496–510.
Bendoraitis, Kristian. "Apocalypticism, Angels, and Matthew." In *The Jewish Apocalyptic Tradition and the Shaping of the New Testament Thought,* edited by Benjamin E. Reynolds and Loren T. Stuckenbruck, 31–51. Minneapolis, MN: Fortress, 2017.
Bengel, John A. *Bengel's New Testament Commentary.* Translated by Charlton T. Lewis and Marvin R. Vincent. 2 vols. Grand Rapids: Kregel, 1981.
———. *New Testament Word Studies.* 2 vols. Grand Rapids: Kregel, 1971.

Benoit, Pierre. *L'Évangile selon Saint Matthieu*. 3rd rev. ed. Paris: Editions du Cerf, 1961.
Bernard Combrink, H. J. "The Structure of the Gospel of Matthew as Narrative." *TynBul* 34 (1983) 61–90.
Bestgen, Yves. "Segmentation Markers as Trace and Signal of Discourse Structure." *JP* 29 (1998) 753–63.
———. "Temporal Adverbials as Segmentation Makers in Discourse Comprehension." *JML* 42 (2000) 74–87.
Bitrus, Sarma A. *Hermeneutic of Mission in Matthew: Israel and the Nations in the Interpretative Framework of Matthew's Gospel*. Cumbria, UK: Langham, 2015.
Black, Max. "Metaphor." *Proceedings of the Aristotelian Society*. NS 55 (1954–55) 273–94.
———. *Models and Metaphor: Studies in Language and Philosophy*. New York: Cornell University Press, 1962.
———. "More about Metaphor." In *Metaphor and Thought*, edited by Andrew Ortony, 19–41. 2nd ed. Cambridge: Cambridge University Press, 1993.
Black, Stephanie L. *Sentence Conjunctions in the Gospel of Matthew: Kai, De, Tote, Gar, Oun, and Asyndeton in Narrative Discourse*. JSNTSup 216. Sheffield, UK: Sheffield Academic, 2002.
Blomberg, Craig L. *Interpreting the Parables*. 2nd ed. Downers Grove, IL: IVP Academics, 2012.
———. *Matthew*. NAC. Nashville: Broadman, 1992.
———. "The Structure of 2 Corinthians 1–7." *CTR* 4 (1989) 3–20.
Blomberg, Craig L., and Sun Wook Chung, eds. *A Case for Historic Premillennialism: An Alternative to "Left Behind" Eschatology*. Grand Rapids: Baker, 2009.
Bock, Darrel L., ed. *Three Views on the Millennium and Beyond*. Grand Rapids: Zondervan, 1999.
———. *Luke 9:51—24:53*. BECNT. Grand Rapids: Baker, 1996.
Bonnard, Pierre. *L'Évangile Selon Saint Matthieu*. CNT 1. Neuchâtel: Delachaux et Niestlé, 1970.
Borg, Marcus J. *Conflict, Holiness and Politics in the Teachings of Jesus*. New York: The Edwin Mellen, 1984.
Bornkamm, Günther. "End-Expectation and the Church in Matthew." In *Tradition and Interpretation in Matthew*, by Günther Bornkamm et al., 15–51. London: SCM, 1963.
Bowman, John Wick. *The Religion of Maturity*. New York: N.p., 1948.
Brandon, S. G. F. *The Fall of Jerusalem and the Christian Church: A Study of the Effect of the Jewish Overthrow of A.D. 70 on Christianity*. London: SPCK, 1951.
Bray, Benjamin J. "A Critique of the Interpretation of Matthew Chapters 24–25 and Luke 17:20–37 by Advocates of the A.D. 70 Doctrine." MA thesis, David Lipscomb University, 1996.
Bray, John L. *Matthew 24 Fulfilled*. Lakeland, FL: John L. Bray Ministry, 1996.
Bridge, Stephen L. *"Where the Eagles Are Gathered": The Deliverance of the Elect in Lukan Eschatology*. JSNTSup 240. Sheffield, UK: Sheffield Academic, 2003.
Broadus, John A. *Commentary on Matthew*. Grand Rapids: Kregel, 1990.
Brown, Jeanine K., and Kyle Roberts. *Matthew*. THNTC. Grand Rapids: Eerdmans, 2018.
Brown, Michael L., and Craig S. Keener. *Not Afraid of the Antichrist: Why we Don't Believe in a Pre-Tribulation Rapture*. Minneapolis, MN: Chosen Books, 2019.

Brown, Raymond E. *An Introduction to the New Testament.* New Haven, CT: Yale University Press, 1997.

Brown, Schuyler. "Faith, the Poor and the Gentiles: A Tradition-Historical Reflection on Matthew 25:31–46." *TJT* 6 (1990) 171–81.

———. "The Matthean Apocalypse." *JSNT* 4 (1979) 2–27.

———. "The Matthean Community and the Gentile Mission." *NovT* 22 (1980) 193–221.

Bruner, Frederick Dale. *Matthew: A Commentary.* 2 vols. Revised and expanded edition. Grand Rapids: Eerdmans, 2004.

Bultmann, Rudolf. *History and Eschatology: The Presence of Eternity.* New York: Harper & Row, 1957.

———. *The History of the Synoptic Tradition.* Translated by John Marsh. New York: Harper & Row, 1963.

———. *Interpreting Faith for the Modern Era.* Edited by Rodger A. Johnson. Minneapolis, MN: Fortress, 1991.

———. *Jesus and the World.* Translated by Louise P. Smith and Erminie H. Lantero. New York: Scribner's, 1958.

———. *Theology of the New Testament.* New York: Scribner's, 1951.

Burnett, Fred W. *The Testament of Jesus-Sophia: A Redaction-Critical Study of the Eschatological Discourse in Matthew.* Washington, DC: University Press of America, 1979.

———. "Παλιγγενεσία in Matt 19.28: A Window on the Matthean Community?" *JSNT* 17 (1983) 60–72.

———. "Prolegomenon to Reading Matthew's Eschatological Discourse: Redundancy and the Education of the Reader in Matthew." *Semeia* 31 (1985) 91–109.

Burney, C. F. "St. Matthew xxv. 31–46 as a Hebrew Poem." *JTS* 14 (1913) 414–24.

Burridge, Richard A. *What Are the Gospels? A Comparison with Greco-Roman Biography.* 2nd ed. Grand Rapids: Eerdmans, 2004.

Buth, Randall. "On Levinsohn's 'Development Units.'" *START* 5 (1981) 53–56.

———. "Ουν, Δέ, Καί and Asyndeton in John's Gospel." In *Linguistics and New Testament Interpretation: Essays on Discourse Analysis*, edited by D. A. Black et al., 144–61. Nashville, TN: Broadman, 1992.

———. "Semitic Καί and Greek Δέ." *START* 3 (1981) 12–19.

Buzzard, Anthony. "Acts 1:6 and the Eclipse of Biblical Kingdom." *EQ* 66 (1994) 197–215.

———. "The Olivet Discourse: Mostly Fulfilled or Mostly Unfulfilled?" *JRR* 12 (2004) 11–22.

Caird, G. B. *The Language and Imagery of the Bible.* Philadelphia: Westminster, 1980.

———. *New Testament Theology.* Revised by L. D. Hurst. Oxford: Clarendon, 1994.

Calvin, John. *A Harmony of the Gospels: Matthew, Mark, Luke.* Translated by A W. Morrison. 3 vols. Edinburgh: St. Andrew, 1972.

Carmignac, J. "Qu'est-ce que L'apocalyptique? Son Emploi à Qumran." *ResQ* 10 (1979) 3–33.

Carson, D. A. *Exegetical Fallacies.* Grand Rapids: Baker, 1984.

———. "Matthew." In *Matthew & Mark*, revised and edited by Tremper Longman III and David E. Garland, 23–670. EBC 9. Grand Rapids: Zondervan, 2010.

———. *Matthew, Chapters 13 through 28.* 1st ed. EBC 2. Grand Rapids: Zondervan, 1995.

Carson, D. A., and Douglass J. Moo. *An Introduction to the New Testament*. 2nd ed. Grand Rapids: Zondervan, 2005.

Carter, Warren. "Are There Imperial Texts in the Class? Intertextual Eagles and Matthean Eschatology as 'Light Out' for Imperial Rome (Matthew 24:27–31)." *JBL* 122 (2003) 467–87.

———. "Kernels and Narrative Blocks: The Structure of Matthew's Gospel." *CBQ* 54 (1992) 463–81.

———. *Matthew and the Margins: A Sociological and Religious Reading*. Sheffield, UK: Sheffield Academic, 2000.

———. *Matthew: Storytellers, Teacher, Evangelist*. Peabody, MD: Hendrickson, 2004.

Case, Shirley Jackson. "The Origin and Purpose of the Gospel of Matthew." *BW* 34 (1909) 390–402.

Casey, Maurice. "Where Wright Is Wrong: A Critical Review of N.T. Wright's *Jesus and the Victory of God*." *JSNT* 69 (1998) 95–103.

Catchpole, David R. "The Poor on Earth and the Son of Man in Heaven: A Re-Appraisal of Matthew 25:31–46." *BJRL* 61 (1979) 355–97.

Charette, Blaine. *The Theme of Recompense in Matthew's Gospel*. JSNTSup 79. Sheffield, UK: Sheffield Academic, 1992.

Charlesworth, James H., ed. *The Old Testament Pseudepigrapha*. 5th ed. 2 vols. Peabody, MD: Hendrickson, 2016.

Charlesworth, Scott D. "Historicist Interpretation of the Olivet Discourse and the Sixth Seal: 1. Medieval Tribulation and Cosmic Signs." *Pacifica* 30 (2017) 111–27.

———. "Historicist Interpretation of the Olivet Discourse and the Sixth Seal: 2. Corrective, Reinterpretation, and Saving the Historical Jesus." *Pacifica* 30 (2017) 240–54.

Chatman, Seymour. *Story and Discourse: Narrative Structure in Fiction and Film*. Ithaca, NY: Cornell University, 1978.

Choi, Sungho. *The Messianic Kingship of Jesus: A Study of Christology and Redemption History in Matthew's Gospel with Special Reference to the Royal-Enthronement Psalms*. Eugene, OR: Wipf & Stock, 2011.

Christian, Timothy J. "A Questionable Inversion: Jesus' Corrective Answer to the Disciples' Question in Matthew 24:3—25:46." *JIBS* 3 (2016) 44–66.

Chrysostom. Translated by Members of the English Church. Oxford: Parker; Rivington, 1851.

Chung, YongHan. "The Temple in Matthew's Eschatology: Matthew's interpretation of the Temple in the Context of First-Century Judaism." PhD diss., Graduate Theological Union, 2011.

Clark, Andrew. "The Role of the Apostles." In *Witness to the Gospels: The Theology of Acts*, edited by I. Howard Marshall and David Peterson, 169–90. Grand Rapids: Eerdmans, 1998.

Clark, K. W. "The Gentile Bias in Matthew." *JBL* 66 (1947) 165–72.

Colani, Timothée. *Jésus Christ et Les Croyances Messianiques de son Temps*. 2nd ed. Strasbourg, Fr.: Truettel et Wurtz, 1864.

Collins, J. J. "Apocalyptic Eschatology as the Transcendence of Death." *CBQ* 36 (1974) 21–43.

———. *The Apocalyptic Imagination: An Introduction to Jewish Apocalyptic Literature*. 3rd ed. Grand Rapids: Eerdmans, 2016.

———. *Daniel: A Commentary on the Book of Daniel*. Hermeneia. Minneapolis, MN: Fortress, 1993.

———, ed. *Apocalyptic: The Morphology of a Genre*. Semeia 14. Missoula, MT: Scholars, 1979.

Conzelmann, Hans. *The Theology of St. Luke*. Translated by Geoffrey Buswell. London: Faber and Faber, 1960.

Cope, O. L. "The Close of the Age: The Role of Apocalyptic Thought in the Gospel of Mt." In *Apocalyptic and The New Testament: Essays in Honor of J. Louis Martyn*, edited by Joel Marcus and Marion L. Soards, 113–24. JSNTSup 24. Sheffield, UK: JSOT, 1989.

———. "Matthew xxv: 31–46: 'The Sheep and the Goats' Reinterpreted." *NovT* 11 (1969) 32–44.

Court, J. M. "Right and Left: The Implications for Matthew 25:31–46." *NTS* 31 (1985) 223–33.

Crosby, Michael. *House of Disciples: Church, Economics, and Justice in Matthew*. Maryknoll, NY: Orbis, 1988.

Crossan, John Dominic. *The Historical Jesus: The Life of a Mediterranean Jewish Peasant*. San Francisco: HarperSanFrancisco, 1991.

Cullmann, Oscar. *Christ and Time: The Primitive Christian Conception of Time and History*. 3rd ed. Translated by Floyd V. Filson. Eugene, OR: Wipf & Stock, 1962.

———. *Salvation in History*. London: SCM, 1967.

Davies, Margaret. *Matthew*. Sheffield, UK: Sheffield Academic, 1993.

Davies, W. D., and Dale C. Allison. *The Gospel according to Saint Matthew*. 3 vols. Edinburgh: T. & T. Clark, 1997.

Deissmann, Adolf. *Light from the East: The New Testament Illustrated by Recently Discovered Texts of the Greco-Roman World*. Translated by Lionel R. M. Strachan. Reprint, Peabody, MD: Hendrickson, 1995.

DeMar, Gary. *Last Days Madness: Obsession of the Modern Church*. 4th rev. ed. Atlanta: American Vision, 1999.

———. "Matthew 24 and 25: How Many Comings?" *Newsletter of Evangelist. John L. Bray*, February 13, 1995.

Denniston, J. D. *The Greek Particles*. 2nd ed. Oxford: Clarendon, 1954.

Derrett, J. D. M. "Palingenesia (Matthew 19.28)." *JSNT* 20 (1984) 51–58.

Deutsch, Celia M. *Lady Wisdom, Jesus, and the Sages: Metaphor and Social Context in Matthew's Gospel*. Valley Forge, PA: Trinity, 1996.

Dlungwana, Mlungisi P. "Jesus' Parousia in the Context of the Crucifixion: An Exegetical Analysis of Mt 24–26:2 Using Semiotic Method." ThD diss., Saint Paul University, 1997.

Dodd, C. H. *The Apostolic Preaching and Its Development*. New York: Clark, 1936.

———. "The Fall of Jerusalem and the 'Abomination of Desolation.'" *JRS* 37 (1947) 47–54.

———. *The Parables of the Kingdom*. London: Nisbet, 1936.

Donahue, John R. "The 'Parable' of the Sheep and the Goats: A Challenge to Christian Ethics." *TS* 47 (1986) 3–31.

Dooley, Robert A., and Stephen H. Levinsohn. *Analyzing Discourse: A Manual of Basic Concepts*. Dallas: SIL International, 2001.

Douglas, R. A. *Matthew*. Int. Louisville: Westminster John Knox, 2009.

———. *The Theme of Jewish Persecution of Christians in the Gospel according to St. Matthew*. Cambridge: Cambridge University Press, 1967.

Down, Martin. "Exegetical Note on Matthew 25:31:46: The Parable of the Sheep and Goat." *ExpTim* 123 (2012) 587–89.

Dubis, Mark. *Messianic Woes in 1 Peter: Suffering and Eschatology in 1 Peter 4:12–19*. New York: Lang, 2002.

Dulling, Dennis C. "The Gospel of Matthew." In *The Blackwell Companion to the New Testament*, edited by D. E. Aune, 296–318. Malden, MD: Wiley-Blackwell, 2010.

Dunn, James D. G. 'Spirit and Kingdom.' *ExpTim* 82 (1970–71) 36–40.

Dyer, Keith D. *The Prophecy on the Mount: Mark 13 and the Gathering of the New Community*. Bern, Switz.: Lang, 1998.

———. "When Is the End Not the End? The Fate of the Earth in Biblical Eschatology (Mark 13)." In *The Earth Story in the New Testament*, edited by N. C. Habel and V. Balabanski, 44–65. EB 5. Sheffield, UK: Sheffield, 2002.

Ehrman, Bart D. *Jesus: Apocalyptic Prophet of the New Millennium*. Oxford: Oxford University Press, 1999.

Ellis, P. F. *Matthew: His Mind and Message*. Collegeville, PA: Liturgical, 1974.

Evans, Craig A. *Matthew*. NCBC. Cambridge: Cambridge University Press, 2012.

———. "Predictions of the Destruction of the Herodian Temple in the Pseudepigrapha, Qumran Scrolls, and Related Texts." *JSP* 10 (1992) 89–147.

Farmer, William Reuben. *Jesus and the Gospels: Tradition, Scripture, and Canon*. Philadelphia: Fortress, 1982.

Farrer, A. M. "On Dispensing with Q." In *Studies in the Gospels: Essays in Honor of R. H. Lightfoot*, edited by D. E. Nineham, 55–88. Oxford: Blackwell, 1955.

Fee, Gordon D. *The First and Second Letters to the Thessalonians*. Grand Rapids: Eerdmans, 2009.

Feuillet, A. "Le Sens du Mot Parousie dans l'Evangile de Matthieu: Comparison entre Matth. xxiv et Jac. v, 1–11." In *The Background of the New Testament and Its Eschatology*, edited by W. D. Davies and D. Daube, 261–80. Cambridge: Cambridge University Press, 1956.

Fiedler, Peter. *Das Matthäusevangelium*. ThKNT 1. Stuttgart, Germ.: Verlag V. Kohlhammer, 2006.

Filson, Floyd V. *A Commentary on the Gospel according to St. Matthew*. Peabody, MD: Hendrickson, 1960.

Fitzmyer, Joseph A. *The Gospel according to Luke X–XXIV*, ABCS 28. New Haven, CT: Yale University Press, 1985.

Ford, Desmond. *The Abomination of Desolation in Biblical Eschatology*. Washington DC: University Press of America, 1979.

Fowler, Harold. *The Gospel of Matthew*. 4 vols. Joplin, MO: College, 1985.

France, R. T. *The Gospel according to Matthew: An Introduction and Commentary*. Grand Rapids: InterVarsity, 1985.

———. *The Gospel of Mark*. NIGTC. Grand Rapids: Eerdmans, 2002.

———. *The Gospel of Matthew*. NICNT. Grand Rapids: Eerdmans, 2007.

———. *Matthew: Evangelist and Teacher*. Downers Grove, IL: InterVarsity, 1989.

———. "On Being Ready." In *The Challenges of Jesus' Parables*, edited by Richard N. Longenecker, 177–95. Cambridge: Eerdmans, 2000.

Freeman Rand, James. "A Survey of the Eschatology of the Olivet Discourse [1]." *BSac* 113 (1956) 162–73.

Fresch, Christopher J. "Discourse Markers in the Septuagint and Early Koine Greek with Special Reference to the Twelve." *TynBul* 68 (2017) 313–16.
Fuller, George C. "The Olivet Discourse: An Apocalyptic Timetable." *WTJ* 28 (1966) 157–63.
———. "The Structure of the Olivet Discourse." ThD diss., Westminster Theological Seminary, 1964.
Funk, Robert. *Language, Hermeneutic, and the Word of God: The Problem of Language in the New Testament and Contemporary Theology*. New York: Harper & Row, 1966.
Gaechter, Paul. *Die Literarische Kunst im Matthäus-Evangelium*. Stuttgarter Bibelstudien 7. Stuttgart, Germ.: Katholisches Bibelwerk, 1965.
Garbe, Gernot. *Der Hirte Israels: Eine Untersuchung zur Isaeltheologie des Matthäusevangeliums*. WMANT 106. Neukirchen-Vluyn, Germ.: Neukirchener Verlag, 2005.
Gardner, Richard B. *Matthew*. BCBC. Scottdale, PA: Herald, 1991.
Garland, David E. *Reading Matthew: A Literary and Theological Commentary of the First Gospel*. Macon, GA: Smyth & Helwys, 2001.
Gaston, Lloyd. *No Stone on Another: Studies in the Significance of the Fall of Jerusalem in the Synoptic Gospels*. NovTSup 23. Leiden, The Neth.: Brill, 1970.
Gench, Frances Taylor. *Wisdom in the Christology of Matthew*. New York: University Press of America, 1997.
Gibbs, Jeffrey A. *Jerusalem and Parousia: Jesus' Eschatological Discourse in Matthew's Gospel*. St Louis: Concordia Academic, 2000.
———. *Matthew 1:1–11*. CC. Saint Louis: Concordia, 2006.
Glasscock, E. D. *Matthew: A Gospel Commentary*. Eugene, OR: Wipf & Stock, 2005.
Glasson, T. Francis. "The Ensign of the Son of Man (Matt. XXIV. 30)." *JTS* 15 (1964) 299–300.
———. *The Second Advent: The Origin of the New Testament Doctrine*. 2nd rev. ed. London: Epworth, 1947.
———. "What Is Apocalyptic?" *NTS* 27 (1980) 98–105.
Gnilka, Joachim. *Das Matthäusevangelium*. 2 vols. HTKNT. Freiburg, Germ.: Herder, 1986.
Grabbe, Lester L. "Prophetic and Apocalyptic: Time for New Definitions—and New Thinking." In *Knowing the End from the Beginning: The Prophetic, the Apocalyptic, and Their Relationships*, edited by L. L. Grabbe and R. D. Haak, 107–33. JSPSup 46. New York: T. & T. Clark, 2003.
Gray, Sherman W. *The Least of My Brothers (Matthew 25:31–46): A History of Interpretation*. SBLDS 114. Atlanta: Scholars, 1989.
Green, H. B. "The Structure of St Matthew's Gospel." In *Studia Evangelica IV. Part I: The New Testament Scriptures*, edited by F. L. Cross, 47–59. Berlin: Akademie Verlag, 1968.
Greg, Carey. *Apocalyptic Literature in the New Testament*. Nashville, TN: Abingdon, 2016.
Gregg, Steve, ed. *Revelation, Four Views: A Parallel Commentary*. Nashville, TN: Nelson, 1997.
Grundmann, Walter. *Das Evangelium nach Matthäus*. THKNT 1. Berlin: Evangelische Verlagsanstalt, 1968.
Guenther, Heinz O. "When 'Eagles' Draw Together." *Forum* 5 (1989) 140–50.
Gundry, Robert H. *The Church and the Tribulation*. Grand Rapids: Zondervan, 1973.

———. *Matthew: A Commentary on His Handbook for a Mixed Church under Persecution.* Grand Rapids: Eerdmans, 1994.

———. *The Use of the Old Testament in St Matthew's Gospel with Special Reference to the Messianic Hope.* NovTSup 18. Leiden, The Neth.: Brill, 1967.

Gupta, Nijay K. "Mirror-Reading Moral Issues in Paul's Letters." *JSNT* 34 (2012) 361–81.

Gurtner, Daniel M. "Interpreting Apocalyptic Symbolism in the Gospel of Matthew." *BBR* 22 (2012) 525–45.

Guthrie, Donald. *New Testament Introduction.* 4th ed. Downers Grove, IL: InterVarsity, 1990.

Hadfield, P. "Matthew the Apocalyptic Editor." *LQHRev* 184 (1959) 128–32.

Hagner, Donald A. "Apocalyptic Motifs in the Gospel of Matthew: Continuity and Discontinuity." *HBT* (1985) 53–82.

———. *Matthew 14–28.* WBC. Dallas: Word Books, 1995.

———. *The New Testament: A Historical and Theological Introduction.* Grand Rapids: Baker Academic, 2012.

Ham, Clay A. "Reading Zechariah and Matthew's Olivet Discourse." In *Biblical Interpretation in Early Christian Gospels,* edited by Thomas R. Hatina, 2:85–97. 4 vols. LNTS 310. New York: T. & T. Clark, 2008.

Hanson, Paul D. "Apocalypticism." In *The Interpreter's Dictionary of the Bible,* edited by Keith Crim, 28–34. Supplementary Volume Edition. Nashville, TN: Abingdon, 1976.

———. "Apocalyptic Literature." In *The Hebrew Bible and Its Modern Interpreters,* edited by D. A. Knight and G. M. Tucker, 465–88. SBLBMI 1. Philadelphia: Fortress, 1985.

———. *The Dawn of Apocalyptic.* Philadelphia: Fortress, 1975.

———, ed. *Visionaries and Their Apocalypses.* Philadelphia: Fortress, 1983.

Harb, Gertraud. "The Meaning of Q 17, 37: Problems, Opinions and Perspectives." *ZNW* 102 (2011) 283–93.

Hare, Douglas R. A., trans. "The Lives of the Prophets." In *The Old Testament Pseudepigrapha,* edited by James H. Charlesworth, 2:380–99. 2 vols. Peabody, MD: Hendrickson, 2016.

———. *Matthew.* Int. Louisville: Westminster John Knox, 2009.

———. "The Testament of Jesus-Sophia: Redaction-Critical Analysis of Eschatological Discourse in Matthew." *JBL* 102 (1983) 644–66.

———. *The Theme of Jewish Persecution of Christians in the Gospel according to St. Matthew.* SNTSMS 6. Cambridge: Cambridge University Press, 1967.

Hare, Douglas R. A., and Daniel J. Harrington. "'Make Disciples of All the Gentiles' (Matthew 28:19)." *CBQ* 37 (1975) 359–69.

Harrington, Daniel J. *The Gospel of Matthew.* SPS 1. Collegeville, PA: Liturgical, 1991.

Hart, John F. "A Chronology of Matthew 24:1–44." ThD diss., Grace Theological Seminary and College, 1986.

———. "Should Pretribulationists Reconsider the Rapture in Matthew 24:36–44? Part 1 of 3." *JGES* (2007) 51–75.

Hartman, Lars. *Prophecy Interpreted: The Formation of Some Jewish Apocalyptic Texts and of the Eschatological Discourse Mark 13 Par.* Lund, Switz.: Gleerup, 1966.

Hatina, Thomas R. "The Focus of Mark 13:24–27: The Parousia, or the Destruction of the Temple?" *BBR* 6 (1996) 43–66.

Hays, Christopher M., et al. *When the Son of Man Didn't Come: A Constructive Proposal on the Delay of the Parousia*. Minneapolis, MN: Fortress, 2016.

Heil, John Paul. "The Double Meaning of the Narrative of Universal Judgment in Matthew 25:31–46." *JSNT* 69 (1998) 3–41.

Hellholm, David, ed. *Apocalypticism in the Mediterranean World and the Near East: Proceedings of the International Colloquium on Apocalypticism, Uppsala, August 12–17, 1979*. Tubingen: Mohr Siebeck, 1983.

Hendriksen, William. *Exposition of the Gospel according to Matthew*. NTC. Grand Rapids: Baker, 1973.

Higgins, A. J. "The Sign of the Son of Man (Matt XXIV 30)." *NTS* 9 (1962–63) 380–82.

Hillary. *Commentary on Matthew*. Translated by D. H. Williams. Washington, DC: Catholic University of America, 2012.

Hill, David. "The Figure of Jesus in Matthew's Story: A Response to Professor Kingsbury's Literary-Critical Probe." *JSNT* 21 (1984) 37–52.

———. *Matthew*. NCB. London: Marshall, Morgan & Scott, 1972.

———. "Son and Servant: An Essay on Matthean Christology." *JSNT* 6 (1980) 2–16.

Hill, Stanford D. "Exceptions to Apollonius' Canon in the New Testament: Grammatical Study." *TJ* 7 (1986) 3–16.

Hirsch, E. D. *Validity of Interpretation*. New Haven, CT: Yale University Press, 1967.

———. *The Aims of Interpretation*. Chicago: University of Chicago Press, 1976.

Hoekema, Anthony T. *The Bible and Future*. Grand Rapids: Eerdmans, 1979.

Holleman, Joost. *Resurrection and Parousia: A Traditional Historical Study of Paul's Eschatology in 1 Corinthians 15*. Leiden, The Neth.: Brill, 1996.

Hood, Jason. "Matthew 23–25: The Extent of Jesus' Fifth Discourse." *JBL* 128 (2009) 527–43.

Huizenga, Leroy Andrew. "Matt 1:1: 'Son of Abraham' as Christological Category." *HBT* 30 (2008) 103–13.

Hultgren, Arland J. *The Parables of Jesus: A Commentary*. Grand Rapids: Eerdmans, 2000.

Hummel, Reinhart. *Die Auseinandersetzung zwischen Kirche und Judentum im Matthäusevangelium*. BET 33. Munich, Germ.: Kaiser, 1966.

Ice, Thomas, and Kenneth L. Gentry. *The Great Tribulation: Past or Future*. Grand Rapids: Kregel, 1999.

Jeremias, Joachim. *The Parables of Jesus*. 2nd rev. ed. London: SCM, 1972.

Jerome. *Commentary on Matthew*. Translated by Thomas P. Scheck. Fathers of the Church. Washington: Catholic University of America, 2008.

Johnson, Andy. "Paul's 'Anti-Christology' in 2 Thess 2:3–12 in Canonical Context." *JTI* 8 (2014) 125–43.

Johnson, Marshall D. "Reflections on a Wisdom Approach to Matthew's Christology." *CBQ* 36 (1974) 44–64.

Juel, Donald. *Temple: The Trial of Jesus in the Gospel Mark*. SBLDS 31. Missoula, MT: Scholar, 1977.

Juza, Ryan P. *The New Testament and the Future of the Cosmos*. Eugene, OR: Pickwick, 2020.

Käsemann, Ernst. "The Beginnings of Christian Theology." *Journal for Theology and the Church* 6 (1969) 17–46.

———. "On the Subject of Primitive Christian Apocalyptic." In *New Testament Questions of Today*, translated by W. J. Montague, 108–37. NTL. London: SCM, 1969.
Keegan, Terence J. "Introductory Formulae for Matthean Discourses." *CBQ* (1982) 415–30.
Keener, Craig S. *Acts: An Exegetical Commentary*. 4 vols. Grand Rapids: Baker Academic, 2013.
———. *Bible Background Commentary (New Testament)*. 2nd ed. Downers Grove, IL: InterVarsity, 2014.
———. *The Gospel of John: A Commentary*. 2 vols. Peabody, MD: Hendrickson, 2003.
———. *The Gospel of Matthew: A Socio-Rhetorical Commentary*. Grand Rapids: Eerdmans, 2009.
———. *Revelation*. NIVAC. Grand Rapids: Zondervan, 2000.
Kik, J. Marcellus. "Matthew Twenty-Four: An Exposition." In *The Eschatology of Victory*, 53–173. Reprint, Nutley, NJ: Presbyterian and Reformed, 1971.
Kingsbury, Jack Dean. "The Figure of Jesus in Matthew's Story: A Literary-Critical Probe." *JSNT* 21 (1984) 3–36.
———. *Matthew as Story*. Philadelphia: Fortress, 1989.
———. *Matthew: Structure, Christology, Kingdom*. Minneapolis, MN: Fortress, 1975.
———. *The Parables of Jesus in Matthew 13: A Study in Redaction Criticism*. London: SPCK, 1969.
———. "The Plot of Matthew." *Int* 46 (1992) 347–56.
Kloppenborg, John S. "Evocatio Deorum and the Date of Mark." *JBL* 124 (2005) 419–50.
Klug, Eugene F. A., ed and trans. *Sermons of Martin Luther: The House Postils*. 3 vols. Grand Rapids: Baker, 1996.
Koch, Klaus. *The Rediscovery of Apocalyptic: A Polemical Work on a Neglected Area of Biblical Studies and Its Damaging effect on Theology and Philosophy*. Translated by Margaret Kohl. SBT 22. London: SCM, 1972.
Koester, Craig. "The Origin and Significance of the Flight to Pella." *CBQ* 51 (1989) 90–106.
Koester, Helmut. "Jesus the Victim." *JBL* 111 (1992) 3–15.
Kolenkow, Anitra Bingham. "The Fall of the Temple and the Coming of the End: The Spectrum and Process of Apocalyptic Argument in 2 Baruch and Other Authors." *SBLSP* 118 (1982) 243–50.
Kon, Kim Ki. "The Signs of the Parousia: A Diachronic and Comparative Study of the Apocalyptic Vocabulary of Matthew 24:27–31." PhD diss., Andrews University, 1994.
Konradt, Matthias. *The Gospel according to Matthew: A Commentary*. Translated by M. E. Boring. Waco, TX: Baylor University Press, 2020.
———. *Israel, Church, and the Gentiles in the Gospel of Matthew*. BMSSEC. Waco, TX: Baylor University Press, 2014.
Kraszewski, Charles S., ed. and trans. *The Gospel of Matthew with Patristic Commentaries*. Lewiston: NY: Mellen, 1999.
Kreitzer, L. J. "Apocalyptic, Apocalypticism." In *DLNTD*, edited by Ralph P. Martin and Peter H. Davids, 55–68. Downers Grove, IL: InterVarsity, 1997.
Krentz, Edgar. "Extent of Matthew's Prologue: Toward the Structure of the First Gospel." *JBL* 83 (1964) 409–14.

Kurz, William. "Acts 3:19–26 as a Test of the Role of Eschatology in Lukan Christology." *SBLSP* 16 (1977) 309–23.
Kynes, William L. *A Christology of Solidarity: Jesus as the Representative of His People in Matthew.* Lanham, MD: University Press of America, 1991.
Ladd, G. E. *The Blessed Hope: A Biblical Study of the Second Advent and the Rapture.* Grand Rapids: Eerdmans, 1956.
———. "The Parable of the Sheep and the Goats in Recent Interpretation." In *New Dimensions in New Testament Study*, edited by R. N. Longenecker and M. C. Tenney, 191–99. Grand Rapids: Zondervan, 1974.
———. *Presence of the Future: The Eschatology of Biblical Realism.* Grand Rapids: Eerdmans, 1974.
———. *Revelation Unveiled.* Grand Rapids: Zondervan, 1999.
———. "Why Not Prophetic-Apocalyptic?" *JBL* 76 (1957) 192–200.
LaHaye, Tim, and Jerry B. Jenkins. *Left Behind: A Novel of the Earth's Last Days.* Wheaton, IL: Tyndale, 1995.
Lakoff, George, and Mark Johnson. *Metaphor We Live By.* Chicago: University of Chicago Press, 1980.
Lambrecht, Jan. "The Line of Thought in Matthew 24:1–35: A Discussion of Vicky Balabanski's Reading." *ETL* 84 (2008) 519–28.
———. *Once More Astonished: The Parables of Jesus.* New York: Crossroad, 1983.
———. "The Parousia Discourse: Composition and Content in Matt 24–25." In *L'évangile selon Matthieu: Redaction et Theologie*, edited by M. Didier, 309–42. BETL 29. Gembloux: Duculot, 1972.
Lampe, G. W. H. "AD 70 in Christian Reflection." In *Jesus and the Politics of His Day*, edited by E. Bammel and C. E. D. Moule, 153–71. Cambridge: Cambridge University Press, 1984.
Lang, T. J. "'Where the Body Is, There Also the Eagles Will Be Gathered': Luke 17:37 and the Arrest of Jesus." *BibInt* 21 (2013) 320–40.
Lassman, Ernie V. "Matthew 24: Its Structure and Interpretation." MSTh thesis, Concordia Theological Seminary, 1991.
Lenker, John N., ed. *Sermons of Martin Luther.* 8 vols. Grand Rapids: Baker, 1983.
Lennartsson, Göran. *Refreshing & Restoration: Two Eschatological Motifs in Acts 3:19–21.* Lund, Switz.: Lund University Press, 2007.
Lenski, R. C. H. *Interpretation of St. Matthew's Gospel.* 2 vols. Augsburg: Fortress, 1998.
Levenson, Jon D. "The Temple and the World." *JR* 64 (1984) 275–98.
Leverett, Gaylen P. "Looking for the Least: An Analysis and Evaluation of Interpretive Issues Which Have Influenced the Interpretation of the Judgment of the Sheep and Goats ('Matthew 25:31–46')." PhD diss., Southeastern Baptist Theological Seminary, 2007.
Levinsohn, Stephen H. *Discourse Features of New Testament Greek: A Coursebook on the Information Structure of New Testament Greek.* 2nd ed. Dallas: SIL International, 2000.
———. *Textual Connections in Acts.* SBLMS 31. Atlanta: Scholars, 1987.
———. "'Therefore' or 'Wherefore': What's the Difference?" In *Reflections on Lexicography: Explorations in Ancient Syriac, Hebrew, and Greek Sources*, edited by Richard A. Taylor and Craig E. Morrison, 325–43. PLAL 4. Piscataway, NJ: Gorgias, 2014.

Licona, Michael. *Why Are There Differences in the Gospels? What We Can Learn from Ancient Biography.* Oxford: Oxford University Press, 2017.
Liebenberg, Jacobus. *The Language of the Kingdom and Jesus: Parable, Aphorism, and Metaphor in the Sayings Material Common to the Synoptic Tradition and the Gospel of Thomas.* Berlin: de Gruyter, 2001.
Lightfoot, J. B. *The Apostolic Fathers: Revised Texts with Short Introductions and English Translations.* London: Macmillan, 1912.
———. *A Commentary on the New Testament from the Talmud and Hebraica.* 4 vols. Peabody, MD: Hendrickson, 1989.
Linnemann, Eta. *Parables of Jesus: Introduction and Exposition.* London: SPCK, 1966.
Lohmeyer, Ernst. *Das Evangelium des Matthäus.* 4. Aufl. Göttingen, Germ.: Vandenhoeck & Ruprecht, 1967.
Lohr, Charles H. "Oral Techniques in the Gospel of Matthew." *CBQ* 23 (1961) 403–35.
Long, Fredrick J. *Koine Greek Grammar: A Beginning-Intermediate Exegetical and Pragmatic Handbook.* Wilmore, KY: Glossa House, 2015.
Longman, Tremper, III, and David E. Garland, eds. *Matthew & Mark.* Rev. ed. EBC 9. Grand Rapids: Zondervan, 2010.
Longstreth, Jason S. "Matthew 24: The Destruction of Jerusalem or the End of History?" MA thesis, Johnson Bible College, 2009.
Lucke, Friedrich. *Versuch einer vollständigen Einleitung in die Offenbarung Johannes und in die gesammie apokalyptishe Literatur.* Bonn, Germ.: Weber, 1832.
Lüdemann, Gerd. "The Successors of Pre-70 Jerusalem Christianity: A Critical Evaluation of the Pella Tradition." In *Jewish and Christian Self-Definition*, edited by E. P. Sanders, 161–73. Philadelphia: Fortress, 1980.
Lunde, Jonathan. "The Salvation-Historical Implication of Matthew 24–25 in Light of Jewish Apocalyptic Literature." PhD diss., Trinity Evangelical Divinity School, 1996.
Luther, Martin. *Luthers Werke: Kritische Gesamtausgabe [Schriften].* 73 vols. Weimar, Germ.: Böhlau, 1883–2009.
Luz, Ulrich. *Matthew 21–28.* Hermeneia. Minneapolis, MN: Fortress, 2005.
———. *The Theology of the Gospel of Matthew.* Translated by J. B. Robinson. Cambridge: Cambridge University Press, 1995.
MacArthur, John F. *Matthew 24–28.* MNTC. Chicago: Moody, 1989.
———. *The Second Coming: Signs of Christ's Return and the End of the Age.* Wheaton, IL: Crossway, 1999.
Maier, Gerhard. *Matthäus-Evangelium.* 2 Bd. Neuhausen, Switz.: Hänssler, 1980.
Manson, T. W. *The Sayings of Jesus.* London: SCM, 1957.
Marguerat, Daniel. *Le Jugement dans L' Évangile de Matthieu.* Geneva, Switz: Labor et Fides, 1981.
Marshall, I. H. *Luke: A Commentary on the Greek Text.* NIGTC. Exeter, UK: Paternoster, 1978.
———. "The Parousia in the New Testament—and Today." In *Worship, Theology and Ministry in the Early Church: Essays in Honor of Ralph P. Martin*, edited by M. J. Wilkins and T. Paige, 194–211. JSNTSup 87. Sheffield, UK: JSOT, 1992.
Marvin, Pate C. *Luke.* MGC. Chicago: Moody, 1995.
Matera, Frank J. "The Plot of Matthew's Structure." *CBQ* 49 (1987) 233–53.
Mawhinney, Allen. "Baptism, Servanthood, and Sonship." *WTJ* 49 (1987) 35–64.

McArthur, Harvey K., and Robert M. Johnston. *They Also Taught in Parables: Rabbinic Parables from the First Centuries of the Christian Era*. Eugene, OR: Wipf & Stock, 1990.

Meier, John P. "Matthew, Gospel of." In *The Anchor Bible Dictionary: K–L*, edited by David Noel Freedman, 4:622–41. 6 vols. New York: Doubleday, 1992.

———. *Matthew*. NTM 3. Delaware: Michael Glazier, 1980.

———. "Nations or Gentiles in Matthew 28:19?" *CBQ* 39 (1977) 92–102.

Merkle, Benjamin L. "Who Will Be Left Behind? Rethinking the Meaning of Matthew 24:40–41 and Luke 17:34–35." *WTJ* 72 (2010) 169–79.

Meyer, Ben F. *Christus Faber: The Master-Builder and the House of God*. Allison Park, PA: Pickwick, 1992.

———. *Reality and Illusion in New Testament Scholarship: A Primer in Critical Realist Hermeneutics*. Collegeville, PA: Glazier, 1994.

Michaels, J. Ramsey. "Apostolic Hardships and Righteous Gentiles: A Study of Matthew 25:31–46." *JBL* 84 (1965) 27–37.

Middleton, Richard J. *A New Heaven and a New Earth: Reclaiming Biblical Eschatology*. Grand Rapids: Baker Academic, 2014.

Mitch, Curtis, and Edward Sri. *The Gospel of Matthew*. CCSS. Grand Rapids: Baker Academic, 2010.

M'Neile, Alan H. *The Gospel according to St. Matthew*. London: Macmillan, 1952.

Montague, George T. *Companion God: A Cross-Cultural Commentary on the Gospel of Matthew*. New York: Paulist, 2010.

Moore, A. L. *The Parousia in the New Testament*. NovTSup 13. Leiden, The Neth.: Brill, 1966.

Morris, Leon. *The Gospel according to Matthew*. Grand Rapids: Eerdmans, 1992.

Morrison, James. *Commentary on the Gospel according to Matthew*. London: Hamilton, 1870.

Moulton, J. H. *A Grammar of the New Greek*. 3 vols. Edinburgh: T. & T. Clark, 1963.

Mounce, Robert H. *Matthew*. NIBC. Peabody, MD: Hendrickson, 1985.

Mullins, Michael. *The Gospel of Matthew*. Dublin, Irl.: Columba, 2007.

Mullooparambil, Sebastian. *Macrostructure of Matthew's Gospel*. Bangalore, Ind.: Dharmaram, 2011.

Murphy, Frederick J. *Apocalypticism in the Bible and Its World*. Grand Rapids: Baker, 2012.

———. *Early Judaism: The Exile in the Time of Jesus*. Grand Rapids: Baker, 2002.

———. *Fallen Is Babylon: The Revelation of John*. Harrisburg: Trinity, 1998.

Mwangomo, Ambilike Anosisye. "A Critique of the Views on the Date and Authorship of the Gospel of Matthew in Recent Decades." PhD diss., Dallas Theological Seminary, 2015.

Neirynck, Frans. "ΑΠΟ ΤΟΤΕ ΗΡΞΑΤΟ and the Structure of Matthew." *ETL* 64 (1988) 22–59.

Nelson, Neil D., Jr. "'This Generation' in Matt 24:34: A Literary Critical Perspective." *JETS* 38 (1996) 369–85.

Neusner, Jacob. "Defining Judaism." In *The Blackwell Companion to Judaism*, edited by Jacob Neusner and Allan J. Avery-Peck, 3–19. Malden, MD: Blackwell, 2003.

Nichole, Allan J. *Jesus' Direction for the Future: A Source and Redaction-History Study of the Use of the Eschatological Traditions in Paul and in the Synoptic Accounts of Jesus' Last Eschatological Discourse*. NGS 9. Macon, GA: Mercer University Press, 1996.

Nolan, Brian M. *The Royal Son of God: The Christology of Matthew 1-2 in the Setting of the Gospel.* Göttingen, Germ.: Vandenhoeck & Ruprecht, 1979.
Nolland, John. *The Gospel of Matthew: A Commentary on the Text.* NIGTC. Grand Rapids: Eerdmans, 2005.
———. *Luke 9:21—18:34.* WBC 35B. Nashville, TN: Nelson, 1993.
Oden, Thomas C., and Manlio Simonetti, eds. *Ancient Christian Commentary on Scripture: Matthew 14-28.* Downers Grove, IL: InterVarsity, 2002.
Orchard, J. B. "Thessalonians and the Synoptic Gospels." *Biblica* 19 (1938) 19–42.
Osborne, Grant R. *The Hermeneutical Spiral: A Comprehensive Introduction to Biblical Interpretation.* 2nd ed. Downers Grove, IL: InterVarsity, 2006.
———. *Matthew.* ZECNT. Grand Rapids: Zondervan, 2010.
Otto, Randall E. "Prophets and Their Perspective." *CBQ* 63 (2001) 219-40.
Pate, C. Marvin, and Douglas W. Kennard. *Deliverance Now and Not Yet: The New Testament and the Great Tribulation.* New York: Lang, 2003.
Patrick, James E. "Matthew's *Pesher* Gospel Structured around Ten Messianic Citations of Isaiah." *JTS* 61 Pt 1 (2010) 43–81.
Patte, Daniel. *The Gospel according to Matthew: A Structural Commentary on Matthew's Faith.* Philadelphia: Fortress, 1987.
Perrin, Norman. *Jesus and the Language of the Kingdom: Symbol and Metaphor in New Testament Interpretation.* Philadelphia: Fortress, 1976.
Pettegrew, Larry D. "Interpretive Flaws in the Olivet Discourse." *MSJ* 13 (2002) 187–88.
Pfleiderer, O. "Über die Komposition der eschatologischen Rede, Mt. 24:4ff." *JDT* 13 (1868)134-49.
Philippe, Rolland. "From Genesis to the End of the World: The Plan of Matthew's Gospel." *BTB* 2 (1972) 155–76.
Pitre, Brant. *Jesus, the Tribulation and the End of Exile: Restoration Eschatology and the Origin of the Atonement.* Tübingen, Germ.: Mohr Siebeck, 2005.
Plevnik, Joseph. *Paul and the Parousia: Exegetical and Theological* Investigation. Peabody, MD: Hendrickson, 1997.
Plummer, Alfred. *An Exegetical Commentary on the Gospel according to St. Matthew.* Grand Rapids: Baker, 1982.
Pond, Eugene W. "Interpretive Issues Pertaining to the Judgment of Sheep and Goats." PhD diss., Dallas Theological Seminary, 2001.
———. "Who Are the Sheep and the Goats in Matthew 25:31–46?" *BSac* 159 (2002) 288–301.
Porter, Stanley E. *Idioms of the Greek New Testament.* Sheffield, UK: JSOT, 1992.
Poythress, V. S. "The Use of the Intersentence Conjunctions De, Oun, Kai, and Asyndeton in the Gospel of John." *NovT* 26 (1984) 312–40.
Price, K. Walker. *Jesus' Prophetic Sermon: The Olivet Key to Israel, the Church, and the Nations.* Chicago: Moody, 1972.
Quarles, Charles L. *Matthew: Exegetical Guide to the Greek New Testament.* Nashville, TN: B&H Academic, 2017.
Rand, James F. "A Survey of the Eschatology of the Olivet Discourse." *BSac* (1956) 200–213.
Reese, Alexander. *The Approaching Advent of Christ.* London: Marshall, Morgan & Scott, 1932.
Reese, Ruth Anne. *2 Peter and Jude.* THNTC. Grand Rapids: Eerdmans, 2007.

Reicke, Bo. "Synoptic Prophecies on the Destruction of Jerusalem." In *Studies in the New Testament and Early Christian Literature: Essays in Honor of Allen P. Wikgren*, edited by David Edward Aune, 121–34. Leiden, The Neth.: Brill, 1972.

Reuss, Joseph, ed. *Matthaeus-Kommentare aus der griechischen Kirche*. Berlin: Akademia-Verlag, 1957.

Reynolds, Benjamin E., and Loren T. Stuckenbruck, eds. *The Jewish Apocalyptic Tradition and the Shaping of the New Testament Thought*. Minneapolis, MN: Fortress, 2017.

Reynolds, Bennie H., III. *Between Symbolism and Realism: The Use of Symbolic and Non-Symbolic Language in Ancient Jewish Apocalypses 333–63 BCE*. Göttingen, Germ.: Vandenhoeck & Ruprecht, 2011.

Richards, I. A. *The Philosophy of Rhetoric*. Oxford: Oxford University Press, 1936.

Richards, I. A., and C. K. Ogden. *The Meaning of Meaning*. 8th ed. New York: Harcourt, 1956.

Ricoeur, Paul. *The Rule of Metaphor: Multidisciplinary Studies of the Creation of Meaning in Language*. Translated by Robert Czerny with Kathleen McLaughlin and John Costello. Toronto: University of Toronto Press, 1977.

Ridderbos, H. N. *The Coming of the Kingdom*. Translated by H. deJongste. Edited by R. O. Zorn. Philadelphia: Presbyterian & Reformed, 1962.

———. *Commentary on Matthew*. Translated by R. Togtman. Grand Rapids: Zondervan, 1987.

Riddlebarger, Kim. *A Case for Amillennialism: Understanding the End Times*. Grand Rapids: Baker, 2013.

Robinson, John A. T. *Jesus and His Coming*. London: SCM, 1957.

———. "The 'Parable' of the Sheep and the Goats." *NTS* 2 (1956) 225–37.

Rollins, Wayne G. "The New Testament and Apocalyptic." *NTS* 17 (1971) 454–76.

Rowland, Christopher. "Apocalyptic Literature." In *It Is Written: Scripture Citing Scripture: Essays in Honor of Barnabas Lindars*, edited by D. A. Carson and H. G. M. Williamson, 170–90. Cambridge: Cambridge University Press, 1998.

———. *The Open Heaven: A Study of Apocalyptic in Judaism and Early Christianity*. London: SPCK, 1982.

Rowley, H. H. *The Relevance of Apocalyptic*. London: Lutterworth, 1944.

Runesson, Anders. *Divine Wrath and Salvation in Matthew: The Narrative World of the First Gospel*. Minneapolis, MN: Fortress, 2016.

Runge, Steven E. *Discourse Grammar of the Greek New Testament: A Practical Introduction for Teaching and Exegesis*. Peabody, MD: Hendrickson, 2010.

Russell, D. S. *The Method and Message of Jewish Apocalyptic, 200 BC–AD 100*. OTL. Philadelphia: Westminster, 1964.

Russell, Stuart J. *The Parousia: A Critical Inquiry into the Testament Doctrine of Our Lord's Second Coming*. 1887. Reprint, Grand Rapids: Baker, 1990.

Sabourin, Leopold. "Apocalyptic Traits in Matthew's Gospel." *RSB* 3 (1983) 19–36.

———. *L'Évangile Selon Saint Matthieu et ses Principaux Parallèles*. Piazza della Pilotta: Biblical Institute, 1978.

Sanders, E. P. *Jesus and Judaism*. Philadelphia: Fortress, 1985.

Scaer, David P. *Discourses in Matthew: Jesus Teaches the Church*. St. Louis: Concordia, 2004.

Schiffrin, Deborah. *Discourse Markers*. Cambridge: Cambridge University Press, 1987.

Schlatter, Adolf. *Der Evangelist Matthäus, seine Sprache, sein Ziel, seine Selbständigkeit: Ein Kommenter zum ersten Evangelium*. Stuttgart, Germ.: Calwer, 1963.
Schottroff, Luise. *The Parable of Jesus*. Translated by Linda M. Maloney. Minneapolis, MN: Augsburg Fortress, 2006.
Schwarz, Hans. *Eschatology*. Grand Rapids: Eerdmans, 2000.
Schweitzer, Albert. *The Quest of the Historical Jesus*. Translated by W. Montgomery. Mineola, NY: Dover, 2005.
Schweizer, Edward. *The Good News according to Matthew*. Atlanta: John Knox, 1975.
Selvanayagam, Israel. "Interpreting a Riddle: Jesus' Subversion of the Davidic Legacy." *BT* 6 (2008) 262–68.
Senior, Donald. *The Gospel of Matthew*. Nashville, TN: Abingdon, 1997.
———. *What Are They Saying about Matthew?* New York: Paulist, 1996.
Sharp, Granville. *Remarks on the Uses of the Definite Article in the Greek Text of the New Testament*. 3rd ed. London: Galabin, 1808.
Shuler, P. L. *A Genre for the Gospels: The Biographical Character of Matthew*. Philadelphia: Fortress, 1982.
Sim, David C. *Apocalyptic Eschatology in the Gospel of Matthew*. SNTSMS 88. Cambridge: Cambridge University Press, 1996.
———"The Gospel of Matthew and the Gentiles." *JSNT* 57 (1995) 19–48.
———. "The Meaning of παλιγγενεσία in Matthew 19.28." *JSNT* 50 (1993) 3–12.
Smalley, Stephen S. "The Delay of the Parousia." *JBL* 83 (1964) 41–54.
———. "Spirit, Kingdom, and Prayer in Luke-Acts." *NovT* 1 (1973) 59–71.
Smallwood, E. Mary. "High Priests and Politics in Roman Palestine." *JTS* 13 (1962) 14–34.
Smith, Christopher R. "Literary Evidence of a Five-Fold Structure in the Gospel of Matthew." *NTS* 43 (1997) 540–51.
Smith, Robert H. *Matthew*. ACNT. Minneapolis, MN: Augsburg, 1989.
Snodgrass, Klyne R. *Stories with Intent: A Comprehensive Guide to the Parables of Jesus*. Grand Rapids: Eerdmans, 2008.
Soskice, Janet M. *Metaphor and Religious Language*. Oxford: Oxford University Press, 1987.
Sowers, Sidney. "The Circumstances and Recollection of the Pella Flight." *TZ* 26 (1970) 305–20.
Stanton, Graham N. *A Gospel for a New People: Studies in Matthew*. Edinburgh: T. & T. Clark, 1992.
Stein, Robert. *Jesus, the Temple, and the Coming of the Son of Man: A Commentary on Mark 13*. Downers Grove, IL: InterVarsity, 2014.
———. "N. T. Wright's *Jesus and the Victory of God*: A Review Article." *JETS* 44 (2001) 207–18.
Stendahl, Krister. *The School of St Matthew and Its Use of the Old Testament*. Philadelphia: Fortress, 1968.
Stone, M. E. "List of Revealed Things in the Apocalyptic Literature." In *Magnalia Dei: The Mighty Acts of God*, edited by F. M. Cross et al., 415–52. Garden City, NY: Doubleday, 1976.
Strauss, David Fredrich. *The Life of Jesus Critically Examined*. Translated by George Eliot. Philadelphia: Fortress, 1972.
Stock, Augustine. *The Method and Message of Matthew*. Collegeville, PA: Liturgical, 1994.

Streeter, H. B. *The Four Gospels: A Study of Origins.* 4th ed. London: Macmillan, 1930.

Sturm, Richard E. "Defining the Word 'Apocalyptic': A Problem of Biblical Criticism." In *Apocalyptic and the New Testament: Essays in Honor of J. Louis Martyn,* edited by Joel Marcus and Marion L. Soards, 17–48. JSNTSup 24. Sheffield, UK: JSOT, 1989.

Such, W. A. *The Abomination of Desolation in the Gospel of Mark: Its Historical Reference in Mark 13:14 and Its Impact in the Gospel.* Lanham, MD: University Press of America, 1999.

Suggs, M. Jack. *Wisdom, Christology, and Law in Matthew's Gospel.* Cambridge: Harvard University Press, 1970.

Talbert, A. H. *Matthew.* PCNT. Grand Rapids: Baker Academic, 2010.

Talbert, Charles H. *What Are the Gospels? The Gene of the Canonical Gospels.* Philadelphia: Fortress, 1977.

Tasker, R. V. G. *The Gospel according to St. Matthew.* TNTC. Grand Rapids: Eerdmans, 1961.

Taylor, Richard A. *Interpreting Apocalyptic Language: An Exegetical Handbook.* Grand Rapids: Kregel Academic, 2016.

Terry, Milton S. *Biblical Apocalypse: A Study of the Most Notable Revelations of God and of Christ.* 1898. Reprint, Grand Rapids: Baker, 1988.

Thatcher, Tom. "Empty Metaphor and Apocalyptic Rhetoric." *JAAR* 66 (1998) 549–70.

Theodoret. *Commentary on the Letters of St. Paul.* Translated by Robert Charles Hill. Brookline: Holy Cross Orthodox, 2001.

Theophilos, Michael P. *The Abomination of Desolation in Matt 24:15.* London: T. & T. Clark, 2012.

Thompson, M. "The Structure of Matthew: A Survey of Recent Trends." *SBibT* 12 (1982) 195–238.

Thompson, W. G. "An Historical Perspective in the Gospel of Matthew." *JBL* 93 (1974) 243–62.

Topel, John L. "What Kind of a Sign Are Vultures? Luke 17, 37b." *Biblica* 84 (2003) 403–11.

Toussaint, Stanley D. *Behold the King: A Study of Matthew.* Portland, OR: Multnomah, 1980.

Trilling, Wolfgang. *The Gospel according to St. Matthew.* 2 vols. New York: Crossroad, 1981.

———. *Das Wahre Israel: Studien Zur Theologie Des Matthäus Evangeliums.* 3rd ed. Munich, Germ.: Kösel, 1964.

Turner, David L. *Israel's Last Prophet: Jesus and the Jewish Leaders in Matthew 23.* Minneapolis, MN: Fortress, 2015.

———. *Matthew.* BECNT. Grand Rapids: Baker Academic, 2008.

———. "The Structure and Sequence of Matthew 24:1–41: Interaction with Evangelical Treatments." *GTJ* 10 (1989) 3–27.

VanderWeele, Tyler J. "Some Observations Concerning the Chiastic Structure of the Gospel of Matthew." *JTS* 59 (2008) 669–73.

Vansina, Jan. *Oral Tradition as History.* Madison, WI: University of Wisconsin Press, 1985.

Varner, William C. "The Didache 'Apocalypse' and Matthew 24." *BSac* 165 (2008) 309–22.

Varner, W. Terry. *Studies in Biblical Eschatology: Background Study to the AD 70 Theory*. Marietta, OH: Therefore Stand Publications, 1981.

Vena, Osvaldo D. *The Parousia and Its Readings: The Development of the Eschatological Consciousness in the Writings of the New Testament*. New York: Lang, 2001.

Verheyden, Joseph. "Describing the Parousia: The Cosmic Phenomenon in Mk 13:24–25." In *The Scriptures in the Gospels*, edited by C. M. Tuckett, 525–50. Leuven, Belg.: Leuven University Press, 1997.

Via, Dan O. "Ethical Responsibility and Human Wholeness in Matthew 25:31–46." *HTR* 80 (1897) 79–100.

———. "Structure, Christology, and Ethics in Matthew." In *Orientation by Disorientation: Studies in Literary Criticism and Biblical Literary Criticism*, edited by Richard A. Spencer, 199–215. Pittsburgh, PA: Pickwick, 1980.

Von Harnack, Adolf. *The Date of the Acts and of the Synoptic Gospels*. Translated by J. R. Wilkinson. CTL 33. New York: Putnam's, 1911.

Von Rad, Gerhard. *The Message of the Prophets*. Translated by D. Stalker. New York: Harper & Row, 1965.

Waetjen, Herman C. *Matthew's Theology of Fulfillment, Its Universality and Its Ethnicity: God's New Israel as the Pioneer of God's New Humanity*. London: T. & T. Clark, 2017.

———. *The Origin and Destiny of Humanness: An Interpretation of the Gospel according to Matthew*. Corte Madera, CA: Omega, 1976.

Walker, Peter W. L. *Jesus and the Holy City: New Testament Perspectives on Jerusalem*. Grand Rapids: Eerdmans, 1996.

Wallace, Daniel B. *Greek Grammar beyond the Basics: An Exegetical Syntax of the New Testament*. Grand Rapids: Zondervan, 1999.

Walvoord, John F. "Christ's Olivet Discourse on the End of the Age." *BSac* (1971) 109–16.

———. "Is a Posttribulation Rapture Revealed in Matt 24?" *GTJ* 6 (1985) 257–66.

———. *Matthew: Thy Kingdom Come*. Chicago: Moody, 1974.

———. "A Review of 'the Blessed Hope' by G. E. Ladd." *BSac* 113 (1956) 289–307.

Ware, Bruce A. "Is the Church in View in Matthew 24–25?" *BSac* 138 (1981) 158–72.

Waterman, G. H. "The Source of Paul's Teaching on the Second Coming of Christ in 1 and 2 Thessalonians." *JETS* 18 (1975) 105–13.

Webb, Robert L. "'Apocalyptic': Observations on a Slippery Term." *JNES* 49 (1990) 115–26.

Weiffenbach, Wilhelm. *Der Wiederkunftsgedanke Jesu. Nach den Synoptikern Kritisch Untersucht und Dargestellt*. Leipzig, Germ.: Breitkopf and Härtel, 1873.

Weiss, Johannes. *Die Prediqt Jesu vom Reiche Gottes*. Göttingen, Germ.: Vandenhoeck & Ruprecht, 1892.

Wenham, David. *The Parables of Jesus*. Downers Grove, IL: IVP Academic, 1989.

———. "Paul and the Synoptic Apocalypse." In *Gospel Perspectives: Studies of History and Tradition in the Four Gospels*, edited by R. T. France and David Wenham, 2:345–75. 4 vols. Sheffield, UK: JSOT, 1981.

———. *The Rediscovery of Jesus' Eschatological Discourse*. Sheffield, UK: JSOT, 1984.

———. "'This Generation Will Not Pass . . .': A Study of Jesus' Future Expectation in Mark 13." In *Christ the Lord*, edited by H. H. Rowdon, 127–50. Leicester, UK: InterVarsity, 1982.

Weren, W. J. C. "The Macrostructure of Matthew's Gospel: A New Proposal." *Bib* 87 (2006) 171–200.

———. *Studies in Matthew's Gospel: Literary Design, Intertextuality, and Social Setting.* Leiden, The Neth.: Brill, 2014.

Westfall, Cynthia Long. "Οὖν in the New Testament: The Minimal Semantic Contribution of a Discourse Marker." In *The Language and Literature of the New Testament: Essays in Honor of Stanley E. Porter's 60th Birthday*, edited by Lois K. Fuller Dow et al., 284–301. Leiden, The Neth.: Brill, 2016.

Whitacre, Rodney A. *John.* Downers Grove, IL: InterVarsity, 1999.

Wilk, Florian. *Jesus und die Volker in der Sicht der Synoptiker.* BZNW 109. Berlin: de Gruyter, 2002.

Wilkins, Michael J. *Matthew.* NIVAC. Grand Rapids: Zondervan, 2004.

Willitts, Joel. *Matthew's Messianic Shepherd-King: In Search of 'the Lost Sheep of Israel'.* Berlin: de Gruyter, 2007.

Wilson, Alistair I. *When Will These Things Happen? A Study of Jesus as Judge in Matthew 21–25.* Cumbria, UK: Paternoster, 2004.

Wilson, Carol B. *For I Was Hungry and You Gave Me Food: Pragmatics of Food Access in the Gospel of Matthew.* Eugene, OR: Pickwick, 2014.

Winer, G. B. *A Treatise on the Grammar of the New Testament.* Translated by W. F. Moulton. 1882. Reprint, Eugene, OR: Wipf & Stock, 1997.

Witherington, Ben, III. *The Christology of Jesus.* Minneapolis, MN: Augsburg Fortress, 1990.

———. *1 and 2 Thessalonians: A Socio-Rhetorical Commentary.* Grand Rapids: Eerdmans, 2006.

———. *The Indelible Image: The Theological and Ethical Thought World of the New Testament.* 2 vols. Downers Grove, IL: InterVarsity, 2009.

———. *Jesus, Paul, and the End of the World: A Comparative Study in New Testament Eschatology.* Downers Grove, IL: InterVarsity, 1992.

———. *Jesus the Sage: The Pilgrimage of Wisdom.* Minneapolis, MN: Augsburg Fortress, 1994.

———. *Jesus the Seer: The Progress of Prophecy.* Minneapolis, MN: Fortress, 2014.

———. *Matthew.* Macon, GA: Smyth & Helwys, 2006.

———. *The Problem with Evangelical Theology: Testing the Exegetical Foundation of Calvinism, Dispensationalism, and Wesleyanism.* Waco, TX: Baylor University Press, 2005.

———. *Torah Old and New: Exegesis, Intertextuality, and Hermeneutics.* Minneapolis, MN: Fortress, 2018.

———. *Women in the Ministry of Jesus.* Cambridge: Cambridge University Press, 1984.

Witherington, Ben, III, and Laura M. Ice. *The Shadow of the Almighty: Father, Son, and Spirit in Biblical Perspective.* Grand Rapids: Eerdmans, 2002.

Wright, N. T. *Jesus and the Victory of God.* Minneapolis, MN: Fortress, 1996.

———. *Matthew for Everyone, Part 2: Chapters 16–28.* 2nd ed. London: SPCK, 2004.

———. *New Testament and the People of God.* Minneapolis, MN: Fortress, 1992.

———. *Surprised by Hope.* New York: HarperCollins, 2008.

———. *Paul and the Faithfulness of God.* Minneapolis, MN: Fortress, 2013.

———. *The Resurrection of the Son of God.* Minneapolis, Fortress, 2003.

Yarbro Collins, Adela. "Apocalypse Now: The State of Apocalyptic Studies Near the End of the First Decade of the Twenty-First Century." *HTR* 104 (2011) 448–57.

Zahn, Theodor. *Das Evangelium des Matthäus*. Wuppertal: Brockhaus, 1984.
Zeichmann, Christopher B. "The Date of Mark's Gospel Apart from the Temple and Rumors of War: The Taxation Episode (12:13–17) as Evidence." *CBQ* 79 (2017) 422–37.
Zetterholm, Magnus. *Approaches to Paul: A Student's Guide to Recent Scholarship*. Minneapolis, MN: Fortress, 2009.

Ancient Document Index

OLD TESTAMENT/ HEBREW BIBLE

Genesis

1:16	199n412
7:1–2	215
7:13–16	220
7:15–16	216
7:16b	271n495
8:22	70n109, 78n162
12:2	23n126
19:11	209n465
19:15–17	219n503
22:3	217n498
22:18	254, 257, 258
31:23	217n498
45:18	217n498
47:2	217n498
47:29—49:33	67n92
49:1	70n110

Exodus

9:18	172n268
10:14	172n268
11:6	172n268
15:14	142n97
19:4	185n353
19:16–18	77
23:16	129n24

Leviticus

11:13	185n348
26:30	169

Numbers

22:41	217n498
23:14	217n498
23:20	217n498
23:22	254n84
23:27–28	217n498
24:8	254n84
24:14	70n110
24:17	254n84

Deuteronomy

2:25	142n97
4:19	198
4:30	70n110
11:12	129n24
13	73n131
14:12	185n348
17:3	198
18:18	248
28:26	182n327
28:49	185n353
30:4	204, 264
31:29	70n110
32:11	185n353
32:8	197n402, 198

Joshua

4:2	217n498
4:8	129n24
23–24	67n92

Judges

20:40	129n24

1 Samuel

8:3	129n24
20:41	129n24
17:44	182n327

2 Samuel

7:10–14	134n58
7:12–16	253

1 Kings

6:12	129n24
6:25	129n24

2 Kings

13:17	129n24
13:19	129n24
16:7	246n45

1 Chronicles

28–29	67n92

2 Chronicles

24:23	129n24
25:11	217n498

Ezra

9:14	129n24
11–12	183n338
14:18	183n338

Nehemiah

9:31	129n24

Job

9:26	182n327
15:23	182n327
26:10	129n24
28:12–28	250n66
30:2	129n24
39:27–30	182n327

Psalms

2	254n85, 256n93, 257
2:6–9	254, 256
18:5	149n136
23	70
23:1	149n136
46:1–3	78n162
58:13–14	129n24
72:7	70n109
79:2	182n327
88:12	149n136
89:2	149n136
92:1	149n136
93:1	78n162
95:10	149n136
95:13	149n136
97:9	149n136
103:25–26	70n109
110:1	227, 256n97, 257
117:26a	124, 126
118	126
118:26	127
118:96	129n24
122:3–5	75, 227
148:6	78n162

Proverbs

6:6	221n512
8:31	149n136
9:14	209n465

Ecclesiastes

1:4	78n162

Isaiah

2:2	70n109

3:1–3	217n498	51:6	70n109, 78n162
4:2–4	217n498	52:11–12	74n133
5:26	200n417	54:10	70n109
6:12	200n417	60:1–5	201
9:1–2	88n12	62:4	149nn135
10:14	149nn135, 136	62:10	200n417
10:23	149nn135	62:11	56n23
11:10	200n417, 203	65:8	73n131
11:12	203, 204, 205, 264	65:17	64n75, 78n162
13	73, 77	66:16	174n276
13:5	149nn135	66:23	174n276
13:6	73n133	66:24	174n276
13:6–13	189n371		
13:8	142n97		

Jeremiah

13:9	70n109, 149nn135
13:9–10	195
13:9–13	73n133, 78n162
13:10	191, 198
13:11	149nn136
14:4	73n133
14:12–15	73n133
14:17	149nn135
14:26	149nn135
18:3	200n417
23:17	149nn135
24:1	149nn135
24:4	149nn135
24:19–20	78n162
26:17–18	142n97
26:19	228n549
27:6	149nn135
27:13	200n417
28:3	200n417
34	77
34:1	149nn135
34:2–5	195
34:3–4	73n133, 189n371
34:4	78n162, 191, 196n397, 198
37:16	149nn135
37:18	149nn135
40:5–6	174n276
40:31	185n353
42:1	254n85
42:1–4	246n45
48:20	74n133
49:22	200n417
49:26	174n276

2:7	155n162
4:1	155n162
4:7	155n162
4:21	200n417
4:23–28	78n162
4:27	129n24
5:10	129n24
5:18	129n24
6:1	200n417
6:11	217n498
6:13–14	70n131
7:4	135
7:10	155n162
7:12	135
7:14	70n131, 135
7:30	155n162
7:33	183
7:34	155n162
8:2	198n407
10:12	149n136
11:15	155n162
12:12	174n276
13:27	155n162
16:18	155n162
22:5	155n162
23:20	70n110
25:11–12	166n234
26:6	135
26:28	129n24
28:15	149n136
29:10	166n234
30:3–9	171n263
30:17–18	217n498

Jeremiah (cont.)

30:24	70n110
32:18	155n162
32:27	174n276
32:31	174n276
39:7	217n498
39:35	155n162
45:4–5	174n276
46:8	70n131
46:10	70n110
48:47	70n110
49:39	70n110
50:6	74n133
50:8	74n133
50:28	74n133
51:6	155n162
51:6–10	74n133
51:22	155, 155n162
51:27	200n417
51:34–36	174n276
51:45–46	74n133
51:50–51	74n133
51:57	74n133

Lamentations

3:2	217n498

Ezekiel

1:1	166n234
1:28	166n234
5:8–12	171n263
5:9	155n162, 172n268
5:11	155n162
5:14	171n263
6:9	155n162
6:11	155n162
7:5–8	155n162
7:12–16	73n131
7:20	155n162
8:10	155n162
10:18	124n6
11:13	129n24
11:18	155n162
11:21	155n162
13:5	70n110
13:13	129n24
17	185n353
20:6	166n234
20:7–8	155n162
20:17	129n24
20:30	155n162
21:4	174n276
21:6–9	174n276
21:10	174n276
21:12	174n276
21:33	129n24
22:12	129n24
24:21	73n131
30:3	70n110
32:4	182n327
32:5–8	73n132, 189n371
32:7–8	196, 197
33:28–29	155
34:10	23n126
36:31	155n162
37	228
38:16	70n110
39:17–20	182n327

Daniel

2:28	70n110
2:38	149n135
3:2	149n135
3:45	149n135
4:28	129n24
4:31	129n24, 217n498
4:34	129n24
6:1	217n498
6:20	217n498
6:29	217n498
7	4, 75, 80, 166n234
7:9	74
7:9–14	227
7:13	74, 78, 204
7:13–14	74, 189, 190n379
7:22	228, 245
7:18	217n498
8:2	166n234
8:9	166n234
8:11	164
8–12	129
8:13	133n49, 158n179, 167

8:13–14	157	13:16	73n131
8:15–17	159n190		
8:17	166n234	**Joel**	
8:19	129n25, 134n56	1:15	70, 70n110
9:12	172n268	2:1–2	70
9:22–23	159n190	2:1–11	78n162
9:24	129n26	2:1–31	70n110
9:24–27	166n234	2:2	172n268
9:26	124n4, 129n27, 157n173	2:10	191, 195, 197
9:26–27	73n132, 134n56, 155n163	2:10–11	73–74n133, 189n371
9:27	7, 129n28, 161n208, 164, 167, 167n241	2:30–31	78n162
		2:30–32	73–74n133
		2:31	197
10:14	70n110	3:1	174n276
11:6	129n24, 134n56	3:1–5	75n142
11:13	129n24, 134n56	3:14	70, 70n110
11:27	129n27, 134n56	3:14–15	73–74n133
11:31	155n163, 158n179, 161n208, 167, 167n241	3:14–16	78n162
		3:21	70
11:31–35	73n132	**Amos**	
11:32	164	1:14	129n24
11:33	159n190	3:3–8	182n332
11:35–36	129n27, 134n56	5:18–20	70n110
11:40	129n27, 134n56	8:8	129n24
11:45	129n28	8:8–9	68
12:1	172n268	8:9	73–744n133, 76, 189n371
12:1–2	171, 173n271		
12:2	226n538	8:9–10	203
12:3	166n234	9:5	129n24
12:4	129n27, 134n56	9:5–6	68
12:6–7	129n27, 134n56		
12:6	133n49	**Obadiah**	
12:9–10	159n190	15	70n110
12:10–11	73n132		
12:11	155n163, 167, 167n241	**Micah**	
		3:12	73n131
12:12–13	151, 152n150	4:9	142n97
12:13	134n56		
Hosea		**Nahum**	
3:5	70n110	1:3	129n24
6:2	228n549	1:8–9	129n24
8:1	185n353	2:11	142n97
11:1	254n84		

Habakkuk

1:8	182n327, 185n353
1:9	129n24
1:15	129n24
3:19	129n24

Zephaniah

1:7–14	70n110
1:15	73–74n133, 189n371
1:18	129n24
3:11–13	217n498
12:5–8	78n163

Haggai

2:6	197
2:21	197

Zechariah

2:6–8	73–74n133
2:10	204, 264
12:15–17	174n276
6:12–13	134n58
12:10–14	203, 204
14:1	70n110
14:1–5	134n57
14:2	73–74n133
14:3–5	73–74n133
14:4	108n123
14:5	78
14:6–7	204n446
14:6–8	78n162
14:9	73–74n133

Malachi

4:5	70n110

OLD TESTAMENT APOCRYPHA

Judith

10:18	176n286

1 Maccabees

1:37	160n192
1:52–58	170n254
1:54	155n164, 157n174, 160n193
1:54–56	73n132
1:59	155n164
1:62–64	73n132
2:7–12	73n132
2:15–28	73n132
3:45	73n132
3:50–53	73n132
4:41–58	157n174
6:7	155n164
9:27	172n268

2 Maccabees

2:18	157
6:1–6	155n164
6:4	160n193
8:12	176n287
8:17	73n132
8:17–19	158n179
13:21	176n287

Tobit

5:4	56n22

Sirach/Ecclesiasticus

6:23–31	250n66
24:8–12	249n61
44:16–17	217n498
51:23–27	250n66

Wisdom of Solomon

9:17	209n465

PSEUDEPIGRAPHA

Apocalypse of Elijah

32	199n416

Apocalypse of Zephaniah

12:5–8	78n163

2 Baruch

3:4–9	133n49
8:2	124n6
11:1	277n69
21:19	133n49
25:2–4	138n77, 141n91
27:2–6	141n88
27:2–13	141n89, 141n90
32:1	78n163
48:34	141n88
53:8–10	179n309
59:3	78n163
70:3	141n88, 141n92
70:7	141n88
70:8	141n89, 141n90
85:10	78n163

1 Enoch

1:3–9	78n163
7:2–6	4
10:4	56n24
25:5	158n179
37–71	75, 223, 223n520
42	249n61
45:4–5	76n152, 78n163
46:3	56n25
46:7	125
48:5	125
48:9	56n24
55:4	125
61:7–11	125
62:3–4	142n96
62:6–16	125
62:10	125
63:1–12	125
69:29	76n152
72:1	76n152, 78n163
72–82	65
80:4	197
80:4–8	78n163
83:2–5	78n163
89:56	124n6
90:1–5	183
90:2	185n353
90:2–4	184
90:6–39	208n461
90:13–20	75
91:11–17	78n163
91:16	76n152, 78n163
94:1	56n25
102:1–3	78n163

2 Enoch

65:6–11	78n163
65:7	76n152
65:10	76n152

4 Ezra

3:18–19	77
3:28	277n69
3:32	277n69
4:33–37	133n49
4:40–42	142n97
4:51–52	133n49
5:1	138n77
5:2	141n94
5:4–5	78n163
5:5–55	78n163
5:10	141n94
6:7	133n49
6:11–12	133n49
6:13–15	141n88
6:20	138n77
6:24–25	141n94
6:25	152n151
7:30–42	78n163
8:63	133n49
8:63—9:13	137n70
9:3	141n88, 141n89
13:29–49	190
13:31	141n88
14:18	78n163
15:15	141n88

Jubilee

1:29	78n163
4:26	78n163
23:11–25	138n77
23:12–13	141n91
23:13	141n90
23:20	141n86
35:17	56n22

Lives of the Prophets

12:10–12	129n30

3 Maccabees

3:17	176n287

Pseudo Philo, Biblical Antiquities

3:10	78n163
11:3	77

Psalms of Solomon

13:11	217n498

Testament of Job

33:3–9	78n163

Testament of Joshua

1:5–20	56n26

Testament of Judah

3:10	56n22
22:2	176n288

Testament of Levi

4:1	198n405
8:15	176n288

Testament of Moses

8:1	172n268
10:1–10	73n133, 189n371
10:3–6	78n163
10:8	183n338

Sibylline Oracle

2:5–9	141n89
2:6–40	138n77
2:20–24	141n89, 141n90
2:154–214	138n77
2:155	141n90
2:165	141n93
3:80–92	78n163
3:675–81	78n163
3:796–804	78n163, 138n77
4:175–92	78n163
5:155–61	78n163
5:211–13	78n163
5:346–49	78n163
5:477–78	78n163
5:512–31	78n163
8:169–210	138n77

PHILO

De aeternitate mundi (On the Eternity of the World)

85–88	228n549

Legation ad Gaium (On the Embassy to Gaius

29:191	134n54

De specialibus legibus (On Special Laws)

1:66–67	134n54

JOSEPHUS

Jewish Wars

1.12	172n268
3.123	183n336
4.151–61	164n223
4.147–63	164n222
4.160	165
4.201	160n192, 168n244
4.202–352	168n245
4.242	168n244
4.278	170n253
4.310–18	168n246
4.311	170n253
4.313–17	170n254
4.387–88	164n222
4.486–90	163n215
4.486–91	161n201, 164n218
4.585–88	163n215
5.3	168n246
5.5.4–5	134n54
5.15–20	168n246

ANCIENT DOCUMENT INDEX 321

5.27–30	170n252
5.394–95	164n221
5.424–38	175n279
5.442	172n268
5.510–19	175n279
5.567–72	175n279
6.5.2	142n100
6.5.3	200n419
6.193–213	175n279
6.288–300	190–91n381
6.316	161n200
6.414–34	175n279
7.11.1	142n100

Jewish Antiquities

3.203	176n288, 180n316
9.152	160n192
11.66	228n549
12.253	155n164, 157n174, 164n221
12.316–25	157n174
12.320–22	155n164, 164n221
18.3.55–59	161n198
18.257–309	73n132, 161n198
20.5.1	142n100
20.164–66	169n250
20.196–99	165n230

Against Apion

2.218	228n549

NEW TESTAMENT

Matthew

1–2	88, 91
1–10	91n27
1–28	252
1:1	95, 253, 254n81, 258
1:1—2:23	89
1:1—4:11	97, 98, 99
1:1—4:16	95, 98, 100, 261
1:2–16	42
1:1–17	41, 108
1:17	47, 47n80, 48n88, 211n473
1:18	49n98, 108, 254
1:18–25	41, 41n41, 98
1:20	206n456, 217n499, 253
1:21	234
1:23	94, 124
1:24	206n456, 217n499
2:1	96, 98
2:2	198, 253, 255
2:6	204n443
2:7	44, 198
2:9	198
2:9–11	198
2:10	13:24
2:11	93n41
2:12–15	237–38n3
2:13	126n18, 206n456
2:13–14	217n499
2:15	253, 254
2:15–18	178n304
2:16	44
2:17	44
2:19	206n456
2:20	204n443
2:20–21	217n499
2:21	204n443
2:22	100n79
3:1	43, 49n98, 101, 253
3:1—4:25	89
3:1—9:11	88
3:2	234, 252n78
3:4–16	43
3:7	100n79
3:7–9	22n123
3:7–10	167n239
3:7–12	123n1
3:8	48n88
3:8–12	90n24
3:10	48n88
3:10–12	252n78
3:11	158n180
3:11–12	248
3:12	207n459, 218, 253, 255
3:13	44
3:15	56n25
3:16	193n386
3:17	253, 254, 255, 258n109
4:1	44

Matthew (cont.)

4:1–11	95, 237–38n3
4:3	253, 254, 258n112
4:5	44, 158, 217n499, 258n110
4:6	206n456, 253, 254, 258n110, 258n112
4:8	217n499, 252n78, 256
4:8–9	253, 258n110, 258n112
4:10	100
4:11	100, 206n456
4:12	95, 96, 100, 101
4:12–13	88n12
4:12–16	95
4:12—11:1	97, 98
4:12—16:20	99
4:12—15:20	88
4:12–17	96, 98
4:13	101, 158n180
4:15	22n122, 144n105, 144n107, 204n443
4:16	100, 101, 253
4:17	49n98, 94, 95, 95n55, 96, 100, 101, 102, 102n84, 234, 252n78, 253
4:17–25	98
4:17—11:1	98
4:17—16:12	103
4:17—16:20	95, 237
4:17—25:46	100, 103, 261
4:18	88n12, 101, 102
4:18—25:46	98
4:20	133n46, 193n386, 217n502
4:22	193n386, 217n502
4:23	88n12, 102, 146, 252n78
4:25—5:2	92
5	105
5:1	43n55, 92n36, 100n79, 102n84, 108, 112
5–7	105
5:1—7:28	89
5:1—26:34	96
5:3	252n78
5:3–12	49
5:5	204n443
5:6	56n25
5:10	56n25, 252n78
5:11	137n68
5:12	234n575
5:13	204n443
5:14	150n140
5:15	93n41
5:17	159n190
5:17–20	57n30
5:18	126n19, 204n443, 230
5:19	48n88, 118n166, 230
5:19–20	252n78
5:20	56n25
5:21	60
5:21–22	252n78
5:21–48	230
5:23	48n88, 118n166
5:23–24	159n184
5:26	126n18
5:35	204n443
5:48	48n88
6:2	48n88, 137n68
6:3–4	234n575
6:5–6	137n68
6:6	234n575
6:8	48n88
6:9	48n88
6:10	82n190, 204n443, 252n78
6:16	137n68
6:17–18	234n575
6:19	204n443
6:22	48n88
6:23	48n88
6:24–26	49
6:28	212n477
6:31	48n88, 118n166
6:32	22n122, 144n105
6:33	56n25, 59n44, 252n78
6:34	48n88, 118n166
7:2	57n33
7:11	48n88
7:12	48n89, 118n167

7:13–14	59n44, 148n129	10:5	22n122, 57n30, 144, 144n104, 144n105, 144n107, 145
7:19	123n1, 252n78		
7:21	252n77, 252n78		
7:21–23	60, 235n579, 248		
7:21–24	235	10:5–6	144
7:22	253, 256	10:6	93n41, 241n20
7:22–23	57n30	10:6–8	234n575
7:24	47, 47n84, 48n89, 118n167, 250n68	10:7	252n78
		10:11	126n18
7:24–27	93n41	10:11–13	234n575
7:26–28	123n1	10:12–14	93n41
7:28	89, 95, 102n87, 104	10:13–15	147n121
8:1	43n55, 100n79	10:14–15	123n1
8:1—9:38	89	10:15	57n33, 158n180, 204n443, 225, 252n78
8:3	193n386		
8:4	146n117		
8:5	100n79	10:16	48n88, 158n180, 250n68
8:6	93n41		
8:10	100n79	10:17–18	137n68, 145
8:11–12	123n1, 204, 252n78	10:18	22n122, 144n105, 144n107, 146n117
8:12	59n44		
8:14	93n41	10:19	137n68
8:18	100n79	10:20–23	54
8:20	245n42, 257n101	10:21	59n44
8:21	132	10:22	151, 151n145, 152, 152n149
8:24	59n44		
8:25	132	10:23	11n55, 12, 12n64, 16, 85, 126n18, 137n68, 144, 144n104, 192, 192n384, 227, 245n42, 257n101
8:29	253, 258n111		
9:6	59n44, 204n443, 245n42, 257n101		
9:6–7	93n41		
9:8	100n79		
9:10	93n41	10:24	144
9:15	137n68	10:26	48n88, 54, 254n86
9:18	49n98	10:26–27	57n33
9:23	93n41	10:29	204n443
9:26	204n443	10:31	48n88
9:27	253, 258n105	10:32	48n88, 252n77
9:28	93n41, 100n79	10:33	252n77
9:31	204n443	10:34	204n443
9:32	109n125	10:34–36	170
9:35	108n120, 146, 252n78	10:34–38	60
		10:40–42	234
9:36	22n124, 100n79	10:41	57, 57n30
9:36–37	92	10:41–42	152n149
9:38	48n88	10:42	230, 231, 231n563, 234
10	144, 145		
10:1	108, 230	11	91n27, 92
10:1—11:1	89		

Matthew (*cont.*)

11:1	89, 95, 102n87, 111n136
11:2–6	96, 98
11:2—12:50	89
11:2—16:12	97, 98
11:2—16:20	98
11:8	93n41
11:10	206n455
11:11–12	252n78
11:12	170
11:16	211n473
11:19	245n42, 250, 251, 257n101
11:20	44, 234
11:20–24	57n30, 57n33, 123n1
11:21	234
11:21–24	226
11:22	252n78
11:23	59n44
11:24	204n443, 252n78
11:25	49n98, 54, 204n443, 252n77, 254n86
11:25–27	250n67
11:25–30	250n66
11:26	252n77
11:27	54, 252n77, 254n86
11:28–30	250n67
12:1	49n98
12:3	159n188
12:4	93n41
12:5	159n188
12:6	124n5
12:8	245n42, 257n101
12:11	22n124
12:12	48n88
12:14	237–38n3
12:18	22n122, 144n105, 252n78
12:18–21	246n45
12:20	126n19, 252n78
12:21	22n122, 144n105
12:23	252n78, 253, 258n107
12:25–26	93n41, 252n78
12:26	48n88
12:28	14, 68n102, 82n189, 158n180, 252n78, 267
12:29	93n41
12:32	59n44, 245n42, 257n101, 268
12:33	22n123, 253
12:33–36	22n123
12:36	226, 233, 252n78
12:36–37	223n523, 235
12:39	211n473
12:39–40	202
12:40	204n443, 224n526, 245n42, 257n101
12:41	57n33, 234
12:41–42	123n1, 211n473, 223n523, 226, 235, 252n78
12:42	204n443, 250, 254
12:43	137n68
12:44	93n41
12:45	211n473, 217n499
12:46	49n98
12:49–50	231, 235
12:50	252n77
13:1	49n98, 88n12, 93n41
13:1–2	106, 108
13:1–3	92, 109
13:1–9	106
13:1–53	89, 94n48
13:5	193n386, 204n443
13:8	204n443
13:10	92n36
13:10–23	106
13:11	59n44, 159n190, 252n78
13:12	57n33
13:18	48n88, 48n89, 118n167
13:19	252n78
13:20–21	193n386
13:23	204n443
13:24	194, 252n78
13:24–30	106, 198, 218, 224, 224n524
13:24–35	106
13:27	48n88
13:28	48n88

ANCIENT DOCUMENT INDEX 325

13:29	219	13:53	89, 95, 102n87, 106, 111n136
13:30	126n18, 185n355, 207n459	13:54	250
13:31	252n78	13:54–56	253
13:31–33	221n511	13:54—17:21	89
13:32	59n44, 137n68	13:56	48n88
13:33	252n78	13:57	67n96, 93n41, 251
13:34–37	104, 105	13:58	104
13:35	59n44, 150n140	14:1	49n98
13:36	44, 91, 92, 93, 93n41, 105, 105n103, 106, 133, 219	14:13	100n79
		14:15	132
		14:22	193n386
		14:24	204n443
13:36–37	92	14:25–26	179
13:36–43	59n44, 106, 198, 218	14:26–31	42
		14:27	193n386
13:36–52	106	14:28	100n79, 132
13:37	245n42, 257n101	14:31	193n386
13:37–43	179, 224	14:33	253
13:38	150n140, 252n78	14:34	204n443
13:38–42	108n124	15:2	137n68
13:39	133, 206, 206n456	15:10–21	93
13:39–40	130	15:12	44, 132, 132n44
13:39–43	268	15:13	252n77
13:40	48n88, 133, 224, 224n526, 252n78	15:15	132
		15:16–17	132
13:40–42	123n1	15:20—18:35	88
13:40–43	25	15:21–28	44
13:41	206, 206n456, 245n42, 252n78, 257n101	15:22	253, 258n106
		15:23	132
		15:24	22n124, 93n41, 144, 144n104
13:41–51	179	15:29	88n12
13:40	252n78	15:33	132
13:42	44, 82n190	15:35	204n443
13:43–45	252n78	16:1	111n136
13:44–45	221n511	16:1–4	202n436
13:46	100n79	16:4	202, 211n473
13:47	185n355, 252n78	16:7	132
13:47–48	207n458, 218	16:7–12	132
13:47–49	207n458	16:8	100n79
13:47–50	123n1	16:9	159n190
13:48	207n458	16:11	159n190
13:49	133, 206, 206n456, 207n458, 268	16:13	100n79, 245n42
		16:13–16	257n101
13:49–50	108n124, 130	16:13–20	103
13:50	252n78	16:13–28	14n78, 96, 98
13:51	133, 133n46	16:13—20:34	97, 98
13:52	252n78		

Matthew (*cont.*)

16:14–17	251n72
16:16	100n79, 103, 103n91, 133n46, 253, 258n113
16:16–17	255
16:17	54, 252n77, 254n86
16:17–19	96
16:18	158
16:18–19	22, 23
16:19	22, 59n44, 204n443, 228, 252n78
16:20	44, 96, 102
16:21	49n98, 59n44, 67n96, 94, 95, 95n55, 96n60, 101
16:21—20:34	99
16:21—25:45	103
16:21–28	98
16:21—28:20	95, 237
16:22	126n19
16:22–23	96, 132
16:24	44
16:26	150n140
16:27	26n152, 59n44, 85, 115, 129, 179, 180, 192, 205, 205n451, 206, 206n456, 245n42, 252n77, 257n101, 262
16:27–28	81, 132n41, 266, 267
16:28	59n44, 85, 96n59, 126n19, 192, 192n384, 205, 205n450, 245n42, 252n78, 257n101
17–23	237
17–25	237n2
17:1	217n499
17:1–6	179
17:1–8	197
17:1–9	59n44
17:4	132
17:5	49n98, 253, 255, 258n109
17:9	237n2, 245n42, 257n101
17:9–12	132
17:10	48n88, 132
17:12	245n42, 257n101
17:13	133n46
17:17	100n79, 115, 137n68, 211n473
17:19	132
17:20	96n59
17:22	109n125, 245n42, 257n101
17:22–23	67n96, 237n2
17:22—19:1	89
17:24	109n125
17:24–27	159n184
17:25	93n41, 204n443
18:1	49n98, 92n36, 108, 132, 252n78
18:1–3	92
18:2	44
18:2–6	230
18:3	96n59
18:3–4	252n78
18:4	48n88
18:4–5	230
18:6	230
18:6–9	56n22
18:6–14	231n563
18:7	150n140
18:8–9	252n78
18:10	59n44, 206n456, 230, 252n77
18:12	22n124
18:12–13	230
18:13	96n59
18:14	230, 252n77
18:15–17	147, 225, 263
18:16	217n499
18:17	22, 245
18:18	204n443
18:18–19	96n59
18:19	204n443, 252n77
18:20	185n355
18:21	44, 105, 132
18:23	252n78
18:23–34	224n525
18:25	109n125
18:26	48n88

ANCIENT DOCUMENT INDEX

18:27	100n79	20:23	67n96, 252n77
18:28	100n79	20:25	22n122, 144n105
18:29	48n88	20:28	224n526, 245n42, 257n101
18:31	48n88		
18:35	252n77	20:30	252n78, 253, 258n105
19	105		
19–22	247	20:31	253, 258n105
19:1	88n12, 89, 95, 102n87, 104, 111n136	20:34	100n79, 193n386
		21	21, 105
		21–23	237n3, 241, 250, 251
19:1—20:34	88		
19:1—22:45	89	21:1	105, 111n136
19:1—26:2	105	21:1–11	105
19:3—22:46	107	21:1–17	96, 98
19:4	159n188	21–25	105, 106n109, 251, 256
19:6	48n88		
19:7	48n88	21:1—25:46	99, 107n117
19:12	252n78	21:1—27:66	98
19:13	44	21–28	88
19:14	252n78	21:1—28:15	97, 98
19:16-17	217	21:2	193n386
19:22	100n79	21:3	193n386
19:23	96n59	21:5	253, 256
19:23-24	252n78	21:9	125, 253
19:26	100n79	21:9-11	127
19:27	217n502	21:10	59n44
19:28	23, 59n44, 96n59, 137n68, 148, 192, 203, 226, 227, 245n42, 257n101	21:11	67n96, 251n72, 253
		21:12	253, 256
		21:12-20	209
		21:13	93n41, 124, 160, 191
19:28-29	199n414		
19:29	93n41, 217n502, 227, 234n575	21:15	100n79, 127, 253, 258n108
		21:16	159n188
19:30	227	21:19	253, 256
20:1	252n78	21:20	209
20:1-16	224n525	21:21	96n59, 100n79
20:2	100n79	21:24	100n79
20:6	27, 212n477	21:25	48n88
20:11	100n79	21:29	235
20:17	217n499	21:30	100n79
20:18	245n42, 257n101	21:31	96n59, 235, 252n78
20:18-19	67n96	21:32	56n25
20:19	22n122, 144n105, 144n107	21:33-41	224n525
		21:33-43	188
20:20	132	21:33-45	22n123, 208
20:20-23	132	21:37-39	237n2
20:21	252n78	21:40	48n88, 137n68
20:21-22	132		
20:22	100n79, 132		

Matthew (cont.)

21:40–43	123n1
21:41	23, 60
21:41–43	23
21:41–45	22
21:42	159n188
21:43	22, 22, 22n122, 22n123, 23n126, 144, 146, 228, 245, 252n78, 263
21:46	67n96
22:1–13	253, 256
22:1–14	147n121, 207n458, 224n525, 245
22:2	252n78
22:4–7	123n1
22:7	60, 67n96, 124, 185, 207n458
22:8–13	219n504
22:9	48n88
22:10	185n355, 207n458
22:11	100n79
22:11–14	123n1, 147n121
22:14	59n44, 206n457, 207n458
22:17	48n88
22:18	100n79
22:18–21	164
22:21	48n88
22:23	49n98
22:28	48n88
22:29	100n79
22:30	206n456
22:31	27, 159n188, 212
22:34	185n355
22:41	185n355
22:41–46	248, 255
22:42–45	253, 255, 256, 256n98
22:43	48n88
22:44	126n19, 198
22:45	48n88
23	22n123, 60, 90n24, 90–91n24, 92, 93, 104, 104n99, 105, 106, 107, 108, 109, 109n126, 110, 159n188, 166, 208, 248
23–25	247
23:1	44, 93, 104
23:1–33	22n123
23:1—24:2	123
23:1—26:2	89, 104
23:1–39	123n1
23:3	48n88
23:8–10	57n30
23:9	204n443
23:12	57n33
23:13	22, 22n123, 124n4, 252n78
23:13–15	22, 23, 23n125
23:13–38	167n239
23:15	22n123, 137n68
23:16–22	159n184
23:20	48n88
23:21	124n3, 191
23:29–39	107n114
23:32—24:2	107n118
23:33	252n78
23:33–37	127
23:34	145n113, 145n114, 146, 208, 249, 250
23:34–35	145, 146, 225, 245, 263
23:35	160, 169n250, 204n443
23:36	96n59, 104, 210, 211, 211n473
23:37	124, 145n114, 186, 186n361, 207, 208
23:37—24:1	146
23:37—24:2	123, 135
23:37–39	253, 256
23:38	22n124, 93n41, 104, 107, 108, 115, 124, 124n4, 133, 157, 160, 210, 211
23:38–39	21, 114, 127, 128
23:39	21n118, 110, 115, 115n156, 124, 124n4, 125, 126, 127, 128, 129, 158n180, 250n69, 262
23–25	104, 104n95, 105, 248

… ANCIENT DOCUMENT INDEX 329

24	3, 12, 13, 14, 15, 16, 17, 19, 24, 25, 33, 53, 104, 107, 109, 121, 132, 138, 144, 144n104, 162, 166, 172, 177, 180, 190, 194, 212, 221, 245, 246–47, 248, 249, 250, 256, 264	24:2	22n124, 96n59, 104, 107, 108, 114, 115, 128, 131, 155, 172, 196n396, 210, 274n56
		24:2–3	120n182, 175
24–25	1, 2, 11, 14n77, 16, 17, 18, 19, 21, 22n124, 23, 24, 25, 33, 34, 35, 50, 51, 52, 53, 54, 57n43, 59, 66, 67, 68, 71, 81, 84, 85, 86, 90n24, 96, 103, 104n99, 105, 106, 106n109, 107, 107n117, 109, 110, 111, 127, 149, 176, 178, 218, 219, 219n507, 232, 235, 237, 238, 239, 240, 241, 242, 244, 246, 247, 248, 249, 151, 252, 252n78, 253, 254n86, 256, 257, 259, 260, 265, 267, 268, 270, 271, 273, 274, 275, 275–76n63, 278, 279, 280	24:3	1, 23, 25, 31, 43n55, 59n44, 92n36, 102n84, 105, 106, 106n105, 107, 107n117, 108, 109, 109n126, 111, 112, 113, 114, 114n150, 115, 115n155, 116n160, 117, 118, 122, 128, 129, 130, 131, 131n40, 132, 133, 135, 136, 137, 137n68, 139, 153, 154, 176n285, 176n292, 181, 192, 199, 200n425, 201, 209, 211, 213, 235, 261, 262, 264, 272
		24:3–4	92
		24:3–14	153
		24:3–31	107n118, 250n69
		24:3–35	213
		24:3—25:46	107n117, 109n126, 113, 212, 261
		24:4	21, 104n96, 107, 107n114, 107n115, 110, 112, 132, 134, 141, 155, 206n457
24–28	111	24:4–5	5, 9, 143
24:1	92n36, 105n103, 107, 108, 111n138, 124, 124n4, 160, 245	24:4–8	26, 31, 59n44, 143
		24:4–13	143
		24:4–14	8, 19, 27, 28, 29, 30, 31, 111, 112, 113, 114n147, 117, 118, 119, 137, 139, 140, 141, 143, 148, 154, 192, 261
24:1–2	108, 109, 109n126, 110, 132n42		
24:1–3	1, 21, 104, 105, 107n114, 107n115, 133, 192		
24:1–4	107n114, 110	24:4–28	29, 30, 210, 210n467
24:1–14	26		
24:1–31	34, 143n103, 150	24:4–31	67, 110, 210, 241
24:1—25:30	25	24:4–35	136, 138, 139

Matthew (*cont.*)

24:4—25:46	110, 112, 261
24:5	134, 148, 192, 247
24:6	1, 120n182, 133, 139, 141, 142, 143, 151, 152, 153, 154, 172
24:6–8	143, 143n103
24:6–14	5
24:6–22	5
24:7	22n122, 113, 144, 144n105, 147, 202n436, 203, 252n78
24:8	120n182, 139, 210
24:9	1, 22n122, 45n68, 113, 119, 143, 144, 144n105, 145, 145n109, 145n114, 147, 172, 173, 193, 194, 198n409, 225, 245, 249n65, 254n83, 263
24:9–12	143, 152
24:9–13	143
24:9–14	31, 143
24:10	45n68, 148, 198n409
24:10–12	59n44, 242
24:11	148, 172, 198n409
24:12	148
24:13	1, 120n182, 151, 152, 152n147, 153, 154, 172
24:13–14	143n103
24:14	1, 4, 6, 8, 22n122, 26, 26n148, 45n68, 113, 136n65, 141, 144n105, 145, 146, 147, 147n122, 148, 149, 150, 151, 152, 153, 154, 178n305, 179, 225, 234, 252n78, 254n83, 262, 263, 266, 272, 280
24:15	4, 15, 21, 28, 48n89, 117, 118, 124n4, 136, 137, 137n68, 137n70, 140, 154, 155, 157, 158, 159n188, 160, 163, 166, 167, 168, 174, 175, 178n303, 194, 205n448, 210
24:15–16	9, 137, 162, 167
24:15–18	21
24:15–20	143n103, 155, 172, 175, 218
24:15–21	7, 29, 30, 266n7
24:15–22	5, 135
24:15–25	117, 118, 119, 121, 122, 152, 154, 155, 170, 174, 193, 261
24:15–28	7, 8, 19, 30, 31, 119
24:15–31	31, 192
24:15–35	26
24:15—25:46	111, 112, 117, 122, 261
24:16	45n68, 137n71, 158, 165, 169, 169n251, 174
24:16–18	28, 208
24:16–19	163
24:16–20	119, 155
24:16–22	152
24:16–31	121
24:17	93n41
24:19	192
24:19–20	120n182
24:19–21	4
24:19–22	174, 193, 194
24:19–31	4
24:20	4, 21, 174
24:20–26	206
24:21	1, 30, 43, 45n68, 118, 137n71, 155, 172, 173, 174, 193, 210, 266
24:21–22	31
24:21–25	155
24:21–28	143n103
24:22	7, 7n31, 30, 119n175, 120n182,

ANCIENT DOCUMENT INDEX 331

	126, 128, 192, 206n457, 208	24:29–30	136n65, 139, 187, 214
24:22–28	119	24:29–31	9, 19, 26, 31, 55, 117, 126, 143, 143n103, 154, 181, 186, 188, 189, 190, 191, 192, 193, 194, 196, 197, 209n466, 210, 211, 213, 250n69
24:22–31	29		
24:23	5, 7, 45n68, 104n96, 119, 137n71, 175		
24:23–24	175, 210, 247		
24:23–25	21		
24:23–26	162, 182		
24:23–31	114n147	24:29–35	209
24:24	40n37, 126, 128, 155, 172, 183, 206n457, 208	24:30	45n68, 59n44, 75n143, 127, 137n71, 139, 148, 180, 181, 188, 189n373, 190n379, 192, 199, 200, 200n417, 201, 202, 203, 204, 205, 205n450, 206n453, 211, 212, 213, 223, 225, 232, 233, 245n42, 247, 254n86, 264, 271n30, 277
24:25	117, 119, 175		
24:26	48n88, 117, 119, 175, 179, 180		
24:26–27	8, 176, 186		
24:26–28	31, 117, 139, 154, 181, 186, 192, 193, 213		
24:26–31	28, 118, 122, 261, 263,		
24:27	1, 14, 27, 34, 59n44, 117, 119, 175, 176, 176n285, 176n292, 179, 180, 181, 182, 186, 188, 200, 201, 202, 212, 213, 224, 245n42, 247		
		24:30–31	8, 192, 195, 195n391, 196, 196n397, 213, 215, 223, 232, 250n69, 264
24:27–28	175	24:31	5, 6, 59n44, 81n182, 117, 120, 126, 128, 186, 187, 188, 195, 199, 200n417, 204, 205, 206, 206n453, 206n456, 206n457, 207, 207n458, 208, 209, 215, 216, 218, 222, 223, 231, 233, 235, 247, 250, 250n69, 264, 271n30
24:27–31	224		
24:28	8, 50, 120n183, 175, 176, 181, 183, 184, 185, 186, 187, 188, 206n454, 207, 207n459, 208, 211, 212, 216n496, 223, 263		
24:29	8, 9, 30, 72, 117, 120n182, 120n183, 139, 176, 181, 188, 190, 191, 192, 193, 194, 195, 196, 196n393, 197, 198, 199, 200, 202, 209, 210, 263		
		24:31–32	207
		24:32	118, 120, 120n182, 136, 209
		24:32—25:46	31, 110, 192
		24:32–33	9, 120, 137n68

Matthew (*cont.*)

24:32–34	209
24:32–35	29, 31, 117, 118, 121, 122, 154, 261
24:32–41	19
24:32–46	28
24:33	40n37, 118, 136, 137, 137n70, 205n448, 209, 210, 210n469
24:34	5, 6, 8, 21, 29, 30n178, 96n59, 104, 126n19, 137, 142n98, 175, 210, 210n469, 211, 241
24:34–35	50, 186n358
24:35	118, 120, 176, 204n443, 210, 211
24:35–36	120n182
24:36	9, 26, 34, 109, 116, 118, 120, 206n456, 211, 212, 213, 214, 219, 252n77
24:36–37	120
24:36–38	194
24:36–42	224
24:36–44	20n113, 29, 212, 214
24:36—25:30	222
24:36—25:46	26, 31, 118, 121, 122, 136, 137, 138, 139, 154, 211, 213, 261
24:37	1, 14, 57n33, 59n44, 118, 176n285, 176n292, 214, 224, 245n42, 247, 257n101
24:37–39	14, 213
24:37–41	215
24:37–42	216
24:38	192, 216, 220
24:38–39	218
24:39	1, 40n37, 59n44, 118, 176n285, 176n292, 192, 214, 215, 217, 217n498, 245n42, 247, 257n101
24:40	45n68, 247, 264
24:40–41	6, 124n2, 214, 215, 216, 217, 217n497, 217n498, 217n499, 218, 232, 270, 271n30
24:40–44	212
24:41	264
24:42	48n88, 192, 213n480, 213n481, 214, 219, 221, 247
24:42—25:30	212
24:43	93n41, 120n182, 121n185, 188, 192, 213n480, 213n481, 216, 220n510, 275, 277
24:43–44	216
24:43–51	266n7
24:43—25:30	224
24:44	14, 192, 213n480, 213n481, 214, 219, 221, 245n42, 247, 257n101
24:45	250n68
24:45–47	220, 221
24:45–51	16, 26n152, 220, 221n512, 224n525, 225n530
24:45—25:30	219, 221
24:45—25:46	152
24:46	192, 213n480, 213n481
24:46–47	50
24:47	96n59, 221
24:48	219, 220
24:48–49	120n182, 121n185, 195n390
24:48–51	220, 221
24:49	222
24:49–50	231
24:50	219
24:51	221
25	25, 90–91n24, 109, 110, 212, 221, 241, 248, 249, 250, 264

ANCIENT DOCUMENT INDEX 333

25:1	45n68, 105, 109, 252n78	25:28	48n88
25:1–12	224n525	25:29	43n54, 57n33, 120n182, 121n185
25:1–13	180, 219n504, 220, 221	25:30	23, 56n24, 59n44, 221, 222
25:1–30	221	25:31	45n68, 113, 120n182, 137n68, 181n320, 192, 201, 205, 206, 206n456, 213, 213n480, 213n481, 216, 223, 227, 245n42, 247, 257n101, 270
25:2	120n182, 121n185, 250n68		
25:3	222		
25:4	250n68		
25:4–6	120n182, 121n185		
25:5	219		
25:6	220		
25:7	45n68	25:31–32	187, 202, 207, 208, 256
24:8–9	250n68		
25:8–12	120n182, 121n185	25:31–34	256
25:10	192, 213n480, 213n481, 216, 216n494	25:31–46	7n32, 15, 24, 24n132, 24n136, 25, 56, 59n44, 60, 71, 102, 102n85, 105, 109, 110, 113, 126, 130, 147, 147n126, 149, 178, 179, 180, 192, 205n451, 212, 218, 222, 222n513, 223, 223n520, 223n523, 224, 224n524, 224n525, 225, 226, 227, 228, 228n550, 229, 229n553, 230, 232, 233, 234, 235, 242, 242, 252, 252n76, 256, 263, 264, 271, 275, 279, 280, 281
25:10–12	218, 220		
25:11	192		
25:12	96n59		
25:13	48n88, 219, 221		
25:14–30	180, 218, 220, 221, 224n526		
25:14–46	26n152		
25:15	120n182, 121n185, 193n386		
25:15–25	27		
25:18	204n443		
25:18–19	120n182, 121n185		
25:19	192, 213n480, 213n481, 219		
25:22	100n79, 120n182, 121n185		
25:21	221		
25:23	221	25:32	22n122, 23, 25, 25n144, 113, 144n105, 149, 178n305, 179, 203, 207n459, 218, 223, 224, 225, 225n534, 226, 226n537, 232, 233, 254n83
25:24	100n79, 120n182, 121n185, 150n140, 185n355, 188		
25:24–27	222		
25:24–30	221		
25:25	204n443		
25:26	100n79, 120n182, 121n185, 180, 185n355, 221n512	25:32–33	218
		25:33	120n182
25:27	48n88, 192, 213n480, 213n481	25:33–46	218

Matthew (*cont.*)

25:34	45n68, 82n190, 235, 252n77, 252n78, 257
25:35–36	56n26
25:36	192
25:37	45n68, 234, 235
25:37–39	137n68
25:38–39	120n182
25:39	192
25:40	96n59, 222, 227, 229, 230, 230n562, 231, 232, 257
25:41	45n68, 206n456, 226, 235n579
25:41–46	219n504
25:44	45n68, 137n68
25:45	45n68, 96n59, 222, 227, 231, 232
25:46	1, 25, 102, 109, 110, 111, 112, 113, 118, 120, 120n182, 130n32, 223, 226, 226n538, 235, 253, 268
26–28	91, 241
26:1	89, 95, 102, 102n86, 104, 106n106, 108n120, 110, 253
26:2	245n42, 257n101
26:1–2	110, 111
26:1–16	98
26:1—28:15	99
26:1—28:20	100, 261
26:2	104, 110, 111
26:3	111, 185n355
26:3—28:20	89
26:3–4	127
26:4	111
26:6	93n41
26:8	100n79
26:10	100n79
26:13	96, 96n59, 146, 150
26:16	43, 95, 101
26:17—28:20	98
26:21	96, 96n59
26:21–25	67n96
26:24	75n143, 245n42, 257n101
26:26	109n125
26:29	137n68, 252n77, 252n78
26:31	44
26:34	67n96, 96, 96n59
26:37	217n499
26:39	59n44, 252n77
26:42	235n580, 252n77
26:45	245n42, 257n101
26:49	193n386
26:51–53	59n44
26:53	206n456, 252n77
26:54	48n88
26:55	49n98, 158n180
26:56	217n502
26:57	185n355
26:58	151n145
26:61	124n5
26:63	253, 255, 258n112
26:64	71, 85, 128, 192, 201, 201n429, 205, 205n447, 245n42, 255, 257n101
26:74	44, 193n386
27:9	44
27:11	253, 257
27:17	47, 48n88, 185n355
27:19	109n125
27:21	100n79
27:24	100n79
27:22	48n88
27:27	185n355, 217, 217n499
27:29	253, 257
27:35	100n79
27:37	253, 257
27:40	124n5, 253, 255, 258n112
27:42	252n78, 257
27:43	253, 255, 258n112
27:45	197, 204n443
27:46	27, 212n477
27:48	193n386
27:51	204n443
27:51–53	197
27:53	158

ANCIENT DOCUMENT INDEX

27:54	253, 255, 258n113	9:31	170n257
27:62	185n355	9:42–48	56n22
27:64	48n88	9:49	274n53
28:1	43n55, 253	10	88
28:1–10	98	10:29–30	268
28:1–20	98	10:32	217n500
28:2	197, 206n456	10:33–34	170n257
28:2–3	59n44	11:1—16:8	88
28:5	100n79, 206n456	11:11	159n183
28:10	231n565	11:15	159n183
28:11	109n125	11:16	159n183
28:12	185n355	11:27	159n183
28:16–20	96, 97, 98, 99, 249n65	12:13–17	114n152
		12:16–27	164
28:18	147, 204n443, 253, 257, 272	12:26	212n477
		12:35	159n183
28:18–20	59n44, 90n24, 95, 145, 145n114, 146, 150, 245, 263	12:41–44	104
		13	2–3n2, 10n47, 13, 14n77, 17, 53, 55, 58, 58n43, 59, 71, 73, 74, 76, 106, 114, 131, 165, 171, 176, 189, 238, 240, 266, 267
28:19	22n122, 23, 48n88, 90, 144n105, 147, 147n122, 178n305, 225, 241n20, 242, 252n77, 253, 254n83, 255		
		13:1	159n183
28:19–20	26, 234	13:1–2	114n152
28:20	94, 108n124, 130n32, 194, 253, 268	13:1–3	109
		13:3	159n183
		13:4	31, 115n154, 181n319, 266
		13:5	73n131
		13:8–10	145n109
Mark		13:10	145
1:4	156n167	13:14	15, 25, 73n131, 157n173, 158n181, 161n207, 163, 164, 165, 178n303
1:1–13	88		
1:1–15	96		
1:15	267		
1:14–15	14		
1:14—7:23	88	13:14–15	14
3:26–27	267	13:14–16	73n132
4:36	217n500	13:17	73n131
5:40	217n500	13:17–20	73–74n133
7:4	217n500	13:18	174
7:24—9:50	88	13:19	266
8:31	170n257	13:20	73n131
8:38	78, 179n307, 266, 267, 270	13:22	73n131
		13:24–25	76, 78n165, 79
8:38—9:1	266	13:24–27	78, 78n167, 189, 190, 206n453
9:2	217n500		

Mark (cont.)

13:24–30	80
13:25–27	55
13:26	75n143, 189n373, 203
13:26–27	78
13:27	250
13:32	212n477
13:37	112n142
13:42–43	66n90
14:33	217n500
14:49	159n183
14:62	71, 75n143
15:33	76
16:15	147n123

Luke

2:1	149n133
2:12	203
2:32	54n10
2:36	148n127
9:10	217n500
9:26–27	267
9:28	217n500
11:20	14, 82n189, 267
11:26	217n500
11:49	249
12:31	56n24
12:32	228
12:35–48	266n7
12:49	274n53
12:49–50	170n257
13:35	128n23
15:13	101n80
17	7
17:20–24	8n36
17:21	267
17:24	14
17:26	14
17:26–27	14
17:30–31	266n7
17:34–35	217n500
17:37	187n362, 188n368
18:8	267
18:29–30	234n575, 268
18:31	217n500
19:27	56n24
19:37–44	128n23
19:42–44	4
20:35	268
21	7, 17, 176, 267
21:1–4	104
21:7	25, 115n154, 266
21:20	162, 166n233, 178n303
21:20–24	175
21:23–24	4
21:24	191n382
21:24–27	267
21:26	149n133
21:27	75n143, 203
22	184n339
22:28–30	227
22:30	148n127
24:26	228
24:47	145n111, 146, 225

John

1:1–8	49
1:11	217n500
2:16	278
2:19	273n43, 275n62, 278
2:21	217n500, 275n62
3:5	276
3:18	227
5:24–25	276
5:25	227
5:28–29	24n132, 276
6:39–40	276
6:47	276
6:54	276
10:28	276
11:24–26	276
13–17	67
14–16	278
14:2	278
14:2–3	277, 278
14:3	217n500, 278
14:23	277
12:48	276
16:2	278
16:11	212n477
16:16–22	278

16:23–26	278	28:23	269, 269n18
16:25	278	28:31	269, 269n18
16:28–29	278		
16:33	278	**Romans**	
17:3	276	1:13	23n125
17:15	278	2:5	54n10
19:16	217n500	4:11	202–3n437
19:16–17	217	8:1	227
21:22–23	276	8:19	54n10
		8:35	271n32
Acts		9:1	101n83
1:3	269n18	10:1	101n83
1:6	139	10:14	45n70
1:6–7	268, 269	10:18	148, 149n133, 150
1:11	180n318, 181n319, 267n12, 269	11:1	148n127
2:1–47	269	11:25–27	125
2:16–21	75n142	12:2	272n38
3:19–21	125, 269, 279n19	12:12	271n32
4:5	149n134	13:1	101n83
6:13–14	158n179	14:17	272n36
8:12	269, 269n18	16:25	54n10
11:28	149n133	16:26	148
13:21	148n127		
13:45–46	269n19	**1 Corinthians**	
13:48	269n19	1:7	54n10
14:22	269, 269n18, 271, 272n37	1:8	150, 154n160
15:39	217n500	1:20	272n38
16:33	217n500	2:6	272n38
17:6	149n133	2:8	272n38
17:31	149n134	3:16	273n43
19:8	269, 269n18	3:17	273n43
19:27	149n133	3:18	272n38
20:25	269, 269n18	4:20	272n36
21:24	217n500	6:9–10	272n37
21:25	212n477	6:19	273n43
21:26	217n500	7:1	212n476
21:28	158n179	7:25	212n476
21:32	217n500	8:1	212n476
23:18	217n500	10:11	129n29, 153n154
23:21	45n70	10:17	272
24:5	149n133	11:23	217n500
25:4	45n70	12:1	212n476
26:9–12	145n113	14:6	54n10
28:5	45n70	14:26	54n10
28:15	180n315	15:1	217n500

1 Corinthians (cont.)

15:3	217n500
15:20–24	228n549
15:23	176n292
15:24	24, 150, 154n160, 272
15:24–25	24n132
15:50	272n37
16:1	212n476
16:12	212n476
16:17	176n290

2 Corinthians

1:4	271n32
1:8	271n32
4:4	272n38
4:17	271n32
6:4–6	271n32
6:16	273n43
7:4	271n32
7:6	176n290
7:7	176n290
8:2	271n32
10:10	176n289
12:1	54
12:7	54

Galatians

1:4	272n38
1:9	217n500
1:12	54n10, 217n500
2:2	54n10
4:3	198
4:9	198
5:21	272n37
6:6	225n530

Ephesians

1:17	54n10
1:21	272n38, 272n39
2:2	272n38
2:7	272n39
2:21	273n43
3:3	54n10
3:9	272n40
3:13	271n32
5:5	272n37
6:12	198

Philippians

1:11	23n125
1:26	176n289
1:28–29	271n35
2:12	176n289
3:5	148n127
4:9	217n500

Colossians

1:6	23n125, 148, 150
1:13	272n36
1:23	148
1:26	272n40
2:6	217n500
2:8	198
2:20	198
4:17	217n500

1 Thessalonians

1:6	271n32
2:12	272n36
2:13	217n500
2:19	176n292
3:3	271n32
3:7	271n32
3:13	176n292, 270, 270n27
4:1	217n500
4:13–17	270
4:13–18	192
4:14	270n27
4:15	176n292, 270n27
4:16	180n318, 270, 270n27
4:16—5:7	271n30
4:16–17	233, 271
4:17	180n315, 270, 271n30
5:9	271
5:23	176n292

2 Thessalonians

1:4	271n32
1:4–7	271
1:5	272n37
1:7	54n10, 270
2	4, 160n193
2:1	176n292, 271n31
2:1–12	272, 273
2:3	161, 162, 178n303
2:4	273
2:7	272
2:8	176n292, 271n31
2:9	176n291
3:6	217n500

1 Timothy

1:17	272
6:17	272n38

2 Timothy

4:1	272n37
4:10	272n38
4:17	148
4:18	272n37, 272n38

Titus

2:12	272n38
3:5	228n549

Hebrews

1:6	149n134
2:5	149n134
3:14	150, 154n160
6:11	150, 154n160
7:13–14	148n127
9:25	158n179
9:28	129n29
10:27	274n53
11:31	158n179
12:25–29	78n165
12:26–27	274n54
12:28	217n500
12:29	274n53

James

1:1	148n127
5:7–8	176n292
5:9	209n465

1 Peter

1:6	273, 273n47, 273n48
1:7	54n10
1:11	273n49
1:13	54n10
1:20	273
4:1	273n47
4:7	150, 154n160, 273
4:12	273n47, 273n49
4:13	54n10, 273n49
4:17–19	273n47
5:1	101n83, 273n49
5:9	273n49

2 Peter

1:1	274
1:3	274
1:6	176n292
1:16	176n292, 274
1:16–18	274n57
1:17–18	197n398
1:19	274
2:4	274n57
2:5	274n57
2:9	274, 274n58
2:20	274n57
3:1	101n83
3:3–5	274
3:4	176n292
3:5–13	78n165
3:6	274n57
3:7	274
3:10	196n397, 274, 274n57
3:10–13	76n152
3:11	274
3:12	176n292
3:13	275
3:14	274
3:15–16	274n57

1 John

2:18	278
2:22	278
2:28	176n292
4:3	278

2 John

1:7	278

Revelation

1:1	54, 66n90, 275–76n63
1:3	66n90
1:4	276
1:7	78, 148n128, 204
1:8	276
2:26	150, 154n160
3:10	149n133, 278, 279
3:12	273n43, 275n62, 278
3:20	209n465
4	279n76
4:8	276
5:5	148n127
5:9	148n128
6:12–13	197, 198n405
7:4–8	148n127
7:9	148n128
7:14	278
11:1–3	275n62
11:9	148n128
12	275–76n63
12–17	78n165
12:9	149n134
13:7	148n128
14:6	148n128
16:14	149n133
17:5	278n75
19:15	199
19:17–18	182n327
19:21	182n327
20:4–6	279
20:6	279
20:11–15	24, 24n132
20:11—21:1–5	275–76n63, 279
21	227–28n548
21:12	148n127
21:23	201
21:23–25	201
22:6	66n90
22:7	66n90
22:10	66n90
22:16	198
22:18–19	66n90

DEAD SEA SCROLLS

Pesher Habakkuk

6.3–5	161n200
111.11	183n338

War Scroll

1:11–12	172n268
1:11–14	141n91
3:13–15	200n417
15:1	141n87

Hodayot or Thanksgiving Hymns

11:19–36	78n163

Rule of the Community

4:2	78n163

Pseudo-Jubilees

1:6–7	78n163

Florilegium or Midrash on Eschatology

2 Sam 7:10–14	134n58

RABBINIC WRITING

Genesis Rabbah

10.7	162n211

GRECO-ROMAN WRITINGS

Aelian
De Natura animalium
2:36	184n344
2.39	182n327
2.46	182n327, 184n344

Aristotle
Historia Animalium (**History of Animals**)
6.5–6	185n348
9.32	185n249

Poetica
21.7–9	82n195

Rhetorica
3.10.7	82n195
3.12	48n90

Diogenes Laertius
Vitae philosophorum
7.140–43	228n549

Lucian
Navigium
1	182n327

Pliny the Elder
Naturalis historia
10.3	185n349
10.5.16	183n336

Pseudo-Sophocles Fragment
2	78n163

Seneca
Epistolae morales
95.43	182n327

EARLY CHRISTIAN WRITINGS

Apollinaris
Fragments
126	182n330

Augustine
Epistles
199.25	5n14

Clement of Rome
1 Clement
5:5–7	148n131

Clement of Alexandria
Stromateis
6.15.128	177n296

Chrysostom
Homiliae in Matthaeun
75–79	5n15
75.2	161n198
76	174n277
76.3	5n18, 182n329, 199n416
77.1	5n19, 211n472

Cyril of Alexandria
Thesaurus de Sancta et Consubstantiali Trinitate
—	4n12

Fragments
266	4n13
269	4n13
271	4n13

Didache
16:4	161n204
16:6	199n416

Eusebius

Demonstration evangelica

4:16	4n11

Historia ecclesiastica

3.5.3–4	161n200, 169n251
3.7	4n11
3.39.14–16	90n18
4.6.3	161n198

Preparatio evangelica

10.8	77n155

Epiphanius

Panarion

29.7.7–8	169n251
30.2.7	169n251

Treatise on Weights and Measures

15.15	169n251

Hillary

Commentary on Matthew

248	4n9

Hippolytus

Matthaeun

24	182n330
205	182n330

IGNATIUS

Ignatius, To the Philadelphians

9.2	177n296

IRENAEUS

Adversus Haereses

4.14.1	182n330
4.33.12	76n150
5.25	4n7

JEROME

Commentariorum in Matthaeum

4.24.28	182n330
269	5n20
270	6n21
271	6n23
272	6n22, 161n198
274	6n21
277	6n24

ORIGEN

Contra Celsium

2:13	4n8

Fragmenta

478	182n330

Theodoret of Cyrus

Commentary on The Letters of St. Paul

118	233n571

NEW TESTAMENT APOCRYPHA

Apocalypse of Peter (Ethiopian)

1	199n416
5:4	198n405

Epistle of the Apostles

16	199n416

Gospel of Peter

39	199n416

www.ingramcontent.com/pod-product-compliance
Lightning Source LLC
Chambersburg PA
CBHW071150300426
44113CB00009B/1154